THE PROSE OF THINGS

THE PROSE OF THINGS

Transformations of Description in the Eighteenth Century

CYNTHIA SUNDBERG WALL

THE UNIVERSITY OF CHICAGO PRESS

CHICAGO AND LONDON

The University of Chicago Press, Chicago 60637
The University of Chicago Press, Ltd., London
© 2006 by The University of Chicago
All rights reserved. Published 2006.
Paperback edition 2014
Printed and bound by CPI Group (UK) Ltd, Croydon, CR0 4YY

23 22 21 20 19 18 17 16 15 14   2 3 4 5 6

ISBN-13: 978-0-226-87158-5 (cloth)
ISBN-13: 978-0-226-21527-3 (paperback)
ISBN-13: 978-0-226-22502-9 (ebook)
10.7208/chicago/9780226225029.001.0001

Frontispiece: "Seeds of Tyme," Robert Hooke, Micrographia (1665). Reproduced by permission of the British Library (shelfmark 1651/1363).

Library of Congress Cataloging-in-Publication Data

Wall, Cynthia, 1959–
    The prose of things : transformations of description in the eighteenth century / Cynthia Sundberg Wall.
        p. cm.
    Includes bibliographical references and index.
    ISBN 0-226-87158-4 (alk. paper)
    1. English prose literature—18th century—History and criticism.
    2. Description (Rhetoric)—History—18th century. 3. English
        language—18th century—Rhetoric. I. Title
    PR769.W35 2006
    828'.5080922—dc22

                                                2005027014

FOR PAUL

CONTENTS

ILLUSTRATIONS

ACKNOWLEDGMENTS

One great pleasure in coming to the last stage of writing a book is thanking all the friends, colleagues, and institutions who helped it along. I am grateful to the American Council of Learned Societies for a year at the beginning of this project to think it out and to the National Endowment for the Humanities for a year at the end to finish it. To the readers for the NEH, Albert Rivero and Anne Coldiron, the readers for the University of Chicago Press, Deidre Shauna Lynch and John Richetti, and my editors at the Press, Alan Thomas and Randolph Petilos, thank you. I am particularly grateful to Joseph Brown, whose extraordinarily accurate and detailed copyediting save this book on detail from a warehouseful of mistakes and infelicities.

As scholars, we all live in and depend on libraries. I spent ten years as a page, desk attendant, reference librarian, and fellow at the Newberry Library in Chicago: I owe decades of thanks to John Aubrey, Robert Karrow, Paul Gehl, Hjordis Halvorson, and Margaret Kulis as well as to my new contacts, John Powell and Will Hansen. Thanks also go to the ever-changing but ever-efficient staff of the British Library; to Robert Lyons at the Institute for Historical Research; to Wayne Furman at the New York Public Library; to Marijke Booth at Christies International in London; and to Bradley Daigle, Heather Moore Riser, and Michael Plunkett in Special Collections at the University of Virginia.

A special conference on "Things" at Texas A&M University in October 2002, run by Margaret Ezell and Katherine O'Brien O'Keeffe, gave me a chance to air the project and to talk "things" with Barbara Benedict and Bill Brown. An invitation to visit the eighteenth-century graduate students at Harvard in April 2003 introduced me to Professor Lynn Festa and to Sophie Gee, with both of whom fruitful intellectual things followed.

Colleagues, students, and staff at Virginia are almost too numerous to name, but I will anyway. I have to begin with Gordon Braden and J. Daniel Kinney, who read the first chapter on classical and Renaissance backgrounds and saved me from some embarrassments. An incomplete, alphabetical list of colleagues to whom I'm grateful for any number of things directly or indirectly related to my project is Steve Arata, Martin Battestin, Ruthe Battestin, Alison Booth, Karen Chase, Ralph Cohen, Greg Colomb, Jessica Feldman, Elizabeth Fowler, Susan Fraiman, David Gies, Lisa Goff, J. Paul Hunter, Clare Kinney, Michael Levenson, Katharine Maus, Peter Metcalf, John O'Brien, Victoria Olwell, Sophie Rosenfeld, Marion Rust, Patricia Meyer Spacks, Anthony Spearing, Herbert Tucker, David Vander Meulen, and Jennifer Wicke. Graduate students whose separate and individual minds helped me think and see differently are Jason Coats, Jim Cocola, Michael Genovese, Neil Hultgren, Kristin Jensen, Ellen Malenas, Kate Nash, Elise Pugh, Jill Rappoport, Megan Raymond, Catherine Rodriguez, Chloe Wigston Smith, Rivka Swenson, and Lauryl Hicks Tucker. Heartfelt thanks as well to Cheryll Lewis, Pamela Marcantel, Lois Payne, and June Webb for making so many parts of daily life so much easier.

And then there are outside colleagues, friends, and family: John Bender, Albert Braunmuller, Linda Bree, Catherine Brighton, Alan Cameron, Anne Cameron, Randall Couch, Mary Ellen Curley, Deirdre David, Lynn Strongin Dodds, J. Alan Downie, Julie Garmel, Anne Goldgar, Warwick Gould, Jeff Greer, Elizabeth Helsinger, Elizabeth Horsley, Christine Krueger, Dee Dee Levine, Joseph Levine, Gail McDonald, Russ McDonald, Tonya Moon, Nicole Pohl, John Price, Kate Glover Price, Carolyn Russell, Richard Strier, Kathryn Temple, Julia Thomas, and Deirdre Twomey. My parents insist that any credit for this book is due to them: Steven and Nancy Johnson and Richard and Jill Sundberg. And, above all, Paul Hunter. I dedicate this book to him.

I *like* the genre of acknowledgments. Like most scholars, presumably, I read others' with great interest. And I would like to chime in with the usual but nevertheless sincere caveat that, with all the helpful suggestions and corrections from friends and colleagues, mistakes and misarguments will inevitably appear, but, for those, the responsibility is mine.

∾

Portions of this book have had an earlier incarnation in print. The bases for chapter 1 first appeared in "Details of Space: Narrative Description in Early Eighteenth-Century Novels" (*Eighteenth-Century Fiction* 10, no. 4 [July 1998]: 387–405) and in "The Rhetoric of Description and the Spaces of Things" (in *Eighteenth-Century Genre and Culture; or, Serious Reflections* on *Occasional Forms: Essays in Honor of J. Paul Hunter*, ed. Dennis Todd and Cynthia Wall [Newark: University of Delaware Press, 2001], 261–79). Some of the arguments about *Clarissa* in chapter 5 rephrase aspects of "The Spaces of *Clarissa* in Text and Film" (in *Eighteenth-Century Fiction on Screen*, ed. Robert Mayer [Cambridge: Cambridge University Press, 2002], 106–22). Some material on eighteenth-century auctions in chapter 6 first appeared in "The English Auction: Narratives of Dismantlings" (*Eighteenth-Century Studies* 31, no. 1 [fall 1997]: 1–25). Some points about *Sir Charles Grandison* in chapter 7 will appear in "Teaching Space in *Sir Charles Grandison*" (in *Approaches to Teaching Richardson*, ed. Jocelyn Harris and Lisa Zunshine [New York: Modern Language Association, in press]). Part of chapter 8 appears in different form in "A Geography of Georgian Narrative Space" (in *Georgian Geographies*, ed. Miles Ogborn and Charles Withers [Manchester: Manchester University Press, 2003], 114–30). My thanks for permission to republish.

INTRODUCTION

Virginia Woolf once wrote that, in *Robinson Crusoe*, "there are no sunsets and no sunrises; there is no solitude and no soul. There is, on the contrary, staring us full in the face nothing but a large earthenware pot."[1] Instead of presenting us with settings, with fully visualized spaces, the early novel describes *things*. Or, rather, it *presents* things; and those things, as Dorothy Van Ghent argued, "are not at all vivid in texture.... In saying that the world of *Moll Flanders* is made up to a large extent of *things*, we do not mean that it is a world rich in physical, sensuous textures—in images for the eye or for the tactile sense or for the tongue or the ear or for the sense of temperature or the sense of pressure. It is extraordinarily barren of such images."[2] To the post-nineteenth-century reader, these "things" seem disconcerting, contextless, isolated in otherwise empty space, not part of *properly* furnished homes with Dickensian detail and Jamesian significance. In classical and Renaissance rhetoric, description had long been an object of suspicion, partly because it behaves too much like an *object* (in 1589, George Puttenham warned that "the Poet or makers of speech becomes vicious and unpleasant by nothing more than by using too much surplusage").[3] As Gérard Genette argues, description was "the ever-necessary, ever-submissive, never-emancipated slave" to narrative.[4] Yet eighteenth-century rhetorical criticism became increasingly anxious about a revolt. Description almost by definition *interrupts* narrative, and, as Samuel Johnson put it, "the mind is refrigerated by interruption."[5] What happened over the eighteenth century to the status of description that transformed Defoe's unvisualized cityscapes and Pope's epitheted spaces into the excruciatingly elaborate landscapes of *The Mysteries of Udolpho* and the familiarly upholstered Victorian novel?

This book argues that the changes in the rhetoric about and the employment of description to accommodate and then absorb the ornamental into the contextual are related to at least four larger cultural changes: experientially, to technologically new ways of seeing and appreciating objects in the ordinary world through the popular prostheses of microscope, telescope, and empirical analysis; economically, to the expansion of consumer culture in the increasing presence and awareness of *things* on the market, in the house, in daily life; epistemologically, to the changing attitudes toward the general and the particular, the universal and the individual; and, narratively, to the perception and representation of domestic space.

Chapter 1, "A History of Description, a Foundling," outlines the rhetorical history of description and attitudes toward it from classical and Renaissance treatises through the nineteenth and twentieth centuries, pointing out the rather sharp critical about-face in the late eighteenth century. The traditionally defined focus of description obviously *is* objects of one sort or another—a shield (in a catalog); a grove or a house (in topography); a face, historical or fictional (in prosopography, prosopopoeia, or portrait); a moral quality (in ethopoeia); or time itself (in chronography)—as opposed to events that are narrated. The spaces of early modern prose and poetry are plentifully stocked with such things, but they tend to function emblematically and in isolation, more pointed out than described. *Things stand in for description in early texts.* This is good, says Johnson; too much "surplusage," too much detail, too many streaks on the tulip, get us away from the "business of a poet," which is "to examine, not the individual but the species; to remark general properties and large appearances."[6] The particular detail is the Aristotelian accidental, of no particular interest to the reader because it is precisely *not me*, not what *relates* but what *separates* human beings. Yet, by the mid-eighteenth century, Thomas Gray, among others, was at the same time insisting that "circumstance ever was, and ever will be, the life and essence of both nature and of poetry."[7] Hugh Blair argued: "No description, that rests in Generals, can be good. For we can conceive nothing clearly in the abstract; all distinct ideas are formed upon particulars."[8]

Chapters 2 and 3 look closely at the nature of "particulars" and their emerging fascination. Chapter 2, "Traveling Spaces," starts with Stow's *Survey of London* (1598) and its contributions to and influence over topographical description, through a century and a half of editions and additions, to Strype's monumental folios of 1720. The details of changing physical space, which is both familiar and increasingly difficult to know, appeal simultaneously to interest, convenience, and aesthetic pleasure, and the *Surveys* run a fine hand over the smallest contours of the city, demonstrating what Philippe Hamon calls the "textual praxis" of description.[9] Cartography maps onto topography, so to speak; John Ogilby's *Britannia* (1675), like his later maps of London with William Morgan, reinitiates a graphic praxis, an arena with room for little trees and local markers, a visual landscape for the reader of maps, the taker of journeys. Bunyan's *The Pilgrim's Progress* (1678) can be read in this context of visualized, particularized, familiarized landscape, as narrativized cartography. Chapter 3, "Seeing Things," addresses the Royal Society and British empiricism, enterprises also reading and marking the natural world, both for its physical secrets and for its spiritual significance. The *Philosophical Transactions* and the society's most widely read and influential members—Robert Boyle, Robert Hooke, John Evelyn, Samuel Pepys— helped engineer what Virginia Woolf considered a cultural difference in perception. Of John Evelyn's diaries, for example, she says: "The general effect of them is that he used his eyes. The visible world was always close to him. The visible world has receded so far from us that to hear all this talk . . . as if the look of things assailed one out of doors as well as in . . . seems strange."[10] Diaries and "occasional meditations" registered and interpreted the things of the world into patterns and texts. The genres of cartography, diaries, journals, lists, and indexes, along with the popular passion for intense observation of the natural world, overlap in their emphases on visualizing, connecting, and resituating the visible world. The extent of this observational emphasis is marked by satire. Swift's *Gulliver's Travels* (1726), like his dressing-room poems and Pope's *The Rape of the Lock* (1714), trains a microscope on some very personal interior spaces precisely in order to make us see differently, to pervert the ordinary into (or expose it as) the grotesque, to destabilize perceptual ground through the act of description.

Chapter 4, "Writing Things," looks at the "empty" spaces of Bunyan and Defoe and the isolation of detail. Early fiction tends to use the detail emblematically, but it frequently invests those emblems with a rich ordinariness, a telling local concreteness, that seems to bolt them more firmly to the here and now than the hereafter. The things in *The Pilgrim's Progress, Part II* (1684), for example, paradoxically transcend their emblematic status and behave more like ordinary things-in-themselves. Defoe's fiction (1719–24) depends heavily on things—earthenware pots, umbrellas, pewter tankards, gold beads, bolts of cloth—and much has been made both of their Puritan emblematicity and of their capitalist commodification. But little attention has been paid to the number of Defoean things that seem to exist for nonfunctional, nonspiritual *pleasure*. The chapter closes with a reading of the

giant Things in Horace Walpole's *The Castle of Otranto* (1764) as exaggerated images of a culture obsessed with things—as the auctiongoing Walpole
knew firsthand.

The spaces occupied by those early things is the concern of chapter 5,
"Implied Spaces." In the culturally representative novels of Aphra Behn,
Eliza Haywood, Penelope Aubin, and Mary Davys, specific interior details
appear precisely—and in isolation—when they are needed, rather than being
presented as connected visual wholes. Windows, closets, and wainscotings
emerge when jumped out of, hidden in, or fainted against, and not a moment
sooner; space is created in the act of narrative. Occasional set pieces of long
description are remarkable for their rarity—and their length. They tend to
visualize the exotic or perform some seductive function for character and
reader. Richardson's novels offer a sort of telescoped history of the eighteenth
century's transformation of narrative space. In *Pamela* (1740), for instance,
the spatial rhetoric is very much that of Bunyan, Defoe, and Haywood: the
detail is emblematic, the space generated *by* action rather than setting up
for action. *Clarissa* (1747–48) is a bit different. Although key actions take
place in the centers of or on the boundaries between rooms, a large portion of
Clarissa's time is spent *deducing* the patterns of space beyond her own field
of vision—because she is voluntarily or involuntarily locked up someplace
or another. For early novels in general, visual detail is a *setting for* narrative
action. (*Sir Charles Grandison* tells of different interiors and, thus, moves
into a later chapter.)

Roland Barthes and others have characterized early modern Europe generally as a "world of goods," and consumerism, commodification, fetishism,
luxury, imperialism, collecting, classifying, packaging, marketing, and trading have been richly mined since the latter half of the twentieth century.
Chapter 6, "Worlds of Goods," looks at how this new interest in the particular connects with the increasing availability of material goods—the
individualized domesticities and spatial differentiation made possible, paradoxically, by mass production. Shops, advertisements, and auctions collect,
arrange, disperse, and textually or graphically "narrate" multiple worlds of
things; having lots of "things" was no longer the perquisite of the rich but a
possibility for the middling sort. Josiah Wedgwood, for example, pioneered
a showroom that emphasized the possibilities in *rearranging* the same set
of objects. But, although class and empire have left an obvious imprint on
all this, what gets less attention is the intensely personal and private possibilities for self-description and self-creation in the choice and care and arrangement of things—a Lockean sense of possession and identification that
derives from labors of intimacy, from knowledge of detail, or even from a

precapitalist conflation of subject with object. Chapter 7, "Arranging Things," folds into the mix interior design, domestic tours, and country-house guides, studying the expanding art of house description as it develops an interest in color, texture, surface, and arrangement. Batty Langley's models for builders, Thomas Chippendale's pattern book for furniture, the tour guides to Stowe, the travel diaries of Celia Fiennes, Mary Delany, and John Byng, all reveal a culture increasingly interested in the curious corners of domestic space. And, as more *things* increasingly occupy interiors, they also increasingly define and make visible narrative space. In *Sir Charles Grandison* (1753–54), for example, spatial boundaries—Harriet's, at least—become clear, articulated, known, occupied. Harriet's detailed descriptions of the interiors of Grandison Hall are virtually lifted from the auction catalog's reworking of probate inventories, highlighting colors, fabrics, and their *visual coordination*—not only filling up space, but connecting it to itself as well.

Richardson's self-conscious literary and printing experiments had, of course, an enormous impact on the various kinds of novels (and works in other genres) fermenting about. Although Harriet's appropriation of the textual praxes of tour books and auction catalogs has offended critics through the twentieth century, I argue that, by simply and massively bringing detailed description indoors, Richardson began its domestication, encouraging its entry into gentility from its past as hired hand. Chapter 8, "The Foundling as Heir," argues that, by the end of the eighteenth century and the beginning of the nineteenth, Radcliffe and then Scott present us with a fully visualized *setting* in which events will occur. We are given the visual world; we no longer extrapolate it. Radcliffe is (in)famous for her extensive landscape descriptions; but she also invests domestic detail with the kind of psychological significance that we expect from nineteenth-century novels: Emily St. Aubert returns home after her father's death and assumes his *space*, sitting in his chair, staring at his hat, touching his lyre, occupying his study. The texture of detailed interiors weaves meanings together that were previously articulated through character, action, and, occasionally, physiognomy. The chapter closes with an examination of how the pressures of particularization—the transformations of narrative space—affected historiography, the writing of time. By the mid-nineteenth century, Macaulay was complaining that historians, unlike historical novelists, were not furnishing us with enough ordinary visual detail, but, in fact, the work of Hume, Gibbon, and others reflected a noticeably expanded emphasis on spatial instead of simply temporal matters. And eighteenth-century translations of the classical historians ladle quite a few more adjectives into their scenes than do their seventeenth-century counterparts. People—readers—were demanding to see the surfaces of their worlds and were prepared to read meaning rather than accident into idiosyncrasies and individualities.

I close with a meditation on Humphry Repton, landscape gardener and house transformer, who argued that "a knowledge of *arrangement* or *disposition* is, of all others, the most useful," both for "external appendages" and for "interior accommodation."[11] Watercolors of his imaginative projects were not enough; he filled in their spaces with detailed written descriptions of what he envisioned. He is the visual figure of the descriptor, who alters places on paper.

Although I address most literary and many nonliterary genres, the novel takes up the most space in this study, in part because it offered the most room for description to expand and intersect with itself. Description in poetry has a largely different trajectory, although poetry was the critical basis for rhetorical change across the generic board. In marking these rhetorical changes, I hope to show cultural and perceptual change across the century. The stable stock of texts and patterns that Michel Beaujour calls the early modern reader's "store of cultural images"[12] disintegrated in the eighteenth century under the pressure of sheer material variety; this project traces the emptying of that cultural storehouse through the stocking of an economic one—through the individuation of domestic space, the familiarization of objects. The *visualness* that Woolf sees assaulting the seventeenth-century subject became absorbed into the nineteenth-century text. Description marked before it mimicked the visual world and, thereby, records differences, not only in literary representation, but also in cultural perception. Different forms of description helped create different textual spaces.

CHAPTER ONE

A History of Description, a Foundling

ETC., tel pourrait être l'emblème de la description.
—*Philippe Hamon*

But *should* "ETC." really be the emblem of description?[1] From the six-teenth century through the late eighteenth, and then again across the middle of the twentieth, the status of description in literary theory and linguistic discourse was generally considered an afterthought at best, an ob-stacle or weakness or danger at worst. And worst tended to win out over best. But, in the later eighteenth century, and throughout the nineteenth, description underwent a sort of rhetorical *amplificatio*, or "enlargement," of its own, along with its stable of figurative means—its own culturally updated versions of accumulation and paralepsis, division and hyperbole,... *etc.* Description, long treated as a static *object* within prose or poetic narra-tives, began to find itself absorbed within narrative lines, at home and in place—only to lose visibility and credibility once again in twentieth-century criticism.

The traditional literary assumption is that description *presents* some-thing, that its primary function is to make us *see*. The *OED* defines it as "the action of writing down; inscription. *Obs. rare*"; "the action of setting forth in words by mentioning recognizable features or characteristic marks; verbal representation or portraiture"; "a statement which describes, sets forth, or portrays; a graphic or detailed account of a person, thing, scene, etc." But some examples of description—from Bunyan in the seventeenth century and Macaulay and Brontë in the nineteenth—will illustrate just how differently things can be seen. The following passage from John Bunyan's *The Pilgrim's Progress* (1678) is typical of late seventeenth- and early eighteenth-century prose place setting in its emblematic quadrants, its fixed coordinates in a fictional geography. What does it make us see? "Just as [Christian and Pliant] had ended this talk, they drew near to a very *Miry Slow* that was in the midst of the Plain, and they being heedless, did both fall suddenly into the bogg. The name of the *Slow* was Dispond. Here therefore they wallowed for a time, being grievously bedaubed with the dirt; And *Christian*, because of the burden that was on his back, began to sink in the Mire."[2] We read the emblems, of course: the Slough of Despond sucks us all in at times, bedaubing us grievously. How vividly do we see it? How are we trained or accustomed to see it? Do we see a particular swamp, a darkening of the green plain, perhaps treeless, the red sun slanting through dreary clouds, the men's arms thrashing, their bodies sinking by inches, panic on their faces? Probably not. Most twentieth-century critics pass along the generalization that the eighteenth-century writers lacked "eye" and, like Dorothy Van Ghent, see a large list of *things* sans context, things that "are not at all vivid in texture…[not] a world rich in physical, sensuous textures—in images for the eye or for the tactile sense or for the tongue or the ear or for the sense of temperature or the sense of pressure. It is extraordinarily barren of such images" (34–35).[3] We have a miry slough that bedaubs and starts to sink two figures: we have the fact of essential details, but not the *details*.

But that is us. Thomas Babington Macaulay, on the other hand, reviewing Robert Southey's 1830 edition of *The Pilgrim's Progress*, finds a text rich in evocative, detailed description:

> This is the highest miracle of genius,—that things which are not should be as though they were,—that the imaginations of one mind should become the personal recollections of another. And this miracle the tinker has wrought. There is no ascent, no declivity, no resting place, no turnstile, with which we are not perfectly acquainted. The wicket-gate and the desolate swamp which separates it from the City of Destruction, the long line of road, as straight as a rule can make it, the Interpreter's house and all its fair shows, the prisoner in the iron cage, the palace, at the doors of which armed men kept guard, and on the battlements of which walked persons clothed all in gold, the cross and the sepulchre, the steep hill and the pleasant arbour, the stately front of the House Beautiful by the wayside, the low green valley of Humiliation, rich with grass and covered with flocks, all are as well known to us as the sights of our own street.[4]

But this is largely *Macaulay's* knitting together of a whole visual scene, from his own very English (as well as biblical) "memory storehouse" (to use the phrase of Philippe Hamon, to which I will return). As a twenty-first-century reader, I am not all that clear on wicket gates and turnstiles myself. It is Macaulay who layers on for himself the details of the spiritual allegory and its visual emblems, connecting them into a fully realized, fully familiar English landscape; it is Macaulay who fills in the empty spaces between visual tags and finds them full and complete representations of his own landscape. Macaulay in the early nineteenth century *sees differently* from us; he sees early English prose narrative in much the way, I will argue, that early eighteenth-century readers were able to see—to fill out, expand on, rehydrate—the local, immediate signs of a shared culture, a shared visual landscape of meaningful, referential detail.

Macaulay lived in a time when one expected to see a novel describe an interior setting in intimate, well-upholstered detail, as in *Jane Eyre*:

> The red-room was a spare chamber, very seldom slept in . . . yet it was one of the largest and stateliest chambers in the mansion. A bed supported on massive pillars of mahogany, hung with curtains of deep red damask, stood out like a tabernacle in the centre; the two large windows, with their blinds always drawn down, were half shrouded in festoons and falls of similar drapery; the carpet was red; the table at the foot of the bed was covered with a crimson cloth; the walls were a soft fawn colour, with a blush of pink in it; the wardrobe, the toilet-table, the chairs were of darkly-polished old mahogany. Out of these deep surrounding shades rose high, and glared white, the piled-up mattresses and pillows of the bed, spread with a snowy Marseilles counterpane. Scarcely less prominent was an ample, cushioned easy-chair near the head of the bed, also white, with a foot-stool before it; and looking, as I thought, like a pale throne.[5]

This is a room made unforgettably familiar to us all, as images pile up for the eye, and for the tactile sense, and for the tongue and the ear, and for the sense of temperature and the sense of pressure, so to speak. There are two points to make here. First, we should compare Jane's description of the red room to an earlier interior, say, Bunyan's House of the Interpreter, for the impact of comparative presences and absences: "Then [the Interpreter] took [Christian] by the hand, and led him into a very large *Parlour* that was full of dust, because never swept; the which, after he had reviewed a little while, the *Interpreter* called for a man to *sweep*: Now when he began to sweep, the dust began so abundantly to fly about, that *Christian* had almost therewith been choked: Then said the *Interpreter* to a *Damsel* that stood by, Bring hither Water, and sprinkle the Room; which when she had done, was swept and cleansed with pleasure" (24–25). The room is large; it is a parlor; it is dusty and uncomfortable until the damsel wets it down and sweeps it out to the pleasure of all. Does it have a sofa? No, because sofas came later.[6] Do we know how many windows it has, or whether it has curtains, or whether its floor is stone or earth? If we lived in 1678, we might. If we live in the twenty-first century, especially if we live in suburban America, we have no idea. There's certainly nothing about snowy counterpanes or walls of soft fawn color with a blush of pink. We know that we're in an interior, and we know the essential things about it: it's dusty and needs cleaning. (And, if we're spiritually attuned, we know that that's an emblem that we *can* easily amplify, especially when the Interpreter adds helpfully: "This Parlor, is the heart of a Man that was never sanctified by the sweet Grace of the Gospel" [25].) Like the Miry Slow, it is an overdetermined place, with certain visual properties as well as its spiritual and ethical meanings. So the first point is that it is *our* job, according to Bunyan, to fill out those spaces with particular meaning; it is our *act*, for Macaulay, that we fill them out with instant familiarity; it is the hope of this chapter to fill out the spaces of different historical perceptions of what visual familiarity might mean.

The second point, coming out of that last clause, is that interior domestic space itself acquires an almost wholly new status in the larger history of description in the late eighteenth century and the nineteenth. Pictorial description has had a long history, but it has mostly devoted itself to landscape or to architectural exteriors, and then largely in terms of the symbolic connections to the landowners and the visual representation of their virtues or vices. Domestic interiors—the furniture and fabric and object details of particularized rooms as part of ordinary life and action—rarely appear in the high-level hierarchies of poetry or prose until later in the eighteenth century, but then dominate nineteenth-century novels and poetry.

This book will try to account for the historical and cultural change in the status and use of description; this chapter will review the history of description from classical rhetoric to nineteenth-century practice. It will show *that* and *how* the rhetoric about and the status of description changed, without trying to reargue the long history of critical work on ekphrasis or word and image. (The subsequent chapters will argue *why* that change appears most prominent in the eighteenth century.) I will first look at some contrasting definitions of *description* to set up some of the dimensions of its historical space. I will then examine the historical rhetoric *about* description, noting particularly that that rhetoric shifts markedly: from talking about description as itself a sort of object, generally getting in the way of (or providing relief from) narrative (a sort of *res non grata*), to talking about description as achieving a primacy of perception, an essential of particularity, as the culture shifts from an emphasis on the universal to a celebration of the particular. The change in description's status involves a change in the culture's awareness of and accessibility to a rather sudden large intake of new *things*, from the expanding English trade markets and the development of a credit economy, to the wider market of readers of English texts and the corresponding evaporation of a shared "cultural storehouse." Description as object was a traditional cultural construct that, over two or three centuries, found itself transformed from something obstructing narrative and refrigerating thought to something absorbed into narrative as the need to *see differently* expanded.

This project obviously marks and, therefore, believes in historical and cultural change. As John Bender and Michael Marrinan point out, one condition governing description is the "historical variability produced when the technology used to register descriptive features changes so dramatically that things previously invisible become newly visible."[7] But such a change is not intended to seem teleological. What interests me is what a particular culture does with its particular inheritance of technological and epistemological revelations, how the culture moves either habitually or inventively both within and beyond its temporal, geographic, and ideological givens. I necessarily cover areas with which I am less familiar than I am with the eighteenth century, but my forays into medieval and Renaissance rhetoric have shown me similar studies of the relation between formal practice in relation to cultural practice, formal innovation underneath traditional decorum. I see the expanding and increasingly intrusive functions of spatial description—most especially the mapping out of domestic interiors—as a late eighteenth-century project, but, along with charting and contextualizing a trajectory, I hope equally to demonstrate the particular agility and richness of early description, an agility and richness that have become more or less invisible to a post-nineteenth-century eye.

Some Definitions of Description

Consider the following dialogic answer from a seventeenth-century distillation of Aristotle and Peter Ramus:

Q. What is Description?

A. Description is a definition defining the thing from other arguments also.

Q. Give an example.

A. This is the description of a man; A man is a living creature, mortall, capable of discipline.

Q. Are not proper circumstances also mingled with common causes sometime?

A. Yes.

Q. Then it seemeth succinct brevity is not always in this kinde.[8]

Although straightforward, to the point, with succinct brevity, and carefully broken down into easily digestible bits, it is not, perhaps, in the end the most helpful way to begin, but it does suggest the difficulty of the task. The history of the *definition* of *description* is at least as convoluted and contrary as that of the practice and importance of description. The *Compendium*'s definition is actually addressing logic, in which description *is* definition of a kind. "[A] description is a sentence which setteth out a thing, even by other arguments," says Thomas Spencer in *The Art of Logick* (1628).[9] Samuel Johnson considers descriptions "definitions of a more lax and fanciful kind" (*Rambler*, no. 143, as quoted in the *OED*), although a 1962 *Dictionary of Philosophy* definition of logical description is neither lax nor fanciful: "Where a formula A containing a free variable—say, for example, x—means a true proposition (is true) for one and only one value of x, the notation (ix)A is used to mean that value of X."[10]

The traditional literary expectation, as noted above, is that description *presents* something, that its primary function is to make us *see*. John Bender has distinguished description from pictorialism by defining *description* as "formally neutral," with a tendency to "reduce and simplify experience" as its "detail accumulates without compelling the reader to a fresh visualization and reevaluation of successive images in a developing context." His focus is on Spenser and the kind of cumulative imagery that creates "intensity and vividness" by its "form and context," producing an "*illusory* sense of comprehensive detail" (emphasis added).[11] Bender's distinction is useful for comparing visual methods: the eighteenth century, I argue, begins systematically to bring in precisely the kind of cumulative detail of description that Bender finds formally neutral and that the nineteenth century would find formally rich. The sense of comprehensive detail would move from "illusory" to very much there. But, throughout this work, I will continue to use *description* as the larger and more economical term, one that can incorporate, or overlap with, or imply *pictorialism*.

The *OED*'s definitions distill meanings prevalent in the Renaissance and the eighteenth century, as in Richard Rainolde's 1563 *Foundacion of Rhetorike*, which defines *descripcion* as something "that collecteth and representeth to the eye, that which he sheweth"; or Henry Peacham's 1577 *Garden of Eloquence*, which defines *pragmatographia* as "a description of thinges, wherby we do as plainly describe any thing by gathering togeather all the circumstances belonging unto it, as if it were moste liuely paynted out in colloures, and set forth to be seene"; or the *Encyclopédie* (1751–65), which declares that description "makes [an object] somehow visible, by lively and animated exposition."[12] Alexander Welsh argues that the eighteenth and nineteenth centuries favored "strong representations," such as Crusoe's detailed description of the Footprint, that made the facts speak for themselves.[13] And Susan Stewart asserts that "all description is a matter of mapping the unknown onto the known."[14] Description in one way or another makes something visible, sets it forth, extracts it from its surroundings, and jabs a finger meaningfully at it; it makes the invisible present, brings the unthought of into awareness, gathers circumstances into meanings.

But, as Michel Beaujour points out, description is also always "Janus-like, always facing at once in two opposite directions" (35). Newton's logical definition in the *Principia Mathematica* (1687) of descriptions ends up being quite literarily and historically suggestive when he notes that they are "incomplete symbols" (quoted in *Dictionary of Philosophy*, 77). And the sense of ultimate incompleteness is elaborated in the *Encyclopédie*: "[C'est une] définition imparfaite & peu exacte, dans laquelle on tâche de faire connaître une chose par quelques propriétés & circonstances qui lui sont particulieres, suffisantes pour en donner une idée & la faire distinguer des autres, mais qui ne developpent point sa nature & son essence" (Description is an imperfect and inexact definition, in which one's task is to make something known by some of the properties and circumstances of its particulars, sufficient to give an idea and to distinguish it from other things, but which does not open up its nature or essence).[15] Aristotle, for example, thought that poetic description should center on things that *ought to be*, rather than things that really *are*: "[T]he poet's function is to describe, not the thing that has happened, but a kind of thing that might happen, i.e. what is possible as being probable or necessary."[16] A hopefulness of essence, perhaps, but imperfect and incomplete (at least by later theoretical standards) by its very hopefulness. Poets and novelists and critics (not to mention scientists) have always been aware that the act of foregrounding articulates absence as much as presence, defining what is left out in the act of inscribing what is within. Edward Casey suggests that any "essences gleaned from description will be *inexact*."[17] Michael Riffaterre argues more pointedly that "description, like all literary discourse, is a verbal detour so contrived that the reader understands something else than the object ostensibly represented."[18] Mieke Bal plunks down the other end of the seesaw when she virtually empties description of either power or deviousness, defining it as "a textual fragment in which features are attributed to objects. This aspect of attribution is the descriptive function.

We consider a fragment as descriptive when this function is dominant."[19] Elizabeth Fowler argues—for Chaucerian description but also description more generally—that, "without ecphrastic conventions, even the most realistic verbal description is more spatially deranged than any Picasso, because the spatial orientation of words in narrative has no similarity to our visual, tactile, and aural experience of bodies in space," but that readers (in Chaucer's time and today) rarely perceive incoherence because "we are skilled at working the bumps of figurative language (here, idioms, similes, and metaphors) into the smooth fabric of propositional statement, and because we know how to catch the conventional signals that set up the topos."[20] We put together the "odd set of objects" (Fowler, 69)—hair, wax, flax, shoulders, cap, eyes, beard, goat, wallet, gelding, mare—that is the Pardoner; the verbal fragments become imaginatively welded. But they remain *fragments*, an "ETC.," something other than what we are all *looking for* in narrative.

Plato, Aristotle, Horace, Puttenham, Chapman, Sidney, Dryden, Locke, Hume, Addison, Lessing, James, Lukács, Jean Hagstrum, W. J. T. Mitchell, Svetlana Alpers, Naomi Schor, Barbara Stafford, John Bender, and many others have extensively considered how the act of narrative visualization is possible epistemologically, how it works psychologically, what it means ideologically. I will not be re-treating those questions but will focus, instead, on the changing cultural and historical perceptions of and rhetoric about description. I will look at description as a cultural phenomenon of making things visible—which things, when, and why. And I will look at the historical discourses about description—how it is treated, when, and why. Each of the following chapters considers the changing function of description in the seventeenth and eighteenth centuries in terms of historical hierarchies; the issues of its dependence and autonomy; the available cultural storehouse; the gradual gentrification of description in matters of "propriety"; the concern with generals or particulars; the relation of emblem and detail to extended allegory and narration and scene setting; the growing approval of surfaces, visuality/nonvisuality, *vraisemblance*, and defamiliarization; the status of Things; the illusion of motion; and the creation of space. Description bobs up and down in literary history, taking up one function and dropping another, looking in more directions at once or over time than, in fact, Janus. In his wide-ranging analysis of "foregrounded description" in literature, José Manuel Lopes concludes that descriptions of space are "masters of disguise" (5), echoing T. H. Smiley—another logician, and one more evocative than Spencer or the *Dictionary of Philosophy*—who concludes that "the interesting thing about descriptions is that so many of them are functions in disguise."[21] It is my hope that, through this book, our experience of the "differently visualized" (or "visually challenged") eighteenth century will shift from a sense of its handicap; after all, says Bal of the general effect of objects filling space, "a cluttered room seems smaller, a sparsely furnished room bigger than in fact it is" (Bal 135). Like Gulliver in his travels, I would like our historical perceptions of literary spatialization to undergo a moment or two of readjustment.

The Rhetorical History of Description

Classical Authority, Classical Components

Until somewhere in the middle of the eighteenth century, the rules for and practices of description in poetry and prose were largely governed—or pretended they were governed—by classical authority. The poet's arena, according to Aristotle, is the probable ("a kind of thing that might happen"); poetry is "more philosophic and of graver import than history, since its statements are of the nature rather of universals, whereas those of history are singulars"; the poet's means are defined by "the imitative element in his work, and it is actions that he imitates"; and his end is vividness (enargeia), for ultimate emotional (and, therefore, moral) effect: "[T]he poet should remember to put the actual scenes as far as possible before his eyes. In this way, seeing everything with the vividness of an eye-witness as it were, he will devise what is appropriate, and be least likely to overlook incongruities" (Poetics, 2:2323, 2328–29, secs. 1451b, 1455a).

The ideal of the universal, the fact of imitation, and the art of vividness shape and define literatures throughout the centuries, but, of course, each comes in cultural contact with place and time and manages to change shape recognizably, without necessarily recognizing or acknowledging the change. Terms are recycled while concepts are reinvented or reapplied; classical categories get rearranged for contemporary convenience. ("[M]ethinks I deserue to be poūded," says Sir Philip Sidney, "for straying from Poetrie, to Oratory: but both haue such an affinitie in the wordish consideratiō, that I think this digression will make my meaning receiue the fuller vnderstanding.")[22] Although vividness seems to retain its sense of literary urgency from Homer to Robbe-Grillet, the meanings and implications of imitation shift recognizably over the centuries as the universal as existent and even as ideal disintegrates.

And even vividness veers wildly. Aristotle does not actually say that the poet should present his scenes vividly to others; he counsels having the

scenes before *himself* in order to order them. Edmund Wilson claims that
"we find so little exact visual observation in Greek poetry," compared to
Latin poetry, because "Greek poetry is mainly for the ear.... [T]he Greeks are
singing about the landscape, the Romans are fixing it for the eye of the mind,
and it is Virgil and Horace who lead the way to all the later picture poetry
down to our own Imagists."[23] We have already seen Macaulay's response
to Bunyan; to some extent vividness is even more a matter of reader (or
auditor) response, an authorial goal achieved when the readers all nod heads
in unison, a matter of a cultural moment or education.

"Description" and "Narration"

In one sense, even talking about *description* is connotatively anachronis-
tic for classical writing. Ekphrasis (Gr. "description"), which *narrowed* in
meaning through history to apply later only to descriptions of works of art,
was originally defined in the Greek *progymnasmata* (school exercises) as
"an expository speech which vividly (*enargōs*) brings the subject before our
eyes" (Theon, second century AD).[24] Ekphrasis was its own self-contained
description of some object (often commonplace—a shield, a cloak, a cup,
a basket, a bedcover) that was inserted into discourse or narrative. Something was displayed or showcased; the object was isolated, as in an auction
catalog. Other forms of description lived primarily in parts, deriving from
distinctions in classical rhetoric. In his *Treatise of Schemes & Tropes* (1550),
Richard Sherry explains that "*enargia*, euidence or perspicuitie called also
descripcion rethoricall, is when a thynge is so described that it semeth to the
reader or heare ye beholdeth it as it were in doyng. Of thys figure ben many
kyndes."[25] *Of thys figure ben many kyndes*: for example, in pragmatographia
("description of thinges") and topographia ("an euident and true description
of a place" [Peacham, Pi]); prosopopeia ("the fayning of a person, that is, to
a Thing senceless or dumme, we fayne a fit persō" [Peacham, Oiii]); prosopographia ("when that as well the person of a very mā, as of a fayned, is by
his forme, stature, manners, studyes, dooings, affections, and such other circumstances ... so described, that it may appeare a playne pycture paynted"
[Peacham, Oii–Oii$_v$]); pathopeia (the "expressyng of vehement affeccions"
[Sherry, Eii$_v$]); or chronographia ("the descripcion of the tyme, as of nyght,
daye, and the foare tymes of the yere" [Sherry, Eiii$_v$]); not to mention similitude, icon or image, dialogue, amplification, hyperbole, paralepsis, distinctions between "feignings" of real persons or animals and feignings of myth,
and division within division, subcategory beneath subcategory, of all the
above.[26]

Both basic kinds of description—the ekphrastic display and the enargiac examples—enjoyed a fairly comfortable companionship with narrative in classical literature. Epics were always happy to pause for long displays of objects, and vivid depictions of "the person... thynges... tymes... places... acttes" (Rainolde, lij) essentially permeated what was later made oppositional: narrative. When Gérard Genette argues the power of "even a verb" to be "more or less descriptive, in the precision that it gives to the spectacle of the action"—for example, "grabbed a knife" versus "picked up a knife" (134)—he is recovering Aristotle, who recommends using verbs of motion, especially present participles, and adverbial phrases in creating vivid representation.[27] And, in fact, Rainolde suggests that "some are of that opinion" that description does not belong among rhetorical exercises simply because it will not distinguish itself generically: "Because that both in euery Oracion, made vpon a Fable, all thynges therein conteined, are liuely described. And also in euery Naracion, the cause, the place, the persone, the time, the fact, the maner how, are therein liuely described" (lj). Indeed, the "descripcion vpon Xerxes" is a history and genealogy: "When Darius was dedde, Xerxes his sonne did succede hym, who also tooke vpon him to finishe the warres... against Greece." And it is also a character analysis: "Xerxes was a cowarde, in harte a childe... last in battaile to fight, and the firste to retire, and runne awaie," although, "when daunger was paste, he was stoute, mightie, glourious, and wonderfful.... He thought hym self a God." Such a "descripcion" of a man does not much resemble Jane's description of Mr. Rochester's craggy brows and stocky body, but it does strike at what the *Encyclopédie* says cannot be caught: "sa nature & son essence."

"Imitation" of the Universal and "Maker" of the Particular

For classical and medieval criticism, the poet is primarily an imitator, and "it is actions that he imitates" (Aristotle, *Poetics*, 2:2323, sec. 1451b). Epic, tragedy, comedy, dithyrambic poetry, flute playing, and lyre playing are all, viewed as a whole, modes of imitation, according to Aristotle, and modes that imitate by language alone: "Imitation is natural to man from childhood, one of his advantages over the lower animals being this, that he is the most imitative creature in the world, and learns at first by imitation. And it is also natural for all to delight in works of imitation. The truth of this second point is shown by experience.... [T]he reason of the delight in seeing the picture is that one is at the same time learning—*gathering the meaning of things*" (*Poetics*, 2:2318, sec. 1448b; emphasis added). Obviously, *imitation* and *originality* become highly contested concepts by the eighteenth century, as much recent work on copyright law and the concept of *genius*, not to mention traditional accounts of romanticism, have outlined. Without reinventing this particular critical wheel (or "imitating" the critics who said it all first and best), it seems useful to revisit its critical turns as they relate to the discourse and status of description. For Aristotle, the poet imitates actions, and the reader, or listener, or viewer gathers from the imitation of actions the meaning of things. The whole point of poetry for the classical world, with its representations of actions and persons and things, is "to prove or disprove, to arouse emotion (pity, fear, anger, and the like), or to maximize or minimize things"; "to describe, not the thing that has happened, but a kind of thing that might happen"; to achieve "universal statements" (*Poetics*, 2:2330–31, 2322, 2323, secs. 1456a, 1451a, 1451b). "The stimulation of inward vision in the imagination and the arousal of concomitant feelings are closely linked.... The immediacy of the effect of subjective representation is more important than the strict truth of its contents."[28] Aristotle claims that "the greatest thing by far is to be a master of metaphor ... since a good metaphor implies an intuitive perception of the similarity in dissimilars" (*Poetics*, 2:2334–35, sec. 1459a). What is "universal" has to do, not necessarily with accurate visual reporting, but with vivid visual evoking, with understanding the invisible potential between things, with the underlying connectedness—with "making our hearers [readers] see things" (*Rhetoric*, 2:2252, sec. 1411b).

The assumption of underlying connectedness, and of classical authors recognizing and articulating that connectedness, shapes the concept of *imitation* in medieval description. Phillip Damon explains that the medieval poet "does not transform, transvalue or otherwise modify the things he selects from the world as objectively given. With minor exceptions for extreme cases, they come to him with their meanings, their truth, and their beauty solidly embedded in them."[29] Douglas Kelly, in his study of description and authorship from Macrobius to medieval romance, notes that "original description implies both a source and a common model." Description in classical and medieval rhetoric and poetry appropriates through imitation a source model and rewrites it for a new context: "Vergil is understood to have 'described' the tempest in the *Odyssey* by drawing it from Homer's version and adapting it to his own story." Description is a form of rewriting, with four technical operations involved in a transformation or appropriation: addition; deletion; replacement; and transmutation. "These operations refer to an art that transforms and recombines compositional blocks, an art, that is, of *belle conjointure*. A new synthesis results from the combined operations of all four of these transformations."[30] In other words, the Greeks and then the Latin writers produced a store of scenes and images—"compositional blocks"—that medieval writers in their turn rearranged and reassembled for different narrative needs and subject matter. Medieval description works with what is already there—not only in the literature itself, but also in the literary memories and experiences of medieval writers' new readers.[31] Description in classical writing and medieval romance might be said to *evoke* images rather than represent them. Chaucer, for example, according to D. W. Robertson Jr., was less interested in "surface reality" than in "the reality of the idea"; thus, the details of his descriptions can seem random.[32] Kelly suggests that a new context alone "may suffice to make a common subject matter resonate differently from its first version" (74).

The term *imitation* absorbed rather different possibilities in the Renaissance as poets began to think of poetry more as a craft or technique than as a sort of Platonic divine madness; the godlike powers seem to invest the poet more directly: "A Poet is as much to say as a maker. . . . Euen so the very Poet makes and contriues out of his owne braine both the verse and matter of his poeme, and not by any foreine copie or example, as doth the translator, who therefore may well be sayd a versifier, but not a Poet. . . . It is therefore of Poets thus to be conceiued, that if they be able to deuise and make all these things of them selues, without any subiect of Veritie, that they be (by maner of Speech) as creating gods" (Puttenham, 1–2). Sidney agrees forcefully. The astronomers, the mathematicians, the musicians, the natural and moral philosophers, the lawyers, the historians, the grammarians, the rhetoricians, the logicians, the physicians, even the metaphysicians, all are bound by *what is.* Everything they do has to take into account "what nature will haue set forth." Only the poet, Sidney says,

> disdeining to be tied to any such subiectiō, lifted vp with the vigor of his own inuention, doth grow in effect into an other nature: in making things either better then [sic] nature bringeth foorth, or quite a new, formes such as neuer were in nature . . . so as he goeth hand in hand with nature, not enclosed within the narrow warrant of her gifts, but freely raunging within the Zodiack of his owne wit. Nature neuer set foorth the earth in so rich Tapistry as diuerse Poets haue done, neither with so pleasaunt riuers, fruitfull trees, sweete smelling flowers, nor whatsoeuer els may make the too much loued earth more louely: her world is brasen, the Poets only deliuer a golden. (Sidney, B4v–C)

This is Protestant reformation; we are losing the priests and nudging against the hegemony of the universal; the pieces of the here and now acquire a

different power. There is less sense of rewriting "Originalls," of reorganiz-
ing compositional blocks, when it is all "contriue[d] out of [one's] owne
braine."[33]

Peter Ramus had largely separated logic from rhetoric in the mid-
sixteenth century, pulling *inventio* (the finding of topics) and *dispositio* (the
organizing of topics) into the discipline of dialectic, leaving rhetoric with
memoria, elocutio, and *pronuntiatio.* But, as Edward Tayler points out, by
the early seventeenth century, "in an age of scientific 'things,' *elocutio,* the
art of tropes and schemes, could not retain its glamour; and in a period dominated by the written word, the oral art of *pronuntiatio* or *actio* had lost most
of its relevance to literature" (24–25). As Puttenham's declaration quoted
above suggests, literary criticism reallocated *inventio,* investing it with new
significance: less the *finding* than the *devising* of arguments. Thus, in 1659,
the rhetorician Obadiah Walker could speak of *fancy* and *invention* as if the
terms were synonymous: "Invention consists in an acute Consideration, and
particular weighing of all circumstances, &c. out of which any argument
may be raised to advance the subject in hand. Therefore your Fancy, in this,
ought not to be committed, and left, to chance; gazing about, and waiting, as
it were, what may by sudden Enthusiasm drop into it, but to be excited and
guided by Reason; diligently beating and examining the Causes, Effects, Ad-
juncts, and whatever may have relation to your subject, that (at least) some
of them may afford materials to your design."[34] The synonymity slid into
literature, in the sense of original creation of plot, or image, or character.
Page duBois notes that one of the changes in the use of ekphrasis from antiquity to the Renaissance lies in the disappearance of the maker of the work
of art;[35] metaphorizing history, the maker slips out of the work of art, out
of imitation, and into the work of maker, inventor, originator, creating god.

Textual Praxes: Lists, Catalogs, Respites, Ornaments

But there is another sense of *work* that surfaces in the history of description
and assumes a less socially impressive curriculum vitae. Philippe Hamon
describes the history of description as a "textual praxis" (4), as serving more
functionary than aesthetic roles. Even in its aesthetic roles, he argues,

> [f]rom Gilles Corrozet (*Les Antiquités chroniques et singularités de
> Paris* 1561) . . . to the recent Michelin guides, . . . description remains sec-
> ondary to economic ends (guides), to military ends (the geographic de-
> scription of sites and landscapes is that of potential military fields), to
> history ("antiques"), to encyclopedic matters, and finally to a number of

inter-semiological re-writings; a description is in fact nothing more than the marginal commentary upon an architectural drawing, upon an allegorical print that requires explanation (cf. the illustrated frontispieces of the great didactic pieces of the eighteenth century), upon a map (where the description becomes the "legend"), upon a painting whose story must be reactivated. (4–5)

Such a sweeping demotion of description to secondary, practical status overlooks the importance of ekphrasis and *enargia* in classical through Renaissance poetry, but it does capture what will become a dominant seventeenth- and early eighteenth-century view of a certain *kind* of detail-oriented description. John Bender categorizes most descriptive poetry as something that "reduc[es] visual experience to simple formulas" and that attempts to be encyclopedic. "The crudest type... would be no more than a list or catalog of things that we might see" (*Spenser*, 34). Description comprises lists, crawls over things, acts as narrative relief, employs figures, behaves as ornament, misbehaves as obstacle, achieves archaeology, to name just a few of its "propriétés & circonstances," its functions and obligations and nuisances that shift shape over the centuries. This functionary history has been considered both as necessary—formally and psychologically—and, with some contempt, as subsidiary, servant-class, sullen, and obstructionist. First, the functions and their cheerleaders.

Gordon Braden has reexamined the epic catalog in its Renaissance self-fashioning, noting that it is "the feature of the genre perhaps least subject to active critical scrutiny, and certainly the feature to which it is most difficult for later generations to give an enthusiastic or even sympathetic reading," as one of the "formal *données* of the classical tradition" and, therefore, "a challenge to the working poetic imagination, a challenge to fit the catalogue into the texture and meaning of a Renaissance poem."[36] From classical to eighteenth-century times (and beyond), lists and catalogs generally served an aesthetic, amplificatory function, as in the following passage from *The Garden of Eloquence*.[37] Peacham demonstrates how a single brief phrase, such as "the citty was ouercome by assault," can be expanded through proper pragmatographia, "a discription of thinges," into a kinetic vision of devastation— "if thou wilt open and set abroade those thinges whiche were included in one word" (Oiiii$_v$). Within one word lies, waiting to spring, all this (Peacham's own version of pragmatographia as catalog):

> [T]here shall appear many fyres and scattered flames upō houses and
> temples, the noyse of houses falling down, one sounde of diuers thinges

& cryes, some flye with great daunger, others hang on their friendes, to bid them farewell foreuer, the scriking of Infantes, women weepinge most bitterly, old men kepte by most unhappy destiny to see that day, the spoyling of temporall and hallowed thinges, the running out of them, that caryed awaye spoyles, and of them that intreated for their owne goods, euery man ledde chayned before his spoyler, the mother wrastling and stryuing to hold her sucking babe, and whersoeuer were great riches, there was great fighting among the spoylers. (Oiiii$_v$)

This word-into-list spills open the horrors of a sacked city through clause after relentless clause, reinforcing, reiterating, or rhetorically creating a sense of vastness, or power, or even, through sheer verbosity, ineffability. Peacham, pointing to Ovid, Virgil, and Cicero (and everyone pointing always to Homer), declares that, "although this word destruction might well comprise all these thinges, yet is it less to declare the whole, which sayeth the citty was taken and destroyed, and no more, but he that rehearseth all thinges orderly, doth much more largely express the same" (Oiiii$_v$). Or, as the 1584 *Artes of Logike and Rhetorike* puts it: "[T]he excellencie or finenesse of wordes or Tropes is moste excellent, when diuers are / Shut vp in one, or / Continued in many."[38] Obadiah Walker reiterates in 1659 that "*Metaphors* (used chiefly in *Descriptions*) which are *similitudes* contracted to a word," and, therefore, the most significant expressions, "are borrowed, and translated to our matter from things amongst which our life is much conversant; as from *Buildings*; *Plants*; *Seasons* of the year; *Navigation*; *Astronomy*; All sorts and all qualities of *Bodies*...which so soon as named, the well-acquainted Auditor with ease, as it were prognosticates the rest of the discourse, and applies them further than the speaker" (54–55). As I discuss in chapters 4 and 5, late seventeenth- and early eighteenth-century narrative description is in some ways much closer to classical practice— and, therefore, immune to nineteenth-century critique—than is generally recognized. So much of early modern description turns out to be a matter of "diverse words or tropes shut up in one" and requiring an intimate readerly *amplificatio*—a well-acquainted reader. The classical and neoclassical view of lists and catalogs, then, is itself a description of narration, a collection of events and consequences and tableaux, sounds and sights, emotions and actions.

It is not much of a coincidence that Peacham's *pragmatographia* of the sacked city concentrates so much on "thinges"—the spoiling of things, the carrying away of things, the entreating for things, the fighting among the spoilers of things—since *things*—objects isolated or caught together—are a common subject of description and, over the centuries, come to shape the rhetoric about it and dominate the criticism of it. A rustic cup, a ship, a drop of water, a shield, almost anything can validly command the attention of the poet. The ekphrasis of the shield of Achilles in book 18 of the *Iliad*—in which Homer enacts the making of the shield and describes as if in motion the scenes carved on it—is the most famous and most rewritten through the centuries. The rewritings of descriptions of things are part of what reveals changes in attitudes toward what constitutes acceptable description. Alexander Pope, for example, in his comments on Homer's catalog of ships in book 2 of the *Iliad*, remarks on the criticism that Virgil's catalogs are shorter than Homer's and accounts for the difference historically and culturally:

> As, that *Homer* might have a design to settle the geography of his country, there being no description of *Greece* before his days; which was not the case with *Virgil*. *Homer*'s concern was to compliment *Greece* at a time when it was divided into many distinct states, each of which might expect a place in his catalogue: But when all *Italy* was swallow'd up in the sole dominion of *Rome*, *Virgil* had only *Rome* to celebrate. *Homer* had a numerous army, and was to describe an important war with great and various events; whereas *Virgil*'s sphere was much more confined.[39]

Although we might at first glance assume that lists and catalogs expand and contract according to the size and needs of their content, Pope suggests that it is just as likely that lists swell and ebb according to the tastes of the times, the appetite for lists, the relish for catalogs. Pope admits to "the addition of a few epithets or short hints of description to some of the places mention'd; tho' seldom exceeding the compass of half a verse (the space to which my author himself generally confines these pictures in miniature)" (*Iliad of Homer*, 131). He creates what J. Daniel Kinney calls a "scenic cohesion" that constrasts sharply with the inventory inclusiveness of nature descriptions in pre-eighteenth-century texts.[40] Rhodes, for example, has "everlasting sunshine bright" (*Iliad of Homer*, 98 [bk. 2, line 795]); "grassy *Pteleon*" is "decked with chearful greens" (99 [line 849]); and Antron has "watry dens and cavern'd ground" (99 [line 852]). This because "a meer heap of proper names, tho' but for a few lines together, could afford little entertainment to an *English* reader, who probably could not be appriz'd either of the necessity or beauty of this part of the poem" (131). The eighteenth-century reader has a different interest in lists, and Pope, like Peacham, is following and "rewriting," in the traditional sense, the poetic obligation to

"[invest] static spatial objects with vitality by transfusing into them its own
rhythmic, temporal succession" (Webb and Weller, 284). Lists and catalogs,
those formal classical données, expand within the expanding conception of
imitation to fill their new textual spaces and new formal textures. Lists are
pieces of description, the tautness of their connections a function of both
what is put in by the poet and culture and what is pulled out by the reader
and culture.

Besides aesthetically expanding and empowering images and effects, lists
and catalogs and description per se were seen to have quite specific readerly
purposes of respite, relief, escape. As *The Art of Poetry on a New Plan* (1762)
explains, in a work as "tumultuous" as the *Iliad*, "whose subject is only
quarrelling, fighting and death, the mind of the reader must have some re-
laxation, some divertisement from a continued scene of horror, or it would
be otherwise rendered torpid and insensible."[41] (As Bertie Wooster puts it:
"I never know when I'm telling a tale of peril and suspense whether to charge
straight ahead or whether to pause from time to time and bung in what is
called atmosphere.")[42] About the same time, Samuel Johnson was objecting
to the intrusiveness of descriptive detail, arguing that the "mind is refrigerated by interruption" ("Shakespeare," 111). But some critics favor a refrig-
erator on a hot day. Thomas P. Roche Jr. explains Spenser's pictorial talents
as a matter of concentration: "[H]e restrains his descriptive talents until he
reaches a place where he can utterly concentrate and intensify those images
that he might have been weaving into the texture of his narrative."[43] Genette
calls "ornamental or decorative description" something that offers a "recreational pause in the narrative, carrying out a purely esthetic role, like that
of sculpture in a classical building" (135). But "ornamental," "decorative,"
"recreational" can seem to belittle the context of, say, "continued scene[s] of
horror," and one line of criticism has always argued for something metaphorically more solid and functional than statuary. The author of the *New Plan*,
for example, also uses an architectural simile ("like beautiful pillars in a
fine building"), but in order to argue that they are, "not *only* ornamental,
but necessary" (emphasis added). His case is stronger than Genette's, or at
least he argues that the aesthetic is more psychologically and structurally
crucial: "The mind cannot always bear the melody of music, however var-
iegated and harmonious, how then should it endure the continual din and
clash of arms? Similes, which at once correspond [to] and differ from the
subject, could only aid *Homer* in this case, for, it is the only mode of writing that can introduce scenes continually new and entertaining, without
taking our attention from the principal object" (2:230). Similes, "figures"
(of thought, language, and speech), lists and catalogs, descriptions—like

architectural pillars—simultaneously separate and unite, reinforce and relieve. They create or evoke a particular image but at the same time underscore the space between the simile and the subject. Although Aristotle's
Poetics does not, in fact, address *figures* or *ornaments* as such—those are Renaissance terms for Renaissance adaptations of classical concepts—it does
deal with "language with pleasurable accessories" (2:2320, sec. 1449b). Aristotle tends to mean rhythm and harmony or song superadded; but such accessories will later become ornaments and, as ornaments, will be redefined
as superficial and obstructionary in the sixteenth and seventeenth centuries,
rediscovered as not *only* ornamental but also *necessary* in the eighteenth,
then redefined again as *not even* ornamental but *substantive* in the late
eighteenth century and the nineteenth.

Object and Obstacle

Page duBois also notes that another change in the use of ekphrasis from
antiquity to the Renaissance lies in the gradual distancing of the precious
object from the body of the hero (92). We have seen in Puttenham the maker
relocated more explicitly in the poet, and we will see below the increasingly
dim view taken of the "work" in art. Meanwhile, the ekphrastic shift itself
could in a way be read as historical metaphor for the discourse of description
itself: from a concentration on objects to its perception *as* object, description
began a sort of migration into otherness.

Genette claims that the "opposition" between description and
narrative—the idea that description simply gets in the way—did not "[enjoy]
a very active existence before the nineteenth century, when the introduction of long descriptive passages in a typically narrative genre like the novel
brought out the resources and the requirements of the method" (133). Certainly, twentieth-century critical rejections of description arose in response
to the elaborate, lengthy nineteenth-century layouts of objects and persons
delineated in detail *and within* a detailed, connected setting. But we can
date the battle earlier. In some sense, the objections were there from the
beginning. Plato, for example, pointed out the bad poet or speaker who "will
attempt to represent the roll of thunder, the noise of wind and hail, or the
creaking of wheels, and pulleys, and the various sounds of flutes, pipes,
trumpets, and all sorts of instruments: he will bark like a dog, bleat like a
sheep, or crow like a cock; his entire art will consist in imitation of voice and
gesture, and there will be very little narration."[44] But the animadversions
really heat up in the seventeenth century, as the nature of description began
to be considered more unified and also more distinct from narration.

Renaissance and seventeenth-century rhetorical advisers frequently
speak of description or its parts in terms of ornament, garnishing, or, in
other words, *objects*. In *The Artes of Logike and Rhetorike*, for example,
rhetoric, the "Arte of speaking finely" (the parent of writing finely), is divided into two parts: "Garnishing of speeche, called Eloquution. / Garnishing of the maner of vtterance, called Pronunciation." In the "garnishing" of
speech, there is, in addition to "[t]he fine maner of wordes, called a Trope,"
"[t]he fine shape or frame of speeche, called a figure" (C4)—all metaphorically images of something attached to or placed within something already
there, something logically and, in some cases, even experientially prior. The
Renaissance conception of the image is itself more of an exemplum than,
as later, "a basis for associative ruminating."[45] The language of object imagery for description seems to increase in the seventeenth century. In 1628,
Thomas Spencer notes that "*Aristotle* doth perpetually forbid accidents to
come within the dores of any Definition" (195). John Smith, in *The Mysterie of Rhetorique Unvail'd* (1657), makes a favorite Renaissance trope
explicit: "A *Figure* in the Greek . . . signifies principally *habitum, vestitu,
& ornatum corporis*, in English, the apparel and ornament of the body;
which by a Metaphor is transferred to signifie the habit and ornament of
words of speech."[46] H. C., in *Aristotle's Rhetoric* (1686), in discussing the
differences and similarities between metaphors and "representations" (by
which he primarily means similes), has a whole long list of examples in
which "representations" are *represented* as objects, things, or people with
things: "Representations therefore are like that which *Androtio* makes of
Idrieus, That he was like a dog let loose from his Chains: For they bite all
they meet. And, that of *Plato*, they who rob the Dead are like to Dogs that
bite the Stones, but never touch them that throw the Stone," like children
that take bread crying, like flints, like frankincense, like beakers, and like
shields.[47]

Some poetic forms actually find themselves transformed into objects. For
example, another kind of list, the blazon, present in classical and medieval
literature and prominent in the Renaissance, started out as a poetic genre
intent on praise or blame but, by the early sixteenth century, was most
commonly a catalogic tribute to female body parts.[48] The body as object was
reverently (or satirically) dismembered into more objects and those objects
reverently (or satirically) rejoined in literary lists.

As "things" with which to garnish and adorn a preexisting text (speech),
figures and ornaments—and, by extension, description—are, in fact, useful
accessories. Boileau asserts: "Without these Ornaments before our Eyes, /
Th' unsinew'd Poem languishes, and dyes."[49] A little more peculiarly,

Sir Thomas Pope Blount declares, in *De re poetica* (1694), that "imagination in a *Poet* is a Faculty so wild and lawless, that like an *high-ranging Spaniel*, it must have *Clogs* tied to it, lest it out-run the *Judgment*."[50] As with the *Compendium*'s (and Aristotle's) idea that a certain amount of ekphrasis provides the reader/listener welcome relief from the din of battles, the exhausting tramp of narrative, so ornament and figure (other body parts of description) prove useful in other ways: holding things together or keeping them down. They have *duties as objects*, to interfere or to coagulate.

But, as objects with duties, as auxiliaries or accessories, ornament and figure also pose difficulties. For one thing, they tend to get in the way when they're not wanted, as well as when they are, and that can have an unfortunate effect on the audience. George Puttenham declares that "the Poet or makers of speech becomes vicious and vnpleasant by nothing more than by vsing too much surplusage" (215). Sidney also finds too much surplusage, too many ornaments, in too many poetic works: "For now they cast Suger and spice vppon euerie dish that is serued to the table: like those *Indians*, not content to weare eare-rings at the fit and naturall place of the eares, but they will thrust Iewels through their nose and lippes, becaue they will be sure to be fine" (I3v). Boileau recounts: "Sometimes an Author, fond of his own Thought, / Pursues his Object till it's over-wrought: / . . . / Of such Descriptions the vain Folly see, / And shun their barren Superfluity. / All that is needless carefully avoid, / The Mind once satisfi'd, is quickly cloy'd" (canto 1, lines 49–50, 59–62). Dryden, fashionably comparing poetry to painting, says that, as a "*Painter* must reject all trifling Ornaments, so must a *Poet* refuse all tedious, and unnecessary Descriptions. A Robe which is too heavy, is less an Ornament than a Burthen."[51] For Thomas Rymer, "Words are a sort of heavy baggage, that were better out of the way, at the push of Action," although he concedes that, to the undiscerning, "there may be something in the buz and sound that like a drone to a Bagpipe may serve to set off the Action."[52]

As objects, descriptions/ornaments can slow things down to a chilly halt. *Frigid* is one way to put it. According to H. C.: "[T]he Writings of *Alcidamus* seem to be frigid. For he does not make use of the Epithites as junkets, but as ordinary viands, frequent, open, and greater then [*sic*] the subject requires. For he does not only say *Sweat*, but *moist sweat*. . . . Not care, but sad care. He hid him not with boughs, but with *the boughs of the Wood*" (174). Redundancy, ordinariness, interruption. And, as Samuel Johnson had declared: "The mind is refrigerated by interruption" ("Shakespeare," 111). Too much relief from the din of battle, and one simply may not want to get up again—or go back to the text.

Decorum

Hand in hand—or, perhaps, hand in glove—with the idea of description behaving both usefully and obstructively is the very idea of its *behavior*. Ideas
of *decorum* begin with classical strictures for diction but escalate into social
significance.

As language is the means of evocation, so diction—choice of words as
logically prior to choice of image or figure or ornament, the *shape* of image or
figure or ornament—becomes central, both in classical and in later Western
traditions. Aristotle declares:

> The excellence of diction is for it to be at once clear and not mean. The
> clearest indeed is that made up of the ordinary words for things, but it is
> mean.... [D]iction becomes distinguished and non-prosaic by the use of
> unfamiliar terms, i.e. strange words, metaphors, lengthened forms, and
> everything that deviates from the ordinary modes of speech.—But a whole
> statement in such terms will be either a riddle or a barbarism, a riddle, if
> made up of metaphors, a barbarism, if made up of strange words.... A cer-
> tain admixture, accordingly, of unfamiliar terms is necessary. These, the
> strange word, the metaphor, the ornamental equivalent, etc., will save
> the language from seeming mean and prosaic, while the ordinary words
> in it will secure the requisite clearness. (*Poetics*, 2:2333–34, sec. 1458a)

Critics apply Aristotle's "rule of moderation" (2:2334, sec. 1458b) in every
cultural moment, but with different cultural commitments. *Proper, decent,
barbarous, uncouth, indecent, mean*—the vocabulary of decorum and gentility marks the various social ascents and embarrassments of description, that
"ever-necessary, ever-submissive, never-emancipated slave" (Genette, 134).
Proper style, proper words for proper topics, proper phrasings and emotions,
had always constituted rhetorical strategy, but, by the eighteenth century,
the term *proper* had absorbed some of its social connotations as well.

Ideas of linguistic barbarity in England go back at least to the sixteenth
century. Richard Sherry offers *A Treatise of Schemes & Tropes very profytable for the better vnderstanding of good authors* (1550) because, he admits, "it is not vnknowen that oure language for the barbarousness and lacke
of eloquence hath bene complayned of, and yet not trewely, for anye defaut
in the tongue it selfe, but rather for slacknes of our coūtrimen, whiche haue
alwayes set lyght by searchynge out the elegance and proper speaches that
be ful many in it" (Aii–Aii$_v$). The author/translator/imitator of *The Artes
of Logike and Rhetorike* agrees about the necessity of speaking finely but

argues that art requires its own interior decorum: "[It] must be shamefast, as it were maydenly, that it may seeme rather to be led by the hand to another signification, then [sic] to be driuen by force" (C4). What contributes to the "vndecent," says Puttenham, is "barbarousnesse, incongruitie, ill disposition, fond affectation, rusticitie, and all extreme darknesse such as is not possible for a man to vnderstand the matter without an interpretour" (208).

The seventeenth century continues the translations of propriety but seems to step up the intensity of the rhetoric and the levels of potential disapproval. The *Compendium of the Art of Logick* (1651) advises that a word (and the putting together of words) be "perspicuous" and "decent": "That is, neither *above*, nor *below* the Thing signified; or, neither too humble, nor too fine," and adds that "*Perspicuous* are all *Words* that be *Proper*" (247). But who defines *proper*? On the one hand, propriety requires a certain gentility, a sense of loftiness. Boileau maintains that some "objects are too mean to stay our sight; / Allow your Work a just and nobler flight" (canto 3, lines 266–67). Sir Thomas Pope Blount insists that "the *Language* [of a poet] must be *lofty* and *splendid*; for the *common* and *ordinary* Terms are not proper for a *Poet*; he must use Words that partake nothing of the *Base* and *Vulgar*" (29). On the other hand, too much loftiness becomes ridiculous or vulgar in itself. Hobbes translates indecent metaphors as those that are "*ridiculous*, as in *Comedies*; or *too grave*, as in *Tragedies*" (105).[53] H. C. has a whole chapter on "Decorum," which lies in not "[bestowing] too much Trimming upon an ordinary word: for that will appear comical … as if a man should say, *Most venerable Colliflowre*" (181). One can be *too* polite; in social terms, perhaps, "affected," or overenunciating your aitches. Rymer (translating Rapin, who is reflecting on Aristotle) reemphasizes that "there is a particular *Rhetorick* for *Poetry*, which the *modern Poets* scarce understand at all; this Art consists in discerning very precisely what ought to be said *figuratively*, and what to be spoken *simply*: and in knowing well where Ornament is requir'd, and where not. *Tasso* understood not well this *Secret*, he is too *trim* and too *polite* in places, where the *gravity* of the *Subject* demanded a more *simple* and *Serious Style*."[54]

Neoclassical criticism shared with the Renaissance a concern with hierarchy, "the concept of decorum function[ing] as a social and metaphysical as well as a stylistic principle, sucking sustenance not only from the authority of classical rhetoricians but also from the structure of society and the universe. In such a context, there is nothing irresponsible or precious in Donne's assertion that 'wicked is not much worse than indiscreet.'"[55] But the neoclassical critics etched the concept even more sharply, and Johnson finds himself appalled by some of Shakespeare's poetic solecisms (although, in general, he believes that Shakespeare catches "the conversation above grossness and below refinement, where propriety resides" ["Shakespeare," 70]). Johnson regrets the historical evaporation of linguistic power in a passage from *Macbeth*, noting the fall into ordinariness of a word like *knife*, now "the name of an instrument used by butchers and by cooks," and the silliness of heaven peeping through blankets. He argues: "Words which convey ideas of dignity in one age, are banished from elegant writing or conversation in another, because they are in time debased by vulgar mouths, and can no longer be heard without the involuntary recollection of unpleasing images."[56]

By the mid-eighteenth century, *New Plan* is declaring that modern poets cannot use with propriety "such rich ornaments" as Homer, Virgil, and Milton did (2:349), and the main concern is a sort of social mixing: "It requires great invention, as well as judgment to assemble low thoughts and images, and dress them in such a manner, that they may mix with propriety among those which are sublime" (2:243). This at a time when social dress connoted the ability to mix socially but no longer necessarily denoted true social status. And, in his 1762–63 lectures, Adam Smith was persuaded that the use of "figures" characterizes "the lowest and most vulgar conversation," that it was always a "secondary means" and only "sometimes proper" in giving elegance to expression, and that, on the whole, it "give[s] no beauty to style."[57] For Hugh Blair, the selection of circumstances is the true art of description, and those circumstances *"in the first place* ... ought not to be vulgar, and common ones" (3:174).

In all this we see shifting concerns with ideas of decorum and propriety. Hamon suggests that to describe is to do, not literature, but the domestic chores within literature: "To describe, then, is 'to describe for'; it is a textual praxis, both coded and aimed, opening onto concrete, practical activities (pedagogical, military; drawing up lists, taking inventory of a stock, archives); or else it is a working between texts (re-writing, rhetorical models, the description of paintings or figurative works of art); or else it is to work in the realm of the verifiable (a description certified from the witness stand; or the traveler's description); and not in the realm of the probably-credible [*vraisemblable*] of a fiction" (6). To do literature, then, he reasons, is to avoid description. Marmontel had complained: "What we call today, in Poetry, the descriptive genre was not known by the Ancients. It is a modern invention, of which, it seems to me, neither reason nor taste approve."[58] Yet, by the late eighteenth century and into the nineteenth, as Susan Stewart argues, "we can see in...realistic novels echoes of two major themes of bourgeois life: individuation and refinement.... The description of the material world, the world of things, is necessary for a description of the hero's or heroine's progress through that world, and the 'finer' the description, the 'finer' the writing." Somewhere within the eighteenth century the workhorse description becomes domesticated, gentrified; it moves back inside narrative, only by now inside out: "The ornament does not dress the object; it defines the object" (28).

The Erosion of the Universal

One of the chief levers for this rhetorical change is the cultural one of difference. As Stewart says: "Refinement has to do with not only the articulation of detail but also the articulation of difference" (29). Classical and medieval description developed agility with its compositional blocks, its rewriting of topoi long in place and long familiar (much like later poets found great room for play within the tight confines of the heroic couplet). Early description compacted poetic culture and iconography such that a word, a phrase, would open up "the reader's store of cultural images" (Beaujour, 28). Richard Sherry drew on the fact that "no lerned nacion hath there bene but ye learned in it haue written of schemes & fygures" (Aiiii$_v$), and authors throughout the centuries have in varying degrees recognized the various extents to which one cultural store of images is adaptable or not to another cultural intersection. As noted above, the *New Plan* advises that the modern poet not attempt to use the rich ornaments of Homer, Virgil, and Milton. Coleridge, comparing poetry to landscape painting, notes to his own period's disadvantage that, for "the great Italian and Flemish masters, the front and middle objects of the landscape are the most obvious and determinate, the interest gradually dies away in the background, and the charm and peculiar worth of the picture consists, not so much in the specific objects," as in the general harmony and larger effects. Modern literature spends too much time on the background, the setting, the specific objects, while the foreground and intermediate distance—the persons, the actions, the ideas—assume and generate less interest. In the Renaissance, Coleridge says, "novelty of subject was rather avoided than sought for."[59]

Coleridge's criticism of his own period's poetry measures the change in status that description in its most essential and traditionally snubbed component—particularized detail, detailed particulars—underwent in the eighteenth century: "In the present age the poet...seems to propose to himself as his main object, and as that which is the most characteristic of his art, new and striking IMAGES; with INCIDENTS that interest the affections or excite the curiosity. Both his characters and his descriptions he renders, as much as possible, specific and individual, even to a degree of portraiture" (2:29). This sense of distaste sustains the traditional criticism of classical and Western religious and philosophical essentialism. Aristotle defined external, individuating traits as "accidentals," matters of little identificatory significance, aspects that revealed little or nothing about inherent meaning or identity or, worse, obscured or distorted some essential truth: "An accident sayth *Aristotle . . . is neither definition, Genus, nor a propertie, and is in the thing. . . . An accident* (sayth he) *is onely that, which is without the subiect, and not caused by the essentiall principles thereof"* (Spencer, 60).

Such definitions and assumptions persisted healthily through the eighteenth century. In poetry, the particularities of *this thing* bogged one down in the finite and local and smacked of vulgar provincialism, self-centeredness, boring prolixity, the *working class*, as Boileau's *Art of Poetry* underscores:

> Sometimes an Author, fond of his own Thought,
> Pursues his Object till it's over-wrought:
> If he describes a House, he shews the Face,
> And after walks you round from place to place;
> Here is a *Vista*, there the Doors unfold,
> Balcon'es here are Ballustred with Gold;
> Then counts the Rounds and Ovals in the Halls,
> *The Festoons, Freezes, and the Astragals.*[60]
> (canto 1, lines 49–56)

For Boileau, the transgression lies in the *technicality* of these details: the poetic tour might as well be conducted by a building contractor.[61] French criticism was (not surprisingly) particularly strong on universals, ferocious on details; Thomas Rymer translated the *Necessary and Universal Rules for Epick, Dramatick, and the other sorts of Poetry* of Rapin in 1694, confirming the dictates of his subject in his prefatory analysis of descriptions of the night in various languages. Apollonius, for example, in his *Argonautiques*, "gives us the Face of things both by Land and Sea, City and Countrey, the Manner, the Traveller, the Door-keeper, the Mistress of the Family, her Child and Dog; but loses himself amongst his Particulars, and seems to forget for what occasion he mentions them" (B4).[62] Addison on the pleasures of the imagination argues that the most powerful description is one that is "apt to raise a secret Ferment in the Mind of the Reader, and to work, with Violence, upon his Passions" so that "the Pleasure becomes more Universal."[63] Sir Joshua Reynolds advises painters to follow the line of poets:

> The grand style of Painting requires this minute attention to be carefully avoided, and must be kept as separate from it as the style of Poetry from that of History.... [T]o mingle the *Dutch* with the *Italian* School, is to join contrarieties which cannot subsist together, and which destroy the efficacy of each other. The *Italian* attends only to the invariable, the great, and general ideas which are fixed and inherent in universal nature; the *Dutch*, on the contrary, to literal truth and a minute exactness in the detail, as I may say, of Nature modified by accident. The attention to these petty peculiarities is the very cause of this naturalness so much admired in the Dutch picturers, which, if we suppose it to be a beauty, is certainly of a lower order.[64]

Samuel Johnson, of course, dictated what oft was thought but ne'er so well expressed: "Nothing can please many, and please long, but just representations of general nature. Particular manners can be known to few" ("Shakespeare," 61). Johnson's sense of the literary cultural storehouse— the *consensus gentium*—is epistemologically universalist, anterior to and justificatory of the "compositional blocks" of classical, medieval, and Renaissance "description" as "rewriting." Edmund Burke articulates the long rhetorical line of poetic duty, where images are just one (and a subsidiary) means to the affective end: "In reality poetry and rhetoric do not succeed in exact description so well as painting does; their business is to affect rather by sympathy than imitation, to display rather the effect of things on the mind of the speaker, or of others, than to present a clear idea of the things themselves."[65] Burke vastly prefers the nonparticularized description of Helen by Priam in the *Iliad* (bk. 3, lines 156–58; or, in Pope's translation, bk. 3, lines 205–8), in which "not one word [is] said of the particulars of her beauty; nothing which can in the last help us to any precise idea of her person," which is much more affectively effective than "these long and laboured descriptions of Helen, whether handed down by tradition, or formed by fancy, which are to be met with in some authors" (Burke, 172). Johnson argues: "The accidental compositions of heterogeneous modes are dissolved by the chance which combined them; but the uniform simplicity of primitive qualities neither admits increase, nor suffers decay. The sand heaped by one flood is scattered by another, but the rock always continues in its place" ("Shakespeare," 70).

Except that, in fact, the rock gets eroded away, and Johnson was standing
on a sandbar. Particulars by definition had always to some extent constituted the nature of description, and, by the middle of the eighteenth century, particularity started absorbing the energy of the universal, to change
its ontology from accidental to inherent. Sidney had argued that the poet
performed the functions of the historian in the "particular truth of things"
and the philosopher in the "general reason of things" (Dv–D2). By coupling
"the generall notion with the particuler example," the poet thus trumped
the philosopher, who merely "bestoweth but a wordish description, which
doth neither strike, pearce, nor possesse, the sight of the soul"; he gives as
his own Gradgrindian example the man who could read all day the philosophical descriptions of an elephant or a rhinoceros and still have no more
than a vaguish idea of one until he saw it "figured forth by the speaking picture of *Poesie*" (D2). To oversimplify what will be expanded in the following
chapters, the inroads of empiricism in Britain, and the new epistemology
of Locke and Hume, changed the format of belief about the construction
and epistemological power of images, and concrete associationism pulled
ahead of a priori recognition. Thomas Gray asserted that *"circumstance
ever was, and ever will be, the life and essence both of oratory and of poetry"* ("Some Remarks," 392–93).[66] Lord Kames argued: "Abstract or general
terms have no good effect in any composition for amusement, because it is
only of particular objects that images can be formed. Shakespeare's style
in that respect is excellent: every article in his description is particular,
as in nature."[67] (Contrast Johnson, for whom Shakespeare's strength lies
in his grasp and representation of the universal.) W. J. T. Mitchell tracks
the decline in the seventeenth and eighteenth centuries of the status of
ornamental "figures" as theories of language, poetry in particular increasingly emphasizing a process of pictorial production. He notes that, in the
eighteenth century, "even abstractions are treated as pictorial, visual objects, projected in the verbal imagery of personification."[68] Even abstractions such as the concept of *description* itself become objects in the critical
vocabulary.

In the light of this conceptual shift, eighteenth-century critics (like their
counterparts any time, any place) can be seen to construct their own revi-
sionist critical histories. Hugh Blair addresses the "considerable place" that
description now not only does but ought to occupy in poetry, and, although
he follows the old general line of choosing the *proper* set of circumstances
(which "ought not to be vulgar, and common ones"), he yet marks the line
diverging from Boileau, insisting that "proper" circumstances are those that

"particularize the object described, and mark it strongly." He makes the ultimate point unmistakably clear: "No description, that rests in Generals, can be good. For we can conceive nothing clearly in the abstract; all distinct ideas are formed upon particulars" (3:173–74). Like Macaulay on Bunyan, Blair goes on to "rewrite" Milton within his own new cultural storehouse of terms and criteria. "L'Allegro" and "Il Penseroso" become "the storehouse whence many succeeding Poets have enriched their descriptions of similar subjects," and this precisely because of their physical particularity, their engagements with objects:

> Here, there are no unmeaning general expressions; all is particular; all is Picturesque; nothing forced or exaggerated; but a simple Style, and a collection of strong expressive images, which are all of one class, and recall a number of similar ideas of the melancholy kind: particularly, the walk by moonlight; the sound of the curfew bell heard distant; the dying embers in the chamber; the Bellman's call; and the lamp seen at midnight, in the high lonely tower. We may observe, too, the conciseness of the Poet's manner. He does not rest long on one circumstance, or employ a great many words to describe it; which always makes the impression faint and languid; but placing it in one strong point of view, full and clear before the reader, he there leaves it. (3:179)

This description of Milton's description operates on several planes at once. Blair emphasizes more strongly than historically critics were wont the importance of particularity, yet he is still within traditional walls of concision of time and text. His view of lengthy, wordy descriptions is on the *impression*, where Johnson's is on the *mind*, yet there is small difference perhaps between feeling faint and languid and being refrigerated. So the general import of this critical appreciation still seems fairly orthodox. But the paragraph is itself a collection of *things*, an enumeration of objects connected to consciousness—moonlight/walk, bell/sound, embers/dying, tower/lonely. And then the description itself becomes an object: for Blair, Milton plunks the image down before the reader, and *there he leaves it*.

In one sense, what Blair is doing (and Macaulay after him) is spelling out the vividness of contemporary experience, the sense of standing inside the cultural storehouse. As Irvin Ehrenpreis notes in his explanation of *negative particularity*, or the phenomenon of detailed description relegated to the low, vicious, or comic in the Augustan world: "What had to be rendered in bright detail was what did not belong to the familiar things of their world."[69]

"Truth" was shared; "truth" and "beauty" and "virtue" were familiar, public matters of common standard (or so goes the doctrine).

But, as we have seen, by the time of Coleridge (at least in the view of Coleridge), modern poetry (with Wordsworth as the prime example) displayed "a laborious minuteness and fidelity in the representation of objects" and "the insertion of accidental circumstances" (*Biographia Literaria*, 2:126). John Graham notes a sharp rise in the use of pathognomy (the "passing expression" and/or signs of the passions) in the novel from about 1760 until, by the late eighteenth century, the particulars of face and expression became "an essential part of character revelation" and "dramatic conflict was expressed through complete and subtle readings of passing expressions."[70] Blake, savaging Reynolds in the margins of his copy of the *Discourses*, insisted more bluntly: "To Generalize is to be an Idiot. To Particularize is the Alone Distinction of Merit.... Singular & Particular Detail is the Foundation of the Sublime."[71] Hazlitt declared that "the greatest grandeur may co-exist with the most perfect, nay with a microscopic accuracy of detail."[72] By 1884, Henry James codified the work of nineteenth-century novelists: "[T]he air of reality (solidity of specification) seems to me to be the supreme virtue of a novel—the merit on which all its other merits (including that conscious moral purpose of which [Walter] Besant speaks) helplessly and submissively depend." For James, it is "the surface" that is the "substance," and "to 'render' the simplest surface" is the complicated artistic obligation of the writer.[73]

We can concretely review the differences in surface detail and connected visualization between the early eighteenth century and the early nineteenth by again comparing two similar scenes, this time of streets rather than houses. In one scene typical of her criminal life, Moll Flanders takes advantage of local opportunity, fixing herself at a general crossroads of time and place, recounting a clear sequence of events, followed by her familiar, loving itemization of booty:

> I was going thro' *Lombard-street* in the dusk of the Evening, just by the end of *Three King Court*, when on a sudden comes a Fellow running by me as swift as Lightning, and throws a Bundle that was in his Hand just behind me, as I stood up against the corner of the House at the turning into the Alley; just as he threw it in he said, God bless you Mistress let it lie there a little, and away he runs swift as the Wind.... I got safe to my Lodgings with this Cargo, which was a Peice of fine black Lustring Silk, and a Peice of Velvet; the latter was but part of a Peice of about 11 Yards; the former was a whole Peice of near 50 Yards.[74]

We have her precise address, the quick interjecting image of another thief, the bundle, and then the bundle unpacked. As we will see in chapters 4 and 5, the economy of things in space in the early eighteenth century is predicated on narrative action. The visual is concise, effective, generated by a few spare details poised briefly together. Moll, even writing retrospectively, saves her reflections and judgments for separate paragraphs.

Some one hundred years later, Oliver Twist is taken firmly in hand by the Artful Dodger and friends and introduced to the criminal interiors of London. This scene, too, is topographically situated, but Oliver pauses to acquire a point of view, to see and hear and smell where he is. (It could be argued from a narratological point of view that the Dodger's experience and account would be more like Moll's, focusing on the absolutism of pragmatics, except that *Moll Flanders*—or Defoe anywhere, for that matter—never presents a visual alternative.) Dickens refashions similar space very differently:

> They crossed from the Angel into St. John's-road; struck down the small street which terminates at Sadler's Wells Theatre; through Exmouth-street and Coppice-row; down the little court by the side of the work-house; across the classic ground which once bore the name of Hockley-in-the-Hole; thence into Little Saffron-hill; and so into Saffron-hill the Great: along which, the Dodger scudded at a rapid pace: directing Oliver to follow close at his heels.
>
> Although Oliver had enough to occupy his attention in keeping sight of his leader, he could not help bestowing a few hasty glances on either side of the way, as he passed along. A dirtier or more wretched place he had never seen. The street was very narrow and muddy; and the air was impregnated with filthy odours. There were a good many small shops; but the only stock in trade appeared to be heaps of children, who, even at that time of night, were crawling in and out at the doors, or screaming from the inside.... Covered ways and yards, which here and there diverged from the main street, disclosed little knots of houses, where drunken men and women were positively wallowing in the filth.[75]

The first paragraph with its topographical directions is no more than what Defoe loved to supply, but the second suggests a different spatial and visual consciousness. Although it is not Dickens's most detailed description and, in fact, retains a classical flavor in its plurals, in its epitomic wretchedness, the direct description of *Oliver looking around* changes the pattern of visualization, slowing down the moment, and opening the sense of space, specifically connecting interrelated images in the midst of Oliver's hasty pace.

And it is precisely this difference, with all its "motivation" ("he could not help bestowing") "making the relationship between elements explicit" (Bal, 41), that leads readers and critics of the nineteenth century to accuse the eighteenth of "lacking eye." Rachel Trickett argues that "we are so accustomed to description as the natural idiom of the novelist in the nineteenth century that the lack of it in Defoe, Richardson, Fielding, and Smollett is at first astonishing" and that its "lack" seems even more remarkable given that "the eighteenth century gave particular weight to the visual arts in its aesthetic theory."[76] Carol T. Christ outlines the standard intellectual history of the change in interest from generals to particulars: "[T]he Augustan suppression of particularity springs from their effort to create art that evokes the sublime." The association of particularity with the accidental, and the accidental with the dangerous as well as the trite, she argues, "is probably related to the emerging climate of realism during the eighteenth century. If the empirical psychology of Locke and Hobbes, the skepticism of Berkeley and Hume, and the emerging form of the novel did not directly help create a growing skepticism about the reality and the knowability of universals, they certainly reflected one." The picturesque, which emphasizes "the pleasures of vision apart from any truth they may contain," segues to the romantics, for whom "the real has become the ideal" and the emphasis lingers, not on the object perceived, but on the mind perceiving. The romantics have their own universality of imagination. But the Victorians "lost the Romantic assurance that there existed universal correspondences among individual imaginations and between the imagination and the sensible world," and Victorian particulars "are not representative of a moment of imaginative experience that becomes in some way universal, like Wordsworth's daffodils, but merely descriptive of a single moment of consciousness, which is portrayed for its own interest and which rarely leads to a statement of universal judgment."[77]

Description again, as a literary category and strategy, sank back into a glamourless and even embarrassed life in twentieth-century critical discourse. Georg Lukács, in "Narrate or Describe?" (1936), found the surface-obsessed literature of the late nineteenth century a bourgeois compensation for "the epic significance that has been lost"; while narration "establishes proportions" and events reveal character, "description merely levels."[78] José Manuel Lopes notes that neither the Russian formalists nor the Anglo-American New Critics paid much attention to the matter, while the discourse linguists of the 1970s and 1980s, by grouping narrative with

"foreground" and description with "background" on the figure-ground opposition of gestalt theory, tended to "perpetuate the notion of literary description as mere background" (Lopes, 9–10, 3). Naomi Schor sees an Enlightenment gendering of detail by Sir Joshua Reynolds that becomes an overall
and overdetermined feminization (trivialization) of the ornamental and the
descriptive, against which the sublime is "a masculinist aethetic designed
to check the rise of a detailism."[79]

Description and detail do have a counternarrative in the twentieth century, both in literature and in criticism. Surfaces resurface—almost violently
in their very stasis—in the *nouveau roman* of Alain Robbe-Grillet and others. Detailed description features prominently in the work of contemporary
novelists such as Nicholson Baker and David Foster Wallace. In the 1980s,
Genette and Hamon, among others, brought description back to the center
of critical interest, Genette arguing that description is, in fact, more indis-
pensable than narration because it is easier to describe without narration
than to narrate without description. Description has regained some of its
nineteenth-century glamour—yet it is very much a postmodern glamour,
more heroin chic than velvet elegance. In the *nouveau roman*, the lavish
supply of surfaces is meant less to heighten significance than to disintegrate
coherence. Genette's reinstatement of description's importance is accompanied instantly by the point that, although one can conceive of description as
independent of narration, in fact it is hardly ever found in a free state—it is
the "ever-necessary, ever-submissive, never-emancipated slave" (134). And,
as Deidre Lynch has pointed out: "[C]urrently it is more than ever the mark
of a successful novel that it should be *frittered away* by detail."[80]

This study, however, is concerned primarily with the transformation
of description and the reshaping of narrative space through the eighteenth
century and into the early nineteenth; description's second decline and revival is someone else's story. One of my two threading arguments is that the
growing perception (and criticism) of eighteenth-century poetry and prose
as visually barren, "lacking eye," is, in part, simply the cultural effect of
the collapse of the memory storehouse. The process of the collapse will be
explored in the assumptions, procedures, and conclusions of empiricism as
well as the empirical interest in differentiation itself; in the material variety
and individuality produced by trade, mass production (paradoxically), and
consumerism; in changing ideas of domesticity, privacy, and architectural
interiors; and in increasing literacy and social mobility and, therefore, diversity of readership. What is no longer shared is no longer familiar, assumed, a
priori *visible*. The world is differently mapped out, and the differences need
new mapping. But adding in more detail, filling in visual space, is building

another storehouse, one just as temporally and culturally contextualized: damask and Marseilles counterpanes might need glossing as well. So one effort of this book will be to somehow rehydrate those visual tags of the early eighteenth century, to re-present the *things* that *people* the spaces of eighteenth-century texts, to supply the visual contexts of windows and doors as well as the literary contexts of allusion and tradition that have almost completely evaporated over time and culture. We might then conclude with Woolf in *"Robinson Crusoe"*: "And is there any reason, we ask as we shut the book, why the perspective that a plain earthenware pot exacts should not satisfy us as completely, once we grasp it, as man himself in all his sublimity standing against a background of broken mountains and tumbling oceans with stars flaming in the sky?" (58).

So the first point is to mark less a change than an adjustment of tradition. But the second point is to reemphasize the change, to maintain the differences between detail and description, emblem and object, thing and setting. And from that angle I will explore the techniques of early fiction in stuffing objects with meaning, in poising objects in space, in generating space through movement, as well as the impact of nonliterary descriptive modes—textual praxes—on the art of literary observation.

Thus, description, always a sort of embarrassing bundle on the literary doorstep, was put to work, called by many different names, left to stand shivering in a corner or cleaning the coal scuttle until sometime in the late eighteenth century, when it was given a wash and told to pay attention to its clothes. By the time of swathed piano legs and upholstered settees, it had become a sort of Tom Jones or Eliza Doolittle, if not Cinderella—still with a dubious, "not quaite-quaite" past lingering about it, but definitely gentrified. The decorum of rhetoric shifted into the decorum of social acceptability, with permission to look around and notice one's surroundings—in print.

CHAPTER TWO

Traveling Spaces

The guide has a Map of all ways leading to or from the City.
—*John Bunyan*, The Pilgrim's Progress, Part II *(1684)*

The seventeenth-century English textual landscape was well populated with the textual praxes of description. Virginia Woolf considered John Evelyn distinctively representative in his modes of observation, both psychological and verbal. The "general effect" of his descriptions, she says, is that "he used his eyes. The visible world was always close to him" ("Evelyn," 81–82). The world was looming visible in some new ways, prompting new or newly adapted forms of observation and representation. Improvements in trade and travel, discoveries and methodologies of empirical science, Puritan habits of self-examination, the passion for collecting and classifying, all found wide-open spaces for description in topographies and maps, micrographies and meditations, lists and catalogs, diaries and satires. This chapter and the next will look in some detail at the *detail* of practical texts that replicated a profusion of material particulars, fell in love with surfaces, and began a practice of filling narrative space with description.

To some extent, these chapters start from the research and conclusions of well-known scholars in well-known areas. Much excellent work has been devoted to tracing out the connections between the discoveries of the Royal Society and the response of the literary; to the influence of Puritan diaries on the novel; to the relation between lists and satire; to the cultural and literary webs between early modern London and early modern literature. Here, I reconsider those cultural contexts and textual praxes in specific relation to their proximity to and influence on literary description. How did the variety of descriptive forms and the passion for minute detail migrate from or become absorbed into self-consciously literary texts? In other words, this

chapter navigates some fairly uncontested ground, but from an undercon-
sidered perspective and with a few new features.

As in the previous chapter, Elizabethan and early seventeenth-century
antecedents are sometimes explicitly and always implicitly presumed to
contextualize (both historically and formally) the "innovations" discussed
here. The first section, "Descriptions and Excavations," in fact begins with
John Stow's *Survey of London* (1598, 1603) precisely because of its direct and perpetual influence on eighteenth-century topographical description through its many editions, particularly Strype's 1720 version. The
Survey attempts "the discouery of *London*" through its "sundry antiquities," a "search of Records to other purposes," "diuers written helpes,"
and Stow's own perambulations of the streets, compiling "such special descriptions of each place, as might . . . make vp an whole body of the English
Chorographie."[1] Stow's "special descriptions" created a definite taste for
description.

In 1675, John Ogilby published his *Britannia*, a comprehensive and
graphically innovative set of road maps and place descriptions that both
opened the opportunities for accurate, oriented travel and made even a paging
through of its leaves a sort of visual, quasi-narrative journey as the eye passes
perspectivized hills and ash trees, stone bridges and rills, "Long greene" and
"Mr Corkins" house. The "maps" themselves are drawn as individual paper
scrolls, each following its own principal road: the effect is narrative in its
graphic emphasis of movement through and on paper; description appears
both in the visual detail occupying the journey's spaces and in Ogilby's added
verbal descriptions of the roads and towns, architecture and curiosities along
the way. This section, "Traveled Spaces," links Ogilby's road maps to John
Bunyan's *The Pilgrim's Progress* in their parallel attraction to infusing description into narrative journeying. Bunyan's work appeared just a few years
after *Britannia* in 1678, and it is the story of a journey that essentially travels
that ribboned-out, emblematized space. I do not pretend to make a direct,
causal, or influential link between the two, but I find it suggestive to read
each in the context of the other, arguing for a kind of shared cultural storehouse of visualization that includes small and spare but pointed and local
detail that spills over into wider meanings for the traveler or reader.

These various categories—the unflagging market for descriptions of
buildings and streets; the linking up of maps, journeys, and topographical
description; and, in the next chapter, the sense of the ordinary dissolving under close inspection; the sense of surfaces imbued with meaning;
the happy fetishization of lists; the entry into interior domestic space—
all contribute over the eighteenth century to the gradual absorption of

detailed description in literature, particularly in prose narrative (fiction, biography, historiography). They also underscore the increasing presence and awareness of *things* in the general culture (and the general culture's spaces). Those things, those spaces, and their significances work to transform emblem and detail into symbol and description in the eighteenth century. Defoe's "earthenware pot," his canoe, his umbrella, his raisins, his limes, the things he makes and surrounds himself with, much like the ordinary, somehow unemblematic things of Christian's journey, begin to combine in their own ordinariness to "make common actions dignified and common objects beautiful" (Woolf, *"Robinson Crusoe,"* 57). The textual praxes of the seventeenth century reflected and endorsed a love of detail and surface, a facility of description, an art of concentration, a habit of collection and connection, a way of visualization—of seeing things—that becomes an early hothouse for the possibilities of narrative description, the growth of interior detail.

Descriptions and Excavations: Stow to Strype

A long history of rhetorical exercises in praise of great cities preceded John Stow's *Survey of London* (1598, 1603), but no physically detailed and purportedly accurate and objective description of London had been written in English by and for the ordinary citizen and reader of London. Historians such as M. J. Power, Valerie Pearl, and Ian Archer have faulted the *Survey* for its inaccuracies and blank spaces: it is concentrated on traders and craftsmen, brief on court and government, silent on a number of social ills, and erratic and impressionistic in its neighborhood descriptions.[2] But, as Patrick Collinson points out, "it was none of Stow's business to tell us how the underlying problem of immigration and overcrowding was being created, addressed, and managed."[3] I am fully prepared to acknowledge Stow's inaccuracies, nostalgias, religious agendas, and historical shortcomings; my business is with the *Survey* and its genre in relation to the art and act of spatial description. The *Survey* was expanded by Stow himself in 1603, then again by his friend Anthony Munday in 1618 and 1633, and habitually pilfered throughout the seventeenth century by topographies of widely different casts—the royalist James Howell's *Londinopolis* (1657), the dissenter Thomas De Laune's *The Present State of London* (1681), Edward Hatton's handy pocket guidebook *A New View of London* (1708)—only to reappear more or less as itself in John Strype's lush folio edition in 1720, which itself went through three more editions in the early eighteenth century.[4] J. F. Merritt examines each of these London topographies in terms of textual

differences arising from cultural and ideological change; I will refollow her
route in terms of descriptive change.

Stow's structure is loosely based on his friend William Camden's *Britannia* (1586 Latin, 1620 English) in that it opens with general sections—
on the antiquity and history of the city, its walls, water supplies, bridges
and ditches, gates and towers, schools and pastimes, churches and charities,
guilds and watches, and the "Honor of Citizens, and worthinesse of men in
the same" (Stow, 105)—and then "get[s] down to the business of detailing
the ground" (Beer, 129). It is a "perambulation" of each of the wards within
and without the City walls, offering "speciall descriptions of each place, as
might...make vp an whole body of the English Chorographie amongst our
selues" (A2–A2v). Richard Helgerson outlines chorography as "the genre
devoted to place, as chronicle is the genre devoted to time[,]...[and the]
repositor[y] of proper names.... [Discursive descriptions also add] ancient
names and place-names; names of places too small to be mapped; names
of particular properties, buildings, and institutions; names of families and
of individual people."[5] Helgerson doesn't spend many words on Stow, but
Barrett Beer notes that Stow "was at work decades before Helgerson's 'culturally uprooted [and elite] young men who began writing England in the
last decades of the sixteenth century'" (146). (Helgerson focuses on Saxton,
Speed, Norden, Camden, Drayton, and others.) Helgerson acknowledges that
chorographies and chronicles are not necessarily mutually exclusive (132),
and Stow, as a writer of both, combined both in the *Survey*.

Stow bricks in physical descriptions around his repository of names and
excavates histories and genealogies as he goes, building a visual territory
of London past and present, east and west, architectural and social. His visual descriptions include etymologies, which superimpose a literal image
from the past onto the physical image of the present, all inscribed within
the streets circumscribing a particular place, as in Faringdon Ward Within:
"Next is Ivie lane, so called of Ivie growing on the walles of the Prebend
houses, but now the lane is replenished on both the sides with faire houses,
and diuers offices be there kept, by registers" (344).[6] He can wax rhapsodic—
and in detail—over architecture:

> [T]he most beautifull frame of fayre houses and shoppes, that bee within
> the Walles of London, or else where in England, [are] commonly called
> Goldsmithes Rowe, betwixt Bred-street end & the Crosse in Cheape....
> the same was builded by Thomas Wood Goldsmith one of the shiriffes of
> London, in the yeare 1491. It contayneth in number tenne fayre dwelling
> houses, and fourteene shoppes, all in one frame, uniformly builded foure

stories high, bewtified towardes the streete with the Goldsmithes armes and the likenes of woodmen, in memory of his name, riding on monstrous beasts, all which is cast in lead, richly painted over and guilt, these he gaue to the Goldsmithes with stockes of money to be lent to yong men, hauing those shops, etc. This saide Front was again new painted, and guilt over, in the yeare, 1594. (347)

Stow can be equally disparaging about uncontrolled growth and bad building. Hog Lane, for example, which once stretched north toward St. Mary Spital and "had on both sides fayre hedgerowes of Elme trees, with Bridges and easy stiles to passe ouer into the pleasant fieldes, very commodious for Citizens therein to walke, shoote, and otherwise to recreate and refresh their dulled spirites in the sweete and wholesome ayre, ... is nowe within a few yeares made a continuall building throughout, of Garden houses, and small Cottages: and the fields on either sides be turned into Garden plottes, teynter yardes, Bowling Allyes, and such like, from Houndes ditch in the West, so farre as White Chappell, and further towardes the East" (128). But that looks like a nice cheery retreat to the greener suburbs. Whitechapel itself, hotbed for the 1665 plague, was once a common field but now "is so incroched vpon by building of filthy Cottages, and with other purpressors, inclosures and Laystalles ... that in some places it scarce remaineth a sufficient high way for the meeting of Carriages and droues of Cattell, much less is there any faire, pleasant or wholsome way for people to walke on foot: which is no small blemish, to so famous a city, to haue so unsauery and vnseemly an entry or passage thereunto" (425–26). Image is everything.

Stow gives *experiential* descriptions of a four-dimensional space in which people once or now walk on foot, meet in carriages, garden, bowl, shoot, and refresh their spirits or otherwise. The descriptions maintain an Elizabethan generality to some extent, with a common storehouse of adjectives (e.g., *spacious, filthy, fair, diverse*), yet those adjectives are applied very particularly, marking one street or building from another, with more individual detail (painting, gilding, carving, stone or wood, thatch or grass) for individual instances. The catalog of the city's various parts is not just a list and description of buildings and monuments, not just a succession of historical anecdotes, but a built-in setting for human existence, for stories, for narrative itself. Stow's richly detailed text is part of the literary and cultural setting for describing narrative spaces that contain and shape narrative plot, character, action.

But Stow rarely goes *inside* anywhere. Churches are explored for their monuments and antiquities (everybody who has a name etched onto a

tablet gets re-recorded in Stow). Houses, prisons, inns, and hospitals just get
the outside treatment: frames; building materials; interesting ornaments.
Poking around interior space in a text is definitely not a sixteenth- or
seventeenth-century preoccupation. But Stow is intrigued by interiors of
a sort: London's historical bowels. He is at his happiest and wordiest *exca-
vating* inner spaces and the things to be found there. On the Roman artifacts
dug up from Spitalfields, for example, he offers positively archaeological lists
and descriptions:

> On the East side of this Churchyard [St. Mary Spital] lieth a large field,
> of old time called Lolesworth, now Spittle field, which about the yeare
> 1576. was broken up for Clay to make Bricke, in the digging whereof many
> earthen pots called *Vrnae*, were found full of Ashes, and burnt bones of
> men, to wit, of the Romanes that inhabited here.... [E]uerie of these
> pots had in them with the Ashes of the dead, one peece of Copper mony,
> with the inscription of the Emperour, then raigning.... [B]esides those
> Vrnas, many other pots were there found, made of a white earth with
> long necks, and handels, like to our stone Jugges: these were emptie, but
> seemed to be buried ful of some liquid matter long since consumed and
> soaked through: for there were found diuerse vials and other fashioned
> Glasses, some most cunningly wrought, such as I have not seene the like,
> and some of Christall.... [S]ome of these Glasses had Oyle in them verie
> thicke, and earthie in savour, some were supposed to have balme in them,
> but had lost the vertue; many of those pots and glasses were broken in
> cutting of the clay, so that few were taken up whole. (170)

This is already a lengthy, thingy description, but Stow is by no means finished, going on delightedly about "diuerse dishes and cups of a fine red
coloured earth, which shewed outwardly such a shining smoothnesse, as if
they had beene of Currell"; a small white earthen pot shaped like a hare; nails
that had (possibly) been driven into some hapless heads; coffin nails with the
wood attached to them "still retaining both the graine, and proper colour";
teeth and jawbones (170–71). This description becomes a several-page paragraphic wheelbarrow of items, each picked up and examined (and tasted) and
put back, each in sets of particularized pots: empty or full; wrought or plain;
earthen or crystal. Stow adds his knowledge of past customs and localized
human behavior. His description allows us to know what is there and why.
The ground beneath us is as full of as many fascinating surprises and secret
histories as Hooke's microscope will reveal sixty years later. The network

below ground is as fully formed as that in the streets above. Description can be a useful thing about once-useful things.

Particularized pots: Helgerson notes that "at the root of all representation is differentiation. A place or person can be represented only if it can be in some way distinguished from its surroundings" (135). Thus, in Richard Carew's chorography *A Suruey of Cornwall* (1602), Dorset is best for the twisted ropes of the navy, Cornwall for pilchards, Pembroke's people are the "shrubbiest," and, where he "'can say little worth the observing for any difference from . . . other shires,' he passes on. Its differences make Cornwall worth describing and Carew's book worth reading. Because of these differences, Cornwall has meaning" (Helgerson, 135). Collinson has argued for Stow's nostalgia as the reason behind the many lengthy mournings over lost open spaces; nostalgia itself, like wonder and discovery, is also a perfectly good motive for differentiating representation because what is lost (as well as what is found or simply differently perceived) wants to be articulated and visualized, resubstantiated.

Stow's text was amplified and cannibalized throughout the next two centuries, and, as Merritt shows, each version tweaks its own ideological slant or formally restructures the material. Anthony Munday provides more information on the current church building and almsgiving, balancing Stow's elegies on the Reformation's destructiveness with descriptions of new church furniture and armorial glass (Merritt, 60).[7] Merritt notes that Howell's *Londinopolis* (1657) "insinuates a defence of episcopacy into apparently straightforward passages of description" (68–69), a development that adds its own dimension to the otherwise standard or even depleted passages from Stow. As in Stow, churches in Howell receive the only interior attention, although Howell is more interested in detail other than tablature. The east part of St. Paul's, for example, "seems to be the newer, and more curiously wrought, having under it a very fair large arch'd Vault. . . . The *West* part, as also the *Cross Isle* are very spacious, high built, and goodly to be seen by reason of such huge Columns, and are marvellously beautified with an arch'd roof of stone." His street-by-street descriptions of the wards are more spare: "Beneath this Saint *Georges* Lane, is the Lane called *Fleet-lane*, winding South by the Prison of the *Fleet*, into *Fleet-street*, by *Fleet-bridge*."[8]

Thomas De Laune's *The Present State of London* (1681) takes a more quantitative approach, supplying bills of mortality, amounts of beer brewed, penny post rates, the rates and orders of coachmen, carmen, and watermen, along with alphabetized descriptions of churches, public structures, and houses of the nobility (Merritt, 60, 68, 70–71). Its format is smaller, handier, portable in a pocket. It includes a number of woodcuts of the gates, prisons, inns of court, churches, and other public buildings and offers plenty of architectural detail and opinion. (Stow had no illustrations.) Of the rebuilding of Bedlam, for example, De Laune notes that, the old structure being "old, narrow, and not very pleasant," a new building was erected "to the great Glory and Ornament of the City, and the great benefit of the Poor Lunaticks." The attention to the visual is relatively detailed:

> It is of a great Length, reaching from Moor-gate, to the Little-Postern, leading out of the North-East part of Moor-Fields, into the City, near the City Walls, with a most Glorious Front towards those Delicate Walks of Moor-Fields; the Architecture is very Regular, Exquisite, and Rich, with a Stately Turret in the midst of a Curious Form, and Fair green Courts, part of which are Paved with broad Stone for walks, environ'd with a very hansom Brick-Wall; there are two Stately Galleries, reaching from one end to the other, on the sides of which, are the Lodgings of the Distracted People, which are very neat and convenient, they are carefully and very decently served with plenty of good wholsom Dyet, and very well attended, by Persons appointed to that purpose.[9]

Stow had, after a history of Bedlam's founding, written only: "It was an hospitall for distracted people . . . the Church and Chappell whereof were taken downe in the raigne of Queene Elizabeth, and houses builded there, by the Gouernours of Christes Hospitall in London" (166). (He adds a bit about a burying ground added and walled in in 1569.) De Laune consistently fills in more architectural details (see, e.g., the description of the Royal Exchange [159]), but, for the most part, physical description still runs a clear second to functional description. "To Describe all particularities relating to this *Royall Seat*" of Whitehall, for instance, "would be too tedious," so he offers instead "a few short Remarks," namely, the mention of the "most Magnificent and Stately *Banquetting-House*" and the *"Delicate Privy-Garden"* (99–100). (The 1690 edition, *Angliae Metropolis*, reprints without change these descriptions.)

Edward Hatton's version, *A New View of London* (1708), also assumed the useful pocket size. It advertises: "In a short time *Proposals* will be published for Reprinting Mr. *Stow*'s large Survey of *London*, improv'd; with very great Additions throughout, and illustrated with about 100 large Copper Cutts."[10] But, in the meantime, its own subtitle establishes its contribution: *Being a more particular Description thereof than has hitherto been known to be published of any City in the World*. It announces that its eight sections cover the names of the streets (and squares, markets, courts, alleys, rows, rents, yards, and inns, with derivations, the quality of buildings and their inhabitants, dimensions, bearing and distance from Charing Cross, St. Paul's, or the Tower); the churches (with vast loads of architectural detail); the companies (and their halls); the palaces and eminent houses; the colleges, libraries, and "musaems"; the bridges and related water things; and the public statues. To this is added a glossary of art terms, a history and survey of London in general, and the arms of the city companies. Hatton refers to the practice common in European countries of publishing guides to their cities, not just for visitors, but for the inhabitants themselves, giving particular credit to *A Guide through Paris*,[11] but says that he realized it was too flimsy a model, that "many more Particulars" would need to be "taken notice of, and more enlarged upon." He observes that, "since the Printing Mr. *Stow*'s latter impression, which is now about 74 Years ago, no tolerable Account of this Famous and Flourishing City has been published" (A2)—presumably suggesting that Howell's and De Laune's are intolerable (he doesn't mention them). He provides old (1600) and new (1707) maps of London and invites us to compare the growth in building; we can also compare the change in representation, from the bird's-eye view of elevations (little Elizabethan houses crowded together) to the two-dimensional street plan, scraped of all but the most famous public buildings and a few boats. Most of the palaces and noblemen's houses don't get much beyond their alphabetical entry: "*Ely House*, against St. *Andrew*'s Church *Holborn*, the Residence of the Bp of *Ely* when in town" (626). There are, however, exceptions. Montague House provides a rare interior glimpse:

> *Montague-House*, is an extraordinary noble and beautiful Palace. situate on the N. side of *Great Russel Str.* near *Bloomsbury*, in the Occupation of his Grace the Duke of *Montague*. It was erected, *i.e.* the Shell, in the Year 1677. The Building constitutes 3 sides of a Quadrangle, is composed of fine Brick and Stone Rustick-work, the Roof covered with Slate, and there is an Acroteria of 4 Figures in the Front, being the 4 Cardinal Virtues.... The Inside is richly furnished and beautifully finished; the Floors of most Rooms finnier'd; there are great variety of noble Paintings, the Staircase and Cupulo-room particularly curious, being Architecture done in Perspective, &c. and there are many other notable things too numerous to insert here. (627–38)

The entry on the Royal Society includes its own museum, with extensive descriptions of human rarities (mummies, a Moor's skin, somebody's veins, skeletons, hair, teeth, a stone voided by a penis), quadrupeds (a stuffed sloth, a tiger's tusk, a hippopotamus skull, porcupine quills), serpents, birds, fishes, whorled and single shells, insects, fruits, petrified animals, gems, minerals, instruments, and the library—an example of both collecting and listing, of stuffing the things of a collection into a text through the sheer pleasure of their iteration. And the streets are deftly sorted into alphabetized descriptions:

> *Scalding alley*, on the N. side of the *Poultry*, near *Stocks market*. *Stow* says, this was formerly called the *Scalding house*, or *Scalding wick*, and *Scalding lane*, as appears by Record of near 300 years standing; because the Poulterers of the *Poultry* there scalded their Fowl, which they sold at their stalls.
> *School house land*, betn the E. part of *upper Shadwel* S. and *Brook str.* N.
> *Scollop court*, a paved passage betn *Puddle dock hill* S. and leads N. into *Creed lane*.
> Scotfords alley, on the S. side of *Petit France, Westminster*.
> *Scotland yard*, about the mid-way betn the statue at *Cha* † [i.e., Charing Cross] and *Whitehall*, near the *Thames*, so called (says *Stow*) for that here were stately Buildings for the Reception of the King, Prince, and Nobility of *Scotland*. (74)

Each new version of Stow, from the reign of Elizabeth to that of Anne, revisualizes the details of the city and restructures the format of the topography in contemporary terms for increasingly wider audiences that needed to know the changing contours of their spaces. True, the increasing detail provides the grist for Boileau's critical mill: unrefined importation of architectural detail into poetry—"[t]he Festoons, Freezes, and the Astragals" (canto 1, line 56)—makes for lummoxy description. But the revisiting of these visual details over and over again, the popularity of these descriptive guides, suggests an increasing appetite for exactly such detail.

John Strype's two large folio volumes of 1720 have struck most critics, historians, and general London readers as the epitome of city description. Most definitely *not* pocket-size, they were designed to impress, recalling Elizabethan versions of the genre and updating them, if not very reliably (see Merritt, 72, 73, 75, 87). The preface addresses the issues of change and accumulated detail, which call for more comprehensive description, and more kinds of description, than Stow's work offered:

[I]t was requisite, that Abundance of Additions should be made to the
former Book, as it was capable of, to render it the more compleat and
useful. As, beside the furnishing it with many more Antiquities, and Observations of Places, Men and Things, belonging to it in former Times;
it was very necessary, that there should be a Continuation of the History of the City, in *Stow*'s Method, down to the present Times[;]...of
the great Enlargements of the Compass of the two Cities; of the Fire of
London, and of the new Buildings thereof, with the new Streets, Courts,
Monuments, Churches, and Alterations.... It was convenint [*sic*] that
the several Wards of the City, with the new Parishes, and eminent Places
lately built in the Suburbs, should have Maps, Plans, and Representations, and such like Illustrations and Embellishments.[12]

Strype's volumes are massive, and there is vastly more visual material,
but the descriptions themselves do not depart radically from Stow's already
careful delineations. We have sketches and outlines more than details; we
have categories of idiosyncracies rather than particularities. Consider these
snapshots of place in Faringdon Ward Without (St. Andrews Holborn), one
savory, one unsavory:

Red Lion Square, a large Place, and much longer than broad. It hath graceful Buildings on all sides, which are inhabited by Gentry, and Persons
of Repute; the Houses having Palisado Pails, and a Freestone Pavement
before them. The middle of the Square is inclosed from the Streets, or
passage to the Houses, by a handsome high Palisado Pail; with Rows of
Trees, Gravel Walks, and Grass Plats within; all neatly kept, for the Inhabitants to walk in. Out of this Square are several Streets which lead to
other Places: Viz. Lee street, Fisher's street, Orange street, Drake street,
North street, Lamb's Conduit passage, Princes street, and Gray's Inn
passage.

Saffron hill... is a Place of small Account, both to Buildings and Inhabitants; and pestered with small and ordinary Alleys and Courts, taken
up by the meaner Sort of People; especially the East side, unto the Town
Ditch, which separates this Parish from St. James's Clarkenwel. And over
this Ditch, most of the Allies have a small boarded Bridge.... Harp Alley, nasty and inconsiderable. Paved Alley, but mean; hath a passage up
Steps into Hatton Garden; and the Entrance into it is but ill, and by some
called Pissing Alley. (1, bk. 3:254, 256)

The narrator pokes down every lane and sums up its physical and social physiognomy. Spaces are treated in parts and as wholes: the image of a neighborhood is constructed in a few telling adjectives and connected phrases.

But, still, no one is going inside. Strype does not noticeably expand on Stow in the matter of interiors. Churches and public buildings will sometimes get a very economical treatment. The parish church of St. Bartholomew the Less, for example (in Faringdon Ward Without), had its inside newly painted in 1622 and its gallery at the lower end rebuilt and enlarged (Strype, 1, bk. 3:238). All the monuments are located and read within the churches. And, at Gray's Inn, the "hall where the Gentlemen of the Society Dine and Sup, is large and good; but the Chappel adjoining is too small; and I could wish that the Society would new build it, and to raise it on arched Pillars, as *Lincoln's Inn* Chappel, and then there would be a good dry Walk underneath, in rainy Weather" (253). We have a *generalized* glimpse of inhabited interiors.

But, although the descriptions in Strype are not noticeably more expansive than those in Stow, relying on many of the same storehoused adjectives, the addition of the ward maps definitely opens things up more visually (fig. 1). Here, we are handed the insides of the ward, the spaces in and between the streets, the shapes of foundations, the beginnings for visual projection. The scene is textured with lines, dots, little trees, and the occasional three-dimensional building, with water in the ditch and grass on the bowling green. Each ward map shows its inhabitants the legal, parochial, and physical boundaries of their immediate world; their own lives fill in the spaces, and they can fill the plan with realities or memories. This map of St. Andrews Holborn shows time as well as space: "References to the New Buildings" (Strype, 1, bk. 12:247 [facing]). When connected with the descriptive text, the map becomes three-dimensional, social, with spacious squares and mean pockets, the human spectrum of narrative possibilities in inns, churches, schools, markets, playing fields, gardens, legal institutions, waste spaces, churchyards.

Vanessa Harding demarcates the spectrum of London topographies from Stow to Strype as analogous to the changed shape of the city itself, from Stow's "compact, integrated, comprehensible" city and text, to Strype's "more prolix, discursive work, infilled, interpolated, and asymmetric," reflecting "an extended, amorphous, ... and almost unmanageably difficult" city. She notes the "important interplay between verbal description, cartographic mapping, and visual representation," an interplay that assists in answering the kinds of questions that invariably arise when a literary scholar embeds a literary text among historical and cultural documents.[13]

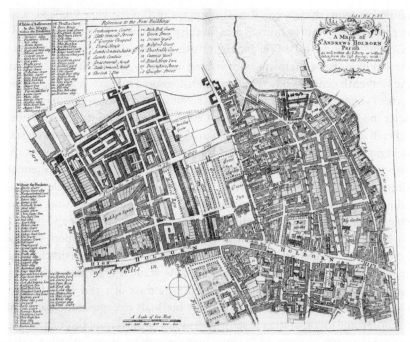

Figure 1. "A Mapp of St. Andrews Holborn Parish," in John Strype, *Survey of London* (1720). Courtesy of Special Collections, University of Virginia Library.

As Richard Helgerson puts it: "How can an atlas and a lengthy poem be considered points on a single line—a line that also passes through an odd assortment of other texts, descriptive and antiquarian?" Because a culture and a history comprise "a dense net of intertextual [and human] relations" (131). A literary author picks up materials from the local world, sees them through situated eyes, and interprets and articulates new things from them in the vocabulary and imagery of the day.

Traveled Spaces: Ogilby, Bunyan

> And then, being encouraged by the King and the Nobility to make an actuall Survey of England and Wales, he proceeded in it so far as to an actuall Survey of the Roads both in England and Wales.
> —*John Aubrey*, Brief Lives

Aubrey's repetition of "actual survey"[14] in his comment on John Ogilby's *Britannia* (1676) could well express some admiring wonder, in part because,

until this map, there were almost no maps of the *roads* of England, and
in part because Aubrey himself was on the project. The fourteenth-century
"Gough" map (so called for its eighteenth-century discoverer) shows numerous roads between towns with staging distances, and it was still used in
the sixteenth century; but "roads were still ignored by Saxton and Speed in
spite of their dependence on them for carrying out countrywide surveys."[15]
After the Great Fire of 1666, in which Ogilby lost all his printing stock ("the
generall and dreadfull Conflagration burn't all that he had, that he was faine
to begin the world again, being then at best worth 5 pounds" [Aubrey, 289]),
he proposed to do for Britain what he had already done for Africa, America,
China, and Japan: compile an atlas.[16] But Robert Hooke, that master of detailed description, was extremely interested in the prospect of an *accurate*
map of Britain's roads and detailed descriptions of its counties and helped
push Ogilby's plans for his new atlas into something rather more than a
heterogeneous collection of wondrous anecdotes and some geographically
challenged maps. Ogilby's *Britannia* set new standards in mapmaking in
England for precision, substituting the statute mile of 1,760 yards for the
old British mile of 2,428 yards, using new methods of computation and delineation, and incorporating descriptive studies of the terrain through which
the roads passed—a series of "natural histories" that became models for the
eighteenth century, as did the road map itself.[17]

At Christopher Wren's suggestion, John Aubrey became part of the surveying team, as Aubrey wrote to Anthony à Wood:

> 'Tis this—Mr. Ogilby is writing the history of all England: the map is
> mending already. Now the Doctor [Wren] told me that if that were all, it
> would be no very great matter. He was pleased to tell him that he would
> not meet with a fitter man for that turne then [*sic*] J. A. Now it's true
> that it suits well enough with my Genius; but he is a cunning Scott, and
> I must deale warily with him, with the advice of my friends. It will be
> in February next before I begin, and then between that and November
> followeing I must curry all over England and Wales.... The King will
> give me protection and letters to make any inquisition, or etc.[18]

Ogilby was never (in fact) planning to write a history of England, the map
even without its attendant descriptions was (in fact) a "very great matter,"
and Aubrey was (in fact) sent to Surrey (not "all over England and Wales").
But Aubrey's loose grip on the facts did not characterize the project as a
whole. Aubrey and the other surveyors were given a questionnaire developed
in 1672 by Hooke, Wren, Ogilby, Aubrey, the engraver Gregory King, and

others that inquired into the use of land, tidal information, local customs, and antiquities, demonstrating an "increasing interest in matters technological, scientific and anthropological" (Van Eerde, 134)—and an increasing interest in observing and recording local surface detail.

Britannia was widely popular: there were four issues in 1675–76, and it was reprinted in 1698; Robert Morden issued packs of playing cards inspired by the maps in 1676; owners cut out individual maps to carry with them; maps and pocket guides by Emanuel Bowen, Thomas Gardner, and John Senex were inspired by *Britannia*'s form and content; and collectors still prize the individual strip maps.[19] Katherine Van Eerde argues that, "in a country whose gentry still had strong attachments to the county of their birth, the detail with which various localities were shown was appealing, and reinforced the growing antiquarianism and appreciation of local history" (137). Given the popularity of the maps and the self-interest that questionnaires can arouse, *Britannia*, it may be argued, functioned as one of the cultural texts generating as well as reflecting a growing absorption with visual and verbal descriptions of ordinary, familiar, physical detail.

Visually, each of the one hundred maps in *Britannia* is a continuous scroll, unwinding luxuriously from the lower-left-hand corner of the double page and curling its end at the upper right (fig. 2). Ogilby based his road maps on the Roman itineraries, which are structured along calculated distances between towns with, according to Howard Marchitello, "a total disregard for orientation. In these maps, the frames correspond not with directions, but simply with the outer edge of concern."[20] Like any other seventeenth- or eighteenth-century endeavor that cast its origins classically, the strip maps simultaneously, perhaps equally, enter and enfold their own very present world. Despite their reference to antiquity, they were pioneering in form and content, and "not until the early nineteenth century were their comprehensiveness and innovations wholly superseded" (Van Eerde, 151).

Ogilby is concerned enough with orientation to install a compass on each strip of the map, and Hooke's influence appears in the exaction. But the "accuracy" is visual and experiential as well as numerical. England is represented in a kind of three-dimensional, *familiarly detailed* abstraction. London is fairly carefully depicted in this first frame, with the empty fields northeast of the City and south of the river, the Tower, St. Paul's, Smithfield, the Exchange, St. James's, all easily recognizable. Then we follow the road "up" (west and a bit north), through the wilds of Hyde Park and the Kensington gravel pits, Shepherd's Bush, Hammersmith, to Acton and Little Ealing, starting again at the bottom of the next strip and passing a brick bridge, a wooden bridge, a pond, Lady Clarke's, a bridge of three arches, a

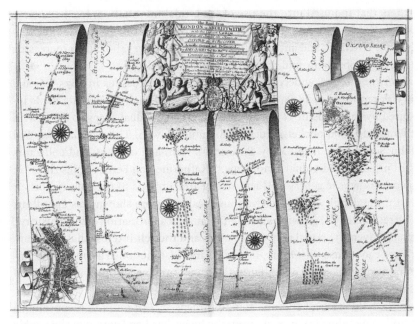

Figure 2. "London to Aberistwith," in John Ogilby, *Britannia* (1675). Reproduced by permission of the British Library (shelfmark 192.F.1).

house and a mill, and so on. As with Strype's ward maps, if you know the territory already, you fill it in even further—the map becomes the metaphor. As Obadiah Walker explained in 1659, "*Metaphors* (used chiefly in *Descriptions*) . . . are *similitudes* contracted to a word," and, therefore, the most significant expressions "are borrowed, and translated to our matter from things amongst which our life is much conversant . . . which so soon as named, the well-acquainted Auditor with ease, as it were prognosticates the rest of the discourse, and applies them further than the speaker" (54–55). The well-acquainted traveler (or reader) colors in the map spaces with personal reality, personal history, or personal possibility.

J. B. Harley has argued that maps constitute *actions* as much as "impassive descriptions," and Denis Wood and Howard Marchitello add that maps are essentially narrative; they tell stories.[21] Jeremy Black demonstrates "an increasing tendency for historical writers and, more important, historical readers, especially in the seventeenth century, to want to relate time to place. Earlier there had been many remarks to the effect that geography was an important ancillary to history—a kind of second eye—but these were essentially rhetorical before about 1580, and possibly later." The "sense of history and of place converging," of narrative and description, is thrown into relief on these opulent, textured pages of Ogilby's, the scrolls themselves both articulating and visualizing a journey.[22] The logic is a little peculiar here since the *backs* of these scrolls must be geographically and chronologically empty; we cannot expect to turn them over and see anything, yet the way the maps are drawn insists, not only that the scrolls have backs to them, but that their fronts roll back and down and up into the next front. (And the scroll splits off into two parts in Oxfordshire, one bit of paper rolling toward Oxford itself.) A later version of Ogilby's scrolls, Emanuel Bowen's *Britannia Depicta or Ogilby Improv'd* (1720–64), gets rid of the scrolls and presents the itineraries in two-dimensional-looking columns (and with quite a bit more marginal editorializing), to a very different (and, to my mind, lesser) narrative effect (fig. 3).

Marchitello calls itinerary maps in nature and desire "entirely narrational: the movement from A to B to C, until one reaches the pre-determined destination, the foregone conclusion. Within the genres of maps, these itineraries correspond to the most formulaic of literatures: they hold no surprises, afford no digressions" (87). And, in fact, Ogilby's accompanying text makes an explicit narrative journey of the scroll, as on the road from London to Holyhead (fig. 2 above):

> At 10′4. Enter *Hartfordshire*, and by an easy Ascent *Barnet, alias* High *Barnet* at 11′6. a well-frequented Town extending 4 Furlongs on the Road, Noted for it's [sic] Medicinal Waters, good Inns, and a Swine-market on *Monday*; and here EDWARD the 4*th*. obtain'd a Victory over the House of *Lancaster*. Having past the Town you re-enter *Midlesex*, and through *Kicks End*, and part of South *Mims*; At 15′3. Enter North *Mims* of 3 Furlongs Extent; and at 16 Miles re-enter *Hartfordshire*, a Mile beyond which a steep Descent conveys you down *Ridg-hill* and shews you St. *Albans*, which (first passing *Coney* at 18′6.) a direct Road brings you to at 21′2. a Town affording a plentiful History.

The seasons enter in: "[A] steep Descent carries you down *Chalk-hill*, thence (if in Winter) a dirty Way leads you to *Hockley*." The old Roman names are cited, as are the local dialects: "[B]y *Potters Perry* End your Road keeps streight, but somewhat Woody, shewing some visible Remains of the old *Roman* way; so by *Cuttle-mill* on the Left and *Havencote* Houses on the Right you come at 60′2. to *Towcester, vulgo Tosseter* and *Toster*, anciently *Tripontium* from its Bridges, a handsom Town, well provided for Reception of Travellers, and has a good Market on *Tuesdays*" (Ogilby, *Britannia*, 42). There you have it: history, geography, personalized to "your"

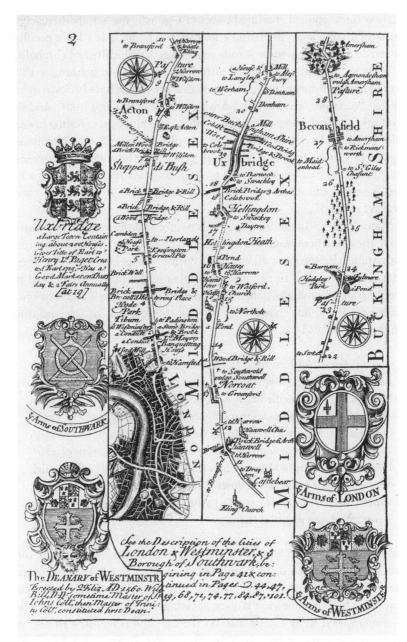

Figure 3. "London to Beconsfield," in Emanuel Bowen, *Britannia Depicta or Ogilby Improv'd* (1720–64). Courtesy of the Institute for Historical Research.

experience, with a local calendar and the promise of a good B&B at the end.

Most map stories, cultural critics argue, are political; Robert Mayhew, for example, finds the fact that all Ogilby's roads "radiated out from London, which was thereby symbolically and geographically constructed as the centre of the kingdom," means that Ogilby's project is essentially a royalist one, confirming rather than effacing the connection between monarch and land, as Helgerson argues for the sixteenth-century maps of Saxton and Speed.[23] Ogilby's text, Mayhew points out, although mostly a list of distances between towns, always managed to elaborate descriptions of loyalist towns, while "displays of Parliamentarian bravery went unrecorded" (79). And Harley claims that the increasing "objectivity" of maps was, instead, a "replication of the state's dominant ideology" ("Silences and Secrecy," 107). (It did not, however, always work out like that; Lisa Jardine recounts Louis XIV's displeasure at the visual reduction of his kingdom on state-sponsored new maps made from Cassini's astronomical observations [*Ingenious Pursuits*, 137–38].)

I don't argue in general with the idea that maps can be as ideologically motivated and influential as the next text, graphic or verbal. But, as Marchitello is primarily interested in tracing the narratival implications of map structures, so I am more concerned with connecting that narrativity to the idea of description. Literally, of course, the strips (or, more aptly, scrolls) neither narrate nor describe anything. A route is drawn, and the landmarks that it "passes" are "realistically" represented. As W. J. T. Mitchell has argued, in the eighteenth century "even abstractions are treated as pictorial, visual objects, projected in the verbal imagery of personification" (*Iconology*, 23). Ogilby's scrolls do not tell stories, and they do not describe places, but they do irresistibly suggest stories and visual spaces—and the connection between the two.

This sense of visualized journey, of narration in description and description in narration, provides another cultural context for John Bunyan's *The Pilgrim's Progress* (1678). The opening poem promises: "*This Book will make a Travailer of thee*" (6). Bunyan's work tells a story and describes Bedfordshire-like places, which critics and local archaeologists have painstakingly mapped—or tried to map—for centuries. Just such "an English highway...as Celia Fiennes might have travelled on," they say, with "fields that are sometimes like those of Bedfordshire, hills that bring the Chilterns vaguely to mind, houses that bear a certain resemblance to English country mansions," and, overall, the "common-place domestic scenes...represented with homely accuracy of detail."[24] But most have also pointed out (in a disappointed sort of way) the fact that, although we could "prove that the famous 'slough' lay near to Dunstable, and that Hill Difficulty rose up six miles from the village of Elstow," the topography runs short: "When the story requires landscape different from the flat Bedfordshire sort, Bunyan, who knew no other, is apt to be extraordinarily vague."[25] The "wide field full of dark mountains" going round the right of the Hill of Difficulty (Bunyan, 35) and the Delectable Mountains, which the group of pilgrims and shepherds casually walk to the end of (100), come in for particular attention in that they demonstrate a particular ignorance of mountainness.[26]

James Turner has persuasively argued that these inconsistencies are not so much faults in Bunyan's knowledge or ability as reflective of a culturally determined mental map that coordinated—or, rather, firmly separated—the terrains of this world and the next. This world—this England surveyed and mapped by Ogilby—represented "a hostile hierarchy of wealth and power founded on *place*—social position and landed estates. [Bunyan] saw place as property. The units of topographical space (heights and depths, lands, fields, hills, houses, and roads) are inseparable in Bunyan's imagination from the social means of their control, from lordship, tenure and sale, trespass actions and enclosure claims." The this-world topography of vivid, familiar detail marks out the dark spaces—the Slough of Despond, the Hill of Difficulty, the Valley of Humiliation, the Valley of the Shadow of Death, Vanity Fair, By-Path Meadow, Doubting Castle ("a vivid reconstruction of a country estate as it is experienced by those excluded from it"). The brighter places along the way, Turner argues—the Interpreter's House, Palace Beautiful, the Delectable Mountains, Beulah, and the Celestial City—are either vaguely described, disproportionately rendered, or of traditional biblical imagery. In the former carnal spaces, the pilgrims are tormented and obstructed; in the latter spiritual estates, "they enjoy lordship of the eye and foot, strolling with 'a pleasant prospect on every side', 'tracing and walking to and fro' in the valley at daybreak." The discrepancies mark "two incompatible 'jurisdictions'" identical in structure but antipathetic in nature.[27]

I am persuaded by almost everything in Turner's essay, but, although he insists that the "trick-picture" topography in The Pilgrim's Progress is "a positive rejection of the carnal rationality which lies behind mapping and surveying" (105), I want to counter that one of the best visual mappings of The Pilgrim's Progress could be made from Ogilby's scrolls of Bedfordshire in Britannia. While I cannot argue for any direct influence and I do for the most part believe with Turner (106) that, for Bunyan, "*all* topographical empiricism is evil if it extends into a second dimension" (the pilgrims have to be "Line-landers" because any straying from the Narrow Way into the surrounding landscape incurs dreadful adventures), nevertheless, the pervasive popularity of Ogilby's rendering of the English roadscapes certainly seems to seep into the contemporary *illustrators'* views of the text and the journey. In fact, the demand for illustrations themselves was so great that, by the sixth edition, an advertisement appeared for thirteen copper engravings, which could be bought separately, and which, by the fourteenth edition, were incorporated into the text itself.[28] In the first several editions, the frontispiece (fig. 4) pictures a portrait of Bunyan lying asleep on a hillside, his dreaming head in his left hand, with the "Denn" (Bedford jail) a cave below him, its gate raised above a lion; over his right shoulder Christian leaves his city of Destruction along a path, climbing toward the wicket gate, a staff and book in hand, a hat on his head, a burden on his back. Clear enough. But the frontispiece for the first edition of *Part II* (1684) (fig. 5) shows as well Christiana, Mercy, and the four boys following a *labeled* road up toward the wicket gate and, off to the right, a maplike city named "Destruction," all looking quite Ogilbyesqe. And, here, even Great-heart carries "in his Pocket a Map of all ways leading to, or from the Celestial City" and consults this "Book or Map," which "bids him be careful in that place to turn to the right-hand-way. And had he not here been careful to look in his Map, they had all, in probability, been smuthered in the Mud." Both the marginal commentary (*"The guide has a Map of all ways leading to or from the City"*) and the Dreamer ("Then thought I with my self, who, that goeth on Pilgrimage, but would have one of these Maps about him, that he may look when he is at a *stand*, which is the way he must take?") heartily enforce the genre and the practice (249).

Even the "evilness" of the topography—the incompatibility of the "two ... 'jurisdictions'"—can be reconciled if we think again of the scrolls *as scrolls*, with an underside or a backside that does not exist (or whereon the journey is simply erased, suspended until it curves back into view); scrolls that suggest text, continuity, movement, journey, narrative; with images that supply local visual detail without exactly representing it, as "a grid to help recall images of things" (Turner, 107): *"Art thou forgetful? wouldest thou remember[?]"* (Bunyan, 6). N. H. Keeble notes Bunyan's skill in combining "the incisively realistic with the typically representative"—in other words, his skill at *fusing* particulars and universals.[29] Sharrock argues that *The Pilgrim's Progress* is less an allegory than a myth precisely because we cannot pare away "the moral significance" from its particularly "sensuous form[s]."[30] And Van Ghent sees a similar fusion in the landscape, which is sometimes that of "dream or nightmare inhabited by our very solid neighbors" and at other times "our solid familiar landscape inhabited by creatures

Figure 4. Frontispiece to John Bunyan, *The Pilgrim's Progress. The Fourth Edition, with Additions* (1679). Courtesy of the Newberry Library, Chicago.

Figure 5. Frontispiece to John Bunyan, *The Pilgrim's Progress, the Second Part* (1684). Courtesy of the Rare Books Division, the New York Public Library, Astor, Lenox and Tilden Foundations.

of nightmare or dream" (31). As in Ogilby, the visual detail *suggests* rather than embodies, which is, Keeble argues, important because it keeps the image or character from becoming a type, remaining an example rather than an incarnation (introduction, xvi). Yet the suggestive detail in each also points to an underlying precision: for Ogilby, the exact measurement of the roads; for Bunyan, the exact directions for the Way (*"If thou wilt its Directions understand"* [6]).[31]

Bunyan's mode of description is largely classical in form, if homely in its particulars; as Sharrock puts it, Bunyan's detail tends to be "the hint of a single figure of speech . . . daringly expanded" (introduction, 25). A century and a half later, Macaulay could still wring his local countryside out of Bunyan's brief, spare, powerful images. I would like to combine the Ogilby way of "seeing things" that became so culturally and cartographically influential with the equally influential vision of Bunyan and follow the road for its evocative familiarities, its suggestive topographies. Ogilby's too, literally and experientially, is a narrow and predominantly straight road (and Bunyan's straight and narrow has its turns and divisions); if you trail off down the line "to Wickham the Coach Way" (see fig. 2 above), you're in a no-man's-land between strips of paper and must return or leap to some other page (which could be a problem if you're traveling and you brought only the one map).

The Miry Slow of Dispond, which lies just along Pliable's house (Bunyan, 12), we know to be a filthy, treacherous mess, but the narrator offers a historical as well as a geographic account of its presence:

> It is not the pleasure of the King that this place should remain so bad; his Labourers also, have by the direction of His Majesties Surveyors, been for above this sixteen hundred years, imploy'd about this patch of ground, if perhaps it might have been mended: yea, and to my Knowledge, saith he, *Here* have been swallowed up, at least, Twenty thousand Cart Loads; yea Millions of wholesom Instructions, that have at all seasons been brought from all places of the Kings Dominions; (and they that can tell, say, they are the best Materials to make good ground of the place,) If so be it might have been mended, but it is the *Slow of Dispond* still; and so will be, when they have done what they can. (13–14)

The fact that the King has surveyors perhaps argues that not *all* topographical science is tainted, although here ineffectual. Here is a textual gloss on a map site, a narratorial expansion of the image, pushing it back into history and deeper into allegorical significance, with the vision of the measurers of ground and the measure of cartloads. Furthermore, the middle of the slough has substantial steps, but, if the weather is bad or the traveler dizzy, "these steps are hardly seen" (14), as Ogilby warns that the descent down Chalk Hill is a dirty way in winter (42).

The "two...'jurisdictions'" may not be so strictly incompatible along the way, either. Chapter 1 looks in some detail at the contemporary realization of the House of the Interpreter; Palace Beautiful isn't as abstract as all that. John Brown argues that it was possibly suggested by the seat of Sir Thomas Hillersdon in Bunyan's village of Elstow, or perhaps by Houghton House, built in 1615 for the Countess of Pembroke by Inigo Jones.[32] Certainly, some of the contemporary illustrations render the palace in Palladian symmetry, while Doubting Castle remains a medieval form (figs. 6.7). Palace Beautiful comes complete with a porter's lodge, which is, perhaps, not allegorically necessary but is, certainly, socially so. Ogilby's map may not feature porter's lodges, but any contemporary traveler would furnish the image if the house were, say, a hall. The "little ascent, which was cast up on purpose, that Pilgrim's might see before them" (Bunyan, 55), and from which Christian shouts out happily to Faithful, "Ho, ho, So-ho!" is as good and useful a landmark for travelers as the "Rocks & Sand" appearing just before you enter Holyhead ("*The Continuation of the Road from London to Holyhead*"), or "a Brick bridge of 3 Arches," or "To Stoaken Church the Coach way" (see fig. 2 above). And the meadow, the stile, and the rising waters of the giant Despair's estate are equivalently rendered in Ogilby by, say, a long stone or a gibbet. As in Ogilby's map, the spaces between iconic landmarks are blank; the point is to get from one rendered image to another, to not mistake the road, to pay attention to the compass, to *see what needs to be seen*, to fill up the empty spaces with personal experience, personal vision. *The Pilgrim's Progress* may not be a map (although Great-heart uses one in the Enchanted Ground), but it is most definitely a topographical guide.

Most readers past and present have found *The Pilgrim's Progress* on the whole to be exceptionally vivid, if not always precisely detailed. But there were notable exceptions. The Baptist Thomas Sherman decided in 1682 to issue his own corrective to the four defects of the original in his *The Second Part of the Pilgrims Progress*, those defects being that "their [sic] is nothing said of the State of Man in his first Creation; Nor Secondly, of the Misery of Man in his Lapsed Estate before Conversion; Thirdly, a too brief passing over the Methods of Divine Goodness," and, last but not least, the problem that some "vain and frothy minds" might actually find "lightness and laughter"

The Palace called Beautifull and Christian afraid of the Lions.

Figure 6. "Palace Beautiful," in John Bunyan, *The Pilgrim's Progress* (22nd ed.), engraved by J. Sturt (1728). Courtesy of the John M. Wing Foundation, the Newberry Library, Chicago.

Page.151.

Chriftian and Hopeful, Efcape from Doubting Caftle.

Figure 7. "Doubting Castle," in John Bunyan, *The Pilgrim's Progress* (22nd ed.), engraved by J. Sturt (1728). Courtesy of the John M. Wing Foundation, the Newberry Library, Chicago.

while reading Bunyan's version. For my purposes, Sherman's first corrective sentence is stunning:

> The spring being far advanced, the meadows being covered with a curi-
> ous carpet of delightful green, and the earth clothed in rich and glorious
> attire to rejoice and triumph for the return of her shining bridegroom, the
> healthful air rendered more pleasing and delightful by the gentle winds
> then breathed from the south, impregnated with the exhilarating fra-
> grancy of the variety of flowers and odoriferous plants over which they
> had passed, and every blooming bush and flourishing grove plentifully
> stored with winged inhabitants, who with a delightful harmony sweetly
> sing forth their maker's praise and warble out their joyful welcomes to
> the gaudy spring, I one day took a walk in the fields to feast my eyes with
> the variety of delightful objects which that season of the year wherein the
> universe bears the nearest resemblance to the happy state wherein the
> immortal God at first created it liberally offers to the view of the admir-
> ing beholders, and thereby lays an irresistible obligation upon heavenly
> minds to spiritualize the several objects they behold, and satiate their
> happy souls with heavenly meditation, by affording them such innumer-
> able occasions of contemplating the divine goodness.[33]

Sherman's is an even more explicit—even plushy—call toward "occasional meditations" (discussed in chapter 3). It is the alternative seventeenth-century landscape discourse, closer to the leisure of the "gentleman
poet"; in Turner's words, "Christian's walk with God becomes the morning
stroll of a tourist, collecting subordinate clauses like souvenirs, each one
testifying to some new excellence or excitement of the place" (91). Sherman
is, according to Turner, in the "decorative" camp (101), which perhaps explains in part why one *Progress* journeyed sturdily through and beyond its
century and the other sank into the Quagg. It is most obviously in large part
a discrepancy of skills: Sherman does not repeat his descriptive performance
noticeably anywhere else in his text, but he does repeat the verbiage, and he
certainly kills the wit. But Sherman's failure may also lie in the cultural and
literary resistance to lengthy visual description *in prose*; what may be fine
for gentlemen poets is not yet welcome within the spaces of fiction. (Sherman, like Dunton, ahead of his time?) Turner argues that Bunyan "could not
achieve the rich breadth of Milton's Eden, nor the sauntering inclusiveness
of Sherman's opening sentence, because it had no basis in his experience,"
an experience in which his relation to the land "was one of bitter strug-
gle and exclusion" (104). But Bunyan's descriptions of the land fit perfectly

comfortably into this other empirical shorthand vision, of the metaphors "contracted to a word" and "borrowed ... from things amongst which our life is much conversant ... which so soon as named, the well-acquainted Auditor with ease ... applies them further than the speaker" (Walker, 55). Bunyan employed and evoked a cultural storehouse of topographical imagery.

Bunyan's pilgrims literally travel the spaces mapped by Ogilby, if spiritually by the Bible; readers of Bunyan's *Pilgrims* included the new travelers encouraged by Ogilby's itineraries. The landscape of England was becoming visually realized and experientially realizable for more of its citizens, and their market hunger for topographical descriptions of its spaces would not have been at odds with, and might even have vivified, the Puritan habit of thinking in metaphoric journeys. The textual praxes of topography and cartography, with their supply *of* local description, contextualized and filtered into literary spaces *for* local description.

CHAPTER THREE

Seeing Things

Not only what is Great, Strange or Beautiful, but any Thing that is Disagreeable when look'd upon, pleases us in an apt Description.
—*Joseph Addison*, Spectator *(1712)*

The Eyes of a Fly in one kind of light appear almost like a Lattice, drill'd through with abundance of small holes.... In the Sunshine they look like a Surface cover'd with golden Nails; in another posture, like a Surface cover'd with Pyramids; in another with Cones; and in other postures of quite other shapes.
—*Robert Hooke*, Micrographia *(1665)*

Bacon's *Novum Organum* (1620) is historically credited with the swing of attention to the material workings of the world (and in some extreme forms: John Aubrey's account of Bacon's death—as told by Hobbes—was that, in his urgent, immediate excitement at the idea that snow might preserve flesh, Bacon leaped out, gutted a peasant's chicken and stuffed it with snow, then lay in a damp bed and caught a fatal cold [Aubrey, 124]). The eighteenth century in general found the seventeenth most observant; Samuel Johnson said of Shakespeare that "he was an exact surveyor of the inanimate world; his descriptions have always some peculiarities, gathered by contemplating things as they really exist" ("Shakespeare," 89). The members of the Royal Society made it their business to describe that material world perambulated by Stow and surveyed by Ogilby, and they presented their findings not only to each other but also to the increasingly interested lay world.[1] This chapter continues the look at descriptive workhorses—the textual praxes of natural history, diaries, and lists. I begin with Robert Hooke's *Micrographia* and Robert Boyle's *Occasional Reflections*, both of 1665. The *Micrographia* renders subspace in breathtakingly (and unexpectedly) lovely detail: the flea, we discover, is a thing of beauty and a joy forever. Boyle renders surfaces, all surfaces, every surface he sees, if not in exhaustive detail, then certainly invested with emblematic meaning. He makes spiritually and textually legitimate the practice of seeing depth in surface. Both these texts worked to astound and expand human perceptions of and assumptions about the ordinary world.[2] But both excited amusement and skepticism as well as wonder, and Swift was swiftest and sharpest to the satiric retort. But, besides finding the microscopic worm in Celia's nose and the absurdity of a broomstick, he also used the jostlings of perspective in a sort of "positive particularity" (to modify Irvin Ehrenpreis's term). *Gulliver's Travels* (1726) supplies a number of notable exceptions to the complaint of visual "barrenness" in early narratives; many of Gulliver's domestic spaces are minutely— and cleanly—described precisely through the new openings in the visual field.

Diaries, like meditations, offer another obvious category for the increasingly popular employment of description, particularly of domestic interiors. In the second section, I look at the descriptions that John Evelyn and Samuel Pepys kept of their own perambulations of the city and country.[3] But, where topographies take us through the streets and micrographies anatomize the material world, diaries can also take us inside. We get rare views of spatial interiors; diaries in a sense carve out a textual space for domestic description. If it's *my* house and *my* diary, I can write about it because only *I* need be interested.

The third section considers *lists* of things as also contributing to the expanding contours of description. The *Philosophical Transactions* of the Royal Society, for example—a serial publication at least as popular and widely known as Hooke's and Boyle's works—functioned as a sort of vehicle for massive and not necessarily related detail in its yearly volumes of recorded travels, experiments, observations, thickly alphabetized indexes, and long, happy lists. Lists proliferated in the late seventeenth century and the early eighteenth; we find them in scientific essays, collectors' catalogs, topographies, mercantile pamphlets, diary accounts, and, of course, satire. Bunyan, Swift, and Pope all absorbed the elastic, bounding list into their descriptive visions.

Subspace and Surfaces: Hooke, Boyle, Swift

Robert Hooke's *Micrographia* and Robert Boyle's *Occasional Reflections* (both 1665) have long been recognized as two of the chief texts popularizing the empirical as well as the philosophical work of the "new sciences" of the Royal Society. The importance of microscopy for natural science is self-evident and has been thoroughly canvassed.[4] Its influence on European art, the British literary imagination, and popular culture has also been admirably outlined.[5] (One could buy a miniature microscope to wear on one's wrist, just in case anything excitingly tiny turned up.) Boyle's contemplative studies of apple parings, clouds, spaniels, coaches, and oysters addressed in part his own issues with scientific methods, discoveries, and theological implications, and his method for observing and recording the "ordinary" world matches gracefully with his colleague Hooke's imagination-stirring volume.[6] In this section, I assume the fundamental importance and well-known history of the *Micrographia* and the *Occasional Reflections* in relation to literature generally but consider each specifically in terms of its function as textual praxis in the literary absorption of description. Each opens further the space for visual re-creation of surfaces, subspaces, and interiors; each pushes effectually for the pleasure of observing and recording detail. The section will close with a brief look at a particularly detailed description of interior space in *Gulliver's Travels* that is *not*, in fact, a clear example of Irvin Ehrenpreis's concept of *negative particularity*, in which microscopically local detail is offered up only in the Augustan service of sharpening our sense of the low, vicious, or comic corners of the surface world; rather, it is an intense focus that unearths neither splendor nor horrors but the contours of familiarity itself.

Robert Hooke (1635–1703)

Robert Hooke, one of the most astonishing members of the Royal Society, was also a talented draftsman who worked on improving the engraving process itself to open up the substructural world of the apparently ordinary. The original charter of the Royal Society (1662) made the organization's official composition include, besides a president, some fellows, and various officers and secretaries, the positions of a "Printer" and a "Graver" as well.[7] The subspace world discovered by the microscope—the territory of surfaces and interiors—demanded illustration, and Hooke's and others' engravings of microscopic (and telescopic) phenomena supplied a form of experiential access. But the title of Hooke's work suggests the importance of its other aspect of depiction: verbal description.[8] Both as text and as illustration, Hooke's beautiful 1665 *Micrographia* was at once a popular publication and the inspiration for the cultural popularity of the microscope and its day-to-day possibilities. It was issued in a splendidly impressive folio form, allowing plenty of space to expand the drama of the invisible. By 1745, when a new edition of Hooke's engravings appeared, its compiler could testify that, since "a Desire of searching into the minute Wonders of Nature is become almost general," the misfortune of the rarity of the *Micrographia* is "considerably alleviated, by a fortunate Preservation of nearly all the *Copper-Plates*, which the Doctor [Hooke], at a great Expence, caused to be engraven for the illustration of his *Microscopical Observations*."[9]

Perhaps the favorite—and, therefore, most famous—of Hooke's microscopic renderings is the flea—that breathtaking foldout toward the end of the volume. Observation 53 opens emphatically: "The strength and beauty of this small creature, had it no other relation at all to man, would deserve a description."[10] No other entry (out of sixty) begins with a declaration that constitutes the entire paragraph[11]—the rest of the description is subordinated to the *deserving* of such. The description then follows in several paragraphs, in which both action and characterization (as well as visualization) are suggestively developed:

> For its strength, the *Microscope* is able to make no greater discoveries of it [the flea] then [*sic*] the naked eye, but onely the curious contrivance of its leggs and joints, for the exerting that strength, is very plainly manifested, such as no other creature, I have yet observ'd, has any thing like it; for the joints of it are so adapted, that he can, as 'twere, fold them short one within another, and suddenly stretch, or spring them out to their whole length....
>
> But, as for the beauty of it, the *Microscope* manifests it to be all over adorn'd with a curiously polish'd suit of *sable* Armour, neatly jointed, and beset with multitudes of sharp pinns, shap'd almost like Porcupine's Quills, or bright conical Steel-bodkins; the head is on either side beautify'd with a quick and round black eye K, behind each of which also appears a small cavity, L, in which he seems to move to and fro a certain thin film beset with many small transparent hairs, which probably may be his ears. (*Micrographia* [1665], 210)

Jardine notes that part of the scientific excitement of the microscope was its revelation of "the intricacy of internal anatomies on a tiny scale," the images of "the actual moving intestines and pulsating heart within the transparent flea or louse" (*Ingenious Pursuits*, 103). She continues commonsensically enough: "That animation could not, of course, be captured on

paper even by the most talented of draughtsmen; it was, however, vital for
an understanding of the mechanics of bodies" (104). Yet Hooke's description
inserts narration of a sort; the flea might well be fixed on his page, but verbs
(Aristotelian, Genettean) free him to fold, stretch, and spring his joints, to
move his hairy auricular film to and fro. As with Stow's perambulations and
Ogilby's strip maps, verbal visualization is matched with narration to try to
create an *experiential* description of something not just seen but imaginatively inhabited.[12]

Although the flea may be Hooke's favorite, the louse (fig. 8) gets even
more characterization and action (albeit pronominally, contemptuously, reduced to an *it* rather than a *he*):

> This is a Creature so officious, that 'twill be known to every one at one
> time or other, so busie, and so impudent, that it will be intruding it self
> in every ones company, and so proud and aspiring withall, that it fears
> not to trample on the best, and affects nothing so much as a Crown; feeds
> and lives very high, and that makes it so saucy, as to pull any one by the
> ears that comes in its way, and will never be quiet till it has drawn blood:
> it is troubled at nothing so much as at a man that scratches his head, as
> knowing that man is plotting and contriving some mischief against it,
> and that makes it oftentime sculk into some meaner and lower place, and
> run behind a mans back, though it go very much against the hair; which
> ill conditions of it having made it better known then [sic] trusted, would
> exempt me from making any further description of it, did not my faithful
> *Mercury*, my *Microscope*, bring me other information of it. (*Micrographia*
> [1665], 211)

While the flea is a happy surprise under scrutiny and so "deserve[s]" description, the louse is so well-known (and well-loathed) that it exempts the
descriptor—except that, in fact, the microscope finds more to be known
(e.g., why the louse scuttles away from light into the dark recesses of our
hair). But well-known as "it" is, the louse still gets his story—pretty much
as story—told. Vivid characterization, the hint of political satire, mock-epic
suspense, and spatialized activity—the "description" of the louse creates
a little, coherent, anthropomorphized world busily existing on the human
scalp, even before we get to *Gulliver's Travels*.

Stewart addresses the general/particular dichotomy of the miniature,
which "offers a world clearly limited in space but frozen and [is] thereby both
particularized and generalized in time—particularized in that the miniature
concentrates upon the single instance and not upon the abstract rule, but

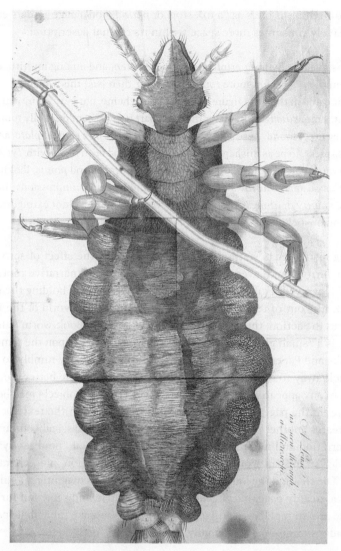

Figure 8. "A Louse," in Robert Hooke, *Micrographia* (1665). Courtesy of Special Collections, University of Virginia Library.

generalized in that instance comes to transcend, to stand for, a spectrum of other instances" (48). While Hooke's engravings of his individual, this-world-specific observations are, indeed, amber-fixed into their clean, otherwise empty pages and, thus, assume some Platonic effects of universality (say, "a Flea" into THE FLEA), his descriptions add narratives that set them moving.

Even something as inert as "a *full stop*, or *period*," on a page gathers energy and actively consumes more space within its textual description:

> I observed many both *printed* ones and *written*; and among multitudes
> I found *few* of them more *round* or *regular* then [*sic*] this which I have
> delineated in the third figure of the second Scheme, but *very many* abun-
> dantly *more disfigur'd*; and for the most part if they seem'd equally round
> to the eye, I found those points that had been made by a *Copper-plate*, and
> Roll-press, to be as mishapend as those which had been made with *Types*,
> the most curious and smothly [*sic*] *engraven strokes* and *points*, looking
> but as so many *furrows* and *holes*, and their *printed impressions*, but
> like *smutty daubings* on a matt or uneven floor with a blunt extinguisht
> brand or stick's end. (*Micrographia* [1665], 3)

A thing disfigured (a static, frozen object) becomes the effect of activity (a hole or furrow) and, even more toward the surface of narrative motion, a gerund (engraved strokes, smutty daubings), with a hand holding the brand or stick just out of textual sight. And returning to the world of the living escalates the action: the silverfish (or "*Silver-colour'd* Book-worm"), for ex-ample, is a "small glistering Pearl-colour'd Moth, which upon the removing of Books and Papers in the Summer, is often observ'd very nimbly to scud, and pack away to some lurking cranney, where it may the better protect it self from any appearing dangers" (208). The scrutinized objects may be held in place on the page, but they are granted movement in the text. Descrip-tion creates another plane of experiential space. The classical combination of description and narration operates in this influential "nonliterary" text to render an unseen world visible and *alive* with motion, plot, characters, space. The flea and the louse may drape themselves as magnificent still lifes across a creamy page, but, in the text, they scuttle and scud and lurk and intrude and trample and spring, generating a visualized, inhabited space in the reader's mind—or, less happily, memory.

Robert Boyle (1627–91)

Boyle, like the other experimental philosophers, found the ordinary world to be stupendously interesting, not only through the technological inten-sification of sensory prosthetics such as the microscope, but also through simple sustained attention: "The bare prospect of this magnificent Fabrick of the Universe, furnished and adorned with such strange variety of curi-ous and usefull Creatures, would suffice to transport us both with wonder and Joy, if their Commonesse did not hinder their operations."[13] Objects, and then events, were being "read" (the metaphor is contemporary) for their divinely revelatory language, for patterns behind and within ordinary existence. The point was to get past the "Commonesse," or, rather, to realize, as did Hooke and Swift, and later Hume, in different ways, that "Commonesse" is more an effect of psychological habit, or inattention, or indifference than an aspect of anything in itself. It is as if we *superimpose* a sense of the ordinary, the common, the uninteresting, across a multitude of vast individualities and smear them all into a generality of sorts. Minute observation and description—actually numbering the streaks of the tulip—will, in fact, get closer to something essential than will pulling away and constructing larger "truths." Meditating on objects and events (surfaces and occasions) becomes a sort of non-equipment-based microscopy—and a widely popularized one at that.

Puritan training in self- and world observation and interpretation was penetrating more widely into the culture at large in the seventeenth century. Edmund Bury, John Flavell, William Spurstow, and Boyle were well-known shapers of the form, in which "the emphasis of the tradition was repeatedly on what could be learned from even the smallest object of contemplation or from the most minute detail" (Hunter, *Before Novels*, 203). Diarists and others were interrupting themselves to occasionally meditate, or to meditate on occasions. U. Milo Kaufmann points out a sustained example of a typical occasional meditation in *Part II* of *The Pilgrim's Progress* (1684), when Prudence catechizes little Matthew: "Several features of this dialogue deserve comment. Its extraordinary terseness stems from the formulaic quality of both question and answer.... Here Bunyan draws upon the conventions of the tradition of occasional meditation and presents a list of observations in a kind of catalogue. It is probable that all of them are clichés of the tradition" (176–77).[14] The clichés, Kaufmann notes, like the punning scenes in Elizabethan drama, work economically and well because "the speakers are availing themselves of the commonplaces of established tradition" (177). The "commonplaces of established tradition" are, in other words, a cultural memory storehouse, busily being stocked from both fresh and familiar sources in scientific innovations and religious traditions.

The surfaces of objects—the surface world—were acquiring an interpretive richness in their own right: "emblems" (made by God) standing in for icons to promise a narrative coherence of meaning. Boyle argues: "The Book of Nature is to an ordinary Gazer, and a Naturalist, like a rare Book of Hieroglyphicks to a Child, and a Philosopher: the one is sufficiently pleas'd with the Oddnesse and Variety of the curious Pictures that adorne it; whereas the other is not only delighted with those outward objects that gratifie his sense, but receives a much higher satisfaction in admiring the knowledge of the Author, and in finding out and inriching himselfe with those abstruse and vailed Truths dexterously hinted in them" (*Naturall Philosophy*, 3–4). The smallest details could provide the profoundest clues; the point was not to misjudge the mean, the low, the common as, well, mean, low, or common: "[T]hough the Thing itself, which sets a mans thoughts a-work may be but Mean in Other regards, yet that which the Reflector pitches upon to consider, may be of another Nature; as though the Glo-worm . . . be but a small and contemptible Insect, yet the Light which shines in his Tail, and which makes the chief Theme of the Meditation, is a noble and heavenly Quality."[15] The point is to make the child into a philosopher.

To that end, the *Occasional Reflections*, like the *Micrographia*, was designed for a wide lay audience, to capture imaginations and produce observers and interpreters. Boyle addresses the work to his sister Katherine Jones, Lady Ranelagh, his closest confidante in intellectual as well as personal matters. She had urged him to publish it during the plague of 1665, writing to him that Londoners "strive to free themselves from [fear] by endeavouring against thinking at all, because they know not how to begin so to think, as by thinking to get themselves relieved from the torments their fears bring them, or those everlasting ones which bring their fears upon them, upon the approach of that disease that scatters death so plentifully round about them."[16] In his long "Discourse Touching Occasional Meditations," Boyle lists a number of reasons for meditating closely on the occasions of the quotidian world; among other things, it supplies us with "store and variety of good Comparisons" (*Occasional Reflections*, 39), which (along with employment, devotion, and disinterestedness) helps free us from prejudice, rigidity, complacency, arrogance, and general human stupidity.

Like Hooke, Boyle appropriates some fictional techniques in his observational works. We have seen the energy of characterization in Hooke's louse and flea; Boyle adds dialogue. In "Upon the eating of Oysters" (Reflection 3 of the Last Section), for example, he employs his pseudonymously named friends Eugenius, Eusebius, Genorio, and Lindamor to debate the cultural relativism of swallowing small, round, slippery, living globs as delicacies. He suggests in his preface that such a technique is "a new thing": "[W]hen I wrote for my own Divertisement, I sometimes took Pleasure to imagine two or three of my Friends to be present with me at the Occasion, that set my thoughts on work, and to make them Discourse as I fancy'd Persons, of their Breeding and Tempers, would talk to one another on such an

Occasion" (*Occasional Reflections*, B2). Such techniques of fiction make for easier cross-pollination: the "scientific" observation already feels welcome among the literary.

Even more to the point is Boyle's similar endowing of surfaces, of Aristotelian accidentals, with meaning. In "Upon his Paring of a rare Summer Apple" (Reflection 7 of Sec. 1), for example, although the description relies heavily, plentifully, and obviously on classical, biblical, and exotic geographic references (Flora, Pomona, Adam and Eve, the Orient), the matter at hand really comes down to the difference between the peel and the fruit of *this apple*: "But those these winning [Green and Red] Dyes delight me strangely, they are Food for my Eye alone, and not my Stomack; I have no Palate for Colours, and to rellish this Fruit well, and know whether it performs to the Taste what it promises to the Sight... all this Gay out-side is cut and thrown away" (so like linguistic ornament, which may delight the ear but must be pruned away to properly relish the Truth) (*Occasional Reflections*, 182). *This apple* comes to stand for *All Apples*, but the equally large point remaining is that any particular apple that I pick up is capable of generating a transcendence by my looking closely at it—or, rather, that *I* can generate a sort of transcendence by describing it. I can pluck this apple out of its ordinary context and give it a new shape simply by looking closely at its shape. I can remake my world by describing it.

Boyle meditates primarily on *things* (and sometimes events), but occasionally he ventures into interior space. Like Swift, he examines a lady's closet and its collection of ornaments, finding an expressive whole (Reflection 9 of Sec. 5); unlike Swift, the expression presumably corresponds to what the lady herself intends by it. Lindamor asks:

> Is not this Closet strangely fine, *Eusebius*? Here is such a variety of pretty and taking Objects, that they do as well distract the Eye as delight it; the abundance, the choice, and the Order, do as well disclose the fair Possessors skill, as Her magnificence, and shew at once, that she both has plenty, and deserves it, by knowing so well how to make use of it. Those things that are here solitary, or single, will scarce be elsewhere matched, and all the rest are so pretty, and so excellent in their several Kinds, that the number of fine things that make up this curious Collection, cannot hinder any of them from being a Rarity. And in a word, the Embellishments, that adorn and ennoble this delightful place, are such, that I believe the Possessor of them, as welcome as she is unto the best Companies, scarce ever looks upon finer things, than she can see in her Closet, unless when she looks into her Glass. (*Occasional Reflections*, 175–76)

The objects, separately and together, reflect not just what the lady owns but how she owns it, how she arranges it, how she deserves it. Lindamor presumably outlines what most possessors feel and think about their possessions. Eusebius isn't quite so delighted, however. Although he would permit ladies—even those not of such high Quality—"to have a retiring place so neatly adorn'd, as may invite them to be alone, and with-draw to it, to read, or meditate," he approves only so long as its "Ornaments be not so costly, as to rob Charity, or so gawdy, as to distract the Devotion they should but accommodate" (176–77). Yet he doesn't draw specific lines; this lady's ornaments—any Ornament—may fit separately or as part of a collection within the sphere of meaningful things, as long as *meaningful* conforms to the *functional*. The equation is general but accommodates particulars.

Jonathan Swift (1667–1745)

Most of Swift's microscopic investigations in poetry and prose achieve the opposite effect from Hooke's delighted wonder in subspace or Boyle's tempered tolerance. The closets and dressing rooms that Swift's speakers explore are notorious for their unearthed filth. What binds objects and images together is a negative aesthetic, a common stickiness. In "The Lady's Dressing-Room" (1730), for example, Strephon finds "a dirty Smock . . . / Beneath the Arm-pits well besmear'd" (lines 11–12), "various Combs for various Uses, / Fill'd up with Dirt so closely fixt, / No Brush cou'd force a Way betwixt" (lines 20–22), and, neither last nor least, Celia's magnifying glass, "that can to Sight disclose, / The smallest Worm in *Celia*'s Nose, / And faithfully direct her Nail, / To squeeze it out from Head to Tail" (lines 63–66).[17] Most critical attention to descriptive detail in *Gulliver's Travels* has dwelt on the repellently rendered Brobdingnagian breasts, cancers, hairs, moles, and pores. Such effluence of detail transforms the ordinary into the monstrous— a nastier move into carnal, secular darkness than Bunyan ever makes. Irvin Ehrenpreis (46–48) has argued that overt dwelling on the ordinary is rare in Augustan poetry or prose, except when the point is satire or the subject is the low, vicious, or comic—whatever did not line up with the accepted universals of truth, beauty, and virtue. His term for such sharp local detail is *negative particularity*. Ehrenpreis's characterization of detail in Augustan poetry corresponds to the contemporary literary suspicion of the ordinary, the everyday, the accidental, which Swift's scab-picking emphasis throws into dark relief.

But even in Swift there are aesthetically and morally neutral examples of microscopic attention paid to the details of this world—or, rather, of Hookean examples of making the familiar strange precisely through familiarity. In book 2 of *Gulliver's Travels* (1726), "A Voyage to Brobdingnag," Gulliver is fitted out with a house that is described in great visual detail:

> The Queen commanded her own Cabinet-maker to contrive a Box that might serve me for a Bed-chamber.... [It was] a wooden Chamber of sixteen Foot square, and twelve High; with Sash Windows, a Door, and two Closets, like a *London* Bed-chamber. The Board that made the Ceiling was to be lifted up and down by two Hinges, to put in a Bed ready furnished by her Majesty's Upholsterer.... A Nice Workman, who was famous for little Curiosities, undertook to make me two Chairs, with Backs and Frames, of a Substance not unlike Ivory; and two tables, with a Cabinet to put my Things in. The Room was quilted on all Sides, as well as the Floor and the Ceiling, to prevent any Accident from the Carelessness of those who carried me; and to break the Force of a Jolt when I went in a Coach.[18]

Swift, like Hooke, is continually inspecting the ordinary in minute, descriptive detail, both in his poetry and in his prose—not just to make us see things, but to make us see things *oddly*.[19] Rather than connecting the strange to the ordinary in his similes, he connects the *ordinary* to the ordinary (a box is "like a *London* Bed-chamber"; Lilliputian geese are like sparrows, Lilliputian larks like flies). Swift deliberately jolts us with his radically relativized perspectives: "[S]ome Eagle had got the Ring of my Box in his Beak, with an Intent to let it fall on a Rock, like a Tortoise in a Shell, and then pick out my Body and Devour it" (131). We come out from the description seeing things *differently* from the way we did when we went in; after each reading, it still takes me a minute to fit Gulliver proportionately back into the landscape of his rescue. (Can't they just pull his box out of the water onto the ship? Oh, right, it's sixteen feet by twelve feet.) Swift's descriptions, like Hooke's, *change us*; they defamiliarize the ordinary world in the apparent act of domesticating it. As Georg Simmel says of microscopic and telescopic technology: "[C]oming closer to things often only shows us how far away they still are from us."[20]

This scene may, in the strict sense, belong to the "low" and "comic" categories of Augustan criticism, but, if so, in a distinctly different way from those detailing Celia's chamber pot or the young nymph's glass eyeball and mouse-skin eyebrows. Swift here uses concrete, recognizable details to create a "clean" realist space, one alienated, not by something nasty in the woodshed, by the familiar made dirtily strange, but precisely by the familiar being hammered in as *familiar*. The familiarity itself, drawn by the description, is beak-lifted out of context and dropped into a readerly perceptual sea (so to speak). Swift is using the textual praxis of microscopic description to open up new possibilities for visual detail and accuracy in narrative prose, shaping what we expect to see, what we are designed to see, what we are able to see.

Diaries and Descriptions: Pepys and Evelyn

Virginia Woolf remarked about John Evelyn, her epitome of seventeenth-century observation and detail: "Wherever there was a picture to be seen by Julio Romano, Polydore, Guido, Raphael, or Tintoretto, a finely built house, a prospect, or a garden nobly designed, Evelyn stopped his coach to look at it, and opened his diary to record his opinion" ("Evelyn," 82). Evelyn's almost clinical passion for detail appalled her; in his account of the man on the rack for robbery (March 1651), she hears a tone that chills her: "Evelyn watched this to the end, and then remarked that 'the spectacle was so uncomfortable that I was not able to stay the sight of another,' as we might say that the lions growl so loud and the sight of raw meat is so unpleasant that we will now visit the penguins." She concludes: "Allowing for his discomfort, there is enough discrepancy between his view of pain and ours to make us wonder whether we see in fact with the same eyes" (81).

But, if, in fact, as Hunter argues, "the early novel's circumstantiality, 'realistic' though it may be, is not so much a device to establish factuality and credibility as it is an outcome of the habit of observing and reporting," then the eyes of the diarists in some ways helped create our eyes. The diaristic habit of observing and reporting "proliferated," according to Hunter, "in Protestant England, Scotland, and America in the seventeenth century and...thus became useful in producing expectations novelists could take advantage of" (*Before Novels*, 200). Those "expectations" would include not only what was seen but also what could be seen and how its visualness could be verbally expressed. Perhaps the most famous seventeenth-century diarists, John Evelyn and Samuel Pepys, although neither in the strictly Puritan diary tradition nor publicly influential in diary writing (both published posthumously—indeed, postcenturously), warrant attention here because, as prominent, self-conscious cultural representatives, they reveal what they were inclined as well as taught to see by the particular emphases of their time and place.[21]

John Evelyn (1620–1706)

So what did they see? Like meditations, diaries record and, in some cases, ponder the diurnal world, finding interest in local spaces and surfaces, and making room for them in their pages. The editor of one edition of Evelyn's diary remarks that it "includes so many details of places and names that to do the diary justice would require a quantity of material equal in size to the text, a task already fulfilled by De Beer" in the standard edition.[22] Evelyn did not divide his manuscript in any particularly orderly, chronological way, and the early entries are compressed memories more than daily recordings. Even the later, fuller entries are, according to De Beer, more a series of memoirs written at various points in Evelyn's life based on his carefully detailed notes, at least until 1684, when the diary assumes a more typical immediacy.[23] The diary itself begins in 1620 (with details of his birth in October, a genealogy, and a description of his family and home) and ends in February 1706, the month of his death. It is short on dialogue and (for the most part) character analysis, its main strength (and for which it has been continually, systematically mined) being description: "Evelyn had a strong visual sense and the ability to paint a verbal picture."[24] And, as Woolf noted, one of his passions was a "finely built house"—including his own family's, Wotton in Blackheath, Surrey:

> The Building after the antient fashion of our Ancestors, (tho' nothing of modish as now the manner is) is not onely very Capacious, but exceedingly Commodious, & almost intirely of Brick: Situated in the most Southern part of the Sheere, and tho' in a Valley, yet realy upon a greate rising; being joynd to one of the most eminent hills in England, for the wonderfull large Prospects to be seen from the Summit of *Lith-Hill*, where one in a bright day may discerne ten, or twelve Counties with a part of the sea, tho' hardly ever taken-notice of, there lying no commone Way for Travilours over it.
>
> The mansion house (built, as I have <said>, according to the mode of those hospitable days) is swetly invironed with those many delicious streames, and venerable Woods, which with the Meadows, render it (in the Judgement of strangers, as well as English-men) accommodated for a greate person & a wanton Purse, capable of being made a noble Seate; for Mounts, Cascades & Fountaines, as the Gardens at present shew, which tho' now, not so perfectly agreaing to the monstrous Expense of this age, is far from despicable, & was lately reckond among the fairest of Surry;

wanting neithe<r> Fountaines, Grots, and other amoenitys, of Ponds; to
which might be added Canales of considerable length.[25]

Description from a nineteenth-century standard does not get very far
in this sketch, which supplies only the staple adjectives *capacious, commodious, delicious, venerable, noble,* and *monstrous.* Perhaps the most individuated piece of information is that the house is of brick. But it is a full
description for its time, as the categories were relatively precise (John Crowley reminds us that *commodious* signaled the comfort of good air rather than
the comfort of good space)[26] and the combination would be telling. Evelyn's
depiction of the return of Charles II adds sound, movement, color:

> This day came in his Majestie *Charles* the 2d to London after a sad, &
> long Exile, and Calamitous Suffering both of the King and Church: being
> 17 yeares: This was also his Birthday, and with a Triumph of above 20000
> horse & foote, brandishing their swords and shouting with unexpressable
> joy: The wayes straw'd with flowers, the bells ringing, the streets hung
> with Tapissry, fountaines running with wine: The Major, Aldermen, all
> the Companies in their liver<ie>s, Chaines of Gold, banners; Lords &
> nobles, Cloth of Silver, gold and vellvet every body clad in, the windos &
> balconies all set with Ladys, Trumpets, Musick, & <myriads> of people
> flocking the streets & was as far as *Rochester,* so as they were 7 houres
> in passing the Citty, even from 2 in the afternoone 'til nine at night: I
> stood in the strand, & beheld it, & blessed God: And all this without one
> drop of Bloud. (3:246 [29 May 1660])

Woolf to the contrary, Evelyn invests this scene with poignance, from the
context of exile to the new paragraph pause for thanks—the indentation for
significance.

Some of Evelyn's most vivid and individualized descriptions are, in fact,
of architectural interiors, as in that of the Duchess of Portsmouth's dressing
room:

> Following his Majestie this morning through the Gallerie, <I> went (with
> the few who attended him) into the Dutchesse of Portsmouths dressing
> roome, within her bed-chamber, where she was in her morning loose gar-
> ment, her maides Combing her, newly out of her bed: his Majestie & the
> Gallants standing about her: but that which ingag'd my curiositie, was
> the rich & splendid furniture of this woman's Appartment, now twice
> or thrice, puld downe, & rebuilt, to satisfie her prodigal & expensive

pleasures, whilst her Majestie dos not exceede, some gentlemens Ladies furniture & accommodation: Here I saw the new fabrique of *French Tapissry*, for designe, tendernesse of worke, & incomparable imitation of the best paintings; beyond any thing, I had ever beheld: some pieces had *Versailles*, St. *Germans* & other Palaces of the French King with Huntings, figures, & Landscips, Exotique fowle & all to the life rarely don: Then for *Japon Cabinets, Skreenes, Pendule Clockes*, huge *Vasas* of wrought plate, *Tables, Stands, Chimny furniture, Sconces, branches, Braseras* &c, they were all of massive silver, & without number, besides of his Majesties best paintings: Surfeiting of this, I din'd yet at *Sir Steph: Foxes*, & went contendedly home to my poore, but quiet Villa. (4:343–44 [4 October 1683])

Both the striking collection of new and dazzling things and Evelyn's being struck by them argue for the culture of things in the creation of descriptions (discussed further in chapter 6). Evelyn makes the rather striking disclaimer that, even though one of the most beautiful women in history is just out of her bed, robed in a loose gown, her hair being brushed, it is still the room itself and its intricate furnishings that capture his eyes (although it *is* rather a long and detailed account of the duchess's dishabille).

Evelyn's several-page description of the Great Fire of 1666 I have examined in detail elsewhere (see *Literary and Cultural Spaces*, 26–28); it is a long, vivid, visual tale of terror and misery and loss, of a ground that burned the soles of his shoes. Long pages are also devoted to the death of his daughter Mary on 14 March 1685. At this entry Woolf recoils: "Though he loved his daughter Mary, his grief at her death did not prevent him from counting the number of empty coaches drawn by six horses apiece that attended her funeral" ("Evelyn," 84). But such a counting occurs after pages of character analysis (remarkable as much for its intensity as for its presence) and biographical recounting: of her piety, learning, reading, writing, translating; her voice and countenance; her modesty and wit; her judgment and orthography; her gracefulness and kindness; the gentlemen courting her; the details of her contracting smallpox; her courage in illness and strength in suffering. There are pages and pages and pages before a paragraph recounts her interment, the noble persons attending, and "others [who sent] their Coaches, of which there were 6 or 7. of six horses viz. Countesse of Sunderland [etc.].... Thus lived, died, & was buried the joy of my life & ornament both of her sex & my poor family: God Almighty of his Infin<i>te mercy grant me the grace thankfully to resigne my selfe & all I have, or had, to his divine pleasure, & in his good time, restoring health & Comfort to my Family" (4:430 [14–16

March 1685]). (Evelyn's prayer continues a few sentences longer.) And then there follows a further biographical revelation, an opening up of the dead daughter's private self from the details of her opened private spaces: "Having some days after opened her Trunks, & looked into her Closset, amazed & even astonished we were to find that incredible number of papers and Collections she had made of severall material Authors, both Historians, Poets, Travells &c: but above all the Devotions, Contemplations, & resolutions upon those Contemplations, which we found under her hand in a booke most methodicaly disposed, & much exceeding the talent & usage of [so] young & beautifull women, who consume so much of their time in vaine things.... But as she was a little miracle whilst she lived, so she died with out Example" (431).

In short, I would say with Woolf that, yes, Evelyn "used his eyes" ("Evelyn," 82). He saw houses, gardens, paintings, events, persons, destruction, reconstruction, joy, pain. In his diaristic habits he recorded the things of the world and occasionally his own and others' responses to them. He accumulated detail and saw importance in circumstance. And he could render pain and suffering with detail as persuasive as that of any Edwardian novelist.

Samuel Pepys (1633–1703)

Samuel Pepys as diarist is almost a cliché in himself; loved and bowdlerized, loved perhaps even more after his debowdlerization, known as the "personal" one when compared to his friend, colleague, and fellow diarist Evelyn.[27] But, like Evelyn's, Pepys's diary is known for its evocative distillation of a world, its "close observation and total recall of detail: it is the small touches that achieve the effect."[28] Pepys's is not a sustained narrative but a vast collection of small bits tellingly visualized. As with Evelyn's diary, while it cannot have influenced contemporary writers directly, Pepys's may be said, on the one hand, to have been influenced by the more widespread contemporary pressure to observe, record, diarize, and, on the other, to have supplied the public literary fabric for the Victorian upholstery to come, being published, as it was, in the early nineteenth century, shortly on the heels of Evelyn's.[29]

Pepys's entries on the theater, music, the Royal Navy, his wife, and his sexual escapades are already well thumbed. Marjorie Nicolson, John Bowle, Guy de la Bédoyère, and others have traced the connections between the diarists and the empiricists and between science and diaristic observation; Stuart Sherman has beautifully analyzed the prose patterns and their cultural contexts; J. Paul Hunter has followed the connections between diary writing and novelistic detail.[30] What remains insufficiently attended to is Pepys's preoccupation with his things and his houses. In telling his diary of those preoccupations, he creates textual space for them.

Pepys is very particular at noticing and commenting on his own and other people's arrangement of household things. On 29 October 1663, he has a meal at the Guildhall, "where under every salt there was a Bill of fare, and at the end of the table the persons proper for that table. Many were the tables, but none in the Hall but the Mayors and the Lords of the privy Councell that had napkins or knives—which was very strange." There ended up being "ten good dishes to a messe, with plenty of wine of all sorts[,] ... but it was very unpleasing that we had no napkins nor change of trenchers, and drunk out of earthen pitchers and wooden dishes."[31] On 26 February 1666, he and Elizabeth are "infinitely satisfied" with their inspection of the King's house, "the neatness and contrivance of the house and gates," "the prospect that is in the balcone in the Queen's lodgings, and the tarrace and walk" (7:59).

Pepys is, of course, dismayed by the general destruction of the Fire, but he is especially discomposed about the state of his things, although much eased when his money and iron chest are in the cellar, the bags of gold and papers and plate carried "to Sir W Riders at Bednall greene," and his wine and "parmazan cheese" put into a hole in the garden (7:272–74 [2–4 September 1666]). But the restoring of things after the Fire is also troubling: "Up, and to work, having Carpenters come to help in setting up bedsteads and hangings; and at that trade my people and I all the morning, till pressed by public business to leave them, against my will, in the afternoon; and yet I was troubled in being at home, to see all my goods lie up and down the house in a bad condition, and strange workmen going to and fro might take what they would almost" (7:285 [14 September 1666]). Pepys wants his things in their places; he wants his interiors intact, his house in its patterns. (This of course is the man who insisted that Magdalene keep his books in exactly the sized pattern that he left them in, on penalty of losing the collection.)[32] And sprucing up his house is as much a pleasure as buying a new suit or a new microscope. On 29 September 1667, he and Elizabeth are talking about "keeping a coach the next year, and doing something to my house which will cost money—that is, furnish our best chamber with tapestry—and other rooms with pictures" (8:455). He is a connoisseur of other people's houses as well: he finds his father's house "altogether ... very pretty—especially the little parlour and the summer-houses in the garden. Only, the wall doth want greens upon it and the house is too low-roofed; but that is only because of my coming from a house with higher ceilings; but altogether is very pretty and I bless God that I am like to have such a pretty place to retire to" (8:469 [9 October 1667]).

Pepys's attention to the details of place, to architecture, furnishings, and the overall effect of the creation of domestic space, is part of what in fact creates domestic space on the page. First seeing, and then choosing, the contours and ornaments of a room, a place, a house, opens up the possibilities in literary space. Accumulating details in diaries, which correspond to observed details in the near world, works into habits of seeing, choosing, recording, and creating visual description.

Collections and Lists: The *Philosophical Transactions*, Swift, Pope

One of the genres to be intensified in and by the seventeenth century was the list. Lists had been around for the life span of literature, of course. The epic catalog was a means of rest and refreshment away from battle narrative. The list as blazon lovingly dismembers the female body. The Rabelaisian list earthily blats vast quantities of things onto the page, filling its textual universe with bodily income and outgo.[33] But, in the seventeenth century, the list comes to occupy more—perhaps all—genres; in some instances, as with Hatton's alphabetized topography considered in chapter 2, the list takes over the form. Lists are historically and generically a part of description at large, in that they gather *things* together to create a visual heap, a heap capable, moreover, of structural meaning. Lists, like the more stitched together description, make grammatical and conceptual connections between objects, connections that we generally find between their commas and within their formal order.

The Royal Society generated its own passion for lists and perhaps helped cultivate a wider cultural obsession. Natural history itself seems to be part of the cause, combined with the increasing interest in antiquities: both natural and artificial artifacts were collected, and investigated, and analyzed, and classified. As Tony Bennett puts it, the new scientific taxonomies emphasized "observable differences between things rather than their hidden resemblances; the common or ordinary object [was] accorded a representative function." As with Boyle's meditations, an individual object is simultaneously isolated for its individual interest and made to stand in for other apples (and truths) like it. But, while Bennett suggests that, at least in some contexts, the ordinary object "was accorded priority over the exotic or unusual," this was not the case for the natural historians or the virtuosi.[34] John

Tradescant's 1656 catalog of his collections—the basis for the Ashmolean Museum—opens with "A View of the Whole," which promises a variety of common and uncommon alike:

1. Birds with their eggs, beaks, feathers, clawes, spurres.
2. Fourfooted beasts with some of their hides, hornes, and hoofs.
3. Divers sorts of strange Fishes.
4. Shell-creatures....
5. Severall sorts of Insects, terrestriall.
6. Mineralls, and those of neare nature with them....
7. Outlandish Fruits from both the *Indies*, with Seeds, Gemmes, Roots, Woods, and divers Ingredients Medicinall, and for the Art of Dying.
8. Mechanicks, choice pieces in Carvings, Turnings, Paintings.
9. Other Variety of Rarities.
10. Warlike Instruments, European, Indian, etc.
11. Garments, Habits, Vests, Ornaments.
12. Utensils, and Housholdstuffe.
13. *Numismata*, Coynes antient and modern, both gold, silver and copper, Hebrew, Greeke, Roman both {Imperiall and Consular[.]
14. Medalls, gold, silver, copper, and lead.[35]

Tradescant's catalog itself—as catalogs tend to be—is one long sorted and alphabetized list of things, the things themselves rarely described in detail. (A few nicely bound books from friends get a wordier attention.) The *Philosophical Transactions* early on provided alphabetized indexes—lists— of their contents that, like Tradescant's catalog, juxtapose the ordinary and the exotic, the things of daily life examined and the things from far away imported: "Air, Ale, Amber, Ambergreese, Analysis, Anatomical Observations, Animals of strange kinds, Answers to Philosophical Inquiries, Antipathy, Ants, Apology, Architecture in China, Artificial Instruments, Asbestus, Asia, Astronomical Remarks; . . . A Wall very vast in China, Whale-fishing, Wicker trees, Winds; Yellow Amber."[36] One sign of the Royal Society's influence on the love for and inclusion of lists is that entry in Hatton's *A New View of London* (1708) on the Royal Society itself, in which the mummies, veins, penises, sloths, tusks, whirled shells, and petrified things take up as much space in the description as anything architectural (see chapter 2). The list of animated nouns produces its own visual field of fascinating plenty.

John Evelyn puts lists together for vivid texture in his tableau narratives, particularly the famous coronation scene, which at the very least is a powerful tribute to his power of memory: "[F]irst went the *Duke* of *Yorks* Horse guards, Messengers of the Chamber. 136 Esquires to the *knights* of the *Bath*, each having two: most richly habited: The knight *Harbinger*, Searjeant *Porter*, *Sewers* of the *Chamber*, *Quarter* Waiters, Six-Clearks of *Chancery*, Cler: of the *Signet*, *Cler*: of the *Privy-Seale* . . . Two Persons representing the *Dukes* of *Normandy & Aquitain* . . . in fantastique habits of that time. . . . " Evelyn goes on, achieving a noun total of over seventy-five (many of them plurals) (2:278–80 [22 April 1661]). Evelyn's procession is more along the lines of Homer's vast catalog of Greek ships, meant, according to Pope, to compliment the many Greek states, than of Virgil's more compact catalog for a more unified territory. Evelyn is reproducing the magnificence of a restored throne in a verbal procession as overwhelming as the actual one.

One of the most popular teaching texts in the seventeenth and eighteenth centuries was Charles Hoole's translation of Johann Amos Comenius's (1592–1670) *Orbis Sensualium Pictus, or The Visible World*, which first appeared in Latin and English in 1659 and reached its twelfth edition by 1777. The text is a series of 150 copperplate illustrations and textual definitions of "A World of Things Obvious to the Senses drawn in Pictures." The preface is Boylean:

> The ground of this business, is, that *sensual objects be rightly presented to the senses*, for fear they may not be received. I say, and say it again aloud, that this last is the foundation of all the rest: because *we can neither act nor speak wisely, unless we first rightly understand all the things which are to be done, and whereof we are to speak. Now there is nothing in the Understanding which was not before in the Sense. And therefore to exercise the Senses well about the right perceiving the differences of things, will be to lay the grounds for all wisdom.*[37]

The editor of the twelfth edition (1777), W. Jones, argues in his prefatory material that "this work of *Comenius* is as far preferable to a common *Nomenclature*, as an habitable building to an heap of loose stones in a quarry, or a burning candle to a dead mixture of grease and cotton."[38] The work begins with a list of the alphabet and its pronunciations: "*The crow crieth á á; The Lamb blaiteth b é é é; The Grasshopper chirpeth cí cí; The Whooppoo saith du du; . . . The dog grinneth err; . . . The Breeze or Horseflie saith ds ds*" (3–4). It is then sorted into numbered sections by category ("II. God," "III. the World," "IV. Heaven," "V. Fire," etc.), with all the things of the world following. Each section has its own engraving, with the various examples

assembled and numbered within in a living picture and the numbered items
named and defined in double-columned lists (English on one side, Latin on
the other) below. Section 26, for example, "Four-footed Beasts, and first those
about the House," shows a room off a hallway, with a squirrel sitting in the
window, a monkey on the table, a cat stalking a mouse, a dog and a puppy
on the floor, and weasels and ferrets trying to get in:

> The Dog, 1.
> with the Whelp, 2.
> is keeper of the House.
> The Cat, 3.
> riddeth the House
> of Mice, 4.
> which also a
> Mousetrap, 5. doth.
> The Squirrel, 6.
> The Ape, 7.
> and the Monkey, 8.
> are kept at home
> for delight.
> The Dormouse, 9.
> and other greater Mice, 10.
> as, the Weesel, the Martin,
> and the Ferret,
> trouble the House.
> (32–33)

The book breaks down the world into 150 categories, from "Serpents and
Creeping Things," "Wild Beasts," "The outward parts of a Man," "The Flesh
and Bowels," "The Dressing of Gardens," "The Making of Honey," "Cook-
ery," "The Blacksmith," "The Box-maker and the Turner," "The Stove with
the Bed-room," "the Booksellers Shop," "the Study," "A Burial," "A Stage-
Play," and "Mahometism" through section 150, "The Last Judgment" (193).
The text closes with an index. We see into rooms and activities and sort
their details. The *Orbis Sensualium Pictus* carefully carves the world into a
visualized text, breaking down its components into charming bits, the great
and the small brought onto the same comprehensible plane of the list.

But the great literary art of lists lies in their satiric use, precisely because
lists can seem such powerful ropes for ordering, on the one hand, and such

bland, inoffensive, offhand, even tedious things on another. (Have I read carefully Evelyn's entire long paragraph of coronation members? Have I *really*?)
As Hunter argues, the "primary allegiance" of lists "is to structure, a process of comparison implied in the thing itself" in which they may "assert
equivalences" but may just as well "imply inappropriate comparisons that
blur distinctions."[39] Tony Bennett, applying Krzysztof Pomian's analysis of
the phenomenological structure of collections,[40] argues that "what can be
seen on display is viewed as valuable and meaningful because of the access
it offers to a realm of significance which cannot itself be seen. The visible is
significant not for its own sake but because it affords a glimpse of something
beyond itself" (35). Bennett is interested in exposing the elitist and exclusionary aspects of such a sorting of the visible in a museum, a sorting that
imposes a classification and directs spectatorial perception—what Barbara
Benedict calls a celebration of "the elite ownership of nature and culture enacted through observation: the extension of material possession to symbolic
possession by means of the eyes."[41]

   While lists and catalogs certainly can have elitist, exclusionary, political
agendas, my interest here is in their larger and multifaceted influences on
and appearances within literary texts in the elastic matter of description. To
consider lists as verbal collections standing in for a series of objects, it makes
sense to pry into those commas for other kinds of significance, significance
that cannot itself be seen. Bunyan, Pope, and Swift all take the scientist's
list, the virtuoso's collection, the human consumption of objects, and wran-
gle out the implications of those various bundles in literary reconstructions
of the list's structure—leveling, roping, identifying, distinguishing, quan-
tifying, qualifying, and generally playing with size, shape, and contextual
significance.

   In *The Pilgrim's Progress*, for example, Bunyan's most famous list appears in Vanity Fair: "Therefore at *this Fair* are all such Merchandize sold,
as Houses, Lands, Trades, Places, Honours, Preferments, Titles, Countreys,
Kingdoms, Lusts, Pleasures, and Delights of all sorts, as Whores, Bauds,
Wives, Husbands, Children, Masters, Servants, Lives, Blood, Bodies, Souls,
Silver, Gold, Pearls, Precious Stones, and what not" (73). Houses and kingdoms, whores and children, souls and pearls, and whatnot—the good, innocent things and the naughty, bad things—are all corralled in this carnal
space, not separated out as in Swift's sort of list, but all tainted (as all topography is tainted for Bunyan, on James Turner's argument ["Bunyan's Sense
of Place," 105–6]). And, appropriately, the list includes goods for sale that
clutter up a *market* space, drawing on another cultural source for pleasurable
listing.

One of the most famous poetic lists is from Pope's *The Rape of the Lock* (1714), cataloging the miniaturized world littering Belinda's dressing table:

> Unnumber'd Treasures ope at once, and here
> The various Off'rings of the World appear;
> . . . .
> This Casket *India*'s glowing Gems unlocks,
> And all *Arabia* springs from yonder Box.
> The Tortoise here and Elephant unite,
> Transform'd to *Combs*, the speckled and the white.[42]

In 1818, William Hazlitt had commented about this poem: "It is like looking through a microscope, where every thing assumes a new character and a new consequence, where things are seen in their minutest circumstances and slightest shades of difference; where the little becomes gigantic, the deformed beautiful, and the beautiful deformed."[43] Pope's poem supplies a double lens: the mock-epic trivializes, but, at the same time, the microscope magnifies. Swift's magnification finds things foul; Pope's celebrates while it satirizes: Japan, China, Arabia, are all employed to produce one cup of coffee; one cup of coffee calls up all the East. The list of luxuries culminates in "Puffs, Powders, Patches, Bibles, Billet-doux" (canto 1, line 138).

Laura Brown demonstrates how Pope employs the textual praxes of mercantile pamphlets—the lists of market space—in displaying clutter. After analyzing the apparent "air of indiscriminacy" in the poetic list as actually "carefully structured in sound and rhythm" (and suggesting some literary sources such as Milton), she then persuasively examines the contemporary discourse of trade.[44] Pamphlets defending mercantilism generally and the East India Company in particular, she notes, specialize in lists of luxury: "*Salt-Petre, Indigo, Muslins, Cotton-Yarn, Cotton-Wool, Ereny-Yarn, Floretta-Yarn, Herba Taffaties, Herba Longees and Callicoes*, besides *Diamonds, Drugs and Spices*."[45] "This is the rhetoric of acquisition," Brown argues. "In each of these catalogues the simple list of goods carries a raw and inherent fascination, an effect that is caught and heightened in Pope's passage by the collective visual attractiveness of the items and the wit that holds them" (12). The "effect" is "caught and heightened" in the commercial passages by a similar, if not, perhaps, as carefully or consciously crafted, sense of alliteration, and pairing, and echoing, and repeating, the verbal equivalent of running masses of gold coins through one's hands.[46]

Swift's devastating lists in *Gulliver's Travels* are more like Bunyan's collection of sins than Pope's scattering of vanities: what is gathered together to ask the Lord's blessing will presumably not get it. In what I consider the most moving and terrible list in all literature, Gulliver proudly collects the infinitely expanding set of weapon nouns and their objective correlatives to display before his Houyhnhnm master. At first, the Master is a little disgusted, but he is primarily skeptical about the list of reasons men go to war with each other: "What you have told me, (said my Master) upon the Subject of War, does indeed discover most admirably the Effects of that Reason you pretend to: However, it is happy that the *Shame* is greater than the *Danger*; and that Nature hath left you utterly uncapable of doing much Mischief: For your Mouths lying flat with your Faces, you can hardly bite each other to any purpose, unless by Consent" (239). But then Gulliver continues:

> I could not forbear shaking my Head, and smiling a little at his Ignorance. And, being no Stranger to the Art of War, I gave him a Description of Cannons, Culverins, Muskets, Carabines, Pistols, Bullets, Powder, Swords, Bayonets, Sieges, Retreats, Attacks, Undermines, Countermines, Bombardments, Sea-fights; Ships sunk with a thousand Men, twenty Thousand killed on each Side; dying Groans, Limbs flying in the Air: Smoak, Noise, Confusion, trampling to death under Horses Feet: Flight, Pursuit, Victory; Fields strewed with Carcasses left for Food to Dogs, and Wolves, and Birds of Prey; Plundering, Stripping, Ravishing, Burning, and Destroying. And to set forth the Valour of my own dear Countrymen, I assured him, that I had seen them blow up a hundred Enemies at once in a Siege, and as many in a Ship, and beheld the dead Bodies drop down in pieces from the Clouds, to the great Diversion of all the Spectators. (239–40)

Gulliver's "description" is a list, a long, long list of nouns, verbs, causes, effects, weapons—the kind of list that any reader in any century is bound automatically to expand. Nothing in this list has disappeared; the picture only gets larger and more precise. This is the list that opens up Peacham's version of pragmatographia as catalog, how a single brief phrase, such as "the citty was ouercome by assault," can be expanded through "a description of thinges" (which in his example is a list) into something infinitely more powerful—"if thou wilt open and set abroade those thinges whiche were included in one word" (Oiiii$_v$). What is revealed beyond the commas is the indefinitely expandable; the rope of grammatical order marks the edge of the abyss.

Leo Spitzer has, in his magisterial way, argued that the cultural shift toward minuter descriptions and filled interiors is a self-protective retreat from such an abyss, an abyss opened up by an epistemological shift in human perceptions of place: "It is in such descriptions of an interior setting that the idea of the 'milieu' (enclosing and 'filled in') is presented most forcefully; we have the *immediate* milieu of the individual. One may remember the vogue which paintings of the same type enjoyed in the preceding century—intérieurs depicting the coziness and comfort of well-furnished human dwellings.... The world-embracing, metaphysical cupola that once enfolded mankind has disappeared, and man is left to rattle around in an infinite universe. Thus he seeks all the more to fill in his immediate, his physical, environment with things."[47] This chapter and the previous one have looked at the way in which the things and the surfaces of the natural world seemed to become more visible, more immediately felt and perceived, in the seventeenth century, the way in which they were mapped, and recorded, and listed, and cataloged, and described, and meditated on in the various textual praxes of topographies, itineraries, micrographies, diaries, and lists. Things occupy texts as they make themselves felt in the world; and, as things come to seem to define the world for the eighteenth century, so eighteenth-century texts adapt to accommodate things in description. The workhorses of textual praxes discover their literary usefulness.

CHAPTER FOUR

Writing Things

> When they came to the Door, they went in, not knocking, for folks use
> not to knock at the Door of an Inn.
> —*John Bunyan*, The Pilgrim's Progress, Part II *(1684)*

A s the physical world was coming into sharp, detailed relief in maps and micrographies, the literary world was also investigating and populating its spaces, if not with a direct *visual* correspondence, then with an experiential one. What folks used not to do at inns—knock—is at once an observation of seventeenth-century custom and a metaphor for seventeenth-century description. In reading, one enters the spare visual space immediately, through the door of a *thing*, a small vivid detail.

One of the characteristics of early novels that most strikes modern readers is the vast heaps of *things* among their pages; Virginia Woolf's image is Crusoe's earthenware pot, but we all remember as well Christian's staff, scroll, and burden; the tasty meals along the way in *The Pilgrim's Progress, Part II*; Moll's bolts of cloth and pewter tankards; the giant helmet and waving feathers in *The Castle of Otranto*. Ian Watt has argued that the proliferation of things in the early novel was a sort of response to the new empiricist epistemology: the "realist" novel attempted to get at the truth of experience by replicating its alleged features, supplying quantities of objects with some sense of immediacy and randomness.[1] What this account does not address is why those objects first appeared in disconnection, as objects without background. Those *things* seem all the more striking because they live and move and have their being in otherwise apparently empty space. Occasionally, we see a bundle *on* a stool *in* an apothecary's shop, but, even then, the prepositions tend simply to connect one object with another, not to a visualized whole. Rather like Hooke's louse, the things stand forth in a sort of glory, surrounded metaphorically by a white page.

This chapter will look at the status and function of things as visual detail, as pieces of description, and as spatial and narrative markers in John Bunyan's *The Pilgrim's Progress, Part II* (1684), Daniel Defoe's *Robinson Crusoe* (1719), *Moll Flanders* (1722) and *Journal of the Plague Year* (1722), and Horace Walpole's *The Castle of Otranto* (1764). The thing, the detail, gradually transforms under early observation. Bunyan's emblems, particularly in *Part II*, are famous for escaping their theological boundaries and behaving much more this-worldly than their allegory directs them. Crusoe's emblems, born in the same spiritual family as Bunyan's, have the same renegade tendencies to prefer life as "real" things. In his later novels, Defoe takes that emblematic energy from the otherworld into the underworld, where the things still stand in a strangely focused light and still throb with some sort of significance, but not the universal sort. And, by midcentury, the palpable presence of things in narratives has become so familiar that Walpole can scoop them up, inflate them to enormous proportions, and wield them as satiric weapons.

Emblems: *The Pilgrim's Progress, Part II*

These are but Generals, said Mr. Great-heart, come to particulars, man.
—*John Bunyan,* The Pilgrim's Progress, Part II

Critics from Coleridge, to Sir Charles Firth, to Dorothy Van Ghent, to Roger Sharrock have considered *The Pilgrim's Progress* as a religious allegory transcended by its own fictional imagination; "his piety was baffled by his genius, and the Bunyan of Parnassus had the better of the Bunyan of the Conventicle," said Coleridge (*Coleridge on the Seventeenth Century*, 475). *Part II* of *The Pilgrim's Progress* (1684) has generally been considered an even more inconsistently sustained allegory than *Part I*, precisely because it more nearly approaches existence as "our first novel" (Keeble, introduction, xxi). Sharrock considers the whole of *The Pilgrim's Progress* to be a less sophisticated allegory than anything from Dante or Spenser; it is too episodic, and its episodes attach to the journey rather than interlock with each other (introduction, 16–17). Proper allegory is a coherent intellectual scheme, a total system of metaphoric words and emblematic images;[2] but, particularly in *Part II*, a number of the objects have been called "merely ingenious and decorative" (Bunyan, 280 n. 190), the scenes simply "incident[s] in the life" of a seventeenth-century Puritan.[3] The "general" system seems to lead more and more into its "particulars" of object and detail, the emblems breaking out of their signifying boxes to become . . . simply, and once again, the objects in the natural world.[4]

C. S. Lewis complained that we have a "pernicious habit of reading allegory as if it were a cryptogram to be translated; as if, having grasped what an image (as we say) 'means', we threw the image away and thought of the ingredient in real life which it represents."[5] That's the wrong way round, he insists. We must go, not out of the book, but *into* it, not figuring out representational significance, inserting equal signs in "a clumsy intellectual operation," as Dorothy Van Ghent says (26), but living *in* the green valley and realizing that humility is quite like that. Left to ourselves, most of us apparently read *The Pilgrim's Progress* the "right" way: from inside. Lewis has claimed that he first read the book as a child without discovering or attaching the allegory to it at all; Talon agrees: "we forget [the allegory] over and over again" (*John Bunyan*, 62). Without in the least discounting the central importance, the necessary condition of the Puritan allegory of *The Pilgrim's Progress* to its entire existence, in this section I want to look at the emblematic objects and scenes as they paradoxically transcend their emblematic status. (Perhaps *escape* or *forget* are better words.)[6] In short, I want to resituate the "common-place domestic scenes" and "homely accuracy of detail" (Van Ghent, 22) of *Part II* within its more "novel-like" effects (C. S. Lewis, 216), to mark another transformation of description into novelistic space. *Part II* is, according to David Alpaugh, "predominantly visual" and abounding in "striking verbal pictures."[7] We will "come to particulars" and watch the emblem return to thing, watch the spaces acquire familiar definition.

In all sorts of ways, *Part II* is a more comfortable, domestic, visualized space.[8] Unlike the first part, it was not written in a "Denn"; Bunyan had been freed from his twelve years in prison in 1672 and was licensed to preach under the Declaration of Indulgence. His Bedford church legally acquired its own barn for Congregational meetings. And, in general, by the 1680s, religious tolerance made for easier lives. The story itself is more communal and comforting, with Christiana, her four boys, and her young neighbor Mercy setting out from the City of Destruction together, with a unified will, unlike Christian, who had to tear himself away from his family and trek across a largely hostile land on his own. And the company grows, with Greatheart being a pretty invincible conductor, the boys growing up to manhood and helping out in fights, their wives coming along, Old Honest joining up, and Fearing, Ready-to-halt, and Feeble-mind bringing up the rear. Unlike in *Part I*, where Faithful is martyred, here the only brutal deaths are those of

giants and their ilk (a really rousing number of heads are put on pikes, and the
bodies of the simple, the slothful, and the presumptuous swing on gibbets
[176]). The very weather seems to help the pilgrims out: they have a good
"sunshine morning"; they make "a shift to get staggeringly over" the steps
in the Slough of Despond (154); they are contented rather than tormented in
the green Valley of Humiliation (196–98); they go through the Valley of the
Shadow of Death in *daylight* (200). But, most of all, they spend far more time
indoors than Christian ever did, and they have more nice things to eat.[9]

Part II might well be characterized by its houses, porter's lodges, and
inns. James Turner has noted that, in *The Pilgrim's Progress*, "[s]ingle aspects of the road and the countryside through which it passes are selected as
the requirements of the allegory arise" (98)—a feature that characterizes non-
allegorical fiction as well, as the next chapter discusses—yet more inns arise
on demand than seems quite strictly necessary for an allegorical pilgrimage.
Most of the group's journey seems spent finding congenial places to stay—
and then staying longer in them than planned. Sharrock has pointed out
that "the friendliness and dignity of the houses of resort along the road owe
much to the entertainment of Christians in apostolic times; ... hints have
been expanded into full-grown fictions" (introduction, 25). Bunyan exhibits
well Henry Peacham's 1577 prescription for powerful pragmatographia, or
"description of thinges," in his ability to "open and set abroade those thinges
whiche were included in one word" (Oiiii$_v$). Bunyan takes those apostolic
places and turns them into increasingly more fully realized and terrifically
pleasant seventeenth-century domestic spaces, with musicians standard.

The Keeper of the Wicket-Gate ushers Christiana, Mercy, and the boys
into a "Summer-Parler below" where they talk comfortably among themselves, and, when they continued on, "the weather [was] very comfortable
to them" (157, 159). At the House of the Interpreter, the significant things to
be shown—the collection of emblems—are not, as for Christian, portraits,
and people, and fires, and palaces, but spiders, and hens, and chickens, and
lambs, and dunged fields, and robins. At first, Mercy can't sleep for happiness, but the Narrator of the Margins assures us of "Mercy's *good nights
rest*" (171). They have a lovely bath the next (sunny) morning and are given
clean white linen clothes and a few becoming ornaments. As they leave,
Mr. Interpreter gives Christiana "a piece of Pomgranate[,] ... a piece of an
Honey-comb, and a little Bottle of Spirits" (179).

At least one illustrator was struck by the prevalence of suppers in *Part
II*. In the twenty-second edition (1728), one of J. Sturt's twenty-two copper
engravings (for both parts) includes "Christiana and her Children at Supper in the Interpreter's House" (fig. 9).[10] The background is spare: plainly

Chriſtiana and her Children at Supper in the Interpreter's Houſe

Figure 9. "Christiana and her Children at Supper in the Interpreter's House," in John Bunyan, *The Pilgrim's Progress* (22nd ed.), engraved by J. Sturt (1728). Courtesy of the John M. Wing Foundation, the Newberry Library, Chicago.

wainscoted walls; a nontransparent window looking out to nothing; a bare floor. But front lit and well detailed are the cloth, the trenchers, the cutlery, the dish of salt, the plates of meat and bread, the pitcher and goblets, a smiling servant bearing a dish of apples, and the candles lighting up the very pleased, expectant faces of Christiana, Mercy, and the boys. Great-heart keeps his helmet on—you never know—and the host looks soulfully upward, presumably in prayer. All have their hands on their plates or utensils, very ready. The details actually correspond better to the elaborate dinner later at Mr. Gaius's house, but they effectively stand for the interior domesticity, the brightness of home details, found throughout *Part II*.

At the Porter's Lodge and then House Beautiful, comfort continues with a nice roast lamb and "accustomed Sauce" (Bunyan, 182), and Christiana asks and is granted "that Chamber that was my Husbands, when he was here" (183). In the morning, Mercy and Christiana have a little discussion about the place, and guest etiquette is strictly observed:

CHRISTIANA. I think it is now time to rise, and to know what we must do.
MERCY. Pray, if they invite us to stay a while, let us willingly accept of the proffer. I am the willinger to stay awhile here, to grow better acquainted with these Maids; methinks Prudence, Piety and Charity have very comly and sober Countenances.
CHRIS. We shall see what they will do. So when they were up and ready, they came down. And they asked one another of their rest, and if it was Comfortable, or not?
MER. Very good, said Mercy. It was one of the best Nights Lodging that ever I had in my Life. (185)

After they have been there a week, we learn that "Mercie *has a sweet heart*" (Bunyan, 187 [marginal commentary]), but the voice from the sidelines is ironic since Mr. Brisk soon loses interest in her because he thinks she spends too much energy on good works, "making of Hose and Garments for others" (188). Mercy says rather defensively: "*I might a had Husbands afore now, tho' I spake not of it to any; but they were such as did not like my Conditions, though never did any of them find fault with my Person: So they and I could not agree*" (188). Here, says Sir Charles Firth, "the allegory disappears altogether. We have simply an incident in the life of a fair Puritan described with absolute fidelity to nature: the actors are ordinary men and women of the time, and the fact that their names have a moral significance makes no difference to the story. We are passing, in fact, from allegory to the novel with an improving tendency" (102).[11]

This scene of courtship and the assurance of a young girl's attractiveness is shortly followed by another scene that irks the allegorical purists:
Matthew's "gripes" from eating the *"Green Plums"* hanging over the wall
at the Wicket-Gate. Colic pains suggest, to begin with, even more graphic
earthiness than, say, being "smuthered with Mud" (Bunyan, 154); but then
we have the actual recipe, which has its referents in Hebrews, John, and
Mark, but which, in its making up and taking, brings us instantly into a
child's sickroom: "'Twas said, [the purge] was made of the Blood of a Goat,
the Ashes of an Heifer, and with some of the Juice of Hyssop, &c. When
Mr. *Skill* had seen that the Purge was too weak, he made him one to the
purpose. 'Twas made *ex Carne & Sanguine Christi.* (You know Physicians
give strange Medicines to their Patients) and it was made up into Pills with
a Promise or two, and a proportionable quantity of Salt" (190). The mother
must talk her son into taking it, tasting it herself, and promising that it's
sweeter than honey, so, finally, Matthew is a good boy: "It caused him to
Purge, it caused him to sleep, and rest quietly, it put him into a fine heat and
breathing sweat, and did quite rid him of his Gripes. So in little time he got
up, and walked about with a Staff, and would go from Room to Room, and
talk with *Prudence, Piety* and *Charity* of his Distemper, and how he was
healed" (191). After a month, it's time to leave, and Mr. Great-heart gives to
Christiana from the Lord some bottles of wine, parched corn, pomegranates,
figs, and raisins (194).

When Fearing finally gets himself pushed and pulled into the House
Beautiful, he too finds himself as comfortable as his nature allows. He is
given "a Bottle of Spirits, and some comfortable things to eat" (Bunyan,
209); and, as Great-heart tells the story, Fearing manages to supply himself
with company of a sort: "I got him in at the House *Beautiful,* I think before
he was willing; also when he was in, I brought him acquainted with the
Damsels that were of the Place, but he was ashamed to make himself much
for Company, he desired much to be alone, yet he always loved good talk,
and often would get behind the *Screen* to hear it; he also loved much to
see *antient* things, and to be *pondering* them in his Mind" (209). Although
Fearing was *"Dumpish at the house* Beautiful" (209 [marginal comment]),
he later tells Great-heart "that he loved to be in those two Houses from
which he came last, to wit, at the Gate, and that of the *Interpreter,* but
that he durst not be so bold to ask" (209). And, here, psychological realism
saturates the spiritual allegory, as Great-heart concludes: "He had, I think, a
Slow of Dispond in his Mind, a *Slow* that he carried every where with him"
(207). The allegorical figure reads the emblematic space as a psychological
symbol.

Bunyan historians have relentlessly tracked down whatever real geography and architecture can be found in *The Pilgrim's Progress*, and they generally agree that the House Beautiful and its interiors were suggested either by the seat of Sir Thomas Hillersond at Elstow or (more probably) by Houghton House near Ampthill, built by Inigo Jones in 1615 for Mary Sidney, Countess of Pembroke (Brown, *John Bunyan*, 18, 323). We have seen in chapter 2 the Palladian-rendered exterior of the house in early illustrations (see fig. 6 above); but, as Sharrock underscores, its interior is visualized as a particular kind of Puritan domesticity: "In the House Beautiful there is more education through symbols and preparation for future dangers; but the chief impression conveyed by the women who tend Christian there is of the human dignity of the best English Puritan household rather than of vague female allegorical personages: Piety and Prudence they may be called, but these very names take us into the middle-class families of Bunyan's time" (introduction, 20). Two seventeenth-century realities converge in the House Beautiful: its architectural realities of spaciousness and plenty imply the spiritual equivalent of the landed estate, the final reward of the afterlife. As James Turner has argued, while Doubting Castle represents the oppressive lords of this world, in the spaces of the House Beautiful, the Delectable Mountains, and Beulah the pilgrims "enjoy lordship of the eye and foot, strolling with 'a pleasant prospect on every side', 'tracing and walking to and fro' in the valley at daybreak" (103). The interior of the house, on the other hand, simultaneously registers the present, the homely, the familiar, the details of family comfort and security.

The dignity and comfort of the House Beautiful are replicated in all the houses along the way. After lingering pleasantly in the Valley of Humiliation, moving with fear (but, as we have seen, in daylight) through the Valley of the Shadow of Death, and watching Great-heart slay Maul the Giant, the pilgrims are all rather exhausted, and "*Christiana* then wished for an Inn for her self and her Children, because they were weary." And lo, says Mr. Honest, "There is one a little before us." It is an inn run by Mr. Gaius (famous for his hospitality, according to Rom. 16:23 and 3 John 1–6), and, "when they came to the Door, they went in, not knocking, for folks use not to knock at the Door of an Inn" (215). And, here, things are exceptionally cosy, the details of food, and conversation, and comfort lavishly laid out.[12] Gaius has a cook (whose name, promisingly enough, is Taste-that-which-is-good), and the cook runs a good kitchen and sets a good table, "sen[ding] up to signifie that the Supper was almost ready, and sen[ding] one to lay the Cloath, the Trenshers, and to set the Salt and Bread in order." Then follows a feast from Levitical law of heave-shoulder and wave-breast ("these two Dishes were very fresh and good, and they all eat heartily-well thereof" [217]), good red wine, a dish of milk well crumbed, a dish of butter and honey, a dish of apples, and a dish of nuts (218–19). There are riddles for when the company get drowsy (220); Matthew and Mercy get married; and Samuel whispers to his mother: "[T]his is a very good mans House, let us stay here a good while.... The which *Gaius* the Host overhearing, said, *With a very good Will my Child*" (219). So everyone stays more than a month.

They next stay at Vanity Fair, also for "a great while," at the house of Mr. Mnason (Bunyan, 231), who also has (this seems to be crucial) "a very fair Dining-Room" (228) and obedient daughters Grace (to marry Samuel) and Martha (to marry Joseph). The better sort of neighbors are called over for supper, and for them to find Christiana on the pilgrim's road was "a very comfortable Surprize." We learn that the neighborhood is now generally quiet (229) and that "*Persecution* [is] *not so hot at Vanity Fair as formerly*" (229 [marginal comment]). No more nasty burnings of people, for example, just good suppers and conversations. On the river this side of the Delectable Mountains was "an House built for the *nourishing* and bringing up of those Lambs, the Babes of those Women that go on Pilgrimage" (234); and there's a dining room in the palace within the Delectable Mountains.

The one time things get dismal, in terms of lodging, is in the Enchanted Ground:

And that place was all grown over with Bryers and Thorns; excepting *here* and *there*, where was an *inchanted Arbor*, upon which, if a Man sits, or in which if a Man sleeps, 'tis a question, say some whether ever they shall rise or wake again in this World.... The Way also was here very wearysom, thorow Dirt and Slabbiness. Nor was there on *all* this Ground, so much as one *Inn*, or *Victualling-House*, therein to refresh the feebler sort. Here therefore was *grunting*, and *puffing*, and *sighing*: While one tumbleth over a Bush, another sticks fast in the Dirt, and the Children, some of them, lost their Shoos in the Mire. While one crys out, I am down, and another, Ho, Where are you? and a third, The Bushes have got such fast hold on me, I think I cannot get away from them. (Bunyan, 248)

However, although there is not one inn, they do find the enchanted arbor, fetchingly detailed, and replete with a sort of sofa: "Then they came at an *Arbor*, warm, and promising much Refreshing to the Pilgrims; for it was finely wrought above-head, beautified with *Greens*, furnished with *Benches*, and *Settles*. It also had in it a soft Couch whereon the weary might lean. This, you must think, all things considered, was tempting; for the Pilgrims already began to be foyled with the badness of the way; but there was not one of them that made so much as a motion to stop there" (248–49). Given these pilgrims' pleasure in comfortable lodgings, it is, of course, even more to their credit that they resist the warm shelter and soft couch; but, in another sense, their discretion increases their comfort. They remember what the arbor does to people, they willingly follow Great-heart's direction, and their consciences remain at peace.

The characters in both parts of *The Pilgrim's Progress* have been admired through the centuries for their refusal to remain types or be captured within their own names. U. Milo Kaufmann has argued that the names "are adjectival in nature rather than substantival, and hence hint at attribute rather than essence" (90). Old Honest, found sleeping under an oak, modestly demurs when he's identified: "Not Honesty in the *Abstract*, but *Honest* is my Name, and I wish that my *Nature* shall agree to what I am called" (Bunyan, 205). But prosopographia enters as well, to thicken psychological characterization with physical details. Feeble-mind is nephew to Fearing, and the family resemblance shows in particulars, as Honest sees: "I am apt to believe also that you were related one to another; for you have his whitely Look, a Cast like his with your Eye and your Speech is much alike" (223–24). Mercy, we learn from her own mouth, has never had a suitor find fault with her person (188). And at the end comes overt prosopographia in earnest, as Honest describes Madam Bubble to Standfast, who applauds his limning skills:

HON. Madam Buble! Is she not a tall comely Dame, something of a Swarthy Complexion?

STANDF. Right, you hit it, she is just such an one.

HON. Doth she not speak very smoothly, and give you a Smile at the end of a Sentence?

STANDF. You fall right upon it again, for these are her very Actions.

HON. Doth she not wear a great Purse by her Side, and is not her Hand often in it fingering her Mony, as if that was her Hearts delight?

STANDF. 'Tis just so. Had she stood by all this while, you could not more amply set her forth before me, nor have better described her Features.

HON. Then he that drew her Picture was a good Limner, and he that wrote of her, said true. (252–53)

Talon argues that the characters in *Part II* are, in fact, *less* novelistic in that they do not change or develop: "Christian's children have no spiritual life, and we hardly believe in their physical existence. Mercy remains the same from beginning to end . . . and Christiana does not develop at all in the course of the pilgrimage" (162). But this is to read "characterization" from the post-nineteenth-century perspective of *expectations* of development—which presumes a different ontological worldview, a different, nonessentialist understanding of personal identity as something capable of change and, therefore, of characters able to be "round." Such an idea of personhood does not develop until the eighteenth century; in Bunyan, the characters are rendered in the sort of minimalist indicative detail that is the typical feature of late seventeenth- and early eighteenth-century novels more generally.[13] The allegorical significance of Madam Bubble is coherent, and her swarthy complexion makes as decodable a sense as Feeble-mind's pale face, but the discussion of description *surrounding* the description floats above the allegorical necessities.

The fight between Great-heart and the giant Maul (playing either the Roman Catholic Church or seventeenth-century rationalism)[14] offers another scene that slips beyond its allegorical bounds into sheer narrative with what C. S. Lewis calls "harsh woodcut energy" (201):

> Then the *Giant* came up, and Mr. *Great-heart* went to meet him, and as he went, he drew his *Sword*, but the *Giant* had a *Club*: So without more ado they fell to it, and at the first blow the *Giant* stroke Mr. *Great-heart* down upon one of his knees; with that the Women, and children cried out. So Mr. *Great-heart* recovering himself, laid about him in full lusty manner, and gave the *Giant* a wound in his arm; thus he fought for the space of an hour to that height of heat, that the breath came out of the *Giants* nostrils, as the heat doth out of a boiling Caldron.
>
> Then they sat down to rest them, but Mr. *Great-heart* betook him to prayer; also the Women and Children did nothing but sigh and cry all the time that the battle did last.
>
> When they had rested them, and taken breath, they both fell to it again, and Mr. *Great-heart* with a full blow fetch't the *Giant* down to the ground. Nay hold, and let me recover, quoth he. So Mr. *Great-heart* fairly let him get up; So to it they went again; and the *Giant* mist but little of all-to-breaking Mr. *Great-heart's* Scull with his Club.
>
> Mr. *Great-heart* seeing that, runs to him in the full heat of his Spirit, and pierceth him under the fifth rib; with that the *Giant* began to faint, and could hold up his Club no longer. Then Mr. *Great-heart* seconded his blow, and smit the head of the *Giant* from his shoulders. Then the Women and Children rejoyced, and Mr. *Great-heart* also praised God, for the deliverance he had wrought. (Bunyan, 203)

I quote this action scene in full for the same reason I quote a long example of prosopographia by Haywood in the next chapter: to emphasize the length itself, the elaboration over time and in space of something that in *Idalia* clearly interrupts the narrative and in *The Pilgrim's Progress* just as clearly sidesteps the allegory *with* pure narrative.[15] In this scene, the Narrator of the Margins offers only one emblematic gloss: *"Weak folks prayers do sometimes help strong folks cries"*; for the most part, the marginal comments have become a Greek chorus, cheering: *"The* Gyant *struck down"*; *"He is slain, and his head disposed of"* (Bunyan, 203). Four paragraphs permit two rounds of fighting, a rest, a moment of fair play, and the salient details of cut and thrust. It is fitting that the giant Maul is the one who talks in generals. "[C]ome to particulars, man," demands Great-heart, and a great deal of particulars follow, including a simile layered on top of the would-be emblem that refuses to be any image but itself: steam from a boiling cauldron. Sometimes, says Sharrock, "Bunyan develops a very slight metaphorical hint in Scripture into a fully-realized allegorical episode" (introduction, 25); sometimes he just develops them into fully realized episodes.

Similes that sprout out of the allegorical structure or emblematic instance in *Part II* create their own indefinite spaces. In the Valley of the Shadow of Death, for example, the group hears "a groaning as of dead men: a very great groaning"; they feel "the Ground begin to shake under them, as if some hollow place was there"; they hear "a kind of hissing as of Serpents; but nothing as yet appeared" (Bunyan, 200). In this murky spiritual space and context, the similes might well point to realities of dead men, treacherous hollow spaces, and snakes. That is, the similes might be connectors to reality rather than to illustrative or explanatory models. In the usual poetic simile, the thing here is compared to something else not here: "When I was ill, I groaned like the dead" compares my actual groaning to something I've imagined, rather than suggesting that the dead were in another room competing with me at the time. Or: *The Pilgrim's Progress... Delivered under the Similitude of a Dream.* But, here, we're not so sure. On the other hand, if these similes operate in the usual poetic way, they stand in for familiar things to concretize the unfamiliar, to give form to the formless and try to neutralize its terror through a grasp at familiarity. But then the horror of what's underneath the patch of ornament and not precisely named—*like* a serpent but *not* a serpent—is doubled.

A bit further down the road in the valley Mercy looks behind and sees, "as she thought, something most like a Lion, and it came a great padding pace after; and it had a hollow Voice of roaring." In this case, the margin confirms the reality: *"A Lion."* Of the previous similes the margin only says

noncommittally: "*Groanings heard*"; "*The Ground shakes.*" Bunyan further
underscores the ambiguous status of the similes here as inexact comparisons
rather than direct representations when, at the next dark bend in the road,
Christiana sees something that defies description even by analogy: "*Christiana said, Methinks I see something yonder upon the Road before us, a
thing of a shape such as I have not seen. Then said Joseph, Mother, what
is it? An ugly thing, Child; an ugly thing, said she. But Mother, what is it
like, said he? 'Tis like I cannot tell what, said she. And now it was but a
little way off. Then said she, it is nigh.*" The Fiend (so the Narrator of the
Margins identifies it) refuses to enter the world of particularity, remaining
instead among the "as ifs"; the space between the abstract and the concrete
seems to wobble, and, indeed, when the Fiend "was just come to [Great-
heart], it vanished to all their sights" (Bunyan, 200). The image ends with
a lesson from James 4:7 ("*Resist the Devil, and he will fly from you*"), but
knowing that Devil = Fiend still doesn't bring either persona into any more
visual clarity than "an ugly thing" does—and so maintains its terrifying
effectiveness.

Jeffrey Kittay argues that a "haunted house... must be narrated [rather
than described], unless one would want to chase the ghosts away. For a house
is haunted to the extent that perceptual contours are uncertain.... It does
not offer a final, nor even a dependably working, manifestness."[16] Bunyan's
spaces, both in described homely detail and in narrated blurred horror, are as
much part of the novelistic expansion of space and transformation of emblem
into thing as they are part of the structure of the most powerful allegory
of the seventeenth century. Indeed, the power of *The Pilgrim's Progress* as
allegory can be considered yet another textual praxis in the transformation of
narrative space, as the Puritan habit of emblematization becomes absorbed
into fictional techniques (see Hunter, *Reluctant Pilgrim*, 29 n. 20). Bunyan
says in his "Apology": "[A]s I pull'd, it came" (1). As he filled his dreamworld
with people and objects and rooms upon rooms, the allegory gained energy,
but the things reinvested themselves with thinginess with an equal—and
equally powerful—energy.

Things (1): Defoe

I found Mellons upon the Ground in great Abundance, and Grapes upon
the Trees; the Vines had spread indeed over the Trees, and the Clus-
ters of Grapes were just now in their Prime, very ripe and rich.... [T]he
green Limes that I gather'd, were not only pleasant to eat, but also very

wholesome; and I mix'd their Juice afterwards with Water, which made
it very wholesome, and very cool, and refreshing.
—*Daniel Defoe*, Robinson Crusoe *(1719)*

Speaking of things in Defoe is a bit like analyzing epistolarity in Richardson or irony in Fielding; what can be said that hasn't already been said?
Nineteenth- and early twentieth-century criticism tended to think of Defoe's imagination and imagery as mercantile: Marx nominated Crusoe *homo
economicus*; Ian Watt calls Moll "in her heart a rentier, for whom life has
no greater terror than when her 'main stock wastes apace,'" someone who
has "picked up the vocabulary and attitudes of a tradesman"; Dorothy Van
Ghent's famous essay treats the "good pearl necklace" and "fine gold watch"
of Moll's cache; one of Maximilian E. Novak's many works on Defoe is titled *Economics and the Fiction of Daniel Defoe*; Sandra Sherman and John
O'Brien have plumbed the credit imagery; Lydia Liu regards Crusoe's earthenware pot as the modern man's fetish because "it carries the symbolic burden of human intentionality that threatens to subdue the natural elements
to his design."[17] Moll the thief, Crusoe the exploiter, H. F. the counting
clerk, all of them are far more obsessed with their (or others') material goods
than with any personal relations, typifying vice more vividly than virtue,
unsensuous and unloving.

But I want to speak up for the melons, the raisins, the limes. Susan Stewart asserts that the "absolute tedium of Crusoe's days is the tedium of this
antiutopia of objects, an island of objects existing solely as their use value"
(15). I disagree. The raisins are too powerful a counterexample. We need
to reinvest Defoean things—and early modern things generally—with some
pleasure that reaches beyond use value or profit. All Bunyan's pomegranates
and figs and honeycombs and well-crumbed milk dishes rehydrate in Crusoe's limewater; Christiana's and Mercy's pleasure in their crisp white linen
and earrings and bracelets is Moll's and Roxana's in clean, comely clothes;
even the bodies wrapped in rugs and thrown in the pits and the windows shat-
tering in the wind share the dark, rich descriptive pleasures of the Valley of
the Shadow of Death. Virginia Woolf's famous *"Robinson Crusoe,"* which
begins by throwing out sunrises and sunsets and positioning "on the contrary . . . nothing but a large earthenware pot," ends by asserting the novel's
ability "to make common actions dignified and common objects beautiful"
(54, 57).

Stewart has claimed about the early novel that "exactness is a mirror,
not of the world, but of the ideology of the world. And what is described

exactly in the realistic novel is 'personal space,' the space of property, and the
social relations that take place within that space" (5). But "personal space"
and personal things are precisely what are *not* exactly described in early
realist novels. The next chapter will look more particularly at the spatial
contours of early novels as *indicated* rather than detailed, and I have written
elsewhere on the details and visualization of domestic spaces of Defoe.[18]
What I would like to resituate here are the ways in which *things* operate in
Defoe as reconstituted emblems—emblems reconstituted back into things
for their own sake, each again a *ding-in-sich*. As Hunter says: "Details are
the coin of novelistic fiction" (*Before Novels*, 308). They behave like pieces
of description; their degree of vividness radiates its own visualness—or at
least its significance—into the surrounding undescribed spaces.

Van Ghent spells out her own sense of Defoe's lack of detail in great
detail:

> [T]hese tangible, material objects with which Moll is so deeply concerned
> are not at all vivid in texture. When Moll tells us that she put on a "good
> pearl necklace," we do not know whether the pearls were large or small
> or graded or uniform in size, or whether the necklace hung low on her
> bosom or was wound around her throat three times, nor do we know if
> the pearls were real or artificial; the word "good" here indicates simply
> that the pearls looked costly to a sophisticated eye, and were of a kind
> that a woman of substantial social position might wear; the "good pearl
> necklace" is mentioned not in a way that will make a sense image for
> us, but only in a way that will suggest the market value of the necklace
> and (through the market value) its value as an indicator of social prestige.
> (34–35)

Yet, in 1810, John Ballantyne said in general of Defoe's descriptive ability:
"[W]hen the power of exact and circumstantial delineation is applied to
objects which we are anxiously desirous to see in their proper shape and
colours, we have a double source of pleasure, both in the art of the painter,
and the interest which we take in the subject represented."[19] Ballantyne actually deplores the "exact and circumstantial delineation" in *Moll Flanders*
(we really don't want to go there, he says), but the novel's vividness for him
is as intense in its own vicious way as is the moral delight in *Robinson
Crusoe*. Part of the problem, as I argue throughout this book, is readerly
expectation. As Arnold Kettle warns about *Moll Flanders*, it "is not to be
judged as though it were an imperfect forerunner of *Pride and Prejudice* or
What Maisie Knew"; one must "not blame Defoe for not being Proust."[20]

Van Ghent, brilliant formal analyst as she is, expects more from Defoean detail than it is prepared to give; or, rather, she does not quite see that it gives everything required by its context and its culture. In the context of emblem rebecoming thing, the Defoean detail is a virtual Argand lamp casting wide light around itself.

Consider the famous scene where Moll steals the gold necklace from the "pretty little Child" and decides not to kill her:

> [G]oing thro' *Aldersgate-street* there was a pretty little Child had been at a Dancing-School, and was going home, all alone, and my Prompter, like a true Devil, set me upon this innocent Creature; I talk'd to it, and it prattl'd to me again, and I took it by the Hand and led it along till I came to a pav'd Alley that goes into *Bartholomew Close*, and I led it in there; the Child said that was not its way home; I said, yes, my Dear it is, I'll show you the way home; the Child had a little Necklace on of Gold Beads, and I had my Eye upon that, and in the dark of the Alley I stoop'd, pretending to mend the Child's Clog that was loose, and took off her Necklace and the Child never felt it, and so led the Child on again. (*Moll Flanders*, 194)

The details are spare, but the paved alley, the close, the dark of the alley, the bending woman, and the way out, all circle hungrily around the little necklace of gold beads that Moll has her eye on. To this extent Van Ghent is exactly right: Moll is interested, not in the length or shape or sentimental value of the necklace, but in its market value, so no other detail is necessary. The main thing looming out of the darkness is a string of shiny gold resellable beads. That is what haunts Moll's memory; that is what we remember. On the one hand, that is all that any early thing detail ever delivers; and, on the other, its bareness is part of the Defoean irony so well articulated by Novak: that's all *Moll* sees, not all there is to be seen.[21]

In this scene, the necklace surfaces in the middle of the narration, more or less at the very moment Moll's hand is reaching for it. The object is the cause of the action, but the detail is embedded within the narration. That is the common habit of early modern detail, as the next chapter will outline. But occasionally in Defoe a small, spare scene is set like a little stage for an actor to enter on—a little cross section of space and time, description and narration, that will swell into descriptive dominance in the nineteenth century:

> Wandring thus about I knew not whither, I pass'd by an Apothecary's Shop in *Leadenhall-street*, where I saw lye on a Stool just before the Counter

a little Bundle wrapt in a white Cloth; beyond it, stood a Maid Servant
with her Back to it, looking up towards the top of the Shop, where the
Apothecary's Apprentice, as I suppose, was standing up on the Counter,
with his Back also to the Door, and a Candle in his Hand, looking and
reaching up to the upper Shelf for something he wanted, so that both were
engag'd mighty earnestly, and no Body else in the Shop. (*Moll Flanders*,
191)

This scene is unusually still and drawn out. The focal point is the white
bundle ("white" makes it gleam a bit more) on a stool, surrounded by the
very key details of the absorbed maid and apprentice, the counter, the door,
and the candle. The scene, like the bundle and Moll, is about to take off. In
Haywood, Aubin, and Richardson, as well as in most of Defoe's narratives,
physical objects and structures appear primarily in the immediate service
of narrative action: windows appear when they need to be jumped out of,
locks when they need to be locked. Things come (literally) to hand as the
character requires. But here, all is presupplied, the scene is a poised, still
whole, *inviting* rather than *responding to* narrative action. The detail of the
bundle appears before Moll's desire to steal it (the gold beads in midtheft).
Things for Defoe may pause or prompt narrative as he designs.

And sometimes his things seem happy just being things. Crusoe's clus-
ters of grapes and green limes and raisins, like the figs and pomegranates
and raisins in *The Pilgrim's Progress*, are emblematic in that they are signs
of God's providence, as the beached canoe emblematizes to Crusoe his own
improvidence, the goat in the cave his own fears. But Crusoe's pleasure in his
raisins, in his "little family" of cats and dogs and goats, in his umbrella, in
his orderly shelves, is a sort of obverse to the Footprint, which, on its own in
the sand, will after several tides simply not attach itself to plausible reality.
The raisins and umbrella give out their pleasures because they *are* reality
and, unlike God's signs, are made by Crusoe himself. Hunter reminds us
not to get carried away with the literary "by-products" of Puritan allegorical
writing; Crusoe is written into a world "where secular activity is meaningful, where history (even the history of every man's trivialities) is somehow
the record of divine activity" (*Reluctant Pilgrim*, 115, 123). But Crusoe is
also written into a world of goods, a mercantile world that provided and celebrated new *pleasures*, the pleasures of buying, making, seeing, and arranging
new things. Things were standing in a light of their own and, on their own
in texts, generated their particular cultural heat. "And is there any reason,"
Virginia Woolf asks as she shuts the book, "why the perspective that a plain
earthenware pot exacts should not satisfy us as completely, once we grasp it,

as man himself in all his sublimity standing against a background of broken mountains and tumbling oceans with stars flaming in the sky?" ("*Robinson Crusoe*," 58).

In addition to presenting themselves as very much there, Defoe's things are also adept at pointing to absences. Description is, as the *Encyclopédie* summarizes so well, "a figure of thought by development of which, instead of simply indicating an object, makes it somehow visible."[22] *Somehow visible*, in many different ways visible. Describing is not just "inscription" or "setting forth in words" or "verbal portraiture," as the *OED* claims; rather, in the act of inscribing or putting forth it creates new presences and absences, it lifts an object or a space into a context, it creates what is *not* about that thing in the act of asserting what *is*—much as the use of description in classical dramatic action *evokes* absence, addressing an action or person offstage (Webb and Weller, 285). Samuel Holt Monk said: "Topographically Defoe is impeccable. But what does he actually show us? Nothing."[23] Perhaps; but "nothing" can be visually powerful: "Passing thro' *Token-House-Yard* in *Lothbury*, of a sudden a Casement violently opened just over my Head, and a Woman gave three frightful Skreetches, and then cry'd, *Oh! Death, Death, Death!* in a most inimitable Tone, and which struck me with Horror and a Chilness, in my very Blood. There was no Body to be seen in the whole Street, neither did any other Window open; for People had no Curiosity now in any Case; nor could any Body help one another; so I went on to pass into *Bell-Alley*."[24] H. F. sees "nothing": no things, no bodies, nobody. In between the precise spaces of two streets is one open window, numberless closed ones, and a disembodied voice crying out over some unseen body or bodies in a moan of unspecific but all too contextualized general concept. This is description in the kinetic sense; as Edward Casey points out: "[T]he surface at stake is always a moving surface" (199). Aristotle and Genette would have approved of the gentle "passing" startled by the "violently opened," the three wordless screeches followed by three crying words, the stillness of "struck," the despairing return to "passing."

We might return to Jeffrey Kittay's haunted house to understand undescribed space. On the one hand, this still moment in *A Journal of the Plague Year* is haunted space in that we see and hear just enough to jump-start horror. But, metaphorically, as twenty-first century readers we tend to look at early fictional narrative as something with uncertain perceptual contours, its doors ajar, its walls permeable, because its boundaries are not set. The relatively few particularized details showing briefly through the narrative curtains presumably conjured up a far more coherent and integrated image for the inhabitants of wicket-gate country. Defoe's *things*—the things of early modern prose—in thus announcing themselves evoke both dim boundaries of space and an emptiness that we have been trained to see.

Things (2): *The Castle of Otranto*

An hundred gentlemen [entered] bearing an enormous sword, and seeming to faint under the weight of it.
—*Horace Walpole,* The Castle of Otranto *(1764)*

Where the things of Bunyan and Defoe domesticate the emblem and make it part of an everyday interior, things in *The Castle of Otranto* do not fit into their allotted space: they are Things. The giant helmet, the mountain of sable plumes, the enormous saber, a gigantic leg, foot, and hand, not only are too large for the castle of Otranto, but also have seemed to many critics from the eighteenth century on to be too large for the text itself. *The Castle of Otranto* has often seemed to faint under the weight of its own sword—its implausible collection of enormous things. Throughout its critical history, *Otranto*'s giant things have blocked the interpretive path. Their object seems to be terror, but their effect ridiculous.

Walpole himself, in the preface to the second edition, marks out the two tracks along which both praise and criticism have run ever since. He claims a Shakespearean precedent in "blend[ing] the two kinds of romance, the ancient and the modern."[25] Thus, the grand supernatural objects of a chivalric past could be reinserted into an age "which only wants cold reason,"[26] and, at the same time, the eighteenth-century preference for psychological realism could be accommodated with characters who "think, speak, and act as it might be supposed mere men and women would do in extraordinary positions" (*Otranto*, 10). But, for two hundred years, critics have found both the supernatural horrors and the psychological characterizations either separately ineffectual or in direct conflict. But, when the things are read as deliberately, satirically inflated grotesqueries, their self-imposed absurdities highlight the equally inflated stereotypes of the characters. Exaggerated things expose exaggerated expectations; a giant finger points to a different reading template. As Bunyan's things comfortably nest in their allegory and Defoe's things light up the spaces of desire and fear, Walpole's giant things squeeze out implications of, on the one hand, the contemporary sentimentalizing characterization and, on the other, the contemporary obsession (especially Walpole's own) *with* things.

Otranto's bifocal reception history began instantly on its publication, the targets of praise shifting over time, but the objects of scorn remaining steadily its *objects*. As one of Walpole's correspondents put it to another: "[The novel] consists of ghosts and enchantments; pictures walk out of their frames, and are good company for half an hour together; helmets drop from the moon, and cover half a family. He [Walpole] says it was a dream and I fancy one when he had some feverish disposition in him" (G. J. Williams to George Selwyn, 19 March 1765, in Walpole, *Correspondence*, 30:177). The *Critical Review* objected witheringly to *Otranto*'s "rotten materials"—especially the picture coming out of its frame, which prompted the speculation that the castle was a "modern fabrick" because "we doubt much whether pictures were fixed in pannels before the year 1243."[27] Clara Reeve, who in 1777 published her own version of the novel, *The Champion of Virtue* (renamed *The Old English Baron* in 1778), more gently critiqued its "violent machinery": "Had the story been kept within the utmost *verge* of probability, the effect had been preserved, without losing the least circumstance that excites or detains the attention."[28] William Hazlitt was less polite: "The great hand and arm which are thrust into the court-yard, and remain there all day long, are the pasteboard machinery of a pantomime; they shock the senses, and have no purchase upon the imagination."[29] Thomas Babington Macaulay frowned: "We cannot say that we much admire the big man whose sword is dug up in one quarter of the globe, whose helmet drops from the clouds in another, and who, after clattering and rustling for some days, ends by kicking the house down"; he also found the characters themselves "commonplace" and "insipid."[30] An early twentieth-century editor argued that it is now "almost impossible, on its intrinsic merits alone, to take the *Castle of Otranto* seriously, or to do anything but laugh at the portions of the gigantic Alphonso which appear from time to time, to the very natural consternation of the inhabitants of Otranto."[31]

But *Otranto*'s collection of objects works with such *consistent* ineffectiveness that the effect is worth considering as the product of design. Elizabeth Napier argues that "the tonal and modal discordances in *The Castle of Otranto* are among the tale's most striking stylistic features ... and the sources of most of the work's comedy." But her reading is, for the most part, unforgiving: "Walpole is unable to arrive at a coherent [justification]"; he "tests the work, feebly, against the familiar conventions of the dramatic unities"; "he evades defining its newness"; its frenetic pace "is the only way of gaining the reader's attention"; and it is "unencumbered by a deeper meaning."[32] But looking for a "deeper meaning" might be the wrong way to go about it: the surfaces themselves clamor for attention.[33] Macaulay describes the entertainment of *Otranto* in terms of things— other things, things in general—as an "entertainment worthy of a Roman epicure, . . . consisting of nothing but delicacies, the brains of singing birds, the roe of mullets, the sunny halves of peaches," which somehow atones for the "absurd . . . machinery [and] insipid . . . human actors" (review of *Letters*, 300). A closer look at Walpole's things as ironically outsized will bring us closer to an epicurean appreciation of its ironically undersized characters and of the work as a whole as less an inadequate gothic parent and more a satire on literary conventions and the culture of things.

There is precedent for reading the characters and things of *Otranto* ironically: the author's own self-portrait, his own love of things. Walpole frequently set himself up as iconoclastic and irreverent, and he is, of course, remembered best as an acid social satirist. His favorite aphorism was his own: "This world is a comedy to those that think, a tragedy to those that feel" (Walpole to Lady Ossory, 15–16 August 1776, in *Correspondence*, 32:315). And he described himself among the thinking comedians: "His humour was satiric," say his third-person *Memoirs*.[34] One of the most enthusiastic auction attenders of his time, he frequently ridiculed, not only the vast clutter of things heaped together for indiscriminate purchase, but also his own participation in such avidity: "Lord Oxford's famous sale begins next Monday, where there is as much rubbish of another kind as in her Grace's history: feather bonnets presented by the Americans to Queen Elizabeth; elk's horns converted into caudle-cups; true copies of original pictures that never existed; presents to himself from the Royal Society etc. etc. particularly, forty volumes of prints of illustrious English personages; which collection is collected from frontispieces to godly books, Bibles and poems; headpieces and tailpieces to Waller's works; views of King Charles's sufferings; tops of ballads; particularly earthly crowns for heavenly ones, and streams of glory" (Walpole to Horace Mann, 3 March 1742 OS, in *Correspondence*, 17:357–58). But he was there to make a bid, nevertheless. He remarks on the mania for auctions spreading into the countryside in a 4 August 1757 letter to Horace Mann: "It was but yesterday that we had a new kind of auction—it was of the orange trees and plants of your old acquaintance Admiral Martin— . . . the plants were disposed in little clumps about the lawn; the company walked to bid from one to t'other, and the auctioneer knocked down the lots on the orange tubs—within three doors was an auction of china—you did not imagine that we were such a metropolis!" (21:121–22). Eventually he sighs to George Montague: "I hope now there will never be another auction, for I have not an inch of space or a farthing left" (25 March 1763, 10:54). W. S. Lewis sees *Otranto* as Walpole's own "gratifying enlargement" of himself; although Lewis meant the phrase in a political sense, it works as well for the exaggerated images of thing culture.[35]

Macaulay made a connection between Walpole's writings and "a profusion of rarities of trifling intrinsic value," claiming that we as readers
respond to his work as if it were "a cabinet of trinkets": "Some new relic,
some new unique [sic], some new carved work, some new enamel, is forth-
coming in an instant.... Walpole is constantly showing us things,—not of
very great value indeed,—yet things which we are pleased to see, and which
we can see nowhere else" (review of Letters, 238–39). Macaulay considered
Walpole a minor writer, nonrepresentative, something of a freak. Yet his
explicit identification between Walpole, Walpole's writings, and Walpole's
things corresponds with Walpole's own view of himself and his dancing
place in an ultramaterial world. Walpole is an *exaggeration* of the state of
things. The idea of things was outsize in Walpole's culture and life; outsizing
them in his novella is a sort of Popean double gesture of love and contempt,
celebration and satire.

The way in which the things in *Otranto* are presented further stages their
bizarre exaggeration into silliness: they are very nearly the only things visible in the text. Walpole noted to William Cole that, in a dream, he saw on the
"uppermost bannister" of an "ancient castle" a "gigantic hand in armour":
"In the evening I sat down and began to write, without knowing in the least
what I intended to say or relate. The work grew on my hands, and I grew fond
of it" (9 March 1765, in *Correspondence*, 1:88). The giant things appear in
isolation, separated as much by their own sharp outlines in the surrounding
visual fog as by their size. Walpole's preface to the first edition, in which he
masquerades as the editor of a found manuscript, disingenuously comments:
"The scene is undoubtedly laid in some real castle. The author seems frequently, without design, to describe particular parts. *The chamber*, says he,
*on the right hand; the door on the left hand; the distance from the chapel to
Conrad's apartment*: these and other passages are strong presumptions that
the author had some certain building in his eye" (*Otranto*, 8). Walpole the
author carries with him his own memory storehouse of spatial detail. The
story provides its gothic landmarks of hide-and-seek in staircases and gates,
subterranean passages and mouths of caves, intricate cloisters and boarded
galleries, latticed windows and recessed oriels (22, 27, 28, 54, 75, 100, 102),
but those architectural details appear and vanish with the kind of narrative economy discussed in the next chapter. The things themselves tend to
command textual and narrative space.

The first of the outsize props is the helmet. Manfred, prince of Otranto,
is waiting in the chapel for his son, Conrad, to appear and be married to Isabella; instead, a servant rushes in, breathlessly shouting: "Oh, the helmet!
the helmet!" (*Otranto*, 18). Manfred goes to the courtyard (the only detail

of passage is the verb *went*): "The first thing that struck Manfred's eyes was a group of his servants endeavouring to raise something that appeared to him a mountain of sable plumes.... He beheld his child dashed to pieces, and almost buried under an enormous helmet, an hundred times more large than any casque ever made for human being, and shaded with a proportionable quantity of black feathers" (18–19). The feathers fringe the episode, and Conrad is reduced nearly to inconsequence, not only by the helmet, but also by the surrounding clauses and his father's relative indifference: Manfred "seemed less attentive to his loss, than buried in meditation on the stupendous objects that had occasioned it" (19). The *proportionable quantity of black feathers*—a nicely measured oddity in a moment like this—dominates the paragraph. And the feathers—less inherently dignified objects than helmets and swords—dominate much of Manfred's relationship with the things in general. These black feathers wave madly about at significant moments, mostly in a sort of pantomimic dialogue with Manfred, as when he tries to pursue Isabella: "[T]he moon, which was now up, and gleamed in at the opposite casement, presented to his sight the plumes of the fatal helmet, which rose to the height of the windows, waving backwards and forwards in a tempestuous manner, and accompanied with a hollow and rustling sound" (25). When the mysterious knights arrive, heralded by a trumpet, "at the same instant the sable plumes on the enchanted helmet, which still remained at the other end of the court, were tempestuously agitated, and nodded thrice, as if bowed by some invisible wearer" (59). The second chapter ends with this feather-nodding. Later appear a "gigantic leg and foot" (37, 39), "the gigantic sabre" (60), a giant hand (102), and a statuesque nosebleed (97). Finally, all the parts reassemble themselves in the form of the "real owner" (17), the usurped and murdered ancestor Alfonso, "dilated to an immense magnitude, in the centre of the ruins" (112).

Virtually all the critics have presumed that such overwhelming special effects were designed to generate terror but simply fail. Lewis staunchly advises that we compare the work to *Siegfried* and *Swan Lake*; in opera or ballet, we are perfectly willing to suspend disbelief over dancing feathers.[36] But the things of *Otranto* really do seem too large and too many to fit onto the stage of serious opera. I suggest that their gigantism be taken seriously in a different way: as a sort of inverse objective correlative to the sizing of the characters and as a metaphorically realistic measure of the presence of things in eighteenth-century culture. Literally, Manfred is besieged and overwhelmed by the things, while Conrad the illegitimate heir and Theodore the rightful heir are underwhelmingly *under* them. What looks like a conservative narrative structure of patriarchal restoration in fact stands in the center of its own ruins. Every single instance of power, terror, tension, tenderness, love, or poignancy is ruthlessly undercut by a close reading. Neither the moral nor the characters are what they pretend to be.

The giant helmet crushing Conrad is one object among many that dwarfs the characters and points to a dwarfing of characterization. Many critics have tried to take Walpole's prefatorial direction at face value and to read realism as well as romance into the story. The *Monthly Review* applauded *Otranto*'s "highly finished" characters and its "most perfect knowledge of mankind"; the *Critical Review* approved the "well marked" characters and the "spirit and propriety" of the narrative.[37] Sir Walter Scott found the finale "grand, tragical, and affecting" and concluded that "the applause which cannot be denied to him who can excite the passions of fear and of pity must be awarded to the author of *The Castle of Otranto*."[38] More recently, Martin Kallich finds that the "plot is united by a common theme of terrifying violence and conflict centered around the defeat of a tyrant. Theodore, the triumphant hero, ... overcomes all dangers and protects the virtuous and persecuted maiden, Isabella."[39] That, indeed, looks like the cast of characters in a conventional romance and the pattern for a gothic future. But, as it turns out, those are only their costumes. As E. J. Clery notes: "[C]loser attention suggests an ambivalence in each of them that verges on irony."[40] *Verge*, I suggest, is a verb too tentative.

The first paragraph of the tale begins a breaking down and sets up a reversal: "Manfred, Prince of Otranto, had one son and one daughter: the latter, a most beautiful virgin, aged eighteen, was called Matilda. Conrad, the son, was three years younger, a homely youth, sickly, of no promising disposition; yet he was the darling of his father, who never showed any symptoms of affection to Matilda" (*Otranto*, 17). That first sentence destabilizes the overall patriarchal order of things. It is the women in this tale, not the men, who get things done and put things in their place. The daughter comes narratively as well as chronologically first, if socially and emotionally second. Only a colon separates her from her father; Conrad—young, sick, small, unpleasant—has already been separated by a full stop and will shortly be stopped altogether.

The reversal of social and textual expectations—of the stereotypes for restitution tales—is consistently carried out. The traditions of patriarchy and romance are continually deflated by the reality of "normalcy," by men and women behaving "as it might be supposed mere men and women would do" (*Otranto*, 10). Close attention does, in fact, disclose *mere* men and women—very much *not* heroes and heroines, or even villains. Theodore, if we watch him closely, is not the romantic hero who overcomes all dangers and rescues the heroines. He's actually an incompetent ass. When Isabella, Manfred's ward, is trying to escape the nefarious political-sexual predations of her guardian, she searches for the trapdoor to safety. Theodore stands by, ready to help, but admits that he is "unacquainted with the castle." Isabella interrupts him, and then *she* finds the trapdoor, opens it, and escapes. *He*, on the other hand, "let the door slip out of his hands . . . and tried in vain to open it, *not having observed Isabella's method of touching the spring*" (30; emphasis added). Isabella is hardly a "weak and indecisive creature" (Kallich, 95, 102), and Theodore, far from being the "triumphant hero," quite thoroughly alerts the enemy by his clumsiness.

Theodore doesn't quite see it this way, of course; he later tells Isabella he was happy to have assisted her: "I have once already delivered thee from [Manfred's] tyranny" (*Otranto*, 76). But then the pattern is repeated: Manfred's daughter Matilda saves Theodore (who is also remarkable for the ease, almost alacrity, with which he is imprisoned). Matilda keeps imploring, "Fly; the doors of thy prison are open: my father and his domestics are absent; but they may soon return" (72), while Theodore keeps saying things like, "Thou are surely one of those angels!" and "Amazement!" Matilda patiently repeats, "Fly, virtuous youth, while it is *in my power to save thee*: should my father return, thou and I both should indeed have cause to tremble," and, "I run no risk but by thy delay. Depart: it cannot be known that I assisted thy flight" (72; emphasis added). She finally—literally—has to shut the door in his face: "He sighed, and retired, but with eyes fixed on the gate, until Matilda closing it put an end to [the] interview" (74). And Manfred, that terrifying tyrant, finds himself in a socially awkward dinner-party moment, trying to converse with silent, helmeted knights (66–68). By the end, it is Isabella who "*took upon herself* to *order Manfred* to *be borne* to his apartment, while she *caused* Matilda to *be conveyed* to the nearest chamber" (110; emphasis added). The actions as well as the verbs of power and decision are hers. But not the happy ending. She marries Theodore, whose "grief was too fresh to admit the thought of another love; and it was not till after frequent discourses with Isabella, of his dear Matilda, that he was persuaded he could know no happiness but in the society of one with whom he could forever indulge the melancholy that had taken possession of his soul" (115). Theodore's undying love is separated only by a semicolon from the warm comforts of Isabella; either he's going to spend a real lifetime droning on about Matilda (lucky Isabella), *or* he's found a convenient way to authorize romantic substitution. Either way, Theodore *cannot* qualify for hero—and that fundamental inadequacy literally closes the story. The giant saber under which a hundred men groan cannot, in fact, be wielded effectually by just one man. It is almost as if, the bigger the phallus, the greater its impotence.

Theodore does, of course, triumph patriarchally in the sense that the end reveals him to be the rightful heir to the usurped house of Otranto; but, even here, the apparent tidiness of patriarchal restitution is dislodged by a second glance at the structure of the whole. The novel opens with Manfred confronting the dire ancient prophecy: "*That the castle and lordship of Otranto should pass from the present family, whenever the real owner should be grown too large to inhabit it*" (*Otranto*, 17). The large gothic body parts collect themselves together in the form of the mighty Alfonso, who had been murdered by Manfred's grandfather Ricardo. So Theodore, Alfonso's grandson, is the rightful heir, obviously. But *Theodore* hasn't grown too large to inhabit Otranto—in fact, he was conspicuously *trapped* under the enormous helmet of his grandfather's image—just like Manfred's son and heir. And how is the prophecy to make logical sense in the first place? When you've grown too big for your house, it's time to find a new one. And, finally, the house inherited stands in ruins, as if caused by the rightful heir's return itself: "*The moment Theodore appeared*, the walls of the castle behind Manfred were thrown down with a mighty force" (112; emphasis added). Under the slightest tug of resistance to the face-value romance reading, the giant things seem designed to dismember themselves, the characters to deconstruct.

The *Monthly Review* of January 1765 said irritably: "That unchristian doctrine of visiting the sins of the fathers upon the children, is certainly, under our present system, not only a very useless, but a very insupportable moral, and yet it is almost the only one deducible from this story."[41] From the eighteenth-century didactic point of view, even the moral of *Otranto* is inadequate. The reviewer is, presumably, sarcastic but may, ironically, have exactly captured the point. Politics and patriarchs might well be said to visit things upon their children and their children's children in regularly unpleasant ways, then and now, as Walpole himself knew at firsthand. As the youngest son of the prime minister Sir Robert Walpole, Horace was, from the start, exposed to faction, backstabbing, and favoritism. His biographers agree that his very problematic relations with his father contributed to his persistent resentment of overt political authority, particularly when condensed into some obvious single source, whether, as Lewis puts it, "the sovereignty, Lords, Commons, clergy, bench, or mob." Such paternal resentment "went underground," according to Lewis (*Horace Walpole*, 72), after Sir Robert was forcibly retired in 1742, shortly after Walpole entered Parliament, but that resentment against his father, along with his resentment against those who deposed his father, continued to influence his attitudes toward the political landscape—and his practices within it.

I discuss elsewhere the specific political disturbances occupying Walpole during the writing of *Otranto*;[42] here, I want simply to suggest that, for Walpole, the sins of the father are visited upon the children every day in real life and that his tale of patriarchal "restitution" in fact portrays a certain realism in its outsize things, undersized heroes, and unexpectedly effective females. *The Castle of Otranto* as romance is a conventional failure; *The Castle of Otranto* as gothic parent is only partly satisfactory; but *The Castle of Otranto* as a sort of Swiftian skein that twists the dark and the comic, the large and the small, the supernatural and the ordinary, into a cultural satire on the *disproportionable* relation between things and people reconciles some of its generic oddities. The giant things are meant to be a bit silly. As Barbara Benedict (175) says, *Otranto*'s metaphors are literalized, but, rather than parodying "Manfred's swollen head" and "the monsterization of male ambition" (although these work as well), we can see the things literally figured as *things*—as the feather bonnets and elk's-horn caudle cups, the tops of ballads and orange pots—that, as we will see in chapter 6, come to fill and dominate domestic space.

CHAPTER FIVE

Implied Spaces

The least and most careless Motion of her Head or Hand, was sufficient
to captivate a Heart. In fine, her Charms were so infinitely above Description, that it was necessary to see her, to have any just Notion of her.
—*Eliza Haywood*, Idalia: or, the Unfortunate Mistress *(1725)*

Most late seventeenth- and early eighteenth-century descriptions of
characters depend just so lightly but fully on a gesture, an indication, "the least and most careless Motion." Rooms, like charms, may be
"above" description in that description itself seems so often superfluous;
the careless, graceful motion of a hand, the economic signpost of a chamber,
tell us all we know, and all we need to know. The rooms and landscapes can
be richly scattered with objects, held together in space more by their emblematic significance than by visual connection; they do need their housing,
and housing is duly supplied. But the rooms themselves, and any particularities of their features, for the most part arise strictly when called on by the
plot—but not quite along the old playwright's rule that a gun introduced in
the first act has to go off in the last. The objects may be lying about waiting
to be picked up, but they are not visible to the reader *until* they are picked up.

As James Turner noted about the places on the road in *The Pilgrim's
Progress* arising, literally, at the demands of allegory, so in other seventeenth-
and early eighteenth-century fiction rooms and balconies and stairways
and windows emerge when a character needs to encounter them.[1] Prosopographia, the description of a person such that "it may appeare a playne
pycture paynted" (Peacham, Oii), is reserved primarily for men or women
of particular beauty (although usually not even then, and men more than
women, presumably because the convention for describing women's beauty

was so much older and more ransacked) or particular hideousness (especially in an older man designed as a husband for a young heroine).[2] When employed for scenery, again it is the extremes that demand attention: a poetically blasted wilderness, an exotic Other place, a wretched prison, or a space manipulated by author or character for seduction.[3] Ordinary interior space rarely zooms into view, unless some extraordinary event explodes within. And, even then, what is viewed is, not the visual entirety of Jane's Red Room, but a floor plan, a two-dimensional and unfocused space called the "Chamber," the "Parlour," or the "Kitchen," rather than a fully realized set of rooms all decked out with someone's choices in fabric, color, furniture, and ornament.

But none of this is to say that domestic space is absent, or clumsily structured, or immaturely developed. On the contrary, early authors of fiction are often adept at creating and employing "implied" spaces, fitting action within carefully chosen contours, their features rising obediently and handily at the first beckoning of plot, time and space in perfect synchronic step with each other. Description per se comes in deft little pieces; no one can accuse it of setting up obstacles or refrigerating things. The relatively few set pieces of description, occasionally long, are meant to be examined because they are few, and they operate with all the revelatory power of an epic catalog.

In the first section of this chapter, I use examples from texts that are not readily available in print or addressed in criticism; the generalizations are meant to apply across the oeuvre-board. (Defoe, e.g., is equally but implicitly covered here.) Aphra Behn supplies the most vivid stage directions in her prose and sets up the template of the visual gesture, with spatial contours, furniture, and objects arising on narrative demand. Eliza Haywood and Penelope Aubin continue the conventions and, with Behn, offer examples of rare extended descriptions in the service of the exotic. Mary Davys works through another textual praxis to insert description into the literary via the familiar letter. All four writers (and others of their time) represent the way in which space—domestic interior space in particular—remains more often implied than described but achieves vividness nevertheless through its very implication by the objects or the floor plans directed by the narrative itself.

In the second section, I look at Samuel Richardson's first two novels, *Pamela* (1740) and *Clarissa* (1747–48), to argue that Richardson very deftly changes the textures of novelistic space. While, for the most part, *Pamela* follows the patterns of the early eighteenth-century novelists in that the contours of and objects within her occupied spaces arise on narrative demand, *Clarissa* plays with borders themselves, essentially dissolving occupied space in apperception, in the characters' (particularly Clarissa's) hypersensitive listening beyond the walls of this room for sounds and implications from the next.

Spaces (1): Behn, Haywood, Aubin, Davys

Aphra Behn (1640–1689)

Aphra Behn shaped her narrative space, not surprisingly, like a dramatist, with a particular eye toward the piece of furniture, the position of a room, the dramatic possibilities of small, enclosed spaces. In fact, all the stage directions that are implicit in her plays tend to emerge almost explicitly in her fiction, to a greater degree than in other novelist-playwrights, such as Haywood later on. Behn has everything necessary to hand: object and space are coordinated to action with a precision and evocativeness of dramatic immediacy.

In *The Fair Jilt* (1688), for example, which takes its plot from the story of Joseph and Potiphar's wife, the reckless, sexually greedy Miranda wants to seduce the young friar Father Francisco (a.k.a. Henrick of Germany). After months of attending church every day and sending him steamy letters and valuable gifts, Miranda decides that her last best trick is to reveal her face in the confessional: "He cou'd not refuse her; and led her into the *Sacriste*, where there is a Confession-Chair, in which he seated himself; and on one side of him she kneel'd down, over against a little Altar, where the Priests Robes lie, on which was plac'd some lighted Wax-Candles, that made the little place very light and splendid, which shone full upon *Miranda*."[4] Father Francisco is taken with her beauty but manages to resist, which really irritates her, goading her into revenge: "[T]hrowing her self, in that instant, into the Confessing-Chair, and violently pulling the young Friar into her Lap, she elevated her Voice to such a degree, in crying out, *Help, help: A Rape: Help, help*, that she was heard all over the Church, which was full of People at the evening's Devotion; who flock'd about the Door of the *Sacriste*, which was shut with a Spring-lock on the inside, but they durst not open the Door" (30).

Miranda commands all that small space, originally designed for thoughts and actions quite opposed to her own. She reshapes it, in fact: "The Fathers had a Door on the other side, by which they usually enter'd, to dress in this little Room: and at the Report that was in an instant made 'em, they hasted thither, and found *Miranda* and the good Father very indecently strugling; which they mis-interpreted, as *Miranda* desir'd" (*Fair Jilt*, 31). And, in fact, that space continues to be misinterpreted by its rightful owners for years; Father Francisco is thrown in prison, and, even when, after innumerable fiendish plots of hers (particularly one embroiling her loving husband, Tarquin, prince of Rome), Miranda herself is in prison and finally confesses about this little episode, Henrick/Father Francisco ends up forgiving her and assisting her husband. That little confessional space remains hers, a failure for sex, perhaps, but dominated and redefined by—penetrated with—her revenge.

Miranda's husband occupies well-defined spaces also, but to different effect. His own *effectiveness* is challenged by described space—his or that of even higher male authority. The scene where Tarquin attempts the assassination of Miranda's inconvenient little sister, Alcidiana, who *will* insist on receiving her portion of 100,000 crowns, is beautifully crafted for its imprecisions of disguise, dusk, thresholds, and mistimed misaims:

> [Prince Tarquin] waited at the Corner of the Stadt-house, near the Theatre, with his Cloak cast over his Face, and a black Periwigg, all alone, with his Pistol ready cock'd; and remained not very long, but he saw her Kinsman's Coach come along. 'Twas almost dark; Day was just shutting up her Beauties, and left such a Light to govern the World, as served only just to distinguish one Object from another, and a convenient help to Mischief. He saw a light out of the Coach, only one young Lady, the Lover, and then the destin'd Victim; which he (drawing near) knew rather by her Tongue, than Shape.... [Alcidiana] stood the fairest Mark in the World, on the Threshold of the Entrance of the Theatre. (*Fair Jilt,* 165)

The prince misses his shot, firing through Alcidiana's train, and he thus creates a very different, much more self-destructive confusion than had Miranda in screaming "Rape!" He's caught, discovered, tried, and sent to his execution. The execution time and space are elaborately detailed; in this case, the description certainly does—deliberately—slow things down and force us to witness each detail of space and action in a clinically observant way (one that very much resembles what chilled Virginia Woolf in John Evelyn's description of the torture chamber):

> When he came to the Market-place, whither he walked on Foot, follow'd by his own Domesticks, and some bearing a black Velvet Coffin with Silver Hinges; the Headsman before him with his fatal Scimiter drawn, his confessor by his Side, and many Gentlemen and Church-men, with Father *Francisco* attending him, the People showering Millions of Blessing on

him, and beholding with weeping Eyes, he mounted the Scaffold; which was strow'd with some Sawdust about the place where he was to kneel, to receive the Blood: For they Behead People Kneeling, and with the Back-stroak of a Scimiter, and not lying on a Block, and with an Ax, as we in *England*. The Scaffold had a low Rail about it, that every Body might more conveniently see: This was hung with Black, and all that State that such a Death could have, was here in most decent Order. (174)

But the agony is not nearly over. The prince says some forgiving and noble things, gives money to the executioner; we learn all about his "white Satten Waste-coat" and "white Satten Cap, with a Holland one done with Poynt under it," the "last Stroak" of the headsman, and the scramble of the multitude for "some of the bloody Saw-dust, to keep for his Memory" (*Fair Jilt*, 175). The details of the prince's clothes, the arena of execution, the motion of his hands, the stroke of the executioner, the cultural differ-ences between executions in Flanders and those in England, the behavior of eager, weeping, sympathetic, bloodthirsty spectators, combine for an exact, drawn-out scene. But Tarquin is not dead yet. And, in fact, the history of the execution spills messily outside the spaces intended for it: turns out, the head isn't severed; the executioner sits the prince on a bench and whips out his clever little "Engine" to twist it off, but just then the prince falls backward over the bench into the mosh pit of a crowd, which bears him jubilantly away and, with the help of the priests, restores him to life. Even-tually, against all the warnings of the priests and the commands of poetic justice, the prince and princess retire to live a peaceful, penitent country life in Holland, occupying a smaller social sphere but a larger—because only geographically defined—space quite happily ever after. The tragedy refuses to inhabit the spaces socially designed for it; Behn allows her characters to redefine the contours of their ending.

Behn is equally at home defining smaller domestic and social spaces and directing their use and abuse. In *The Lucky Mistake* (1689), the young and superlatively beautiful Atlante and Rinaldo, neighbors in Orleans along the river, work energetically with balconies and bay windows to sustain their eternal love in the face of the usual cast of tyrannical fathers and unpleas-antly older men. Atlante is designed by her poor but blood-proud father for his friend Count Vernole, to whom she is invariably polite, to the point where her younger sister, Charlot, inquires: "What is it, said She, that charms you so, his Tawny Leather Face, his extraordinary high Nose, his wide Mouth and Eye-brows, that hang Lowring over his Eyes, his lean Carcass, and his Lame and Haulting Hips."[5] Definitely Ehrenpreis's negative particularity here; Vernole is offered as a sharp, detailed, repugnant foil to the soft hands, languishing eyes, and delicate person of the teenage Rinaldo. Atlante does, of course, prefer Rinaldo, and they exchange love letters and engage in love conversations from their respective jutting balcony and jutting window. But, with two proud fathers opposed to the match and a jealous Vernole sleeping in the chamber below, matters are arranged to come to a head. After one steamy but sexually innocent meeting in her chamber, Rinaldo visiting her from his exile in Paris, Atlante finally sends him away at dawn, and none too soon:

> [H]e was no sooner got over the Balcony, and she had flung him down his Rope, and shut the Door, but *Vernole*, whom Love and Contrivance kept waking, fancied several times he heard a noise in *Atlante*'s Chamber.... [H]e came up in his Night-Gown, with a Pistol in his Hand. *Atlante* ... turned her self to her dressing Table, where the Candle stood, and where lay a Book open of the Story of *Ariadne* and *Thesias*. The Count turning the Latch, entered halting into her Chamber, in his Night-Gown clapped close about him, which betrayed an ill-favoured Shape, his Nightcap on, without a Perriwig, which discover'd all his lean withered Jaws, his Face pale, and his Eyes staring, and making altogether so dreadful a Figure, that *Atlante*, who no more dreamt of him than of a Devil, had possibly have rather seen the last. She gave a great Shriek, which frightned *Vernole*; so both stood for a while staring on each other, till both we[re] collected: He told her, the care of her Honour had brought him thither; and then rolling his small Eyes round the Chamber, to see if he could discover any Body. (383–84)

Vernole's person is redescribed in vivid, denigrating detail; the room picks up its necessary objects of dressing table, candle, book, latch; Vernole himself scans the room for the details he will not find; Atlante has erased the space and erected her alibi. Things heat up, and Atlante manages to grab Vernole's pistol and train it on him; a natural coward, he apologizes and retreats but then spends the next several pages hunting down Rinaldo with hired assassins. The penultimate action scene has Rinaldo hovering by "the corner of the dead wall" of the monastery where Atlante and Charlot both are immured when Vernole comes on him and, seeing his back turned, sets his "Bravoes" on him; in the confusion of a fight scene, the young lady who emerged to elope with Rinaldo, and who would have run back into the garden except that "the Door fell too [sic] and lockt," is taken off by Vernole

(*Lucky Mistake,* 398, 399). But it turns out to be Charlot, who wants to escape from the monastery. Vernole, realizing that Atlante will love only Rinaldo, decides to marry Charlot, the fathers decide that all is working out for the best, and there's a double wedding. The balconies, bay windows, and corner walls have done their job of uniting lovers. Both in tragedy and in comedy, Behn supplies explicit stage directions that, if not visually rendering all details of a space, give exactly everything needed for visualization.

Eliza Haywood (1693?–1756)

Haywood's early fiction is itself a floor plan for early eighteenth-century uses of fictional space. Part of her contemporary popularity and her lively recent revival in print and on syllabi is due to her sure narrative hand, which produced tautly paced plots, succulent ambiguities, and deftly defined spaces for the occasionally spirited but usually standard heroines to move along, among, within. *Fantomina, or, Love in a Maze* (1724) has received particular attention in reprintings and criticism.[6] Its beautifully crafted structure has the unnamed heroine moving through the basic female roles available through the social scale (country girl, prostitute, maidservant, widow, court lady) in pursuit of the wonderfully obtuse Beauplaisir; there is a central, crucial interruption by the narrator in godlike voice, answering the (male) reader's skepticism about the possibility of being so sexually deceived by the same woman; and it ends with the playful ambiguities of a "hero" silenced, a heroine who had never dreamed of marriage in the first place being sent to a "monastery" in "France" (with all the contemporary connotations possible, both sexualized and "straight"), and a decidedly non-judgmental final sentence. I had to get in my own praise of *Fantomina* as a work of true literary art, but, because it has become so well-known and available, I will pay attention here to a lesser-known work, *Idalia: or, the Unfortunate Mistress* (1725), because it offers both the standard Haywoodian presentations and uses of novelistic space and the more rare extended description.

Haywood most often and most consistently presents the basic interior floor plan for action, with other rooms or a few key objects rising up obligingly when called on by the plot. Idalia—typically young, beautiful, vain, and headstrong—is first flung into trouble by being unable to resist a declaration in a love letter and slipping out to meet the writer on her way to vespers. On finding herself trapped in the house of the amorous Don Ferdinand, she tries to escape, but he finally convinces her to stay by "repenting," telling her it's

too late to go home, and giving her the key to lock herself into a bedchamber.
Of course, Idalia trusts too much in locks and surface appearances:

> She had look'd on herself as safe where she now was, as in her *Father's*
> House, thro' the double Security of her *Lover's* Conversion, and having
> the Key of the Door: But, alas! she too soon discover'd her Mistake. She
> had not been an Hour in Bed, before she felt the Clothes thrown off, and
> something catch fast hold of her. The Voice and Actions of the Person told
> her it was no other than Don *Ferdinand*, as did his own Behaviour and
> Confession afterward, that the Story of his Repentance was but forg'd,
> the easier to betray her, and the Delivery of the Key only an Artifice to
> engage her Trust, there being a Back-Door to the House, by which he
> immediately enter'd, and came into the Chamber thro' a Closet, which
> had a Passage into another Room.[7]

The key is a false object; the bedchamber suddenly has a closet that suddenly
has a passage to a newly appearing room connecting to the previously un-
mentioned back door. Where a character is, is only where she might be; the
unnamed spaces around her can be as important as the designated spaces that
she occupies; bits of furniture can be bumped into, so to speak; bedclothes
appear in order to be thrown off.

Occasionally, Haywood will throw in a dash of scenic ambience, as when
Idalia is taken to a place of asylum by a servant of Don Myrtano's (Don Myrtano is the brother of Henriquez, who had earlier rescued her from Ferdinand;
Ferdinand and Henriquez have by now killed each other in a duel; Idalia is
now in love with Myrtano [and he with her]; Myrtano is engaged to Ardella;
Ardella, jealous, had ordered a servant to kill Idalia; the servant has rescued
her instead):

> [T]hat Evening about Sun-set [Idalia and the servant] arriv'd at a neat, but
> small Dwelling, such as the Poet describes to be the Abode of *Baucis* and
> *Philemon*: A good old Man and Woman, pretty near the same Age, came
> forth to welcome her . . . and shew'd her to a Chamber, which, tho' it could
> boast no Finery, was extremely clean and decent, and had every Thing in
> it fit to charm a contemplative Mind. The Windows were cover'd with
> *Fillarée* and *Jessamine*, only where here and there Spaces were cut to
> give the Eye a most delightful Prospect o'er distant Meadows, Fields, and
> Vineyards; a sweet Confusion *without* fill'd the whole rural Scene, and
> fed extensive Thought with all the Charms of Nature:—*Within*, a vast

Variety of collected Books, and choicest Maps, brought to the View the
spacious Universe, improving Reason with the Aids of *Art*. (*Idalia*, 62)

Idalia is in three parts, a longer novel than most of Haywood's fiction, and
she does use the space to provide more space, so to speak. J. Paul Hunter has
characterized novels in general as attentive to "the meanings of stasis" as
well as to those of motion. Novels embark on a "conquest of space" through
travel and print.[8] There is room in a novel to spread out, to look longer at
things, to let the visual unfold in space as well as time.

And that in part accounts for a really tremendously long description in
part 2. Idalia decides to leave the cottage and find her way back to her father,
a journey that involves a sea voyage. But the ship on which she is traveling
is attacked by Barbary Corsairs—conveniently so, it turns out, since the
attack occurs just as the amorous Captain Rickamboll is on the point of
raping her. The leader of the Corsairs, Abdomar, is a gent and rescues her,
giving her as a servant to his beloved Bellraizia. Bellraizia, as a representative
of an Exotic Land as well as of female virtue and beauty, gets three pages of
prosopographia pretty much all to herself, which I quote in their entirety for
the visual effect as a whole:

> *Abdomar* led [Idalia] immediately into a Cabin, adorn'd with the choic-
> est Curiosities which Art could produce in all the various Climates of
> the habitable World; the Floor was cover'd with the most rich, as well as
> most beautiful Tapestry that ever was seen; the Ground was Silver, on
> which were so dextrously interwoven all manner of fine Flowers, that
> they seem'd more the Handywork of Nature than of human Skill; the
> Windows, which *without* were fenced from the dashing of the Waves
> with Chrystal in the manner of half Globes, *within* were chequer'd with
> green and gold Twist, each Square being join'd with precious Stones: Di-
> amonds, Rubies, Emeralds, Chrysolites, and Saphirs, with their various
> colour'd Lustre, spread such a dazzling Glory round the Room, that it
> even pain'd the Eye to look upon it: The greatest Magnificence that ever
> *Idalia* had beheld in *Venice*, than which no City in the World can boast
> of more, was so infinitely short of what now met her Eyes, that she had
> longer and more heedfully regarded it, had not a greater, and yet sur-
> passing Wonder appear'd to attract her Admiration; it was the charming
> *Bellraizia*, Mistress of *Abdomar*, who, rising from a Couch of Crimsom
> Taffety embroider'd with Gold and Pearl, stepp'd forward to meet and
> congratulate her Lover on his Victory. (*Idalia*, 75)

And that's just the first half. The description of the interior space of the cabin
is as richly detailed as any Byzantine description of Hagia Sophia—with
slightly different objects for worship. The move to describe Bellraizia that
follows interweaves the specifics of color and fabric within more generalized
detail ("something," "Form," "all," "sort," "seem," "as much as Decency
would permit"):

> She spoke to him in the Language of their own Country, but there was
> something so sweet, so soft, so engaging in her Voice, that render'd it
> an Impossibility to hear her, without feeling some Part of that Pleasure
> which the looking on her did in a great abundance bestow. To the most
> lovely and enchanting Form that Nature ever made, there was also added
> all the Embellishments of Art:—Had she been in a Court where it was
> the sole Business of all about her to study what would most become her,
> she cou'd not have been dress'd with greater Elegance: Her Hair, which
> was whiter, and more shining than Silver, and hung down in Tresses be-
> low her Waste, was only kept from falling o'er her Face by a Fillet of
> Diamonds; but as the greatest *Art* is to appear *artless*, this seeming Neg-
> ligence had in it something so infinitely beyond the formal Ornaments
> of the *Europeans*, that whoever would desire to please, must covet to
> look like this lovely *Barbarian*. On the Middle of the Fillet there was
> fix'd a sort of a little Tree of Gold, on the Branches of which hung Jewels
> of a prodigious Largeness, but such a Height above her Head that (the
> Springs on which they were fastn'd being shaded by some loose Hair,
> which flew out as tho' disdainful of Restraint) made it seem to the Eye
> as tho' they were self-poiz'd, and form'd Constellation like *Ariadne*'s
> Crown. On her slender and fine proportion'd Body, she had a close Jacket
> of Gold Stuff; but the Sleeves were large, and tied up before almost as
> high as her Shoulders, with small Sky-coloured Ribband mixed with Sil-
> ver, and discover'd, as much as Decency would permit, her lovely Arms,
> which were encompass'd with Bracelets of several sorts of Jewels. In fine,
> her whole Appearance, her Face, her Shape, her Hair, her Habit, was sur-
> passing what the most extensive Imagination can figure out, and forc'd
> *Idalia* (who was not over quick-sighted to the Perfections of her own Sex)
> whether she would or no, to confess within herself, that she had never
> seen any Thing so beautiful! so glorious! (75–77)

I have quoted this at length in part because of its length. The details of
the cabin, of Bellraizia's hair, clothes, and jewels, are luxuriously recounted.
But it is worth noting that it is the ornaments of room and person—the

things—that get the telling. The dimensions of the cabin, walls, floor, and windows, are themselves described, not in terms of size or color or shape, but in terms of the curiosities that adorn them—the tapestry, the fencings, the jewels that cover and connect them. Not Bellraizia's nose, mouth, or eyes, but her odd white hair, its fillet, and her jacket get visualized. Her face and arms and shape are "lovely"; her sleeves are tied up with blue and silver ribbons. The reason for the description is partly the novelty, the exoticism, the prefiguring of an important new character, and the presentation of Idalia's new perspective on things (other countries, other women's beauty); the nature of the description fastens on the things that occupy the space. The space itself—including a face—remains implied by its things.

Penelope Aubin (1679–1731)

All these early romance novels[9] depend heavily and happily on extraordinary adventures for their extraordinarily beautiful heroines; Aubin loves to throw in masses of coincidence as well. In *The Life of Madam de Beaumont* (1721), for example, each house (or domestic space) that a character enters is connected to or occupied by some other character closely connected by plot or family relation, no matter how geographically or temporally far-flung those houses and connections might be. Mr. Luelling, a Welshman, falls in love with the daughter of a cave-dwelling Frenchwoman, Madam de Beaumont, whose portrait is in his parlour because *his* father was in love with *her*; her husband, the count, captured in Sweden by Muscovites, escapes to a little cave occupied by a Capuchin friar sent to tell him about the escape of his wife; the (by now) Marquis and Mr. Luelling (now married to young Belinda and having successfully found her father in France) get lost in Wexford and find shelter with a man who turns out to be Belinda's London uncle, a Jacobite under an assumed name, who is also the father of the young man who offered protection to Belinda when she escaped her abductor.

There are more coincidental connections, but that's enough to go on with. For the most part, beyond this web of space-plot connections, interior space follows the early narrative program that I have been sketching out. Objects appear when they are needed; rooms appear on the floor plan drawn by the characters' motions, as when the count describes his escape from the Muscovite prison with another desperate gentleman:

> [W]e took a Resolution to kill our Goaler, and fight our way out. Accordingly the next Morning we seiz'd him as he enter'd my Chamber, and having knock'd him down with the Bar of a Door that we found in my

Room, we dispatch'd him, took the Keys, and rush'd by the Centries who
kept the Out-Gate; and not knowing where to go, we fled o'er the Mountains towards a Wood in *Tartary*, to which he guided me, where none but
Robbers and Out-Laws lived. My Fetters much hinder'd my Speed, being
extremely weak, but Fear gave me Strength, so that we reached the Wood
before night.[10]

They found a handy door bar when they needed one—the room was not
previously described with its number of doors with bars, dimensions, windows, position relative to the "Out-Gate," position relative to mountains or
woods. As they run, the starting point the chamber, the passing point the
gate, the end point *away*—mountains, woods, whatever—unroll moment by
moment in the narrative as well as actual journey.

One extended interior is described, that of the cave in which the
Huguenot fugitives Madam de Beaumont and her daughter, Belinda, live
for fourteen years, as viewed in amazement by their (until now unknown)
neighbor Mr. Luelling:

> The Ladies consenting, they went back together to the Cave, the inside
> of which was most surprizing to Mr. *Luelling*; there he found five Rooms
> so contrived, and so richly furnish'd, that he stood amazed. "In the Name
> of Wonder, *said he*, Ladies, by what Inchantment or Art was this Place
> contrived, from whence is this Light convey'd that illuminates it, which
> seems without all cover'd o'er with Earth, and is within so light and
> agreeable?["] The Lady answer'd, "When you have heard our Story you
> will be satisfied in all. At our landing on this Place, we found a Cave, or
> little Cell, but not like what it now is; the Seamen belonging to the Ship
> that brought us here, contrived and made it what you see; the Damask
> Beds, Scrutores, and all the Furniture you find here, I brought with me
> from *France*: the Light is from a Skylight on the top of the Hill, covered
> with a Shutter and Grate, when we think fit to shut day out; a pair of
> Stairs leads to it in the midst of the Rooms which you see lie in a kind of
> round: the Building is contriv'd an Oval, part lined with some Boards, to
> defend the Damps from us; but yet in Winter 'tis no pleasant Dwelling.["]
> (*Madam de Beaumont*, 16–17)

The description is domestically detailed with items familiar to the eighteenth-
century reader—damask beds and escritoires, grates and stairs—but the women occupy a *cave*. As with Gulliver's traveling box, the peculiarity of the
space itself justifies and even delights in the ordinariness of its furnishings.

Other structures get the quick touch of pragmatographia (the description of things) when wanted: a "poor Clay Cottage" is "neat"; the host offers the marquis and Mr. Luelling "Venison-Pasty, Wine, and dry'd Tongues" (*Madam de Beaumont*, 96); the upstairs room is remarkable because "they could but just stand upright for the Ceiling; but the Softness of the Bed, and Fineness of the Sheets, made amends" (98); there is more than one "ruinous old Castle" (40, 63); Luelling's drawing room has its pictures, his parlour its dining table, and his bedchamber its bed (42, 54, 53); a robbers' hideout in a ruined chapel is filled with the disguises of "old ragged Coats, Shoes, Hats, &c. being Beggars Habits" as well as soot, grease, and oaken sticks (117). And, when the young Belinda is nearly starving in the course of her escape from the robbers, when she's really desperate, she's enabled to snatch and kill a goat kid, drink its blood, and eat its flesh raw. As with the "Clay Cottage," the narrative spaces in Aubin are (coincidentally) never "destitute of Necessaries" (96) when the characters require them.

Mary Davys (1674–1732)

Davys's novels follow similar spatial patterns—the quick brushstroke sufficing to depict a room, an architectural feature, an object to hand. But one early work, the *Familiar Letters betwixt a Gentleman and a Lady* (1725), offers another sort of textual praxis, another way into the domesticating trend of fictional description. Although structured as a plot-cumulative series of letters between Artander and Berina (letters that begin with them professing themselves eternal platonic friends and, in general, enemies to love and end with Artander seriously wooing Berina and she more or less revealing that she'll eventually give in), each individual letter reads more like an essay from the *Spectator*, either offering political arguments or delineating scenes from daily life with a moral punch. These latter—like a number of the *Spectator* or *Rambler* essays[11]—inject quite a bit more visual detail than is found in the usual novel format. The quality and quantity of detail are more or less the Ehrenpreisian negative particularity, spelled out lusciously for comic relief or didactic improvement.

On the comic side, Artander offers—partly as a tactful diversion from an increasingly heated argument between his Toryism and her Whiggism, partly as a sign of his luck with the ladies—an account of a visit he'd paid to an elderly lady:

When I first enter'd, I found the Lady in her Parlour, set in an easy Chair, with her Feet upon a Cricket, which rais'd her Knees almost as high as her

Mouth; she was dress'd in a black Cloth Gown, over which she had a dirty
Night-rail, and a coarse Diaper Napkin pinn'd from one Shoulder to the
other; upon her Head two yellow *Scotch*-Cloth Pinners, and over them
a black Gauze Hood, ty'd under her Chin, one Hand in her Pocket, and
t'other scratching her head.... [I] turn'd to take a Survey of the Room and
Furniture, which was no way inferiour to herself: Upon her Tea-Table,
instead of a Set of China, stood a Paste-board, with a piece of fat Bacon
upon it; and on the Seat of the Sash-window, a red earthen Pan, half full
of Pease-pudding, which I guess'd to be the Remains of her Dinner. Upon
one of the Silk Cushions were three greasy Plates, and in the Chimney-
Corner, a Black-Jack all dropp'd with Candle-grease; upon the Squab lay a
great Dog gnawing a Bone, whom she commanded off, and desir'd I would
take his Place, but I had too much respect for my Clothes, to accept of her
Offer. However, as I was walking to and fro, watching the Cobwebs that
they did not fall into my Wig, I slid over a piece of Bacon-Swerd, which
threw me directly into the Lady's Lap, and over-set her Cricket: She grew
very merry at the Accident, and I very much out of Countenance.[12]

This seems to be comedy for comedy's sake; Artander pretends to use the
incident as confirmation of his inherent bachelor tendencies. But it is clearly
also meant to make Berina (and the reader) laugh—detailed description employed as wooing device, a more leisurely, middle-class, homey version of
the quicksilver Restoration (aristocratic) wit.

Berina responds (after a studied silence) with a didactic anecdote of her
own, one related by her family doctor, who is called on to treat an ailing peer
in the country. The doctor is first ushered into a kitchen—"(if it may be call'd
one, where no Victuals is stirring)"—that is poorly lit by "a glimmering
Light" and occupied by "three or four Fellows who were sate upon a Log
of Wood before a Hatfull of Fire" and who were remarkably filthy (*Familiar
Letters*, 281). When he is finally brought upstairs to see his patient (lit up the
stairs by a farthing candle in a wooden candlestick holder, rather than a wax
taper in a silver one), he finds the ailing peer "within a Suit of Moth-eaten
red Serge Curtains, where he look'd more like one swinging in a Hammock
than lying in a Bed: The ponderous Weight of his own Carcass having sunk
the Cords even to the Boards: so that whoever wou'd have seen my Lord,
must have peep'd under the Bed." Of the four chairs in the room, "one stood
upon three Legs, another wanted its Back, a third had lost his Bottom, and
the fourth was half cover'd with a red Rag, and the —— upon it" (282). The
doctor spends a supperless night in

a Room much like an old Goal, where there was a Bed, but no Curtains;
Windows, but no Glass; and a Door, but neither Lock, Bolt, or any thing
to make it fast with. I was still apprehensive of some Danger; so drew all
the Lumber in the Room to the Door, and then wrapt myself up in my
Cloak, and laid me down, with a design to sleep till the Moon got up, to
light me home; but the Fleas, who wanted their Suppers as much as I did,
surrounded me on all sides, and fed so heartily, that they sav'd me Half
a Crown to a Surgeon for bleeding me, and that was my Fee. As soon as
Dawn of Day appear'd, I left my wretched Bed, and posted home without
either Coach or Company; and soon after heard my Lord was dead, which
all that lov'd him rejoiced at: He having gamed away his whole Estate,
his very Clothes and Furniture of his House. (283)

What is absent (light, wax tapers, bedcords, curtains, glass, bolts, food,
warmth, comfort) as well as what is present (filth, darkness, ——, fleas)
combine to produce the effect of wretchedness much more vividly than the
available stock adjectives could. The doctor has a moral: "And thus, Madam,
continu'd he, I have given you a true Account of my Lordly Patient; which
I have not done with a design to expose Quality, but to shew the miserable
Effects of that bewitching Vice which ruin'd him" (*Familiar Letters*, 283).
But the moral derives its power from the scene itself, the loading of details,
the implicit stark contrast to the expectation of wealth and luxury, the kind
of interior not yet usually described. Robert A. Day notes that this "British
middle-class realism" of "furniture, food, and the difficulties of day-to-day
life is as rare as a sense of humor in the early English novel" and that Davys's
"eye for physical detail" gives her "a claim to be a pioneer in the approach to
fiction improved by Fanny Burney and perfected by Jane Austen."[13] I would
agree; the visual details are not just satirical negative particularity, nor yet
quite "clean" Swiftian perspective shifting (as in Gulliver's traveling box),
but a sort of *domestication*. Where the prose works of Behn, the early novels
of Haywood, and the fiction of Aubin all generally practice the production
of implied space, Davys's familiar letters are more like the periodical essays
in bringing more leisurely description of ordinary spaces and ordinary life
(well, realistic spaces and quirky life, perhaps) into familiar generic territory.

Spaces (2): *Pamela, Clarissa*

In 1756, Catherine Talbot visited Samuel Richardson (1689–1761) at his
countryseat, Parson's Green, and for the most part reported admiringly: "His

Villa is fitted up in the same Style his Books are writ. Every Minute detail attended to, yet every one with a view to its being useful or pleasing. Not an inch in his Garden unimproved or unadorned, his very Poultry made happy by fifty little neat Contrivances, his House prepared not for his Family only but for every friend high or low to whom Air & Recess may be of Benefit."[14] Richardson, delighting in domestic details, constantly pushing the possibilities of print technology, and attentively conscious of literary trends,[15] crafted three enormously influential novels that, in their new fashionings of detail, their print innovations, and their formal patterns, carved out distinctly new spaces for the eighteenth-century novel. In fact, I will argue, *Pamela* (1740), *Clarissa* (1747–48), and *Sir Charles Grandison* (1753–54) together construct a formal trajectory that embodies the larger literary shift in attitudes toward and employments of (in particular) spatial description. *Pamela* follows, but also more intensely focuses, the patterns set up by Bunyan, Haywood, and Defoe: the details of Pamela's spaces emerge as the action demands, but, often, little heaps of things collect even more noticeably than in *The Pilgrim's Progress* or *Moll Flanders*. In *Clarissa*, Richardson plays more imaginatively with space, exploring its elasticity, the power of the place just around the corner, just beyond the line of sight. The intensity of location in *Clarissa* is created precisely by Richardson's more consciously submerging the visual and heightening both Clarissa's and the reader's apperception of the implicit. And, as the following chapters will show, *Sir Charles Grandison* pushes more decisively forward in opening up domestic interiors and visually filling their spaces, bringing the worlds of goods and the textual praxes of traditional forms and functions of description right into the parlor.

Pamela (1740)

Richardson printed not only the works of Defoe but also a number of stage comedies and prose fictions by Haywood, including the third edition of her *Secret Histories, Novels, and Poems, in Four Volumes* (1732). Keymer argues that we should more properly consider Richardson as "engaged, for all his originality, in a project of selective appropriation and conversion" rather than, as has traditionally been assumed, "operating in lofty ignorance of popular fiction" (introduction, xxi). *Pamela* employs the now-familiar structure of particular space constructed by specific narrative need as well as the sudden fastening on emblematic objects that characterizes late seventeenth- and early eighteenth-century novels.

All the many *things*, especially clothes, that Pamela itemizes and fetishizes have been thoroughly recataloged by critics. I will lay by her "Shoes and Stockens" and "*Flanders* lac'd Headcloths," then, except for one brief glance at her famous three bundles.[16] Pamela has just laid out in front of Mrs. Jervis a sort of past, present, and future in the packages of clothes that her deceased mistress had given her, those lately from Mr. B, and those she plans to take back with her to her parents' house. Of the first, she says: "I went on describing the Cloaths and Linen my Lady had given me"; of the second: "I particulariz'd all those in the second Bundle"; of the third: "Now, Mrs. *Jervis*, comes poor *Pamela*'s Bundle, and a little one it is, to the others. First, here is a Calicoe Night-gown, that I used to wear o' Mornings.... Then there is a quilted Callimancoe Coat, and a Pair of Stockens, ... and my Straw-hat with blue Strings, [and so on]" (1:96 [78]). It is only in the third instance that she enacts description and particularization. As Harriet will discover in *Sir Charles Grandison* (or Lovelace about Clarissa, for that matter), it is much more satisfying to describe your own things than someone else's; "*Pamela*'s Bundle" gets the act of description and particularization, while the things from others, the things she plans to leave behind, get packed back up in a single word, a single bundle, in an inverse pragmatographia.

The particular contours of Pamela's habitations have had less attention. The broad screen of the Bedfordshire countryside is sharply evoked in the characters' dialect; Keymer says that we find Bunyan in Pamela's "deviations from polite usage" into a dialect "unfamiliar enough to need definition in a glossary of Bedfordshire words that was published a few decades later" (introduction, xvii). Such energetic coloring from the likes of "Clog," "Mort," "Curchee," "Blood-pudden," and "Beechen Trencher" (like Bunyan's use of "Slabbiness," "Snibbeth," and "pelting") suggests another form of spatial creation: a particular local landscape (and, therefore, specific readerly expectations or associations) rises from the realm of dialect. (At least in the first edition. Later editions routinely sanitized the rusticisms [see Keymer, introduction, xvii].)

Particular local house details also rise from Pamela's words and actions. Shortly after the summerhouse scene, when Mr. B pops in on Pamela writing (as tends to happen), she makes a tearful petition on her knees after being called "Boldface and Insolent," at which "he seem'd to be moved, and rose up, and walked into the great Chamber two or three Turns, leaving me on my Knees; and I threw my Apron over my Face, and laid my Head on a Chair, and cry'd as if my Heart would break, having no power to stir" (*Pamela*, 1:30 [31]); suddenly, the "great Chamber" is mapped out, and a chair in Pamela's closet materializes. When Mr. B comes back and tries to fondle her, the energy of her indignation combines with the force of the plot to call up new objects, new spaces: "He then put his Hand in my Bosom, and the

Indignation gave me double Strength, and I got loose from him, by a sudden Spring, and ran out of the Room; and the next Chamber being open, I made shift to get into it, and threw-to the Door, and the Key being on the Inside, it locked; but he follow'd me so close, he got hold of my Gown, and tore a Piece off, which hung without the Door" (1:31 [32]). Although we can count on Pamela's bosom being pretty much a constantly visualized, always present object(s), things like locks and keys and next-door chambers are the sort of early modern fictional features that depend for their very existence on a character's immediate action. When Pamela is fairly convinced that she is, in fact, leaving shortly and she, Mrs. Jervis, and Mr. Longman are in some unspecified room with Mr. B, talking about estate management and Pamela's departure, Pamela makes a weeping prayer that calls up her master's "Elbow Chair" for her support as well as the wall, lobby, hall details through which she moves in exiting:

> But indeed, my dear Father and Mother, my Head was so giddy, and my Limbs trembled so, that I was forc'd to go holding by the Wainscot all the way, with both my Hands, and thought I should not have got to the Door: But when I did, as I hop'd this would be my last Interview with this terrible hard-hearted Master; I turn'd about, and made a low Curchee, and said, God bless you, Sir! God bless you, Mr. *Longman*! And I went into the Lobby leading to the great Hall, and dropt into the first Chair; for I could get no further a good while. (1:91 [75])

The unnamed wainscoted office with a door to a lobby stocked with more than one chair and leading to a hall—all these things rise around Pamela and become visible as she moves through them, vanishing again once she's gone. She lives a charmed life in terms of apertures. So to speak.

One of the most drawn-out and artfully choreographed scenes of architectural occupation—architectural *dance*, really—is when Mr. B's vinegary sister, Lady Davers, and her pert nephew Jackey show up unexpectedly shortly after Pamela and Mr. B marry, while Mr. B is at a neighbor's expecting his bride. Pamela is trapped socially: she does not think it her place to announce their marriage, nor can she tell or act an outright lie; all her arts of answering a question with a question, or evading the direct monosyllable, are called on as the pair launch an inquisition on her sexual status. And she is trapped physically: at one point Lady Davers "gave [her] a Push, and pull'd a Chair, and setting the Back against the Door, sat down on it" (*Pamela*, 2:228 [382]); when she rises and walks angrily about, Pamela would have moved the chair and left, "but her Nephew came and sat on it" (2:230 [384]); she is tapped, and slapped, and nearly boxed on the ear; and then Jackey "set his Back against the Door, and put his Hand to his Sword, and said, I should not go, till his Aunt permitted it. He drew it half-way" (2:246–47 [395]).

All this time, Pamela moves from window seat to window seat, fanning herself and biting her fan, until she finds just the right window:

> I was quite sick at Heart, at all this passionate Extravagance, and to be hinder'd from being where was the Desire of my Soul, and afraid too of incurring my dear Master's Displeasure; and, as I sat, I saw it was no hard matter to get out of the Window, into the Front-yard, the Parlour being even with the Yard, and so have a fair Run for it; and after I had seen my Lady at the other End of the Room again, in her Walks, having not pulled down the Sash, when I spoke to Mrs. *Jewkes*, I got upon the Seat, and whipt out in a Minute, and ran away as hard as I could drive, my Lady calling after me to return, and her Woman at the other Window. (*Pamela*, 2:250 [398])

Here, the space is measured by Pamela's quick eye, and we get a rare glimpse *through* the window to the "Front-yard." (Philippa Tristram claims that Richardson's characters "tend to treat windows as though they are closets whose walls are opaque.")[17] The outside is specifically connected to the inside, and Pamela finally gathers enough energy and attention to break the bounds of both—as well as of convention. Sash windows, after all, were not constructed for ladies to leap out of.

The most obvious spaces of *Pamela*, of course, are the "secret" or side-lined ones that Mr. B hides in to watch Pamela in various states of physical or mental undress: the closet in Mrs. Jervis's bedroom; the closet in the green room; the shadowy corner where the faux figure of a drunken "Nan" pretends to sleep. Mr. B is watching constantly, reading over her shoulder, reading between her lines, listening to her private conversations, plotting things in every corner of her background. But, in at least one place, things are reversed, and Pamela eavesdrops, intrudes, and causes *Mr. B* to slam the door on *her*. When she is preparing to leave the Lincolnshire estate, after he has proposed marriage and she draws his wrath for still doubting, he orders her back to her parents:

> So down I went, and as I went by the Parlour, [Mrs. Jewkes] stept in, and said, Sir, you have nothing to say to the Girl before she goes? I heard him say, tho' I did not see him, Who bid you say *the Girl*, Mrs. *Jewkes*, in that Manner? She has offended only me!... let her go, perverse and foolish as she is; but she *deserves* to go honest, and she shall go so!

> I was so transported with this unexpected Goodness, that I open'd
> the Door before I knew what I did; and I said, falling on my Knees at
> the Door, with my Hands folded and lifted up, O thank you, thank your
> Honour a Million of times! . . .
> He turn'd from me, and went into his Closet, and shut the Door.
> (2:34–35 [244])

Pamela has learned some of Mr. B's tricks—and, perhaps, some of his mistakes. When one thinks one is occupying the center of a space, it is disconcerting for the margins to break open.

Pamela's spaces tend to form around her, as with any good early
eighteenth-century heroine; she takes advantage of what comes narratively
to hand and makes it visual. The pressure in *Pamela*, as in all Richardson's
works, is on *locality*.

Clarissa (1747–48)

Where the spaces and details of *Pamela* follow the patterns set up by Bunyan,
Behn, Haywood, Defoe, and the other early novelists, those in *Clarissa* are
made into something else entirely, spatially speaking. Where we might say
that the action of *Pamela* and the early novels depends on or calls into being
the various architectural features of doors, windows, staircases, wainscotings, and gardens, in *Clarissa* some of the most powerful spaces are those
that we—or Clarissa—never see at all. I have argued elsewhere about the
ways in which Clarissa manages center space, particularly in her parlor (as a
mark of honored family status at the beginning and as a dominating corpse at
the end) and in the dining room at Mrs. Sinclair's, where she continually and
successfully resists Lovelace.[18] Here, I want to examine the spaces outside
Clarissa's occupation, spaces beyond the known or apprehended, as sites of
deduction and interpretation because so much implicitly happens.

But, before visiting the implicit, I want to contextualize the explicit acts
of description. Richardson employs full-scale description in a few rare moments in *Clarissa*. The most famous of those moments is the prison scene,
which I will not quote here, but which is familiar as an example of negative
particularity in that Belford finds it so utterly shocking to see "the divine
Clarissa" in that small, sordid space that he has to punish Lovelace with its
detailed horrors.[19] Tristram singles this interior out as "the *in*appropriate
context that needs description" (6–7). That prison room—that description—
is, in some ways, the logical conclusion of the confinement implied in this
epistolary example itself; as John Bullen argues, the "objects associated with

[the composition of letters]—the pens, ink, paper, desks, chairs, locked doors, hiding places—; the physical conditions that influence the writer—lighting, privacy, health—; and the activities included in the writing—alluding, quoting, cross-referencing, enclosing—all convey aspects of imaginable environment to the reader" and "[postulate] confined space."[20] But equally telling in relation to the narrative plot is Lovelace's long example of prosopographia, detailing Clarissa's physical characteristics and, even more, her clothes, to an extent that exceeds any descriptions of Pamela and even the elaborate description of Bellraizia in Haywood's *Idalia*—matched in Richardson's own work only, perhaps, by Harriet's descriptions of Grandison Hall on her entrance as its mistress.

The context for the description is a quasi abduction. Lovelace has peopled the spaces just out of sight of the garden gate with fictional pursuers, suspecting that Clarissa might have changed her mind about fleeing: "They are coming! They are coming!—Fly, fly, my beloved creature, cry'd I, drawing my sword with a flourish, as if I would have slain half an hundred of them" (*Clarissa*, 3:55 [399]). Now he's got her, and his motives for the luxuriance of the detail reflect Harriet's pride of ownership:

> HER wax-like flesh . . . by its delicacy and firmness, answers for the soundness of her health. . . . I never in my life beheld a skin so *illustriously* fair. The lily and the driven snow it is nonsense to talk of: her lawn and her laces one might, indeed, compare to those: But what a whited wall would a woman appear to be, who had such a complexion which would justify such unnatural comparisons? But this lady is all-alive, all-glowing, all charming flesh and blood, yet so clear, that every meandring vein is to be seen in all the lovely parts of her, which custom permits to be visible.
>
> Thou hast heard me also describe the wavy ringlets of her shining hair, needing neither art nor powder; of itself an ornament, defying all other ornaments; wantoning in and about a neck that is beautiful beyond description.
>
> Her head-dress was a Brussels-lace mob, peculiarly adapted to the charming air and turn of her features. A sky-blue ribband illustrated that. . . .
>
> Her morning-gown was a pale primrose-colour'd paduasoy: The cuffs and robings curiously embroider'd by the fingers of this ever-charming Ariadne [Arachne], in a running pattern of violets, and their leaves; the light in the flowers silver; gold in the leaves. A pair of diamond snaps in her ears. A white handkerchief, wrought by the same inimitable fingers,

concealed—O Belford! what still more inimitable beauties did it not conceal!...

Her ruffles were the same as her mob. Her apron a flower'd lawn. Her coat white satten, quilted: Blue satten her shoes, braided with the same colour, without lace; for what need has the prettiest foot in the world of ornament? Neat buckles in them: And on her charming arms a pair of black velvet glove-like muffs, of her own invention; for she makes and gives fashions as she pleases. Her hands, velvet of themselves, thus uncover'd, the freer to be grasp'd by those of her adorer. (3:53–54 [399–400])

Description in Lovelace's case is, of course, power; he owns Clarissa in the verbal recapitulation, which reflects the leisure he has—and takes—to stare closely at all the details of his new objet d'art, down to the braid on her shoes and the gold-shot leaves in her robes (the kind of thing you presumably don't notice when you're running off in the darkness from nonexistent pursuers). Lovelace's detailed portrait of Clarissa does the opposite of what her family had already begun, but to the same effect. They erase her; he fixes her.

The family erases Clarissa from its rooms and its sight. She is forced to spend much of her time deducing the spatial patterns of events beyond her own field of vision primarily because she spends much of the novel being locked up in one place or another. But the image of (in a sense) *pushing space away* comes in Clarissa's first encounter with her family after having refused Mr. Solmes's proposals:

I was sent for down to tea. I went with a very cheerful aspect: but had occasion soon to change it.

Such a solemnity in every-body's countenance!—My mamma's eyes were fixed upon the tea-cups; and when she looked up, it was heavily, as if her eye-lids had weights upon them; and then not to me. My papa sat half-aside in his elbow-chair, that his head might be turn'd from me; his hands folded, and waving, as it were, up and down; his fingers, poor dear gentleman! in motion, as if to the very ends of them. My sister sat swelling. (*Clarissa*, 1:47–48 [63])

Clarissa is decentered by the gestures of her family, emptied out of her place by averted eyes, waving hands, swelling bodies.

Then she is literally banished. Her brother, James, orders: "You are not to be seen in any apartment of the house, you so lately govern'd as you pleased, unless you are commanded down. In short, are strictly to confine yourself to your chamber" (*Clarissa*, 1:154 [121]). Just before this edict, Clarissa had

listened to and tried to interpret the new silences of space, visually marked
in her letters by stars dividing her paragraphs:

★ ★

MY father is come home, and my brother with him. Late as it is, they
are all shut up together. Not a door opens; not a soul stirs. Hannah, as
she moves up and down, is shunn'd as a person infected.

★ ★

THE angry assembly is broke up. My two uncles and my aunt Hervey
are sent for, it seems, to be here in the morning to breakfast. I shall then,
I suppose, know my doom. 'Tis past eleven, and I am order'd not to go to
bed.

Twelve o'clock.

THIS moment the keys of every thing are taken from me. It was proposed to send for me down: But my papa said, he could not bear to look
upon me.—Strange alteration in a few weeks! Shorey was the messenger.
The tears stood in her eyes when she deliver'd her message. (1:146 [115])

The servants, Hannah and Shorey, move between floors and family members; trapped in her room, Clarissa can mark space and time on the page,
but it's the nature of the epistolary novel that events break through the
page itself: twelve o'clock marks an intrusion into her space and a confirmation of her banishment. Her father, no longer not looking at her presence,
refuses to have her present to avoid. Clarissa frequently notes (as consequence and cause of various familial machinations): "All is in a hurry below
stairs." Both at Harlowe Place and in London, Clarissa's perspective is that
of imprisoned and, therefore, imperfect apprehension of spaces beyond her
immediate boundaries, and, thus, she needs to interpret motives, events, and
possibilities by deciphering the *sounds* coming out of those spaces—pacings,
shoutings, door closings, silences. Both Clarissa and the reader always have,
in Tristram's words, "a vivid sense of location—whether in rooms, on stair-
cases, in passages, or as forming the containment of a house" (229), but the
locations are rarely described and more often implied than named. The occupied space often visually disappears in the strain to *apperceive* surrounding
space.

But, in a sense, all the characters function within and against these odd
implied spaces; all are listening for or waiting on Clarissa. Clarissa's account
seems to give everyone else a clearly defined and understood space: the father
and brother issuing orders from Below Stairs; the lover plotting in the Next

Room; the best friend reading helplessly At Home; the aunt and mother shrinking into the Window. But all those spaces are positionally dependent on Clarissa's; everyone else is as acutely aware as she is of the boundaries, and their apparently central spaces are all implicitly facing the banished center of Clarissa herself, wherever she is.

Lovelace in particular demonstrates a moment-by-moment, place-by-place inversion of Clarissa's apparent spatial powerlessness. When Clarissa has fled to Hampstead, he tries to recapture her by repossessing her spaces, touching her things: "I HAVE been traversing her room, meditating, or taking up every-thing she but touched or used: The glass she dressed at, I was ready to break, for not giving me the personal image it was wont to reflect.... From her room to my own; in the dining-room, and in and out of every place where I have seen the beloved of my heart, do I hurry; in none can I tarry; her lovely image in every-one" (*Clarissa*, 4:323 [740]). Like Clarissa reconstructing the actions and decisions of her family by listening for their steps or the sounds of their doors, Lovelace tries (even less successfully) to evoke Clarissa from her rooms and their objects, to demand her image from her mirror.

His powerlessness, his waiting in the wings or occupying abandoned rooms, is not always a side effect. Both before and after the rape, when virtually a prisoner of Lovelace's, Clarissa, like any good guerrilla fighter, takes advantage of the weapons and strategies usually employed against her for her own ends, in this case immuring herself in her room after the play and insisting on one whole day to herself:

★ ★

HE was very earnest to dine with me. But I was resolved to carry this one small point; and so denied to dine myself....

He was very busy in writing, Dorcas says, and pursued it without dining, because I denied him my company.

He afterwards *demanded*, as I may say, to be admitted to afternoon tea with me.... However, I repeated my promise to meet him as early as he pleased in the morning, or to breakfast with him.

Dorcas says, he raved. I heard him loud, and I heard his servant fly from him, as I thought. (*Clarissa*, 4:139 [640–42])

In this case, Clarissa can keep him out, rather than being kept in. And, after the rape, Lovelace is reduced to the same spatial helplessness, depending on servants and sounds to gauge Clarissa's state of mind: "JUST now Dorcas tells me that what she writes she tears, and throws the paper in fragments under the table, either as not knowing what she does, or disliking it: Then gets up, wrings her hands, weeps, and shifts her seat all round the room: Then returns to her table, sits down, and writes again" (*Clarissa*, 5:233 [889]). Clarissa's final triumph is, of course, to escape Lovelace's sight altogether, having left her poor haven at the Smiths' before he comes looking for her:

> CURSE upon my stars!—Disappointed again!
>
> It was about eight when I arrived at Smith's—The woman was in the shop.
>
> So, old acquaintance, how do you now? I know my Love is above.—Let her be acquainted that I am here, waiting for admission to her presence and can take no denial. Tell her, that I will approach her with the most respectful duty, and in whose company she pleases; and I will not touch the hem of her garment, without her leave.
>
> Indeed, Sir, you're mistaken. The lady is not in this house, nor near it. (6:398–99 [1219])

Lovelace indeed takes no denial and essentially ransacks the house, but is she gone yes she is gone alas.

But never more powerfully present than in the coffin returned to Harlowe Place:

> But when the corpse was carried into the lesser parlour, adjoining to the hall, which she used to call *her* parlour, and put on a table in the middle of the room, and the Father and Mother, the two Uncles, her Aunt Hervey, and her Sister came in (joining her Brother and me, with trembling feet, and eager woe) the scene was still more affecting.... And now seeing them before the receptacle that contained the glory of their family, who so lately was driven thence by their indiscreet violence (never, never more to be restored to them!) no wonder that their grief was more than common grief. (*Clarissa*, 7:275 [1398])

After all their expulsion, her submission, her rebellion, her sacrificiality, it is this central occupation of internal domestic space—*her* parlor in her "father's" house—that Clarissa reclaims symbolically at the end. That body implied (not seen) in the coffin, like the woman immured in her upstairs room or imprisoned in Lovelace's house or in the jail, is the reason for every gesture, every decision, every movement, every emotion.

Thomas Keymer has argued that Richardson "was not only familiar as a printer with prior novelists like Haywood [and Aubin], but also a close observer of the emergent genre, and of competing trends within it" (introduction, xxi). *Pamela* collected the "things" of the early novel and distributed them carefully but plentifully throughout the plot-sponsored architecture. *Clarissa* attempts more with boundaries themselves. Implied space crystallizes around Clarissa. Virtually everyone around her wants to push her into corners, and the description of interior space consequently blurs. But Richardson's manipulation of this space into excruciatingly articulated *vagueness* makes our awareness of narrative space that much more intense, and the more visible elasticity of that narrative space will paradoxically make more room in his next venture for a new articulation of *precision*.

CHAPTER SIX

Worlds of Goods

> While they were at breakfast, they were again visited by Miss Larolles. "I am come," cried she, eagerly, "to run away with you both to my Lord Belgrade's sale. All the world will be there; and we shall go in with tickets, and you have no notion how it will be crowded."
>
> "What is to be sold there?" said Cecilia.
>
> "O every thing you can conceive; house, stables, china, laces, horses, caps, every thing in the world."
>
> "And do you intend to buy any thing?"
>
> "Lord, no; but one likes to see the people's things."
>
> —*Frances Burney*, Cecilia *(1782)*

In the eighteenth century—as, perhaps, in every other—one indeed liked to see people's things, and new ways of (and reasons for) seeing things were invented, or recycled, or perfected. The things of the house—china, laces, caps, "every thing in the world," began to emerge as visible, *connected* objects within novelistic spaces, in part because of a new profusion of things, of ways and means to collect and arrange as well as to disperse and disassemble them. Chapter 3 discusses the passion for collecting and listing; this chapter moves into other spaces created by and for objects found and arranged in other ways. Shops, advertisements, and auctions—all significantly popular and either new or newly fashioned—displayed and made available the vast new world of goods, responding to and creating new needs, desires, and readerly expectations.

Horace Walpole, like Frances Burney's Miss Larolles, was a pillager at heart. He, too, saw "all the world" (almost) at the auction, although he was less socially pleased about it: "Gideon the Jew and Blakiston the independent grocer" were suddenly part of this world (Walpole to Horace Mann,

18 June 1751 OS, in Walpole, *Correspondence*, 20:268). Like the auction catalogs (and the guidebooks and travelers' journals of the next chapter), he details as well as acquires (and so anticipates) the spoils of Poynton, so to speak. And detailed description is a sort of itemization, which actually or metaphorically breaks up a whole into distinct, perceptible, and, in some instances, purchasable bits. Detail in the eighteenth-century world of houses proliferates—and migrates into textual spaces. Perhaps acquisitiveness does, indeed, engineer the change, as Carole Fabricant argues;[1] "Lord Belgrade's sale," in Burney's *Cecilia*, as well as the breakup of the Harrels' estate[2] may well be, as Julia Epstein demonstrates, part of Burney's attack on the materialistic obsessions and consequent cruelties of society.[3] But acquisitiveness is creative as well as destructive, a way to "nest," to create new forms of inner space and comfort and delight. What remains critically underappreciated is the extent to which eighteenth-century English society was also deeply interested in the plastic possibilities of personal habitation.

This chapter looks at some of the details that produced details: the phenomena of shopping, shopwindow displays, and advertising that promoted the desire for and possibility of variety; the auction, that very English, very eighteenth-century phenomenon of competitive exchange, of dismembering and reassembling household objects from whole estates into new households; and auction catalogs, which described and offered pieces for new possibilities. Things are described in catalogs, inventories, letters, guidebooks; things are acquired by shopping, collecting, bidding; things are arranged and rearranged in private spaces, both in the world and in texts; and the *idea* of things *visibly* inhabiting real and textual space becomes increasingly socially acceptable—gentrified. Acts of dispersion, dismemberment, fragmentation, are countered by acts of collection, assemblage, collage—description.

Worlds of Goods

Consumption and the World of Goods; Virtue, Commerce, and History; The Ends of Empire; Painting for Money; The Invention of Comfort; The Economy of Character; The Improvement of the Estate; The Birth of the Museum; Early Modern Conceptions of Property; Married Women's Separate Property; The Romantic Ethic and the Spirit of Modern Consumerism; The Cultures of Collection; The Property of a Gentleman; A History of Everyday Things; "Le monde-objet"; On Longing.

It has become more or less a commonplace that the eighteenth century was a world of goods, awash in mercantile choices, obsessed with "the various

Off'rings of the World" on Belinda's dressing table—the "glitt'ring Spoil" (Pope, *Rape*, canto 1, lines 130, 132) of ivory and tortoiseshell, Arabian perfumes and Indian gems, japanned furniture and chinaware. Standard accounts of the changing economic and social systems in Britain cite its emerging dominance in world trade; a credit economy; increasing urban populations; improvement in inland transport, with better roads, more navigable rivers, and the construction of canals; a nationwide carrier system; the development of the postal system; the widespread advertising of newspapers; the introduction of banks, bills, and promissory notes; more disposable income among workers; more mobility among populations; a faster tempo of industrial and mercantile activities with a quickening of commercial information; and, thus, along with all this, an increased demand for and consumption of both home-manufactured goods and foreign imports.[4] As Deidre Lynch puts it: "[R]eaders had to negotiate the experience of a marketplace that was chock-full of strange new consumables and that beggared description" (4). Except that, in the end (and as the consequence), the beggar Description comes out full handed and well dressed.

Many accounts of the early modern "world of goods" are explicitly or implicitly critical of the phenomenon of acquisition, seeing a hegemonizing of the "bourgeoisie";[5] the self-justification of empire; the rise of an unrepentantly materialist, novelty-ridden, feverishly consumerist society; and a false consciousness that "encourag[ed] people to think and act in ways that went against their own (material and class) interests" (Fabricant, 257). The idea of a culture so deeply invested in *things*, of people interested only in achieving a social status as reflected by others' admiration for or (better yet) envy of their things, seems to some inherently shallow. Roland Barthes's famous critique of Dutch still-life painting, "Le monde-objet," sets a standard for identifying a culture obsessed with appearances and their prices. As Simon Schama explains: "For Barthes all these elaborate arrangements of objects, visualized with almost fanatical attention to detail, suggested not just a form of cultural encyclopaedism but an exercise of power: art mobilized to service the appropriation of matter. The 'empire of things' is the reduction of cosmology to catalogue: whatsoever may be measured, enumerated, exchanged, priced, processed and marketed."[6] Certainly, plenty of contemporary critics also saw the dangers of superficiality, acquisitiveness, covetousness, spendthriftiness, foppishness, and the general moral slough of luxury—the *Spectator*, the *Rambler*, the whole host of moral critics, the whole luxury debate from Mandeville to John Brown.[7] But, as a number of other critics point out, and as this chapter will presume, sometimes— many times—a thing is more than just an object or a status symbol. For one

thing, as Peter Stallybrass and Ann Rosalind Jones argue, when writing from
our own ideologically and historically situated centers, we are apt to "get
the past absolutely wrong. It is not the capitalist present that has suddenly
started to obsess about the value of things. On the contrary, capitalist cultures are often squeamish about value, attempting to separate cultural value
from economics, persons from things, subjects from objects, the priceless
(us) from the valueless (the detachable world)."[8] For the eighteenth century,
as for the Renaissance, things could still be interpreted as intertwined with
persons, objects with subjects.

The eighteenth century of course mingled many cultural, economic, political, religious, and social values within its traditions and innovations. One
way of thinking about change in terms of things might be, in fact, to use a
metaphor of things. Elizabeth Burton notes about furniture in great and middling houses: "A new piece of furniture might replace an old piece in the
saloon or 'eating' room, but the style of the room was probably a mixture
ranging from elaborate Charles II to plain Queen Anne, with perhaps an inherited white elephant in the shape of an Elizabethan or Jacobean stool or
chest." For the most part, she explains: "[I]t was not easy to tell new furniture
from old[;] . . . design in general during the reign of George I remained much
the same as in Queen Anne's day."[9] In some sense, I will be arguing that the
romance of eighteenth-century Britain with all its new things is as much
or more a part of the Renaissance investiture of meaning into things, of the
resistance to a cultural separation of value between us and the things of this
world as it is a product of commercialization, materialism, or capitalism.

Chapters 2 and 3 explored the Puritan and empiricist fascination with
the things of the natural world and the meanings, religious or otherwise, to
be read in them. The new things of trade and manufacture had an equal, if
not exactly similar, appeal. Chandra Mukerji puts it neatly: "Material novelties . . . were so varied and so new to European travelers and traders that they
created a crisis of meaning only solved by new attention to the material
world, i.e., by envisioning ways to explain and use it."[10] The commercial
and urban tendencies of eighteenth-century society produced the rise of various arts; the culture of things was as much aesthetic as material.[11] The
"consumer"—the person who saw, desired, bought, and arranged things—
was not simply a passive swallower of advertising gimmicks or a passive
consumer of retailer-driven trends; "changes in demand resulted in changes
in production, rather than vice versa."[12] Furthermore, as Lorna Weatherill
argues: "[T]here is no evidence that most people of middle rank wanted to be
like the gentry, although they may have wanted some of the new goods for
their own purposes."[13] Those purposes could include the fashioning of new

identities through the inventive accumulation and arrangement of color, texture, pattern, material. The remarkable expansion of *choice* in determining, among other things, the domestic interior involved an imaginative exercise in spatial variability, in the tone and nuance of object ordering, in playing with traditional social boundaries, and in creating the simple, self-sufficient satisfaction in personal expression so fully felt later by Wemmick in his tiny gothic cottage with its tiny moat, tiny drawbridge, tiny gothic door "almost too small to get in at," and a hundred little contrivances.[14] As T. H. Breen suggests: "The very act of appropriating goods generated meaning."[15] And, as we will see in the travel accounts of John Byng and Mary Delany in the next chapter, descriptions of *other* people's spaces, *other* people's things, constituted analysis and self-construction rather than some simple absorption of a status quo or reification of imposed ideologies.

We are already well versed in the commodification of the eighteenth century; the following analyses of shops and auctions and tours, of furnishing and arranging and sharing interiors, examine the potential for meaning in domestic spaces and how that meaning comes to shape narrative space to accommodate the cultural interest in things. And, from that perspective, I am willing to take Barthes's critique of the still life and reinvest it with a different significance for the literary as well as the social world:

> Des objets, il y en a dans tous les plans, sur les tables, aux murs, par terre: des pots, des pichets renversés, des corbeilles à la débandade, des légumes, du gibier, des jattes, des coquilles d'huitres, des verres, des berceaux. Tout cela, c'est l'espace de l'homme, il s'y mesure et détermine son humanité à partir du souvenir de ses gestes: son temps est couvert d'usages, il n'y a pas d'autre autorité dans sa vie que celle qu'il imprime à l'inerte en le formant et en le manipulant. (20)

> [Objects on the tables, the walls, floor, pots, pitchers overturned, a clutter of baskets, bunches of vegetables, a brace of game, oyster shells, pans.... All this is man's space; in it he measures himself and determines his humanity, starting from the memory of his gestures, his *chronos*[;] ... there is no other authority in his life but the one he imprints upon the inert by shaping and manipulating it. (Translation from Schama, 478)]

"L'espace de l'homme" is also the novel in which characters measure themselves by their gestures within and movements through it, shaping (or manipulating) their spaces as they go.

Theories of Description

Chapter 1 traveled over a history of theories about the relation of detail to
narrative, of the particular to the general. In this section, I concentrate on
some specific twentieth-century arguments about the relative lack of visual detail, especially of domestic interiors, in the eighteenth- versus the
nineteenth-century novel. For two critics, in particular, ignorance or alienation explains absence. Warren Hunting Smith argues that most eighteenth-
century authors simply didn't know what the elevated interiors their characters inhabited actually looked like; James H. Bunn claims that the new
superabundance of things in the eighteenth century estranged the world,
making it too difficult to encompass visually with words.[16] I will argue, on
the one hand, that both claims are inadequate to explain the apparent textual
emptiness and, on the other, that they misinterpret textual visualization as
empty.

   Smith posits that the middle-class author of the eighteenth century had
no real intimacy with—even idea of—the "castles" or great houses of his novels' heroes and that, "preoccupied as he was with the nobility and gentry,"
he "had little occasion to describe the type of house with which he himself
had intimate associations—consequently his buildings are not personalities"
(204). (For *personalities* read *detailed descriptions*; Smith discusses as contrast the living features of windows, doors, floors in Dickens.) The author,
by virtue of class, knew little more than the tourist: "When Mrs. Radcliffe
describes a castle, it is with the awe of a sightseer who is being conducted
on a visitors' day through those rooms which are occasionally thrown open
to the public. The aged housekeeper who guides the Gothic heroine through
her castle is suspiciously like the women who conduct parties of tourists
through the state room of such places as Knole and Penshurst. One expects
to hear the clink of a shilling at the end of the hour" (204–5). The author
simply visits his or her interiors and points out the obvious sites of public interest; intimacy requires experience, and unfamiliarity breeds textual
reserve.

   On the other hand, Bunn argues that it was an increasingly unknown
world that, in the nineteenth century, prompted visual fullness in an attempt
to rein in and familiarize a new experience of alienation. Too many things
had been pulled from their originary contexts, Bunn insists, and were fed into
collections and museums with a "polyglot effect" of having been "randomly
purchas[ed]." He suggests: "In reaction perhaps to the estranged place that
England had become, poets like Wordsworth and Burns, novelists like Jane
Austen and the Brontës, naturalists like Gilbert White and later Charles

Darwin, began to write about minutely observed exchanges within intensely localized terrains" (204). To describe is to reacquaint, to know, to possess or repossess.

There are three problems with Smith's argument. First, by the later eighteenth century, tourists' acquaintance with the great houses was far more extensive than Smith imagines, as Fabricant demonstrates (and as I articulate more fully in the next chapter). Second, many of the early and midcentury novelists had plenty of firsthand intimacy with such places already. If they did not occupy those places themselves, they had friends and connections who did (Behn, Defoe, Richardson). And, third, most novels concerned themselves primarily, not with the great, but with the middling sort who might wander across class boundaries and their architectural thresholds (e.g., Moll Flanders, Robinson Crusoe, H. F., Pamela, Tom Jones, Humphry Clinker, Emily St. Aubert, and Elizabeth Bennet). The novelists knew enough to describe their inhabited spaces if they wanted.

One problem with Bunn's argument is similar; to writers such as Wordsworth and Burns, Austen and the Brontës, White and Darwin, the English landscape and social world were already so immediately and consistently grounding them, so constantly under their observation, that it is more reasonable to argue that it is their literary attention that lifts the landscape out of the ordinary, rather than that the ordinary had suddenly become alien and unmanageable. As I have argued so far, the awareness of the proliferation and strangeness of both natural and artificial things had been a source of keen observation and attention since at least the late seventeenth century. These later writers were absorbing the kinds of "minutely observed exchanges within intensely localized terrains" that had already become the staple of topographies and meditations, diaries and micrographies. Narrative attention to the spatial relation of objects in interiors, to movement within boundaries, adapted increasingly to the presence of more objects in interiors, more patterns of movement within more architectural boundaries. Leaping from a bed to a passageway would increasingly become leaping from *this* brocaded bed to *that* dark, twisting passageway. By the time of Austen (post-Richardson, post-Radcliffe), the author could actually focus on the boring and ultraordinary of the social rather than the material world and lift it out of its ordinariness rather than rein it in: a Mr. Collins or a Miss Bates—agony to be with in a real room in real time—can enchant through the sheer *perfect* depiction of boredom. Austen performs on the bore what Hooke had already done for the flea.

Philippa Tristram brushes aside the "they didn't have it in their repertoire yet" explanation for the absence of detail, offering instead two claims very similar to my own: first, that the availability of actual interior detail directly informs the presence of literary interior detail; and, second, that the so-called rule of taste applied: "Just as a gentleman was defined by his likeness to other gentlemen, so a house should resemble other houses of a similar standing; it would therefore be redundant to describe what every courteous author must assume was already known to his readers." Tristram points out that the eighteenth- and early nineteenth-century house was "to a modern eye... extremely bare," using as evidence Repton's drawings of "'an old-fashioned cedar parlour' and 'a modern living room'" (see fig. 10). She then draws an extremely apt conclusion: "The room, in consequence, is dominated not by its furniture but by its structural features—walls, floor, and ceiling; windows, doors, and fireplace. As a result, the novelist tends to sense, rather than see, domestic environments, registering the definition of space and not its detail" (5). She notes, on something like Ehrenpreis's negative particularity line, that it is "the *in*appropriate context that needs description, like the room in which Clarissa is imprisoned for debt" (6–7).

I will, in fact, be arguing along Tristram's theoretical lines—that, frequently, eighteenth-century novelists "register the definition of space" through its detail—but with both historical and theoretical expansions. First, an eighteenth-century or Regency room, when compared with its Victorian successors, might, indeed, strike us as remarkably bare, but this view depends on the hindsight of a post-nineteenth-century perspective. It does not take into quite enough account the extent of interior changes—the quantity and resonance of things new and old and their new and old forms of dispersal and arrangement. Changes in size, weight, amount, variety, and arrangement, as well as the increasing availability, of furniture and ornaments for middling houses; the lines of trade and the patterns of retail; the pattern books and mass production; the phenomenon of the auction as a social as well as a commercial and imaginative site—all these phenomena produced *by midcentury* the possibilities for widely different, detailed, and textilely coordinated interiors. *Things* gather together in Richardson as for an interior decorator in what Deidre Lynch calls "the eloquence of the material surface" (38).

And that is part of my second move in further contextualizing Tristram's intelligent analysis. The way in which space is theoretically inhabited—as, in Henri Lefebvre's words, "the individual situates his body in its own space and apprehends the space round the body" through "concatenations of gestures"—marks historically a change in perception in literary representation between "natural space" and "social space." Natural space

INTERIORS

Figure 10. "Old-fashioned Cedar Parlour and modern Living Room," in Humphry Repton, *Fragments on the Theory of Landscape Gardening* (1816). Courtesy of the Newberry Library, Chicago.

"juxtaposes—and thus disperses: it puts places and that which occupies them side by side"; "[i]t particularizes [where social space] implies actual or potential assembly at a single point, or around that point"; "everywhere there are privileged objects which arouse a particular expectation or interest, while others are treated with indifference."[17] In other words, the social spaces of early novels were created in response to the gestures and motives and actions of characters who found room enough to move in *narrative itself*. Social space changed; the particularities of natural space (in the sense of background, what exists as you arrive, whether in nature or in a space made or arranged by others) achieved or demanded a different focus, a different value. More things made more shapes; shape and surface acquired interest, began to seem, not to lead to meaning, but to house it. The things of an interior became *part of their narration*. Narration in the eighteenth century caught up with the experience of a fullness of things. What could be acquired and displayed in the world found new ways to be acquired and displayed in texts.

Shopping and Advertising

> The man's name, at whose house I lodge, is Smith—A glove-*maker*, as well as seller. His wife is the shop-keeper. A dealer also in stockens, ribbands, snuff, and perfumes.... Two neat rooms, with plain but clean furniture, on the first floor, are mine; one they call the dining room.
>
> When I came into the shop, seeing no chair or stool, I went behind the compter, and sat down under an arched kind of canopy of carved-work, which these proud traders, emulating the royal nich-fillers, often give themselves, while a joint-stool perhaps serves those by whom they get their bread: Such is the dignity of trade in this mercantile nation!
> —*Richardson*, Clarissa *(1747–48)*

Clarissa Harlowe and Robert Lovelace present two polarized takes on the English shop: the respectable and the mean. Clarissa, raped, vulnerable, and, as she thinks, dishonored, finds and describes a place of ordered exchange, plainness, and profusion, a place of *supply*, a place that understands need and structures daily life. Lovelace obsessively hunts her down at the Smiths', where she returned after her imprisonment (although, by this time, she has actually left the house). He sees the shop's accoutrements, but, having no place there himself (the Smiths more or less evicted him from his fruitless search of the house), he tries to assume the space of ownership and empty

it of its social and even commercial significance—to take its meaning away
from Clarissa (not to mention the Smiths).

Lovelace plays the shopkeeper, yet not the shopkeeper, pushing on the
dissonance between his gentlemanly appearance and the spatial expectations
within the shop, breaking the customer contract but keeping the customer's
money: "The wench was plaguy homely; and I told her so; or else, I said,
I would have treated her. She in anger (No woman is homely in her own
opinion) threw down her peny; and I put it in my pocket" (*Clarissa*, 6:391
[1214]). He sees "a pretty genteel lady" and becomes himself the profusion
of things, raising desires and anticipating exchange:

> What do you sell, Sir, said she, smiling; but a little surprised?
>
> Tapes, ribbands, silk-laces, pins, and needles; for I am a pedlar: Pow-
> der, patches, wash-balls, stockens, garters, snuffs, and pin-cushions—
> Don't we, Goody Smith?
>
> So in I gently drew her to the compter, running behind it myself,
> with an air of great diligence and obligingness. I have excellent gloves and
> wash-balls, Madam; Rappee, Scots, Portugal, and all sorts of snuff....
>
> Madam, said I, and stept from behind the compter, bowing over it,
> now I hope you will buy something for yourself. No-body shall use you
> better, nor sell you cheaper. (6:391–92 [1215])

But, like the "dagged females" in Swift's *Description of a City Shower* (1710),
Lovelace cheapens goods—and never buys. He doesn't exactly believe in fair
exchange or paying market price. He prefers the "air" of the spatial situation
rather than its substance.

The contrasting representations in *Clarissa* of shops and shop space capture prevailing attitudes. Addison and Steele, Defoe, and Adam Smith all
approve the retailer's part in the English economy, but there is an equal literature weighing in against the cheats and impositions of shopkeepers. Here,
however, I am interested not so much in the overall integrity of the English
shop as in certain facts about its existence and the articulation of its space
as it offered itself—its things—to its expanding clientele.

Most historians of the English shop and retailing practices have fastened
on the nineteenth century as the space of innovation and energy. But, as
Hoh-cheung Mui and Lorna Mui have argued, many of those innovations,
and the growth of "fixed-shop" retailing itself, were well established in the
eighteenth century: "Convention links a great increase in retail shops with
industrialization, either concomitant or trailing after, and with urbaniza-
tion. In England, at least, that increase appears to have taken place before

the industrial sector had achieved revolutionary changes and when the proportion of the population living in urban centres of 5,000 or more may have been no more than 20 percent" (44–45).[18] John Brewer notes that "by 1750 more people worked in industry, trade, commerce and services than in agriculture. England had already become a nation of shopkeepers" (xxvii). Swift's phrase (or Adam Smith's, or Samuel Adams's, or Napoleon's)[19] originated in contempt, but a contempt that rose from the proliferation of shops—an intricate network of shops, argue the Muis, and, among them, "not the least important was the small back-street shop" (3).[20]

The fixed shop really became a fixture by the early eighteenth century, replacing much of the trade carried out in street markets, through itinerant peddlers, or from the "bulk stalls"—a board acting as a shutter over a window that would unhinge down onto a set of legs to make a table, with a little "pent roof" overhead. In the sixteenth and seventeenth centuries, many more craftsmen began to use the front rooms or the ground floors of their houses as workshops and salesrooms; by the eighteenth century, many purposely built shops were incorporated into uniform, street-building facades. J. B. Jefferys has claimed that, by the mid-nineteenth century, "the developments in the techniques of selling took the form of transforming the fixed shops from units that existed solely to fulfill customers' wants to units designed and planned to attract customers and create wants."[21] But, in the 1725 *Complete English Tradesman*, Defoe noted:

> It is a modern custom, and wholly unknown to our ancestors, who yet understood trade, in proportion to the trade they carried on, as well as we do, to have tradesmen lay out two thirds of their fortune in fitting up their shops. By fitting up, I do not mean furnishing their shops with wares and goods to sell ... but in painting and gilding, fine shelves, shutters, boxes, glass-doors, sashes, and the like. ... It is true, that a fine shew of goods will bring customers; ... but that a fine shew of shelves and glass windows, should bring customers, that was never made a rule in trade 'till now.[22]

Defoe arrows in on early eighteenth-century urban spaces very much designed to attract customers and create wants, purely through the detailed attention to appearance, and the *appearance* of things through the medium of *appearing*, on fine shelves and in fine windows.

The image of the London shop front has delighted and upset both shoppers and social critics since the institution of the fixed shop, but it seems to be the shopwindow in particular that stirs up so many passions. The concept of literal transparency, of visual accessibility, seems to set up expectations that have been persistently—and, in odd ways, consistently—exceeded as well as defeated. As Lefebvre argues: "The illusion of transparency goes hand in hand with a view of space as innocent, as free of traps or secret spaces" (28). For what is a window? "Is it simply a void traversed by a line of sight? No. In any case, the question would remain: what line of sight—and whose? The fact is that the window is a non-object which cannot fail to become an object" (209). The shopwindow was its own most immediate and vivid advertising medium, playing on that transparency, that social creation of ingenuousness. We have already seen the increasing amount of narrative attention paid to the window in Behn, Defoe, and Richardson as the window becomes culturally prominent.

Glass windows came into shop vogue in the early eighteenth century, at first in small panes (Defoe says twelve by sixteen inches), made of Crown bullion glass—a bubble of glass spun until flattened, with the little knob remaining in the center.[23] Glass windows prompt displays; innovations in display prompt improvements in glass technology. Defoe notes a pastry shop in 1710 that boasted

> SASH windows, all of looking-glass plates, 12 inches by 16 inches in mea-
> sure; ALL the walls of the shop lin'd up with galley-tiles, and the Back-shop
> with galley-tiles in pannels, finely painted in forest-work and figures;
> Two large Peir looking-glasses and one chimney glass in the shop, and one
> very large Peir-glass seven foot high in the Back-shop; Two large branches
> of candlesticks, one in the shop, one in the back-room; THREE great glass
> lanthorns in the shop, and eight small ones; TWENTY five sconces against
> the wall, with a large pair of silver standing candlesticks in the back room,
> value 25£; ... Painting the ceiling, and gilding the lanthorns, the sashes,
> and the carv'd work, 55£. (*Tradesman* 314–15 [formatting altered])

Already the detail that Defoe accords here to display the art of display, although far more than he ever uses in his novels (Moll might well have noted the number and value of candlesticks in a shop, but she never provides such a visual interior sweep), is enough to describe the state of supply, the extent of furnishings, the art of commercial seduction. As Deidre Lynch argues: "The microcosm of teeming social detail that was exposed to view in the windows of the typical English print shop captured metonymically what many liked to cast as a peculiarly English world of abundance" (60). Print shop, pastry shop, millinery shop; and not just abundance, but mimetic possibility. By 1786, Sophie von la Roche, visiting London shops, exclaimed: "[B]ehind the great glass windows absolutely everything one can think of is neatly, attractively displayed.... There is a cunning device for showing women's materials. They hang down in folds behind the fine high windows so that the effect of this or that material, as it would be in a woman's dress, can be studied."[24]

The shopwindow and display shelves presented integrated possibilities; like the presentation of auction catalogs, discussed below, they suggest almost kernel narratives—*as it would be* if it were mine. In 1767, Josiah Wedgwood was also playing with the re-creating of space as mimetic suggestion, planning a display in his London warehouse and showroom of his wares set out as if for meals "in order to *do the needfull* with the Ladys in the neatest, genteelest, and best method. The same, or indeed a much greater variety of setts of Vases sho^d. decorate the Walls, & both these articles may, every few days be so alter'd, revers'd, & transform'd as to render the whole a new scene, Even to the same Company, every time they shall bring their friends to visit us."[25] Wedgwood made black teapots to show off white hands; his wares were distinctly designed for the wearers. He also specialized in turning social phenomena and events (Methodism, the slave trade, Keppel's acquittal, the peace with France) and persons (Garrick, Johnson, Priestley, Mrs. Siddons, Captain Cook, as well as Greeks, Romans, poets, painters, scientists, historians, actors, politicians) into *things*—images in ceramic (McKendrick, 422). Wedgwood presented his world of pottery for acquisition and representation, along with the *possibilities of change* in acquisition, of variety through rearrangement of the same objects. His showrooms dramatized different effects with the same things, the magic of decoration, alteration, reversal, transformation.

Besides arranging themselves seductively on shelves and in windows, the new things of the world showed up in new worlds of advertising, as parts of everyday *texts*. In the seventeenth century, shopkeepers relied primarily on their shops' signs and their local reputation within the more or less stable communities of London and beyond for advertising. But newspapers soon took over part of that office. The earliest known advertisement appeared in the *Weekly Relations of Newes* (23 August 1622), concerning two back editions of the *Newes*, but it appears "almost as an afterthought, and is of little significance."[26] In 1667, the *Mercury* advertised the possibility of advertising itself:

> **The Mercury Numb. 21.** From Thursday *August* 15. to Monday *August* 19.
> Publishing Advertisements of all sorts: as, Of Persons run away, lost or
>   spirited; Horses, or other Things lost or stoln, &c.

For the prevention of Escapes, and discouragement of Evil-doers.
And of Books to be sold; Lands or Houses to be Lett. And the Several Prices
    of both Foreign and English Commodities in *London*, and all other
    Places of Trade in all Parts of *England*, with all common Accidents.
And an Office for the publishing Merchants Goods, where to be sold in
    London or the Out-ports; where Purchasers and Purchases are to be
    found, &c. As also all manner of Servants and Services, Apprentices, or
    Apprenticeships, Seamen, Souldiers, Nurses dry or wet, &c. (*Mercury*,
    15–19 August 1667)

Peter Briggs counts the rise in advertisements in London's *Daily Advertiser*
from about 15 per issue in the early 1730s to 200 in the 1780s; C. Y. Ferdinand
tracks the country: the *Salisbury Journal*, for example, went from an annual
average of 296 advertisements in the 1730s to nearly 2,500 in the 1760s and
over 3,000 in 1770.[27]
    Sometimes advertisements simply listed things:

To be SOLD,
    This present Tuesday the 22d Instant, a House of Goods in Red Lion-
street, Holborn, over-against East-street. Consisting of China and Pictures, India Cabinets, and Tea Tables, Book Cases and Buerows, large
Peer Glasses, Sconces, and Chimney Glasses in Gold Frames, Carpets
and Tapestry, good Bedding, and all other Sorts of Furniture. The lowest
Price is fix'd on every Particular. (*Daily Post*, 22 December 1724)

Sometimes they described them:

Lost Ten Days since in and about Covent-Garden, a Black and White
Springing Spaniel Dog, with some small Spots, and Mottled in the Feet,
Seven Months Old, and commonly call'd of King Charles's Breed. Whoever will bring the same to Mr. Cornwall's at the Castle In Drury-Lane,
shall receive Ten Shillings Reward. (*Daily Post*, 22 December 1724)

Breen notes that an anonymous American pamphlet appropriated the formal
patterns of the contemporary journal advertisement to list the goods stolen
by a gang of thieves in Philadelphia in 1750, the list reading like any of Moll's
lists of her booty: "'two Silk Gowns, two other Gowns, three fine Aprons,
a Tea Chest, some Cambrick Hankerchiefs and other Things, which one
of his Companions carried to New York for sale.'"[28] Such a list, he argues,
becomes "a lexicon whose very complexity reveals a growing sensitivity

to the possibilities of an expanding consumer market—tea kettles, wearing linen, silver spoons, coats and hats, table cloths, iron boxes, a coffee mill, a pewter basin, a pair of stays, a calico gown, a necklace, a silk waistcoat, a scarlet long cloak, a camblet cloak, a blue cloth jacket, a pair of black silk stockings and two pairs of pumps" (253).

Jonathan Lamb notes of advertisements what I have elsewhere argued for auction catalogs: that lexicons supply narratives.[29] He reads a particular description of a missing snuffbox for its sensual appeal and narrative pull:

> Lost on the 1st Instant, a Snuff Box about the Bigness and Shape of a Mango, with a Stalk on the Lid, it being a West-India Bean of a reddish Colour, and like Shagreen; the End of the Stalk tipped with Silver, opens with a Hinge, and the Inside lines with Lead. Whoever brings it to Tom's Coffee-house Cornhill, shall have a guinea Reward, and no Questions asked; it being three times the Worth of the Silver. (*Daily Courant*, 10 January 1718)

Lamb explains: "In one sense this must be considered an aesthetic exercise, an account of the appeal of the thing's fashion that justifies its price of thirteen shillings and eightpence. In another sense it is like the beginning of a narrative—something about life in Jamaica or Barbados and a journey to London—except that the story speaks of the thing itself, while for his part the owner retires into necessary silence, bent merely upon evoking the motive power inherent in the snuffbox he hopes will cause it to return to him" (158). Simply the comparison of the snuffbox with a *mango* flatters the reader with exotic acquaintance and widens and connects the variant worlds of things. Briggs also argues for the rhetorical strategy of advertisements in their very "incompleteness," which encouraged "speculat[ion] about the doings, attitudes, needs, and habits of others—all made at least partly visible in the ads" (36); the connections, the background, the narrative would be supplied by the reader/consumer.

These detailed descriptions of objects and spaces in *The Complete English Tradesman* and the newspaper advertisements are still part of the *utility* landscape. They are textual praxes, in Hamon's sense—yet, in another sense, not quite. As Nevett argues, most advertisements featured, not commonplaces, but novelties: "Newspaper advertisements, however, were only concerned with a limited range of products. While some categories of consumer goods appear in the advertising columns ... their incidence tends to be fairly low. Common foods are largely absent, as are large brewers, while luxury products, such as tea and chocolate, seldom appear once their initial novelty value has worn off" (20). Mango-like snuffboxes and spotted-foot dogs stand out; already in a position of self-advertisement by their appearance on a page, in a space designed to advertise, they jostle for further notice with boldface letters, capitals, and their suggestiveness for fictional narrative:

> *The Daily Advertiser*, May 1780.
>
> MADNESS
>
> Whereas a crazy young lady, tall, fair complexioned, with blue eyes and light hair, ran into the Three Blue Balls, in ——street, on Thursday night, the 2d instant, and has been kept there since out of charity. She was dressed in a riding habit. Whoever she belongs to is desired to send after her immediately. She has been treated with the utmost care and tenderness. She talks much of some person by the name of Delvile.
>
> *N.B.* She had no money about her. (Burney, *Cecilia*, 901)

Burney's Cecilia is herself found an object of description in an advertising narrative that encloses its kernel story with its own emotional and structural meaning. The advertisement, like a novel, has a title, a heroine, a setting, a personal description, a foreshortened present, an all too obviously missing past, and an undisclosed future—presumably to be shaped by this advertisement.

The acts—or, rather, the pieces—of description were accumulating; the world of goods encroached from every direction. Pattern books were published and circulated by tradesmen, along with their trade cards, which offered better opportunities for illustration—the graphic description of visual representation (Nevett, 20). Anywhere the paper went, the consumer could be produced, could act, for, as Ferdinand points out, "the paper's carrier also undertook to deliver the dyed silks, the hats, the serial books, the tea, the medicines, and the silver watches it advertised, as well as the notices for distant services and leisure events, plus the transportation to get there" (398). The traveler John Byng (later fifth Viscount Torrington, 1742–1813) asserts: "I am ever greedy, when travelling, to read the county papers, and the account of sales, races, concerts and pastimes."[30] The images, the descriptions, the ideas of *things* multiplied around the eighteenth-century consumer, the eighteenth-century reader. The increasing acts of description among many different genres and in many different venues accumulated imaginative power, intensity, vividness, in a way that created a common landscape of things, a common possibility for their acquisition, and also the common possibility for difference and individuation in their arrangements and rearrangements.

Auctions and Catalogs

As James Ralph satirically asserts: "Just as I had resolv'd to shut up this my last ESSAY, upon our publick Diversions, I recollected, that I was about disobliging five Parts in Six of the numerous Inhabitants of this *Metropolis*, by neglecting to make honourable Mention of our *Publick Auctions*; which of late Years are become one of the principal Amusements of all Ranks, from the Duke and Dutchess to the Pick-pocket and Street-walker."[31] Auctions were yet another increasingly popular way to redistribute things, from duchesses to pickpockets or, as Horace Walpole says, from "Gideon the Jew" to "Blakiston the independent grocer." Although at the end of March 1763 Walpole hopes "now there will never be another auction, for I have not an inch of space or a farthing left" (Walpole to George Montagu, 25 March 1763, in *Correspondence*, 10:54), by the end of May he declares himself to be "the first man that ever went sixty miles to an auction" (Walpole to Montagu, 30 May 1763, in ibid., 10:76). He seems perhaps most fascinated with the inchoateness, the inherent disorganization, the implicit disintegration, of a collection of things coming from or going under the auctioneer's hammer:

> Lord Oxford's famous sale begins next Monday, where there is as much rubbish of another kind as in her Grace's history: feather bonnets presented by the Americans to Queen Elizabeth; elk's horns converted into caudle-cups; true copies of original pictures that never existed; presents to himself from the Royal Society etc. etc. particularly, forty volumes of prints of illustrious English personages; which collection is collected from frontispieces to godly books, Bibles and poems; headpieces and tailpieces to Waller's works; views of King Charles's sufferings; tops of ballads; particularly earthly crowns for heavenly ones, and streams of glory. There are few good pictures, for the miniatures are not to be sold, nor the manuscripts; the books not till next year. There are a few fine bronzes, and a very fine collection of English coins. (Walpole to Horace Mann, 3 March 1742 OS, in ibid., 17:357–58)

Forty years later, still avidly buying, he writes to Mann again: "Philosophers make systems, and we simpletons collections and we are as wise as they—wiser perhaps, for we know that in a few years our rarities will be dispersed at an auction; and they flatter themselves that their reveries will be immortal, which has happened to no system yet. A curiosity may rise in value; a system is exploded" (26 August 1785, in ibid., 25:604). "Who knows how soon my playthings may fall under Mr Christie's hammer!" (Walpole to Lady Ossory, 16 July 1793, in ibid., 34:184).

The relevant facts about the English auction include its primarily eighteenth-century genesis and its enormous eighteenth-century popularity; its public-spheredness, it being in most cases literally open to all members of the public, whether bidding or not; its arena of surprise competitiveness, in which the eventual ownership of an object is never predetermined by class or gender or wealth; and its inexhaustibly elastic boundaries of things to be sold. Auctions had appeared in England (as well as Holland and France) since the reign of Henry VII, and book auctions in particular were fully established and popular since the Restoration.[32] By the early eighteenth century, Henry Fielding, like James Ralph, was able to satirize the social phenomenon of the auction (Mr. Hen, the figure of the auctioneer Christopher Cock, sends up for popular bidding a "catalogue of curiosities" that features political honesty, patriotism, modesty, courage, wit, a clear conscience, and interest at court).[33] Peter Briggs shows how advertisements "brought large crowds to the estate sales of the prominent" outside London (39)—John Byng appends a number of Christie's sale advertisements throughout his journals. Within the capital, Samuel Baker in 1744 and James Christie in 1766 fully professionalized auctioneering, founding the formal auction houses of Sotheby's and Christie's, respectively.[34] Each had formal auction rooms in London where they conducted art and book auctions, but each also dealt—and, in the early years, primarily—in household auctions. Household auctions, most relevant here, have a separate history from book and art auctions, which almost by definition have a different and more limited clientele—either learned, wealthy, or both. The household auction, on the other hand, appealed to the ordinary shopper as well as to the connoisseur; acquisition could be as much for use as for display, and personal need, desire, or taste could count more than expertise in a purchase. And auctions could be simple entertainment—no purchase required. John Brewer includes attending an auction as part of the overall social performance in which audiences actively incorporated "culture" in a simultaneously public and personal way (69).

In "The English Auction," I focused primarily on the dismembering effects of household auctions and catalogs; here, I want to pick up on the thread of narrativized rhetoric in the catalogs and their relation to the ways in which auctions could present a fully imagined, fully filled domestic space—most obviously because the auction usually took place on the premises of the estate to be sold off, but also because it sometimes reassembled the

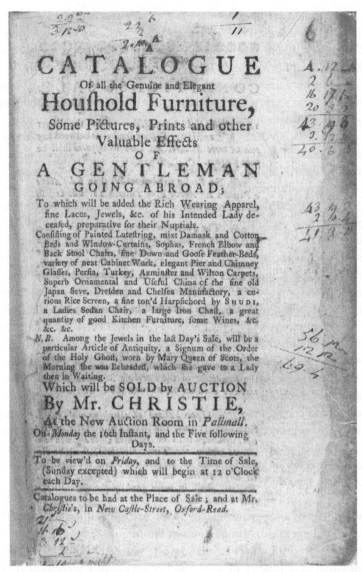

Figure 11. "Valuable Effects of a Gentleman Going Abroad," 16 March 1767. Reproduced by kind permission of Christie's; © Christie's Images Limited.

furniture in the auction house itself, rather like Wedgwood's suggestive breakfast services.

The title pages of Christie's auction catalogs, like the newspaper advertisements, structure their own narrative spaces of possibility in the combination of the implicit story of the former owner and the setting out of

his or her goods in a little interesting heap, while the interior of the catalog becomes a tour of the house, all visual details of color, texture, and
arrangement ready-made. The 16 March 1767 auction of the "Genuine and
Elegant Houshold Furniture . . . of a Gentleman Going Abroad," for example,
includes "the Rich Wearing Apparel, fine Laces, Jewels, &c. of his Intended
Lady deceased, preparative for their Nuptials" (fig. 11). Strictly speaking,
that is more than we need to know in order to view and purchase "Painted
Lutestring, mixt Damask and Cotton Beds and Window-Curtains, Sophas,
French Elbow and Back Stool Chairs, fine Down Goose Feather-Beds," or the
"Superb Ornamental and Useful China of the fine old Japan Seve, Dresden
and Chelsea Manufactory, a curious Rice Screen," or the "fine ton'd Harpsichord by SHUDI." But knowing that "she" died and that "he" can't seem to
bear the house without her casts shadows of a presumably pleasant vicarious
sadness over the beds, the dinners, the music of their unlived life together.
A gentleman "lately returned from India" has decided to sell his "Dressing
Boxes, *fine India paper*, Muslin, Soy, [and] fine Batavia Arrack" (30 November 1767). Some are quitting housekeeping, some are going abroad, some are
just dead. The condensed descriptive paragraph on the title pages that gathers the goods into a representative list is a collection of things from Tompion
watches, to tent wine, to anchovies and reads like the sporadic indexes of
the *Philosophical Transactions*, except insofar as it implies someone else's
whole. And, in some cases, that implicit whole of a house remains intact
and becomes visible on the title page:

A

PARTICULAR

OF A

compleat and convenient House and Garden, delightfully situated in the
Lane leading from *Waltham-Green* to *Hammersmith* Turnstile, at *North
End, Fulham.*

    Premises consist of two Parlours, Kitchen, Brew-house, and Wash-
house, three Bed-chambers, Servants [Rooms], and good Cellerage, with
Coach-House and Stabling for four Horses; together with about an Acre
and a Half of Pleasure and Kitchen Garden, with a neat Green-House, the
whole wall'd in; neatly laid out, and stock'd, and Plenty of good Water,
together with . . . Coppers, Ranges, Dressers, Shelves, Locks, . . . Grates,
&c. &c. as in the Schedule annexed to the Lease. The Premises are in
good Repair, and sold for a Term, whereof Eleven Years were unexpired
at Michaelmas last, at the Yearly Rent of Twenty-two Pounds. (22 July
1767)

The whole estate is drawn before us; the description itself is neatly laid out and well stocked with all the necessaries, in a logical order of desirability—location, size, amenities, condition, with some detail of inventory. This could be yours; you could step into the *whole thing*—the lease life of this gentlemanly estate. In some cases, that unexpired lease comes with even more additional benefits, as in the catalog for the "real, genuine, and Rich Household Furniture" of "Mrs. Thornton, At her House, the Fourth Door from the *Strand*, on the West Side of *Northumberland Street*," whose unexpired term of twelve years leaves a *"much improved Lease* of the said Premises, now in elegant and perfect Repair, and Number of valuable and requisite Fixtures" (15 November 1769).

As with a number of the newspaper advertisements, the auction catalog title pages were "deliberately intriguing by virtue of their incompleteness, and a pre-sociological and pre-electronic age had time to speculate about the doings, attitudes, needs, and habits of others—all made at least partly visible" (Briggs, 36). But, in a household auction and its catalog, even more pieces are present; that a narrative existed, first, in the arrangement and, now, in the dispersal of these things is obvious, even if its details are not. Opening the catalog and paging through it further connect the pieces; that little paragraphic jumble of goods on the front gets spread out in an orderly, visually connected way within the text. The catalog for the most part moves room by room, rather than by the kind of items to be sold or their value. As Albert Braunmuller points out, such an arrangement "precisely duplicates the inventory system in use . . . during the lifetime of the house's owners ('Has Lucy been lifting linen napkins?' 'How many hampers are there?' etc.)" and is also "the way the possessions were inventoried if . . . the possessions were to be seized legally or royally at the owner's death. People of quite modest means would know about this system (at least they'd know the post-mortem inventory, only the wealthiest would do knock-down room-by-room inventories under any other circumstances), and therefore lots of auction audiences would have the sense of death-and-transition from the very printed catalogue they read or held."[35] Braunmuller is speaking primarily about the period 1500–1640 but rightly believes that procedures didn't change much, except for the constituency of the bidders, who included the middle classes in knock-down room-by-room auctions—those middle classes who, in the satiric eyes of Walpole and Ralph, included streetwalkers and pickpockets, Jews and grocers. The stories of death- (or departure-) and-transition are embedded in the title pages of auction catalogs; the miniature narratives reassemble someone's past, and the goods for sale promise to reassemble in your future. All these household goods are, not just itemized, but visually described and sorted into semireal, semifictional settings within the catalog text.

See, for example, the auction catalog of the sale of the Earl of Chesterfield's estate in 1782 (figs. 12–13). While from late in the century, it is a representative sample of Christie's catalogs from the 1730s on, for both gentry and aristocracy. In a way, those and other auction companies' catalogs more or less took over the unified and preservationist formats of probate inventories, which became rare after the 1720s (Weatherill, 208), but which were essentially structured, as Braunmuller notes, like this example, in terms of a room-by-room inventory of movable goods. Room "No. II," for example, the "Field Bed Chamber," contains a "blue check throw over furniture," chairs with "yellow damask and blue check cases," a "night chair, with horse hair seat," a "square glass in a gilt frame," and much mahogany, walnut, and rosewood. In room "No. III," the "Housekeeper's Bed Room," we find yellow "harrateen furniture" and "festoon window curtains," plenty of chairs, some upholstered, that popular post-1750 item the couch, and the newly popular chest of drawers, replacing the simple chest of the seventeenth century. Room "No. IX," "Lord Chesterfield's Bed Chamber," boasts the escalated elegance of "fine chintz patterns," "elegant cornices lined and fringed" matching the green silk fringe of the bed, "superfine blankets," an "elegant pier glass" with "burnished gold frame," a Wilton carpet, and lots of "neat mahogany." Oh yes—he also has a "Closet adjoining," with "an excellent mahogany wardrobe with cedar sliders and drawers complete" and a "ditto corner cupboard" with a "carpet plan'd to the floor." And—oh no!—something (What? we wonder) happened to the "Venetian blind." Lord Chesterfield, not surprisingly, lived well, but his housekeeper didn't do so badly in terms of interior decoration. Important guest bedrooms are designated by color: "The Crimson Damask Bed Chamber" ("No. VII") might as well be Jane Eyre's Red Room, with crimson silk damask furniture and counterpane ditto, a white Manchester quilt, and plenty of mahogany, presumably highly polished. Objects from Italy, Japan, Scotland, China, France, and the worlds that England produced internally occupy the house, and all get careful attention, much more so than the "*Pictures*," for example: "A landscape, *Italian*"; "A famous drawing, after *Domenichino*, by *Blancher*." Pictures, in fact, even in art sales, rarely received detailed attention (although they tend to dominate the early guidebooks and journal accounts); the focus was on the things that make a house—the things that people collected and organized to define and present themselves. We will see in the next chapter (on domestic tourism) that pictures often get best billing in travelers' letters, and it is characteristic of book auction catalogs that,

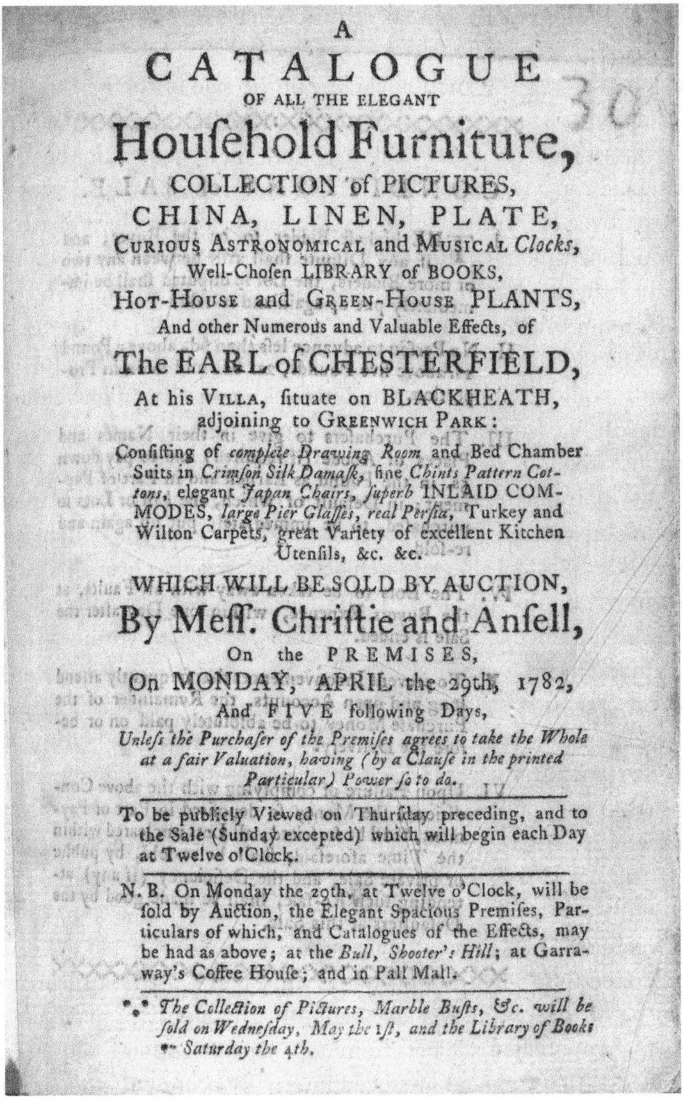

A

CATALOGUE

OF ALL THE ELEGANT

Houfehold Furniture,

COLLECTION of PICTURES,

CHINA, LINEN, PLATE,

CURIOUS ASTRONOMICAL and MUSICAL *Clocks*,

Well-Chofen LIBRARY of BOOKS,

HOT-HOUSE and GREEN-HOUSE PLANTS,

And other Numerous and Valuable Effects, of

The EARL of CHESTERFIELD,

At his VILLA, fituate on BLACKHEATH,
adjoining to GREENWICH PARK:

Confifting of *complete Drawing Room* and Bed Chamber
Suits in *Crimfon Silk Damafk*, fine *Chints Pattern Cot-
tons*, elegant *Japan Chairs*, fuperb INLAID COM-
MODES, *large Pier Glaffes*, *real Perfia*, Turkey and
Wilton Carpets, great Variety of excellent Kitchen
Utenfils, &c. &c.

WHICH WILL BE SOLD BY AUCTION,

By Meff. Chriftie and Anfell,

On the PREMISES,

On MONDAY, APRIL the 29th, 1782,

And FIVE following Days,

*Unlefs the Purchafer of the Premifes agrees to take the Whole
at a fair Valuation, having (by a Claufe in the printed
Particular) Power fo to do.*

To be publicly Viewed on Thurfday preceding, and to
the Sale (Sunday excepted) which will begin each Day
at Twelve o'Clock.

N. B. On Monday the 29th, at Twelve o'Clock, will be
fold by Auction, the Elegant Spacious Premifes, Particulars of which, and Catalogues of the Effects, may
be had as above; at the *Bull, Shooter's Hill*; at Garra-
way's Coffee Houfe; and in Pall Mall.

⁎ *The Collection of Pictures, Marble Bufts, &c. will be
fold on Wednefday, May the 1ft, and the Library of Books
⁎ Saturday the 4th.*

Figure 12. "A Catalogue of all the Elegant Household Furniture...of The Earl of Chesterfield," 29 April 1782. Reproduced by kind permission of Christie's; © Christie's Images Limited.

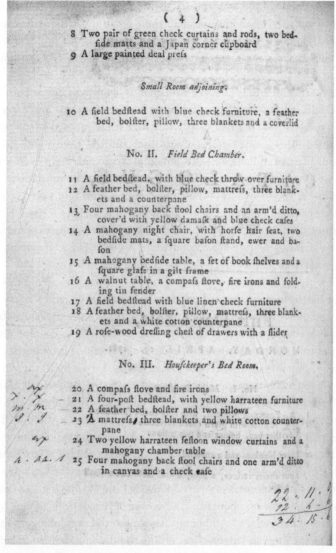

(4)

8 Two pair of green check curtains and rods, two bed-
side matts and a Japan corner cupboard
9 A large painted deal prefs

Small Room adjoining.

10 A field bedftead with blue check furniture, a feather
bed, bolfter, pillow, three blankets and a coverlid

No. II. *Field Bed Chamber.*

11 A field bedftead, with blue check throw-over furniture
12 A feather bed, bolfter, pillow, mattrefs, three blankets and a counterpane
13 Four mahogany back ftool chairs and an arm'd ditto,
cover'd with yellow damafk and blue check cafes
14 A mahogany night chair, with horfe hair feat, two
bedfide mats, a fquare bafon ftand, ewer and bafon
15 A mahogany bedfide table, a fet of book fhelves and a
fquare glafs in a gilt frame
16 A walnut table, a compafs ftove, fire irons and fold-
ing tin fender
17 A field bedftead with blue linen check furniture
18 A feather bed, bolfter, pillow, mattrefs, three blankets and a white cotton counterpane
19 A rofe-wood drefling cheft of drawers with a flider

No. III. *Houfekeeper's Bed Room.*

20 A compafs ftove and fire irons
21 A four-poft bedftead, with yellow harrateen furniture
22 A feather bed, bolfter and two pillows
23 A mattrefs, three blankets and white cotton counterpane
24 Two yellow harrateen feftoon window curtains and a
mahogany chamber table
25 Four mahogany back ftool chairs and one arm'd ditto
in canvas and a check cafe

Figure 13. "No. II. *Field Bed Chamber*," from "A Catalogue of all the Elegant Household Furniture...of The Earl of Chesterfield," 29 April 1782. Reproduced by kind
permission of Christie's; © Christie's Images Limited.

while they may have interesting introductory prefaces, "as bibliographical catalogues they have," as John Lawler says, "no value—a single line
in most instances sufficing for description."[36] The kind of visual detail that
would come to occupy domestic novels emerges most fully in the auction
catalog.

Auction catalogs and auctioneers also seem to have done something in the way of gentrifying themselves and their position. Although, according to one rival, James Christie came from modest origins, his professional trajectory with its august connections landed him in the life of a gentleman:

> Philips said Christie is Son to a Scotsman & woman—He was born in Round St. Strand,—His Father a feather bed beater—He is abt. 63 or 4 years old.—Is now married to 4th wife.—First He married [blank] she deformed—He expected a fortune was disappointed—lived 3 yrs.—2d. a servant married in Pallmall had 8 children—3d. [blank]—4th. widow of Mr. Urquhart wine merct. of Adelphi—eldest Son very amiable—good scholar—music—languages—drawing—Commissions one year £16000 another £11000, another more than 10,000—ought to have been enormously rich—domestic—but kept three houses—besides watering place—still expenditure not accounted for—said to game—no proofs.— very good head for scheming—but wants education.[37]

Half the battle to gentility was getting your son or daughter music, languages, and drawing as well as acquiring those three houses (besides the watering place) and the society of the well-placed and well-to-do. One also has to talk the talk. Ralph's satire *The Touch-Stone* (1728) at least noted the aspirations to gentility of Christopher Cock: "He is allow'd by all the World, to be a very Clever Gentleman in his Business, and manages his little Hammer as much to the Purpose as any Instrument can possibly attain to: His Flourishes are genteel, yet significant; his Manner of Address easy and well-bred, but intrepid; his Phrases manly without Rudeness, and expressive without Obscurity, or Circumlocution. Not *Tully* himself could fill a *Rostrum* with more Grace, or Eloquence" (233–34). A contemporary of Christie's described that "successful disposer of property of every kind" as having "an easy and gentleman-like flow of eloquence," a "power of persuasion," and a "gentle refinement of manners."[38] And James Boswell noted that Johnson's making of an era in the English language (according to Edmond Malone) meant that "everybody wrote in a higher style now, even Christie in advertisements."[39] (Christie could name among his friends most of Johnson's circle.) But, while Johnson may have gentrified the language of a Christie, Christie, I argue, gentrified the language of description, bringing the visual detail of interior space visibly and connectedly into textual space.

The sense of visual connectedness, of a textual praxis becoming a textual aesthetic, will emerge in the next chapter's discussion of *Sir Charles*

Grandison in terms of the domestication and gentrification of description, but worth emphasizing here is the full dimensional permeation of auctions into literary texts—as fragmenting and disruptive and tragic as well as cumulative and enabling and reconfiguring. Miss Larolles trips toward Cecilia in Burney's novel, exclaiming: "So you would not go to the auction? Well, you had a prodigious loss, I assure you. All the wardrobe was sold, and all Lady Belgrade's trinkets. I never saw such a collection of sweet things in my life. I was ready to cry that I could not bid for half an hundred of them. I declare I was kept in an agony the whole morning. I would not but have been there for the world. Poor Lady Belgrade! you really can't conceive how I was shocked for her. All her beautiful things sold for almost nothing" (*Cecilia*, 44–45). Miss Larolles subsumes the real loss, the real agony of Lady Belgrade's real story (as well as, presumably, the real delight of bidders grabbing at the "collection of sweet things" for "almost nothing") into her own tragedy of terminally incomplete acquisition; Burney, like Fielding, Ralph, and half the time Walpole, exposes—to use an auctioneer's term—the disintegrating and dismembering effects, in both senses, of the auction. The very table of contents of *Cecilia* (a nineteenth-century editor's compilation of Burney's chapter headings)[40] marks a lengthy list of separated, titled *things*—adventures, events, emotions, characterizations, social dealings, tragedies, comedies. It is a list of *humanized objects* made disparate as narrative tags, very much in contrast to Fielding's mininarratives in the chapter headings of *Tom Jones*. The following example from volume 1 of *Cecilia* is structurally repeated in volumes 2–5 (the whole comprising ten books):

VOLUME I
Book I

I   A Journey
II   An Argument
III An Arrival
IV   A Sketch of High Life
V   An Assembly
VI   A Breakfast
VII A Project
VIII An Opera Rehearsal
IX   A Supplication
X   A Provocation
XI   A Narration

Book II

The table of contents ends with: "X. A Termination."

One of Burney's contemporary critics, Choderlos de Laclos, author of *Les liaisons dangereuses* (1782), noted in a 1784 critique of *Cecilia* that Burney followed the English rather than the French novelistic method of introducing and describing characters before any action occurs;[41] but, in the chapter headings at least, Burney characterizes events, actions, emotions, to *encapsulate* and, therefore, anticipate action. Her breakdown of enormous and complicated content into simple nouns is one of many rhetorical ways of characterizing the enormous proliferation of things up for grabs, of possibilities for rearrangement, for narrativization. Even while the 1770 novel by Mrs. A. Woodfin, *The Auction: A Modern Novel*, has precisely two small, unrelated auction scenes that have no apparent bearing on plot or character, it is nonetheless full of severed toes, amputated legs, poked-out eyes, licked blood, and disjointed stories—all sorts of dispersions of personal property, all sorts of rearrangements of personal habitations.[42]

The idea of estates for sale, of household goods up for grabs to the highest or luckiest bidder, is part of a culture that was absorbing and performing its culture in front of itself, for flagrantly social and competitive reasons, or for (perhaps in many cases) personal and self-defining ones. The auctions, the shops, and the advertisements made a profusion of things imaginatively as well as actually available to buyers, readers, and the makers of homes. Catalogs and showrooms, descriptions and shopwindows, displayed both the sheer quantity of "parts" and their various promises of "wholes." Choice generated individuality and difference, and differences would ask to be compared and described.

CHAPTER SEVEN

Arranging Things

She looked about her with due consideration, and found almost everything in his favour, a park, a real park five miles round, a spacious modern-
built house, so well placed and well screened as to deserve to be in any
collection of engravings of gentlemen's seats in the kingdom, and wanting only to be completely new furnished.
—*Jane Austen*, Mansfield Park *(1814)*

Mary Crawford, eyeing Tom Bertram's prospects (before she finds herself falling for the younger brother), simply wants what everyone
these days is wanting: to completely new furnish a house. The auction catalogs, newspaper advertisements, and shopwindows were matched in popularity and availability by the design catalogs of Batty Langley, William Kent,
Thomas Chippendale, Josiah Wedgwood, and the brothers Adam, which outlined in detail the fine art of combining furniture, textiles, and ornaments to
create an individualized yet fashionable interior, a space for the eye to travel
in delight. And that eye traveled both metaphorically and literally from room
to room, county to county, as the great houses began opening themselves up
with a will for the new middle-class tourist, detailed guidebook in hand. And,
as tourists increasingly explored and felt free to comment on other people's
houses, the interest in the construction of interiors increased throughout
the country and across class lines. The mass production of pottery, fabrics,
carpets, and furniture paradoxically made interiors more individuated, at
least in the quantity and, therefore, the possible patterns of arrangements of
their things. With increasing varieties of interiors, the cultural storehouse of
visual expectation diminished, and detailed description in print supplied its
place. The textual praxis of the house guide combined with published travel
accounts to bring description even more into cultural consciousness, even

more into public demand, even more into literary space. The arranging of things and the touring of arrangements brought description further toward gentrification.

Carole Fabricant has defined Fanny Price as the ideal visitor from the landowner's point of view (unlike Mary Crawford). Fanny could visit Sotherton and eagerly view its rooms, prospects, and treasures "without making any material claim upon it, the acquisitiveness suggested by the description taking place on an aesthetic and metaphorical level only" (254). She is the good tourist, who sees and appreciates and reaffirms the value of the whole. But perhaps that in part explains why Austen's novels are more classical in description than other contemporary authors' when it comes to interiors. Her novels are, in that sense, closer to Defoe's or Fielding's than to Radcliffe's; we know about Fanny's geraniums and books in the East room and the cramped, stifling, chaotic dimness of the Portsmouth house as well as (and only as well as) we know of Moll's pewter tankards and Crusoe's raisins. Austen contents her heroines with the minimal tags.

But sometimes she looks in the other available direction, where details were beginning to be spelled out. When Fanny tours Sotherton, for example, she naturally hopes much from the chapel: "They entered. Fanny's imagination had prepared her for something grander than a mere, spacious, oblong room, fitted up for the purpose of devotion—with nothing more striking or more solemn than the profusion of mahogany, and the crimson velvet cushions appearing over the ledge of the family gallery above." Edmund reassures her, pointing out the newness of the building, but Fanny was looking for Elizabethan details; the mahogany and velvet here are, disappointingly, from James II's time. The few details locate the space in a time, and Fanny displays the cultural consciousness of the late eighteenth and early nineteenth centuries in the act of looking for those historical details of furniture and fabric. But, for the most part, even the toured Sotherton remains abstractly intact, with "many more rooms than could be supposed to be of any other use than to contribute to the window tax, and find employment for housemaids."[1] If a viewer's acquisitiveness lies in detail, then Fanny (like Austen) does, indeed, leave the estate intact—on its own and in her nonexistent desires.

But not so the many contemporary tourists, such as Mary Delany and John Byng, who relished both the tour of a house and the critical review afterward. Other people's choices, other people's constructions, come under sharp scrutiny. Fabricant argues that the rhetoric of tour guides created the tourist every bit as much as the tourist created the market for detailed descriptions of great houses, "helping to shape...aesthetic judgments" as well as to reinforce the ideology of a landowning hierarchy (260). Part of that aesthetic judgment included the expanded range of possibilities for domestic interiors and the textual articulation of their detail, as the middle and upper classes began entering the great houses to examine them (sometimes in a two- to three-hour visit), the guidebooks in their hands supplying a critical vocabulary. But some tourists went far beyond the tour guide in the imaginativeness and originality of their descriptions and judgments— not surprisingly, since the house guides were a sort of limping prose version of the country-house poem, written to point out and celebrate the taste and glory of the owner. The tourist was always free to disagree with the preformatted description of the house. As with the auctions, where the buyer, defined by an instance of purchase rather than by a predetermination of class or wealth, picked up pieces from dismantled estates and reassembled them along his or her own private lines, so with the house tours, the tourist in viewing and judging managing to exhibit as much freedom from a particular ideological framework as any subservience to it. "I would have arranged things differently" is a perfectly possible and, indeed, very common bit of judgmental rebellion.

The auction catalog and the house guide combine in Samuel Richardson's *Sir Charles Grandison* (1753–54) to bring interior description right into the front parlor for tea. Harriet Byron employs the current practical rhetorics to fill her newly acquired Grandison Hall with *coordinated* descriptions of matching fabrics and furniture, not only to define specific interior spaces, but also to redefine herself in a newly visualized space. Unlike Clarissa, who is defined through negative space—where she is not and others are—Harriet finds herself anew among the more richly detailed spaces of Grandison Hall. Clarissa intuits, Harriet describes; Clarissa retreats, Harriet occupies. Richardson domesticates the guidebook and the auction catalog, bringing more textual praxes of description deeper into novelistic space.

Furniture and Arrangements

All sorts of Windsor Garden Chairs of all sizes, painted Green, to be sold at John Brown's at the Three Chairs and Walnut-Tree in St. Paul's Churchyard near the School. (1730)
—*Moss Harris and Sons*, The English Chair *(1937)*

Furniture was going retail, along with so much else. There were, of course, many furnituremakers with workshops and a crew of craftsmen, but the number of furniture *shops* increased, with retailers buying and reselling but not themselves making the objects. And furniture began stocking rooms in a noticeable way. Lisa Jardine notes that "there were comparatively few items of furniture even in an affluent Renaissance home—chests for storage, tables and a few chairs and settles."[2] The objects might well be decorated, even lavishly, particularly the family bed, but, for most people through the seventeenth century, items of furniture would be few, heavy, permanent, and functionally significant. Occasionally, the "found object"—such as "the vertebra of a whale used as a stool or the log of wood which traditionally provided a seat on one side of the central or 'roundabout hearths'"—would inhabit a smaller house, but things like beds, "dishboards" (large cupboards for displaying pewter plate), chests, and even chairs would, generally, be massive in size or weight.[3] Until the eighteenth century, basic shapes, basic functions, and basic materials varied little (although local woods and local talent frequently combined to produce local beauty).[4] The Windsor chair in particular (deriving its name from, presumably, the Windsor area and shipped to London via the Thames in great numbers) has remained popular from the early eighteenth century to the present for its unusual comfort (sans upholstery): its lightness and curves offering a happy change from the standard rectilinear rigidities of basic carpenter-made chairs (Ayres, 171–74). The chair retained its aura of special seating—raised from the floor or hearth—into the seventeenth century (Ayres, 175) and, as Daniel Roche argues, "between the sixteenth century and the eighteenth, conquer[ed] the social space" (173). (We will see in chapter 8 how Emily St. Aubert, in her delicate, ladylike way, very firmly comes to conquer her father's chair.)

Thomas Chippendale (1718–79) published *The Gentleman and Cabinet-Maker's Director* in 1754 and was the first Englishman to have an entire furniture style named after him. He brought English furnituremaking to the exquisite levels of the French *ébénistes*, who, until the French Revolution, were regarded as Europe's finest craftsmen. His was the first published pattern book devoted to the design of every conceivable piece of domestic furniture, from writing tables to shaving tables, from bookcases to candlestick holders, from enormous beds to fire screens, from sofas to coffins—but, perhaps most famously, chairs (fig. 14). The *Director*, as its title implies, made designs adaptable to a range of consumer budgets. Chippendale generally recommended mahogany—a newly popular and recently more widely available import from the West Indies (the heavy duty on colonial wood having been abolished in 1721), replacing French walnut, on which an embargo was imposed in 1720 (Burton, 122)—but one could substitute deal (a kind of

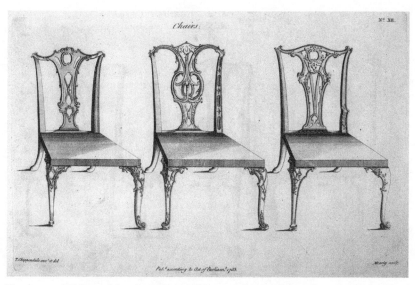

Figure 14. "Chippendale chairs," in Thomas Chippendale, *The Gentleman and Cabinet-Maker's Director* (1754). Courtesy of the Newberry Library, Chicago.

pine) and paint or lacquer it, using more or less ornamentation as taste and pocketbook directed. The possibilities for individual taste were built into the pattern-book designs; the notion of *difference* came paradoxically from *patterns*—much as Wedgwood's displays of his dishware in his showrooms suggested alternatives from rearrangement.

Chippendale set up his workshop in St. Martin's Lane in London in 1749 and, by 1755, had as many as twenty-two workmen in his shop. In 1760, he was elected a member of the Royal Society of Arts. He visited France in 1768 and imported unfinished French furniture. He thus began to shape English interiors over the second half of the eighteenth century, first in the wake of William Kent, and then in tandem with Robert Adam. The aristocracy and gentry would come to London for the season and ship his furniture back to their estates. Europe and the colonies were also excellent customers—some of the famous Philadelphia cabinetmakers came from Chippendale's shop. Chippendale introduced the rococo (what he called the "Modern Taste"), characterized by delicate, asymmetrical scrolls; the gothic (influenced by Horace Walpole's Strawberry Hill; fig. 15); and the popular "Chinese" patterns based both on imported designs and on a sort of escapist interpretation of those designs. As Burton points out: "'Chinese Chippendale' is neither Chinese nor [Chippendale's] invention, nor is 'Chippendale Gothic'. But what Chippendale *did* do was to English the new styles" (130).

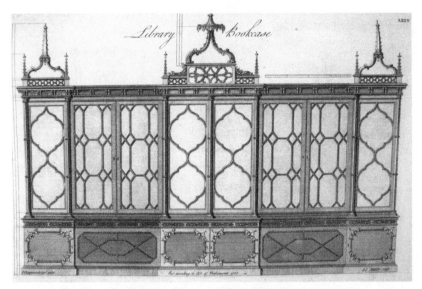

Figure 15. "A Gothic Library Bookcase," in Thomas Chippendale, *The Gentleman and Cabinet-Maker's Director* (1754). Courtesy of the Newberry Library, Chicago.

But it was William Kent (1684?–1748) who first regarded furniture "as an essential part of interior decoration," who believed that "each room should be a separate individual work of art," and without whom, according to Burton, "the English interior might have remained an uncoordinated hodge-podge" (110–11). As in the auction catalogs, fabrics and colors and their variously particular coordinations began to assume prominence in guide-books' and tourists' notice. In her first visit to Houghton Hall in 1756, Caroline Lybbe Powys (1756–1808), then Caroline Girle, was entranced by Kent's rooms, which she found "very superb": "[T]he cornishes and mouldings of all the apartments being gilt, it makes the whole what I call magnificently glaringly, more especially as the rooms are, instead of white, painted dark green olive." She notes, however, in the spirit of arranging things, that "this most likely will be soon altered."[5]

Alongside Kent and his systematic attention to interior detail and coor-dination for the gentry and aristocracy was Batty Langley (1696–1751), who published a number of popular trade books for builders and their clients out-lining an elementary spatial theory. Langley's father was a gardener in Twick-enham, and Batty himself started out as a landscape gardener, one of his first books being *New Principles of Gardening* in 1728. He and his brother Thomas, an engraver, opened up a school of architectural drawing in Soho, in London, for young carpenters and workmen in the various building trades.

But he made his mark in architectural writing with such titles as *Practical Geometry* (1726), *The Builder's Chest-Book* (1727), *The Sure Guide to Builders* (1729), *The Young Builder's Rudiments* (1730), *The Builder's Jewel* (1741), and *The City and Country Builder's and Workman's Treasury of Designs* (1740). Architecture itself was acquiring a new popular appeal, with a number of architectural treatises appearing, not only for builders, but also for the layperson. Renaissance architects such as Andrea Palladio (1508–80) and classical architects such as Vitruvius Pollio (fl. 40 BC) were enthusiastically translated and architecturally revived. Langley's work clarifies for the beginner the importance of proportion in relation to human habitation and gesture. He underscores, for example, the rule that one should always be able to end a flight up or down the staircase with the same foot that began it. Gesture as symmetry is part of properly—and comfortably—inhabiting a house. The later descriptions of the various parts of houses give the reader a very-much-from-the-inside tour of what to visually and spatially understand from the references to galleries, and halls, and chambers in eighteenth-century novels and poetry.

Langley directs attention to space, light, symmetry, and rhythm in dialogues—approaching narrativity—between apprentice and master:

Of GALLERIES.

M. *What Proportion should the length of a Gallery have to its breadth?*

P. Not less than five times its breadth, nor more than eight.

M. *What height ought Galleries to have?*

P. Their height ought to be equal to their breadth.

M. *What is the best Aspect for Galleries?*

P. The North, because its light is best for Paintings, &c. which they are generally adorn'd with.

M. *Is it not possible to make Galleries too narrow or too wide?*

P. Yes, and therefore their breadth should never be less than sixteen Feet, nor to exceed twenty four feet....

Of CHAMBERS.

M. *What Situation is best for Chambers of Delight?*

P. The *East*, provided that any other hath not a better Prospect....

Of STAIR-CASES.

Great care ought to be taken in the placing of the Stair-Case of any Building, but commonly the Stairs are placed in the Angle, Wing or middle of the Front....

... The Landing of Stairs, should be large and spacious for the convenient Entrance into the Rooms: In a word, Stair-Cases, should be spacious,
light, and easy in ascent....

In making of Stair-Cases this Rule should be observed, that the number of Steps at every Landing be odd, and not even, for thereby, when you
begin to ascent with your right Foot first (as all Persons generally do) you
will end with the same Foot also.[6]

Galleries for paintings (the focal point of country-house guides), chambers for
delight, staircases for pedestrian symmetry—Langley articulated the spaces
(the sizes, the dimensions, the locations, the views, the inhabiting gestures)
of the eighteenth-century house with the same pattern-book economy as
Wedgwood and Chippendale, one that supplied standards yet accommodated
difference. These are the spaces outlined for a reading public that would be
inhabited—with spatial consciousness—first by consumers/readers and then
by the characters they read about.

Where Kent established the symmetry and proportion of rooms, Robert
Adam later in the century introduced diversity. Round, square, rectangu-
lar, divided, curved—each room in the house might be differently shaped.
Colors were lightened, lines more delicate, and above all (for my purposes):
"*No detail was too small* for Mr Adam, everything, right down to door furniture, comes under his designing eye" (Burton, 134; emphasis added). He
and his brother James in fact expressed their mission to bring about "a kind
of revolution in the whole system of this useful and elegant art" of domestic interior architecture.[7] Adam felt responsible for interiors and considered
that too many architects left the owners of their houses with structures
alone. Adam designed and advised on furniture of all sorts—harpsichord
cases, sedan chairs, carpets, embroidery, en suite coordination. Mary Delany
(née Granville, then Pendarves; 1700–88) very much approved of Adam's alterations of Luton, the home of Lord and Lady Bute, when she visited in
September 1774:

The furniture well suited to all. The beds, damask and rich sattin, green,
blue and crimson; mine was white sattin. The rooms hung with plain
paper, suited to ye colour of ye beds, except mine which was pea-green,
and so is the whole appartment below stairs. The curtains, chairs and
sophas are all plain sattin. Every room filled with pictures; many capital
ones.... The chimney pieces in *good taste*; no extravagance of fancy;
indeed throughout the whole house that is avoided. Fine frames to the

pictures but very little guilding besides, and the cielings elegant and not loaded with ornament.[8]

Horace Walpole was less enamored: "From Kent's mahogany we are dwindled to Adam's filigree. Grandeur and simplicity are not yet in fashion" (Walpole to William Mason, 29 July 1773, in Walpole, *Correspondence*, 28:102). Like Byng, some of whose complaints about modern fashion are recorded below, Walpole preferred the sturdiness of the old—although he was one of the most prominent configurers of the new.

In general, Adam's designs as well as colors were lighter, and, in furniture, that meant *mobility*. Says Daniel Roche: "In furniture are embodied ways of ordering things assembled, histories marked by the ordinariness of everyday actions, the need for privacy, the valorisation of what is contained by what contains it" (170). What happens to social space, to textual space, when it can easily be reconfigured? What happens to the space of individual gesture? Burton remarks that, although the introduction of oil floorcloths meant a nuisance for cleaning (all the furniture had to be removed so that the cloths could be polished with milk and turned), at least "furniture had by now become a good deal lighter—although more of it was used than in the days of George I and II—and was considerably easier to move, to rearrange or regroup as the owner wished" (136). Even by the owner himself. Adam Smith declares: "When a person comes into his chamber, and finds the chairs all standing in the middle of the room, he is angry with his servant, and rather than see them continue in that disorder, perhaps takes the trouble himself to set them all in their places with their backs to the wall."[9] John Byng, an indefatigable traveler and inveterate lover of all things old, does not approve the change. At Raby Castle, not only are the windows "modernly glazed" and the floors made of deal, but, in the drawing room, "instead of large chairs rolling upon casters there is nothing to be seen but little light French chairs," and "French linen festoonings" replaced the now-traditional Kent-style curtains of rich velvet or damask. Tables were no longer "substantial and immovable" but "little" and "skuttling"—too easily moved around to different strategic positions (3:156–57). In *Mansfield Park*, Tom Bertram very mistakenly insists that to rearrange his father's house—to move a bookcase or a pianoforte—is no matter of moment ("absolute nonsense," in fact) (152). And, by 1864, we have Boffin's Bower in Dickens's *Our Mutual Friend*, with his'n'her sides of the room, neatly divided down the middle: "There was a flowery carpet on the floor; but, instead of reaching to the fireside, its glowing vegetation stopped short at Mrs. Boffin's footstool, and gave place to a region of sand and sawdust."[10] As with Wedgwood's interchangeable, mix-and-match china services, the domestic interior space became a sort of palette, offering more elasticity of self-expression and an invitation to design—and, to some, a threat to order and stability.

Surfaces themselves became part of the design. Glass of all sorts created and enhanced the emphasis on surface. Windows, for example, had low architectural priority in medieval houses; glazed windows in Tudor England were primarily found in aristocratic and wealthy houses and even in the seventeenth century were the province of the well-to-do (Ayres, 69–74). The combination of sashes with glazing promoted larger windows afforded greater light, air, prestige, increasing their aesthetic and social prominence— as in the shopwindows. The sash window that Pamela so readily hops out of became a signature feature of gentry housing, pointing to high ceilings (the windows were taller than they were wide); high ceilings, like the empty space on a page of poetry, represented a luxury of space ostentatiously unoccupied. Looking glasses reflected other kinds of images, including a sort of gentrification. John Crowley notes that, in 1675, fewer than 10 percent of English households outside London (30 percent in London) appeared to have looking glasses; "fifty years later they were the most frequently listed item of furnishing besides beds, chairs, and tables" (122). He argues that the placement of mirrors was designed more for public display than for personal grooming: "[T]he conjunction of mirrors and candlelight accorded with a desirability for sheen and luster in interior decoration, whether in paintings, metals, fabrics, or furniture finish" (129). The emphasis on surface as itself a creator of space that Defoe tracked in the shops of the 1720s was imported into the domestic interior as well. Mirrors amplify space, light, patterns, things; one seems to have even more of everything. And, while such a display seems to demonstrate most obviously *ostentation*, with an admiring audience presumably essential to its effect, surely the compellingly strange world that Alice found through the looking glass was no less strangely compelling for someone with any imagination at all alone in his rooms in the eighteenth century. Reflection as well as arrangement produced new planes of habitation.

Attention to color and arrangement increasingly occupies more social and textual space throughout the century. Mary Delany's early correspondence and autobiography spend little time describing interiors; her early attention focuses more on gardens. But, once she makes a trip to Ireland, the details of place take up increasingly more space throughout her long years of observing and recording. An early example of her new detail, from a trip to Dublin, describes the house of the bishop of Killala:

Mrs. Clayton [the bishop's wife] opened her apartment and admitted all
her acquaintance. I will describe to you how they are disposed and furnished. First there is a very good hall well filled with servants, then a
room of eighteen foot square, wainscoted with oak, the panels all carved,
and the doors and chimney finished with very fine high carving, the
ceiling stucco, the window-curtains and chairs yellow Genoa damask,
portraits and landscapes, very well done, round the room, marble tables
between the windows, and looking-glasses with gilt frames. The next
room is twenty-eight foot long and twenty-two broad, and is as finely
adorned as damask, pictures, and busts can make it, besides the floor being entirely covered with the finest Persian carpet that ever was seen. The
bedchamber is large and handsome, all furnished with the same damask.
(1:305 [21 October 1731])

She is very taken with the yellow Genoa damask. As with the auction catalogs, color and fabric could signal as much to a purchaser/reader as the size
and kind of furniture.

Color connects. Kent's windows were thematically linked to doors with
matching looped velvets; and Caroline Lybbe Powys was impressed with
the fact that his rooms at Houghton were, "instead of white, painted dark
green olive" (6). Color also resonates socially, historically. Jane Schneider has
shown how the dominant blacks and whites of Elizabeth's court (and "the
'sad,' dark colors of prestigious Londoners during her reign") signaled, not
only support for the queen (black as opposed to the vivid colors of European
courts, white for the queen's virgin purity), but also "England's determi-
nation to hold its own in the lively textile rivalries of the time." Scarlets
and crimsons were the ceremonial color, and, according to a royal statute
of 1552, "true," rather than false and deceiving. Other royally validated colors included "a host of non-descript shades including brown-blue, orange-
tawny, russet, marble, sheep's color, lion's color, motley or iron gray, something called 'new sad color' and something called 'puke.'" Other specifically
English-made colors included "rat's color," "horseflesh," "pease-porridge
tawny," and "gooseturd."[11] Homemade magnificence lay more in shape than
in color until the seventeenth century, when the Puritans, of course, rejected color itself. But trade and colonization brought in more possibilities
for dyes (cochineal, brazilwood, indigo), and immigrants from Flanders, Germany, Portugal, and Huguenot France taught the English dyers and weavers
what to do with them. As Italians began to dress more in black, the English then played increasingly with color and the lighter "new draperies."
Small wonder that the peacock colors of home and the rich yellow damask

of Genoa should both win out over "gooseturd" and "puke" over the next century.

All this attention to surface and interior detail could not, of course, miss the obvious social criticism of shallowness, appearance, image, illusion, vanity. But it is interesting to watch how even the concern over detail ushers in more detail. In Samuel Johnson's *Rambler*, no. 200 (15 February 1752), Asper complains to Mr. Rambler of the unpleasant effects that Prospero's rise to fortune have had on his personality and their friendship. On arriving for an invited visit, Asper is kept waiting at the door, then brought upstairs by the footman, who shows him "the staircase carefully secured by mats from the pollution of my feet." He is taken to a back room:

> On the floor where we sat, lay a carpet covered with a cloth, of which Prospero ordered his servant to lift up a corner, that I might contemplate the brightness of the colours, and the elegance of the texture, and asked me whether I had ever seen anything so fine before? I did not gratify his folly with any outcries of admiration, but coldly bade the footman let down the cloth.
>
> We then sat down and I began to hope that pride was glutted with persecution, when Prospero desired that I would give the servant leave to adjust the cover of my chair, which was slipt a little aside to show the damask; he informed me that he had bespoke ordinary chairs for common use, but had been disappointed by his tradesman. I put the chair aside with my foot, and drew another so hastily that I was entreated not to rumple the carpet. (5:279)

Then follows a display of tea and china. Mr. Rambler quotes Pythagoras and suggests that Prospero should not be hated for "little faults": "[S]urely, he, upon whom nothing worse can be charged, than that he mats his stairs, and covers his carpet, and sets out his finery to show before those whom he does not admit to use it, has yet committed nothing that should exclude him from common degrees of kindness" (5:281). Color, fabric, texture, and light, kickable chairs were everywhere, defining elegance or ostentation, individuality or vanity—and the delight in the manufacturable beauty of everyday space. Paul McGlynn notes that, throughout the *Rambler* and *Idler* essays, "the details are often so particular and exact that one wishes Johnson had been more receptive to the novel as it was then developing into a mimetic narrative form."[12] But Johnson's attention to contemporary interior detail can equally be read as part of the cultural investment in such spaces that spilled back into and between prose narratives of all sorts, newly

charging their spaces. In Virginia Woolf's words, the prose attention to prosaic things—Crusoe's earthenware pot—manifested the ability "to make
common actions dignified and common objects beautiful" ("*Robinson
Crusoe*," 57).

Domestic Tours

*A Short Account of the Principal Seats and Gardens in and about Rich-
mond and Kew.* Printed and Sold by P. NORBURY, near the Market-Place,
and GEORGE BICKHAM, in Kew-Lane, Richmond. Where may be had, a Description of the House and Gardens of Blenheim, Ditchly, and Stow; likewise a Description of Kensington, Hampton-Court, and Windsor. (n.d.)

Virginia Woolf considered John Evelyn a sort of eyes and ears for his time,
the quintessential observer of the strange and the familiar: "Wherever there
was a picture to be seen by Julio Romano, Polydore, Guido, Raphael, or
Tintoretto, a finely built house, a prospect, or a garden nobly designed, Evelyn stopped his coach to look at it, and opened his diary to record his opinion"
("Evelyn," 82). Travelers' diaries and country-house guidebooks represent
perhaps two of the most important textual praxes in the development of
novelistic description.[13] The narrative descriptions of interiors in travelers'
journals and country-house guidebooks were distinctive eighteenth-century
phenomena in their widespread popularity. Traveling, and writing about it,
had, of course, existed before the eighteenth century (as in John Leland's
1538 *Laboriouse Journey and Serche for Englandes Antiquities*), but both
the practice of touring country houses and the genre of the guidebook flour-
ished in the second half of the century, only to die out in the next. "The
Victorian country house guide did not exist," John Harris asserts, and, "except for the few very great houses, the mansions of our Victorian ancestors
were generally closed to the public."[14] Access to other people's houses, both
personally and textually, coincided with the increased attention to interior
detail in novels; and novelistic description further increased in a sort of
compensation as, by the 1840s, the houses closed up and the guidebooks
disappeared.

England began touring itself in earnest from about 1700. Roads improved
gradually over the century, as did coaches (springs helped) and personal security. As we saw in chapter 2, John Ogilby's *Britannia*, first published in 1675
and republished in many forms throughout the eighteenth century, gave the
traveler an almost narrativized sense of travel in the visual effects of the
itinerary, not to mention a useful means of finding places without getting

lost. And great houses to see were being built all over the country with the
new mercantile wealth. Celia Fiennes, in the preface to her travel journals,
"To the Reader," advises:

> if all persons, both Ladies, much more Gentlemen, would spend some
> of their tyme in Journeys to visit their native Land, and be curious to
> inform themselves and make observations of the pleasant prospects, good
> buildings, different produces and manufactures of each place, with the
> variety of sports and recreations they are adapt to, would . . . form such an
> Idea of England, add much to its Glory and Esteem in our minds and cure
> the evil itch of over-valueing foreign parts; at least furnish them with
> an equivalent to entertain strangers when amongst us, or inform them
> when abroad of their native Country, which has been often a reproach to
> the English, ignorance and being strangers to themselves.[15]

Know your country, Fiennes says; know its land and houses and manufactures and interconnections. Her journals are exceptionally detailed; she was
every bit as much the observer as Evelyn or Defoe. Christopher Morris characterizes her as "most a woman when she is describing gardens or domestic
architecture."[16] Well, perhaps. John Crowley argues that, from Tudor times,
domestic space lost some of its social status as male servants in aristocratic
households were replaced by female servants (43–56), so a female might be
expected to care more about female space. But, as Harris notes, Fiennes was
something of an exception among travelers in 1700 as a woman often traveling more or less alone and traveling virtually everywhere. By the time of her
death in 1741, she "literally saw the exception become the rule" ("Country
House Guides," 59) of English travelers. I would also argue that Fiennes is an
exception for recording interior domestic detail, a practice that also becomes
the rule by the second half of the century.

Fiennes describes at great length the situation, exterior, and interior of
Chatsworth, home of the Duke and Duchess of Devonshire, rebuilt between
1681 and 1707. She notes of the duchess's closet: "[It] is wanscoated with the
hollow burnt japan and at each corner are peers of Looking-glass, over the
Chimney is Looking glass an oval, and at the 4 corners, after this figure 'O',
and hollow carving all round the glass; the roomes are all painted very finely
on the top, all the windows the squares of glass are so large and good they
cost 10s. a pannell; there was sweete tapistry hangings with small figures and
very much silk, they look'd as fresh as if new tho' bought severall yeares,
there were no beds up." She is also fascinated by the "batheing roome"
with walls of blue and white marble, the bath itself (big enough for two and

"deep as ones middle") with "two Cocks to let in one hott the other cold water to attemper it as persons please" (106). Although, like Defoe, Fiennes is, perhaps, even more interested in manufactures, roadways, waterways, mines, local produce, and gardens, she was as meticulous in detailing colors and fabrics, carvings and windows, as any auctioneer.

Defoe, on the other hand, stays outside Chatsworth (and most buildings) in his *Tour thro' the Whole Island of Great Britain* (1724–26). From that standpoint, he finds it "the most regular piece of architect I have seen in all the north part of England; the pilaster seventy two foot high to the foot of the ballaster on the top; the frize under the cornish is spacious, and has the motto of the family upon it.... The sashes of the second story we were told are seventeen foot high, the plates polish'd looking-glass, and the woodwork double gilded; which, I think, is no where else to be seen in England."[17] Defoe is primarily interested in what the exterior of a house can publish to a viewer and in how various houses relate to their surrounding counties. His *Tour* represents the more widely available access to house visualization in the early eighteenth century, in tour books as well as in fictional narratives.

Defoe's was virtually the only published guide to Britain in the first half of the century, and there were almost no guidebooks to single places, as there were in Italy. Benton Seeley published a description of the gardens of Stowe in 1744, and George Bickham published a rival guide in 1750. But it wasn't until 1759, when Seeley paired up with the printer J. Rivington to produce a new guide to Stowe, that a text ushered visitors inside, offering, according to George Clarke, "an entirely new feature, a tour of the principal rooms in the house with details of the pictures and the interior decoration." Clarke pronounces Seeley's 1763 edition "a work of outstanding merit in its own right" with a "well documented tour of the house and gardens" among its plans of the garden and illustrations of the buildings.[18] He gives Seeley primary credit for the evolution and perfection of the guidebook in virtual isolation by 1763. Harris calculates the bibliographic count of the rise in guidebooks for the rest of the century as twelve in the 1760s, three in the 1770s, fourteen in the 1780s, ten in the 1790s, fourteen in the first decade of the new century, twenty-four in the 1810s, nineteen in the 1820s, twelve in the 1830s, nine in the 1840s, and then their virtual disappearance for a while ("Country House Guides," 69). By 1822, he argues, the structure of the guidebook was well in place and possessed "three essentials: a study of the genealogy of the family, a description of the garden, then of the house and finally a room-by-room account of the pictures" (68).

House guides become more detailed about their subjects' interiors as they rise in popularity. Bickham's guide to Stowe focuses mainly on the gardens and their buildings, one example of which marks a certain limited attention to spatial detail, along with a rather profuse musing:

The SLEEPING PARLOUR

This Temple is situated at the Bottom of a lovely Recess, contrived with all imaginable Art, in the Middle of a cool dark Grove; far from all Noise, and breathing, as it were, Tranquillity and Repose. Six Walks centre in this Building, which is of Free-stone; and contains only a middling Hall, where commodious Canopies invite you to sleep; and the Walls are adorned with most charming Fresco's of the *Caesars* Heads, with several Festoons of Fruit, &c. On the Frise is this Inscription.

Cum omnia fiut in incerto, fave tibi.
Since all Things are uncertain, indulge thyself.

I must confess, that I think *Ovid* himself could scarce have buried the senseless God in an happier Retirement. This gloomy Darkness, these easy Couches, and that excellent *Epicurean* Argument above the Door, would incline me wonderfully to indulge a little, if these beautiful Ornaments did not keep my Attention awake: But there wants a purling Stream, to sing a *Requiem* to the Senses; though the Want is in some measure made up by the drowsy Lullabies of that murmuring Swarm, which this Shade has invited to wanton beneath it; and, I must own, Sleeping is a Compliment as much due to this Place, as Admiration and Attention are to *Raphael*, at *Hampton-Court*.[19]

Bickham's musings probably fill in the spaces left empty by personal observation; Clarke shows that he pirated most of his material but concludes that, although *"The Beauties of Stow* may be a disreputable little volume, . . . it remains a milestone in the development of tourist literature" (xi).

Bickham's later guidebooks offer more in the way of visualizing interior texture. For example, *A Short Account of the Principal Seats and Gardens in and about Richmond and Kew* (published sometime before 1771, according to Harris ["Country House Guides," 72]) offers crisp little paragraphs about the homes along the Thames, both great and small:

Mr. BARLOW's, at *Twickenham*,

is small, but the extreme neatness of the Outside, which is perfectly White, makes it a striking Object from the River: a large Room with a fine Bow-Window to the Water, hung with Buff Colour and adorn'd with

Prints, cut out and elegantly disposed, is its chief Ornament; the Garden is laid out to as much Advantage as so small a Piece of Ground is capable of.

Walpole's Strawberry Hill gets more extensive treatment; Bickham seems fascinated by the lilac color scheme and, in general, the gothic style, which has "all the noble Simplicity yet Magnificence of Antiquity, without its Decay"—quite the opposite of Ann Radcliffe's anachronistically ruined Udolpho (discussed in the next chapter). And Mrs. Pritchard's house in Twickenham ("called *Ragman's Castle* from its original Builder") supplies almost a narrative in the "moving Picture" of the river prospect artfully reproduced by mirrors:

> [IT] STANDS behind three very fine lofty Trees, which fence it from the Sun and Wind, without intercepting the Prospect; tis situated exactly opposite to *Ham-Walks*, which, together with the woody Side of *Richmond-Hill*, give it the Advantage of a very rich Prospect: The Front of the House is very pretty, being covered with Gravel, and the best Room (with a handsome Bow Window) forms a very uniform Appearance: This Appartment is hung with India Paper, dispos'd in a most elegant Taste. It represents a Chinese Pavilion supported with Lilac Pillars. In several Parts there are Looking Glasses so artfully placed in the Chinese Houses, that the Prospect is seen by every Person, from every different Part of the Room, which in the Afternoon, when the Barges are coming up, presents the most beautiful moving Picture imaginable.[20]

Like Delany, in a sort of cultural interweaving that may argue Fabricant's mutual influencing between visitors and guidebooks, and like the auction catalogs, emphasis here emerges on color, texture, and arrangement, all providing a kinetic set of prospects for "every Person," whether within or without the house. Those who arranged their colors, their textures, their spaces, their things, had in mind an audience that enjoyed as well as critiqued those arrangements.

By 1793, William Mavor's *New Description of Blenheim* will argue that it is "impossible" to do the tapestry and paintings "adequate justice in any general description," so Mavor proposes to conduct his readers "through the grand suit of rooms, usually open to public inspection, in the order they are shewn."[21] Each description of the room more or less begins with a color-fabric setting for the descriptions of the paintings; the Bow Window Room, for example, has window curtains and furniture of blue silk damask (31);

the Duke's Dressing Room is done in "straw-coloured flock paper, with a rich border; the furniture is chintz" (31); the East Drawing Room is crimson damask (33).

Paintings do get first billing, presumably as part of the absorption of culture noted by John Brewer (*Pleasures*; see also Solkin), although Elizabeth Burton notes that "paintings are often commissioned with subject matter and size of canvas specified *to suit the decor and to fit into an exact space in a room*" (134; emphasis added).[22] Guidebook writers and tourists may be scavenging for Art, but the owners were beginning to subordinate art to interior space—perhaps a flip from what Lisa Jardine recognizes in the affluent Renaissance house, where the art itself became a "meticulous visual inventory of consumer goods" and was as prominently displayed as the "comparatively few items of furniture" (*Worldly Goods*, 9, 16). The profusion of objects, the arrangement of space in a house, became more than a setting for paintings (although Mavor's textual arrangements and travelers' descriptive emphases suggest multiple focal points in domestic observation)—more an integration of the visual, in which paintings were meant to enrich and enhance rather than compel focus on their own.

The rise in house guides is matched by increasingly elaborate accounts of house interiors in diaries and published journals by travelers such as Mary Delany, Caroline Lybbe Powys, and John Byng. Esther Moir notes that tourists of the English country house "gave painstaking accounts of even the most minute details of furnishing and decoration" and that "a great part of the pleasure of touring houses lay in passing judgement upon the architecture and criticizing the internal décor."[23] The tourist was not necessarily a passive absorber of country-house ideology; he or she often felt perfectly comfortable as imaginative critic or prospective tenant. The increasing play of light, color, and texture in the great houses—and the easy rearrangement of these plays—invited visitors as well as owners to *play*. At Raby Castle, John Byng has plans for a grand staircase to ascend to a charming room above stairs, "with old windows, and a lofty wooden roof": "'Lord D, will your lordship permit me, a stranger, to lay out £20,000 for you? And I, then, think that I could make your house a wonder of beauty; . . . the hall should be in eternal warmth; I should build a chapel; and a Gothic stair-case; and I should render that great room, fitted up with cedar, and glazed with stain'd glass, one of the grandest libraries in the universe'" (3:75). In general, Byng scorns the use of guidebooks: "In all my descriptions I have trusted to my own eye sight, and opinions, without borrowing from any touring books; of these I have read but few; and now for the pleasure of my own pen, and that I may not accuse myself of plagiarism, I totally abstain from them" (1:229n).

But he lavishly supplies his own descriptions and evaluations of the houses and inns, gardens and roads, cities and villages he visits. He is one of the few eighteenth-century tourists who prefers the old (Moir, 63); he mourns the new industries, the felling of forests, the modernization and "Frenchifying" of ancient houses. In thinking back on his visit to Raby Castle in 1792, Byng gets a little fierce: to make a fine hall "a thoroughfare street, is wretchedness indeed!" (It was very cold in that hall.) And all that little skuttling furniture: "I love large, firmly-fix'd writing tables in my library; and to have my breakfast, and dining tables substantial, and immoveable: and when I say immoveable, it is because my rooms, and every part of them, should be of an equal warmth; and there should be no need, as I see at present, of little skuttling tables being brought before a hearth.... People spend fortunes, and waste great estates, without ever having passed one hour in a comfortable room, or in a good bed. A good bed is a great rarity" (3:156–57).

Mary Delany had inscribed a very approving description of Luton Hoo, quoted earlier in this chapter; in general, she says of the house: "The only objection to yᵉ house is 42 stone steps, which you must ascend whenever you go up to yᵉ lodging appartments. When you are there there is no fault to find" (5:35). But she is quite capable of finding fault, of rejecting as well as appropriating interiors. When she visits Mr. Bateman at Old Windsor in 1768, which had been converted from the "Indian" to the "Gothic," she calls the exterior "venerable," but, in an echo of Defoean disapproval, she finds that

> the inside of the old monastery (for such it is to represent), is not so easily described; it is below stairs divided into four very small rooms, and a passage, all filled with an innumerable collection of china, japan, and knickknacks. The walls are embossed with undescribable oddities brought from all corners of the world; the chairs, the tables of all forms and sizes. His windows are glazed with as much variety as a glazier's sign, but he has picked up a vast quantity of pretty old painted glass. His library is indeed as *fribbish* as himself, and so furnished with looking-glass that had it the property of representing to him his inside as well as outside, it might read him a better lesson than he could find in his whole collection of books, and shew him his own insignificancy. (4:176–77)

Mirrors for the visitor sometimes offer up reflections other than those the owner might have suspected.

Delany's own first habitation as a married woman at age seventeen shocked her. She had been pressured by her uncle, George Lord Lansdowne, to marry Alexander Pendarves of Roscrow (in Cornwall), a man three times her age. She records to her friend the Duchess of Portland:

> The castle is guarded with high walls that entirely hid it from your view. When the gate of the court was opened and we walked in, the front of the castle terrified me. It is built of ugly coarse stone, old and mossy, and propt with two great stone buttresses, and so it had been for threescore years. I was led into an old hall that had scarce any light belonging to it; on the left hand of which was a parlour, the floor of which was rotten in places, and part of the ceiling is broken down; and the windows were placed so high that my head did not come near the bottom of them. (1:36)

This was 1717, long before the gothic novel, but Delany lived a gothic horror. She spent the rest of her life recording and manufacturing things of beauty, especially the cut-paper flowers for which she has become famous. She would later be startled by the general Irish disinterest in interior comforts: "The people of this country don't seem solicitous of having *good dwellings* or more furniture than is absolutely necessary—*hardly so much*, but they make it up by *eating and drinking!* I have not seen less than fourteen dishes of meat for dinner, and seven for supper" (1:351). Delany's later attention to interior detail was premised to some extent on firsthand observation of absence.

Caroline Lybbe Powys is generally not one to complain; as a writer and traveler, friend and wife, she delights in just about everything (except, perhaps, the Norfolk landscape). She defers speaking of "Mrs. Freeman's, Fawley Court, Bucks," even though she was a frequent visitor in 1771 (where her brother-in-law had the living), "till it was more finish'd" because, "though always an excellent house," it "had no ornaments till now, when Mr. Freeman has laid out £8000, I believe, in inside decorations, besides having the celebrated Mr. [Lancelot, a.k.a. Capability] Brown to plan the grounds" (145). She particularly notes the individuality of each room, "each in a different style" (146). But she does remark of home embroidery: "One is seldome partial, I think, to ladies' work of this kind" (147). Another tiny criticism, this time of Knole, the seat of the dukes of Dorset, is simply a sigh of regret: "One goes through the apartments with concern that this young Duke cannot refit the furniture of each. One longs to repair every old chair, table, bed, or cabinet, exactly in its former taste" (149). She enjoys "a droll visit to see an odd house" and a "still odder Mr. Spilman" and rejoices in the house's singularities: "You ascend a flight of twenty-one steps, which, as they don't spread out as usual towards the bottom, seems as if you were mounting a perpendicular staircase; you enter a hall, striking from its strange dimensions, being five cubes of eighteen feet, so it's ninety feet long by eighteen! and might rather be termed a gallery" (7). And she is capable of finding a vicarage house "despicable": "'Tis literally a poor cottage, and even thatched" (5). Although one might argue that her criticisms, à la Fabricant, tend to reinforce the fashionable norms, even in the greatest houses she exercises the tourist's prerogative to imaginatively rearrange.

Moir and Harris both argue that, until the end of the eighteenth century, the joys of tourism were limited to the aristocracy and gentry: "Even if a labourer could afford the entrance fee and exorbitant tips (amounting to several pounds in present-day value [this in 1968], the gate lodge of a Stowe or Strawberry Hill would have been firmly closed to him" (Harris, "Country House Guides," 59; see also Moir, 58). But Carole Fabricant finds a much wider scope for eighteenth-century tourism as "functioning on multiple socioeconomic and ideological levels and implicating a range of different social classes, including tradesmen (booksellers, innkeepers, etc.) who profited from the tourist business and members of the lower orders who were... allowed to visit places like Stowe and The Leasowes along with their 'betters'" (256). She argues that, while the rise of domestic tourism created a market for house guides and topographical prints of estates, those texts in turn helped create the tourist, "[shaping] his aesthetic judgments, and artificially (in both eighteenth- and twentieth-century senses of the word) stimulating hitherto nonexistent needs and desires" (260). The wider scope of tourists—or native English persons aware of or involved in the new industry—meant, among other things, a wider cultural awareness of the insides of other people's houses, a knowledge of their things, and a license to describe, to judge, and to re-create them in their own image. In a sense, the visiting and describing of English country houses contributed to an interest in and the art of describing fictional houses; entering intimately into someone else's house, spending "a leisurely two or three hours wandering through the place at will, catalogue in hand, unharassed by attendants and free to inspect everything from the kitchens to the chapel" (Moir, 59), whetted appetites for interiors. Tourists, the readers of the guidebook texts, were also, of course, the readers of novels.

Domestication

In *Sir Charles Grandison* (1753–54), when Harriet Byron first arrives at Grandison Hall, now blissfully married to the hero, she promptly informs us in

startling detail (historically speaking) about *detail*. The dining room, she
notes,

> is noble and well proportioned: It goes over the hall and dining-parlour.
> It is hung with crimson-damask, adorned with valuable pictures. The
> furniture is rich, but less ornamented than that of the Lady's drawing-
> room.
>   The best bed chamber adjoining, is hung with fine tapestry. The bed is
> of crimson velvet, lined with white silk; chairs and curtains of the same.
> Two fine pictures drawn by Sir Godfrey [Kneller], one of Sir Thomas, the
> other of Lady Grandison, whole lengths, took my eye.[24]

The rooms are *full of things*, thing after thing, and, moreover, *matching*
things—"chairs and curtains of the same." We have visual continuity; we
find ourselves looking, with Harriet, *around the room* instead of *at a thing*.
In Bunyan's *The Pilgrim's Progress* (1678), Christian and the Interpreter had
"reviewed" the very large, dusty parlor for "a little while" before entering
it and having it swept; Harriet grabs that subjective moment, that point
of view, and pours in more precisely what that moment, that view, that
perception of space contains.

Harriet's extended descriptions of the interior spaces of Grandison
Hall (and her cousin Lucy's descriptions of its gardens) have not been
favorites with either readers or critics. Malcolm Kelsall remarks: "The
meticulous particularity of [Richardson's] description of his 'good man's
house' ... provides a veritable checklist of desirable features given local habitation and a name. It runs the risk, however, of making the ideal ridiculous by
too much detail. Richardson rarely knows when to stop."[25] Kelsall is essentially repeating the centuries' worth of distrust toward description, outlined
in chapter 1, as a generally subservient textual praxis—the workhorse of
geography and topography, of catalogs and guidebooks, of nonliterary life.
Harriet, Kelsall complains, tells us too much about too little; she might as
well be drafting a guidebook for tour groups.

And so she is: "I will give you a slight sketch of the house and apartments,
as I go along." She gives us the situation of the house, an elevation ("It is
built in the form of an H; both fronts pretty much alike" [pt. 3, p. 271 (vol. 7,
letter 5)]), the various kinds of rooms, the furnishings, the glass cases, the tea
sets, and, of course, the paintings. Cousin Lucy, she says, "loves to describe
houses, furniture, gardens, and such like" (and is employed on the garden
descriptions here), but Harriet herself runs a loving hand over the interior
now her own. That is part of the point. Interior space is not overwhelmingly

or even consistently described in this novel; Harriet's room at her cousin's house in London at the beginning is "extremely elegant" and with "a well-furnish'd book-case" (pt. 1, p. 17 [vol. 1, letter 4]), but, for the most part, it is Clarissa-space—the space of gesture and social meaning, as when Sir Charles renegotiates the status of the former housekeeper-cum-mistress of his late father by seating her in a "chair not distant" from the snubbing sisters (pt. 1, pp. 362–64 [vol. 2, letter 19]).[26] But, when Harriet enters the life—and house—of her choice, when after hundreds and hundreds of pages she gets what she wants, she takes visual as well as actual possession: "O my dearest, dearest grandmamma! Here I am! The declared mistress of this spacious house, and the happiest of human creatures!" In that order? Sir Charles shows her around, affirming: "The whole house, my dear, said he, and every person and thing belonging to it, is yours: But this apartment is more particularly so. Let what is amiss in it, be altered as you would have it." This initiates the country-house guide: this room, particularly her own, is a drawing room "elegantly furnished. It is hung with a light green velvet, delicately ornamented; the chairs of the same; the frames of them gilt; as is the frame of a noble cabinet in it" (pt. 3, p. 269 [vol. 7, letter 5]).

I want to conclude in this chapter that Richardson is beginning to absorb into his text the kind of spatial detail that by midcentury was permeating public consciousness in the advertisements, shopwindows, newspapers, satires, auction catalogs, and country-house guides. Susan Stewart has argued: "We can see in eighteenth- and nineteenth-century realistic novels echoes of two major themes of bourgeois life: individuation and refinement.... The description of the material world, the world of things, is necessary for a description of the hero's or heroine's progress through that world, and the 'finer' the description, the 'finer' the writing" (28). From this perspective, Harriet's meticulous cataloging of the colors and textures and lived geometry of Grandison Hall is not *just* a textual praxis, not *just* a guide to a country house, but a textual reproduction of the spaces of her identity. Bringing the workhorse of description into novelistic space becomes an act of domestication and gentrification; these are fine spaces Harriet's got herself into. Kelsall and others might still consider the newcomer awkward, rustic, a little too obvious, but Richardson's well-known influence on contemporary and later novelists would plausibly include his innovations in spatial construction and description. Household description absorbs the catalogic into the space and meaning of narrative, reassembling and reuniting the *things* of a house into the *meaning* of a house.

This absorption comes in response to what T. H. Breen calls the "unprecedented size and fluidity [of the eighteenth-century world of goods], its

openness, its myriad opportunities for individual choice that subverted traditional assumptions and problematized customary social relations" (251). In
1678, Bunyan's tag "a very large Parlour" could instantly be rehydrated into
a fairly specific set of images because the contents of the image were more
confined, the boundaries of interiors more uniform and uniformly available. But, throughout the eighteenth century, Langley, Kent, Chippendale,
Wedgwood, the Adams, all were redefining English interiors at a prodigious
and commercial rate. Ironically, sturdier houses were filled with more disposable furnishings (Shammas, 178). More disposable, more differentiated,
more idiosyncratic, more available to recombinations and multiple personal
meanings—thus more in *need* of description for readerly visualization, less
the common property of a cultural storehouse available to Bunyan's readers.
Bill Brown has said that, for the modern and postmodern world, "we begin to
confront the thingness of objects when they stop working for us: when the
drill breaks, when the car stalls, when the windows get filthy, when their
flow within the circuits of production and distribution, consumption and
exhibition, has been arrested, however momentarily" (4). But it is equally
the case, for eighteenth-century things, that they appear when they *start*
working—when the skuttling chairs, and the black teapots, and the afford-
able glass, and the "new draperies" start filling and then *differentiating*
houses, with the result that a domestic interior was no longer, as Tristram
says, "what every courteous author must assume was already known to his
readers" (5). The market for and arrangement of things in the world created
the space for the description of things in texts; interiors produced interiors;
surfaces produced meanings.

CHAPTER EIGHT

The Foundling as Heir

Sometimes an Author, fond of his own Thought,
Pursues his Object till it's over-wrought:
If he describes a House, he shows the Face,
And after walks you round from Place to Place;
Here is a Vista, there the Doors unfold,
Balcones here are balluster'd with Gold;
Then counts the Rounds and Ovals in the halls,
The Festoons, Freezes, and the Astragals.
—*Boileau,* The Art of Poetry *(1683)*

By the end of the eighteenth century, the festoons, friezes, and astragals had come to stay. Harriet Byron (Lady Grandison) walked us round and round her new place, counting the rounds and ovals in the hall; Ann Radcliffe is generally credited with pioneering detailed landscape description, but, as is less often recognized, she also moves comfortably indoors—not just to mark a vista from the windows, but to inhabit a visualized interior. Walter Scott acknowledges Radcliffe's influence—and the influence of gothic romance generally—on his own work. In the Waverley novels and *Ivanhoe* (1819), what would have been the nineteenth-century habit of preparing an elaborately described setting for the characters to enter and act within gets firmly established. Thomas Babington Macaulay is, presumably, thinking primarily of Scott when he complains that historians do not pay the same attention to prosaic, ordinary, visual details as the historical novelists. But even the historians were feeling the pressures of things filling space and demanding recognition. The wider cultural interest in interiors and in the relations between objects and persons within them seeped into the sense of

boundaries, and contours, and detail in eighteenth-century historiography
as well. The genres of time, we might say, made more room for space.

The title of this chapter alludes to Tom Jones, who, raised by Squire
Allworthy and aspiring to Sophia Western, is sent spiraling across the
countryside by the envious misrepresentations of Blifil and the proprietorial
rage of Squire Western. But Tom turns out to be the son of Blifil's mother,
and, therefore, the nephew of Squire Allworthy, and becomes the legitimated
heir to property and love. Just like young Mr. Description. Except that the
allusion would seem to be only semiapt because Henry Fielding's *Tom Jones*
(1749) is not what one would call a physically descriptive novel. The head-
ing of chapter 4, book 1, volume 1 warns: "*The Reader's Neck brought into
Danger by a Description.*" Yet the description proves classically untreacher-
ous: "The *Gothick* Stile of Building could produce nothing nobler than Mr.
Allworthy's House. There was an Air of Grandeur in it, that struck you with
Awe, and rival'd the Beauties of the best *Grecian* Architecture; and it was
as commodious within, as venerable without."[1] The essential moral qualities of the squire are worthily dimensioned in the essential architectural
qualities of his house—the standard "inside answerable to the outside," in
Defoe's phrase, that architectural theory and country-house poems had always promoted. But the actual interior remains implicit, like the interior
spaces of Behn, Defoe, and Haywood; the rest of the description records the
position of the house and the view "seen from every Room in the front" (*Tom
Jones*, 43). Rachel Trickett claims that "the self-consciousness itself warns
us that Fielding is thinking of such description as a convention, but a high
poetic convention, like the epic battle, not a convention of simple narrative.
His attempt at it is clumsy and confusing; he is ill at ease with description,
with any attempt to depict natural beauty" (247). But that criticism forgets
conceptual history. Fielding is "ill at ease with description" insofar as he
is a good classical scholar (or, rather, the classically trained gentleman), for
whom the vocabulary of as well as the conceptual space *for* spatial detail
is prescriptively and (non-self-)consciously limited. Fielding follows Boileau
and will not count the rounds and ovals in the hall. The classical strain of
antidescription, or, perhaps better, of *curbing* description, survives healthily
in the nineteenth and twentieth centuries; the Russian formalists and the
Anglo-American New Critics had little time for description, Marxists dis-
trusted its materiality, and the discourse linguists of the 1970s and 1980s
theorized it into the mere background of gestalt theory.[2] And that is why I
think of literary description as a foundling. Tom Jones never acquires birth
legitimacy; he is adopted by legitimacy, marries into it, inherits a bit of it,
but more by acquired and demonstrated virtue than by patriarchal right.

THE FOUNDLING AS HEIR

This chapter will watch description as it upholsters itself within narrative in the late eighteenth century and the early nineteenth. I choose more well-known names and texts partly because of their overt influence on each other and on the literary market generally and partly to avoid the exhaustive catalogic approach of investigating a conceptual treatment: "In 'Cecilia' (1782) there is no use of Nature."[3] Much of what I show and argue here will apply to other novelists and historians of the period, but always with the awareness of the many permutations of "cunning" and "great discretion" that George Puttenham says go into the making of "creating gods" (199). Description shifts in meaning, function, purpose, and practice, not only across the centuries, but also intensely within the eighteenth, as the product of the newly coinciding textual praxes of land description and house description in travel narratives, diaries, topographies, auction catalogs, and house guides.

The Gothic: Reeve and Radcliffe

Philippa Tristram argues that the later eighteenth-century revival of gothic architecture might have been expected to have an impact on the description of houses in literature because "it is the antithesis of the classical: its inspiration is indigenous, not foreign; Christian, not pagan; medieval or even Tudor, not antique. Its structures, moreover, are irregular, supposedly answering to the needs of those within, not dictated from without by standards of symmetry." But in fact, she claims, its influence was minimal: "The Gothic . . . invited description, but in terms that are generalized and atmospheric rather than particular and domestic" (7). In one sense, this seems apt: Radcliffe, known *particularly* for her lavish landscape descriptions, achieved her best effects, according to an early nineteenth-century reviewer, "by a series of hints, glimpses, or half-heard sounds. . . . The clang of a distant door, a footfall on the stair, a half-effaced stain of blood, a strain of music floating over a wood, or round some decaying chateau . . . became in her hands invested with a mysterious dignity . . . by a train of minute details and artful contrasts, in which all sights and sounds combine to awaken and render the feeling more intense."[4] Horror and sublimity are achieved by indication, by the presence of the ultimately unsensible, and Radcliffe masters the art of the fragment, the hint, the atmospheric. But this is what she is known and remembered for; it is not by any means all she does. I will argue in this section that the gothic does, indeed, bring us intimately inside, not only in its moments of fear and oppression and horror—although, in these moments, it makes far more use of connected specific detail than do the rape or chase scenes of Behn, Haywood, or Defoe—but also in the happy little spaces of domestic retreat.

Recent critical work on the gothic novel has closed the apparent thirty-year gap between Horace Walpole's *The Castle of Otranto* (1764) and Ann Radcliffe's *The Mysteries of Udolpho* (1794), which was claimed to set off a twenty-year spree.[5] Part of the effort of filling in the context lay in recovering works such as Clara Reeve's *The Champion of Virtue, or, The Old English Baron* (1777, 1778) from a critical dump site. Reeve modeled her work explicitly on *The Castle of Otranto*, but Walpole's response was to call it "the most insipid dull thing you ever saw" (Walpole to William Cole, 22 August 1778, in Walpole, *Correspondence*, 40:379). Scott described it as "tame and tedious, not to say mean and tiresome" (*Novels of Sterne...*, lxxxv). Its first major twentieth-century editor, James Trainer, claims that it never "really [comes] to life" because its author fails "to establish sufficiently the milieu in which the events are placed."[6] Nevertheless, the novel went through thirteen editions by the end of the nineteenth century, was translated into French and German, and was reworked for the stage (Trainer, xii n. 2). James Watt argues well for its original and revived claim to fame as a notable contributor both to gothic fiction and to romance revisionism, "[staging] the ascendancy of a distinctly 'bourgeois' set of values" in its careful redistribution of property and poetic justice.[7] I want to emphasize here how it repossesses the giant *things* of *Otranto* into a domesticated (if gothic) setting, laying the less visible tracks for quietly smuggling interior detail in the boxcars of special effects.

Most of the criticism of *The Old English Baron* takes aim at its prosaic detail. "Nowhere else [in gothic literature] do we find knights regaling on eggs and bacon and suffering from the toothache," said J. M. S. Tompkins.[8] Scott, of all people, complained of the "prolix... and unnecessary details," the "grave and minute accounting" (*Novels of Sterne...*, lxxxvi). John Dunlop in 1814 found the "gigantic and awful features of romance" crowded out by the mundane affairs of "settlements, stocking of farms, and household furniture."[9] James Trainer echoes Dunlop: "A little subterranean groaning, some impressive nocturnal thuds, doors which open unaided... is the sum total of supernatural activity.... It is far outweighed by more tangible reliques of the deceased, armour, necklace, and seal, as well as by the characters' concern with mundane business affairs such as the settling of petty debts, the apportioning of farm stock, the furnishing of apartments, and the quest for general respectability" (ix). Reeve, like Richardson, Radcliffe, and, to a lesser (contemporary) extent, Scott, was critically scolded for her domestic details and prolix descriptions. Nevertheless, she described

away, like Richardson, Radcliffe, and Scott; their popular fictions opened
many new doors for the descriptive habit.

Such a claim can still be considered relative. Trainer finds Reeve's
work undervisualized even as it is overdetailed in prosaic concerns: "This
economy, one might almost say parsimony, of means extends into the creation of historical and local atmosphere. Apart from the generalities of the
opening sentences . . . there is no regard for historicity just as there is a total
absence of the rich and detailed nature descriptions to which Mrs. Radcliffe
devoted so many pages. On only one occasion, in the portrayal of the moth-
eaten fabrics and decaying furniture of the secret apartments, does she afford herself the luxury of atmospheric description" (xi). As *The Old English
Baron* preceded *The Castles of Athlin and Dunbayne* (1789) and *A Sicilian
Romance* (1790) by more than a decade (and *The Mysteries of Udolpho*—
the real debut of Radcliffe's landscape descriptions—by fifteen years), Reeve
should hardly be held to a nonexistent standard. Nor should this particular
description be said to rely on "formulaic effects" (Watt, introduction, xi).
Such "effects," such a "formula," did not yet exist, even in *Otranto*. Trainer
recognizes that this description of an "abandoned wing of a castle with its
dilapidated rooms and reputation for mystery [would become] one of the
most frequent scenes of incident in later Gothic tales" (xi).

But the scene itself is asking to be seen. The hero, Edmund Twyford, has
agreed to sleep three nights in an apparently haunted apartment of Baron
Fitz-Owen's castle:

> He then took a survey of his chamber; the furniture, by long neglect, was
> decayed and dropping to pieces; the bed was devoured by the moths, and
> occupied by the rats, who had built their nests there with impunity for
> many generations. The bedding was very damp, for the rain had forced
> its way through the ceiling; he determined, therefore, to lie down in his
> clothes. Three were two doors on the further side of the room with keys in
> them; being not at all sleepy, he resolved to examine them; he attempted
> one lock and opened it with ease; he went into a large dining-room, the
> furniture of which was in the same tattered condition; out of this was a
> large closet with some books in it, and hung round with coats of arms,
> with genealogies and alliances of the house of Lovel; he amused himself
> here some minutes, and then returned into the bed-chamber. (*Baron*, 36)

The picture is of a resolute, cheerful young man in a deteriorating room.
When he opens a door, and the draft extinguishes his lamp, and he hears
a rustling in the darkness, "just then, all the concurrent circumstances of

his situation struck upon his heart, and gave him a new and disagreeable sensation" (36)—of fear. Edmund's situation is like the reader's: the author *combines* "concurrent circumstances" for a "new . . . sensation." In Richardson's *Clarissa*, Belford's long, detailed description of Clarissa's prison room also combines those circumstances of decay and filth, but for purposes of pity, for the sense of insupportable contrast between where Clarissa is and where she ought to be. In a sense, the horror of Belford's description is on a continuum with Reeve's: the occupants of the description in a sense *don't belong there*. As Susan Stewart puts it, "refinement" in writing "has to do with not only the articulation of detail but also the articulation of difference" (29). Throughout most of description's history, what did not need to be described was *home*, the setting of belonging, the background from which a character emerged into danger, alienation, exoticism, discomfort. (Or the reverse: if the whole life route of a pilgrim is danger and weariness, the differences to be described are the moments of domestic peace and comfort, the inns of *The Pilgrim's Progress*.) Only if home was unusual—a cave, say, or a traveling box neatly appointed, or an exotic ship's cabin—would it call for a graphic representation. What Harriet Byron began forcefully to do is what the gothic and late eighteenth-century novel in general would continue: spin the readerly gaze into the domestic interior, to think about what *at home* means.

The rest of the scene in the "haunted" apartment gets cozier and cozier. Edmund's friend-manservant Joseph arrives "with a light in one hand, a flaggon of beer in the other, and a faggot upon his shoulder" to light, warm, and air the room as well as to supply a ground plan for the rest of the wing: a door leads "upon a passage that ends in a staircase that leads to the lower rooms; and there is likewise a door out of that passage into the dining-room"; there are likewise the same rooms below as above (*Baron*, 37). And, when the ghosts arrive, they turn out to be Edmund's loving parents:

> [Edmund] thought that he heard people coming up the staircase that he had a glimpse of; that the door opened, and there entered a Warrior, leading a Lady by the hand, who was young and beautiful, but pale and wan: The Man was dressed in complete armour, and his helmet down. They approached the bed; they undrew the curtains. He thought the man said,—Is this our child? The woman replied,—It is; and the hour approaches that he shall be known for such. They then separated, and one stood on each side of the bed; their hands met over his head, and they gave him a solemn benediction. (38)

They tell him to sleep sweetly, and, in fact, he already has because the narration of what turns out to have been a dream is cozily inserted *after* we learn that Edmund wakes up to sunshine.

At home, of course, has a lot to do with property, and it is also a critical commonplace that most novels of the later eighteenth century and the nineteenth concern themselves with the acquisition and disposal of property. (Well, so do *Moll Flanders* and *Colonel Jack* and, in spite of itself, *Robinson Crusoe*, but, in Defoe, the property is generally of a more portable variety, and, in Haywood and Behn, money and property tend to be givens.) The occupying of houses, genealogically and actually, rightfully or otherwise, also obviously informs an interest in distinctions *among* houses, as in Sophia Lee's *The Recess* (1785), Charlotte Smith's *The Old Manor House* (1793), and any Jane Austen. Matthew Lewis wrote to his mother after reading *The Mysteries of Udolpho*: "I am sure you will be particularly interested by the part, when Emily returns home after her father's death."[10] He doesn't say why; but we do know that his mother had left his father for a music master in 1781 and "moved from place to place to avoid Mr. Lewis."[11] The obverse of Emily? But I, too, am interested in that scene, partly because of the *way* it defines interiors, and I will look at it carefully below.

More generally, the critical tradition about Radcliffe points to her pioneering landscape descriptions and assumes a straightforward set of parallels between scenery, characters, and a Burkean, aesthetically gendered hierarchy. What I hope to show here is that, in Radcliffe's hands, description is more than simply a stuffing of the newly popular subgenre into the already popular dominant genre and more than just a way of highlighting character traits and gender distinctions. Radcliffe's descriptions are there to be read *closely*, and, the more carefully they are read, the more they weave themselves into a consistent counterhierarchy, a character map against the grain, opening up a sophisticated fault line underneath the obvious and accepted Burkean reading. Her masculine heroes prove every bit as incompetent as Walpole's Theodore, her fainting heroines every bit as effective as Matilda and Isabella.

Radcliffe is and was famous for her descriptions: all the early reviews mention them, the *British Critic* pointing to "the lady's talent for description" and the *Gentleman's Magazine* to her "great frequency of landscape-painting." The *Critical Review* reported that "[t]he Mysteries of Udolpho are indeed relieved by much elegant description and picturesque scenery," the *Analytical Review* that "the descriptions are chaste and magnificent," and the *Monthly Review* that "[t]he descriptions are rich, glowing, and varied."

But not all notice was positive; most of the same reviewers who favorably remarked on the descriptions also complained about their length and frequency: "much too frequent" (*Analytical Review*); "to excess" (*British Critic*); "minute even to tedious prolixity" (*European Magazine and London Review*); "wearies the reader with repetitions" (*Gentleman's Magazine*).[12] From the critical perspective, classical precepts still dominated. Radcliffe was opening the door far too wide.

From the start, Radcliffe was considered a pioneer in the art (or excess) of description. Anna Laetitia Barbauld claimed her as the first to introduce elaborate scenic description into fiction. Sir Walter Scott appointed her "the first poetess of romantic fiction" because she was "the first to introduce into her prose fictions a beautiful and fanciful tone of natural description and impressive narrative, which had hitherto been exclusively applied to poetry."[13] But most modern critics like to point out that Radcliffe more or less lifted her descriptions of scenery from travel narratives and then repeat the early line that there's just too much of it and that it doesn't do much but *depict*. Her descriptions do, however, have a few twentieth-century defenders. Clara McIntyre, for example, shows that, in using Hester Thrale Piozzi's *Observations and Reflections made in the Course of a Journey through France, Italy and Germany* (1789), Radcliffe expands the details to include "atmospheric conditions ... odors and sounds ... [and] those things which appeal to the sense of sight."[14] Rhoda Flaxman considers Radcliffe as one of the first English novelists to seriously extend and elevate prose descriptions of landscape, approaching Victorian word painting—but only when her imagination, "thoroughly aroused by her concept of sublime landscape, struggles to free itself from generalized description to achieve an almost scientific particularity of observation." Flaxman, in fact, reads the opening paragraph of *The Mysteries of Udolpho* as an example of *ineffective* (i.e., "eighteenth-century") description, with "generalized diction," an unidentified observer, an improbability of that observer's perceptual experience, a passive voice construction that "allows no rhythmic enlivening of the stilted, choppy phrases that built [*sic*] complex, often confusing, sentences," and nonspecific verbs, adjectives, and adverbs.[15] In other words, Flaxman offers another teleological metanarrative designed to explain how the eighteenth century finally flung off those clanking generalist chains and leapt mature into the nineteenth. The eighteenth century in general, and Radcliffe in particular (along with Scott), is more or less accused of being eighteenth century in its practices and predilections. But to go back to the two strands of central argument of this book: (1) this account does not see what is actually there; and (2) this account does not understand the concept of seeing differently.

I will argue that Radcliffe actually puts her "lifted" descriptions to quite sophisticated work.

The Mysteries of Udolpho begins, after its epigraph:

> On the pleasant banks of the Garonne, in the province of Gascony, stood, in the year 1584, the chateau of Monsieur St. Aubert. From its windows were seen the pastoral landscapes of Guienne and Gascony, stretching along the river, gay with luxuriant woods and vines, and plantations of olives. To the south, the view was bounded by the majestic Pyrenées, whose summits, veiled in clouds, or exhibiting awful forms, seen, and lost again, as the partial vapours rolled along, were sometimes barren, and gleamed through the blue tinge of air, and sometimes frowned with forests of gloomy pine, that swept downward to their base. These tremendous precipices were contrasted by the soft green of the pastures and woods that hung upon their skirts; among whose flocks, and herds, and simple cottages, the eye, after having scaled the cliffs above, delighted to repose. To the north, and to the east, the plains of Guienne and Languedoc were lost in the mist of distance; on the west, Gascony was bounded by the waters of Biscay.[16]

This first paragraph essentially captures the entire 672 pages of Dobrée's Oxford edition of the novel. Perhaps "our ability to visualize the scene is hampered by the illogical perspective and the inert passivity of the language" (Flaxman, 11), but our ability to *interpret* should be charged by the multiple and contradictory perspectives afforded by windows that transmit "the eye." This eye sees a view twice *bounded* and twice *lost*, in a novel obsessed with boundaries of all sorts, with things seen and unseen, with fragments as partial and frequent as its clauses. The stark contrasts of pastoral and sublime slide syntactically into each other in this paragraph, as they do conceptually in the novel. The pastoral is bounded by the sublime, but also by itself. That first paragraph unfolds a vast visual universe in its rolling general gaze; Radcliffe's form in fact *gloves* its content rather than loinclothing it.

Twentieth-century criticism invariably connects the scenery with characterization, and that characterization follows predictable Burkean lines. "Radcliffe's striking scenery not only reflects and enhances the plot," says Deborah Rogers, "it also serves to define character, evoking the heightened emotions and spirituality associated with sensibility. (Only the good guys appreciate nature.)"[17] Daniel Cottom agrees: "This parallel between landscape and character may become so close that at times Radcliffe's characters themselves experience difficulty distinguishing between them."[18]

Landscape does, in fact, prove an accurate map of character in *Udolpho*, but it is a map that has been consistently read upside down. We are given the map in the first chapter: "It was one of Emily's earliest pleasures to ramble among the scenes of nature; nor was it in the soft and glowing landscape that she most delighted; she loved more the wild wood-walks, that skirted the mountains; and still more the mountain's stupendous recesses" (6). Soft and glowing landscapes equal the Burkean feminized beautiful equals Emily's third choice.[19] Second runner-up is the (skirted) "wild wood-walks." First prize: the Burkean masculine sublime. How, then, do the landscapes and the plot combine to rank the characters in Emily's ultimate estimation?

Daniel Cottom points to Emily's early memories of Valancourt as associated with the sublime, and this for critics has generally been regarded as Valancourt's identity badge for heroism: "The grandeur and sublimity of the scenes, amidst which they had first met, had fascinated her fancy, and had imperceptibly contributed to render Valancourt more interesting by seeming to communicate to him somewhat of their own character" (*Udolpho*, 89). We read the memory, and we remember "grandeur," "sublimity," "fascinated," "interesting." But a few key facts about Valancourt leaven the description, and other words bubble to the surface. Valancourt, on their first meeting, was "in hunter's dress"—he was not actually a hunter (31). On meeting him, St. Aubert says approvingly, "This young man has never been at Paris" (36, 41)—but he shortly will. And, throughout Emily's long travails, Valancourt is most emphatically *not there*. The reader, like Emily, is led to believe that he might be the hidden musical presence cheering and strengthening her in her captivity in Udolpho, but he is not. He never once actually rescues her. Given that early and explicit hierarchy of Emily's tastes, Valancourt at best is down there among the beautiful, a soft and glowing landscape sort of man; the sublimity of scenes *contributes* to make him *more interesting*, and even yet they only *seem* to communicate *somewhat* of their own character. Without those stupendous mountain recesses reflecting beams of glory on him, Valancourt might not have made quite the lasting impression he did on Emily's heart.

Emily's father doesn't fare any better. Although he is presented as the wise, benign patriarch, to whom Emily devotes her entire love and obedience, a bird's-eye view of his general behavior proves him disastrous as a guardian. He is first killed off by sublimity. Emily had reservations about her father's judgment from the outset of this trip across the mountains, although she would never directly express them: "Emily seldom opposed her father's wishes by questions or remonstrances, or she would now" (*Udolpho*, 25).

The narrator backs her up along the way, confirming the ineptitude of St. Aubert, who, "instead of taking the more direct road" (27), chooses for its scenery another that he is not well enough to endure and that imperils the whole party. Emily laments that her father "had taken a road so ill provided" (33); when he tries to get the muleteer to stop to find out whether they're close to a village in which they can rest, "the distance, and the roaring of waters, would not suffer his voice to be heard" (44). He manages "accidentally" to shoot his daughter's new love interest (38). And, if he had simply died in the mountains, Emily would have been bereft but free; instead, he appoints as guardian someone who would make the next three volumes of her life miserable because he "had no alternative" (81) but to choose his sister-in-law, Madame Cheron. (What was wrong with the sturdy, reliable neighbor, M. Barreaux?) For that choice, Emily very loudly (textually speaking) will not criticize him: "Though her affection would not suffer her to question, even a moment, the propriety of St. Aubert's conduct in appointing Madame for her guardian, she was sensible, that this step had made her happiness depend, in a great degree, on the humour of her aunt" (98). Not for a moment would she question, but the narrative takes a moment to bring the point explicitly home. This was a father who needed to be overcome.

And so he would be, both in Emily's return home and in the larger spaces of the novel. Emily's home, La Vallée, gets less attention than the descriptions of Udolpho, but, in some ways, it functions as an equally powerful space for Emily-reading and is, therefore, every bit as detailed. As an interior, it is occupied—its objects determined, its contours shaped—first by the father, but then by the daughter. When Emily first arrives home after her father's death in the mountains, she is overwhelmed by the memory of St. Aubert; he owns and fills up every bit of space, historically and metaphorically:

> Not an object, on which her eye glanced, but awakened some remembrance, that led immediately to the subject of her grief. Her favourite plants, which St. Aubert had taught her to nurse; the little drawings, that adorned the room, which his taste had instructed her to execute; the books, that he had selected for her use, and which they had read together; her musical instruments, whose sounds he loved so well, and which he sometimes awakened himself—every object gave new force to sorrow....
>
> Having passed through the green-house, her courage for a moment forsook her, when she opened the door of the library; and, perhaps, the shade, which evening and the foliage of the trees near the windows threw across

the room, heightened the solemnity of her feelings on entering that apartment, where every thing spoke of her father. There was an arm chair, in
which he used to sit; she shrunk when she observed it, for she had so
often seen him seated there, and the idea of him rose so distinctly to
her mind, that she almost fancied she saw him before her.... She walked
slowly to the chair, and seated herself in it. (*Udolpho*, 94–95)

Shortly after, the maid Theresa prepares a little supper for Emily in "the
common sitting parlour," and, although she had grown up in this house,
"Emily was in the room before she perceived that it was not her own apartment" (97). She sits down at "the little supper table," but not for long: "Her
father's hat hung upon the opposite wall; while she gazed at it, a faintness
came over her. Theresa looked at her, and then at the object, on which her
eyes were settled, and went to remove it; but Emily waved her hand—'No,'
said she, 'let it remain. I am going to my chamber'" (97). Her father's presence
still overpowers the room—and her. But Emily seating herself in her father's
chair on that first day is just the first small gesture of a reappropriation, as
she quietly usurps his patriarchal position. (Between the sixteenth and the
eighteenth centuries, as Daniel Roche argues, the chair "conquers the social space" [173].) In time, "she could bear to read the books she had before
read with her father; to sit in his chair in the library—to watch the flowers
his hand had planted—to awaken the tones of that instrument his fingers
had pressed, and sometimes even to play his favourite air" (*Udolpho*, 99).
Ownership of this domestic interior and these domestic objects has been reversed; instead of St. Aubert awakening her instruments, she awakens his,
so to speak. Emily makes herself *at home*.

   But, by the end of the novel, *at home* is somewhat problematized once
again by Emily's hierarchy of values, by Valancourt's place on that hierarchy,
and, perhaps, by the implicit position of the most obviously "sublime" character, Montoni. Montoni is the villain, of course, but Emily tends to behave a
little revealingly around him. He is initially described as uncommonly handsome, manly, and expressive, with a haughtiness of command and quickness
of discernment, plus a general silence, that put him easily into the sublime
category. During her captivity, as he tries to wrest her estate from her, Emily
grasps his knees (*Udolpho*, 314) and nearly faints thinking about him "ex-
piring at her feet" (316). Like Pamela, she has "no idea of escaping from her
room" (317); when Montoni orders her to be removed from the castle, as it is
about to be besieged, she exclaims "thoughtlessly": "'Of safety!... has, then,
the Signor so much consideration for me?'" (398). As she leaves the castle,
she often looks back on its "blue point" (400). She wonders why Montoni

sent her to such an "enchanting spot" (411). Even Count Morano thinks that she's in love with Montoni (265). The first sublime description of Udolpho suggests the reason:

> "There," said Montoni, speaking for the first time in several hours, "is Udolpho."
>
> Emily gazed with melancholy awe upon the castle, which she understood to be Montoni's; for, though it was now lighted up by the setting sun, the gothic greatness of its features, and its mouldering walls of dark grey stone, rendered it a gloomy and sublime object. As she gazed, the light died away on its walls, leaving a melancholy purple tint, which spread deeper and deeper.... Silent, lonely, and sublime, it seemed to stand the sovereign of the scene.... As the twilight deepened, its features became more awful in obscurity, and Emily continued to gaze, till its clustering towers were alone seen, rising over the tops of the woods....
>
> The extent and darkness of these tall woods awakened terrific images in her mind...she saw, she judged.... Beyond these all was lost in the obscurity of the evening...Emily gazed with awe.... (226–27)

Emily gazes, and gazes, and gazes at rising towers and spreading purple tints over the tops of woods and is *awakened* to terrific images. That, and the description of her room with its "steep, narrow staircase" that has "no bolts on the chamber side, though it had two on the other" (235) and can be easily penetrated by a man (261), hand-deliver with chocolates a psychosexual reading.[20]

Emily's displays of strength throughout the novel outweigh in number and effectiveness her bouts of fainting and helplessness. Cottom claims that, "even when they are not paralyzed, unconscious, or physically abducted and confined by others, [Radcliffe's] heroines frequently find their bodies beyond their control" (52)—a standard assumption about gothic heroines, but one that, in fact, rarely holds up under scrutiny. For one thing, the heroes tend to be equally paralyzed, powerless, emotionally overcome, and/or inept, as we have seen in *Otranto* (chap. 4). But, more important, Emily holds up in all the "sublime," "masculine" roles of resolve, courage, consistency, resistance, self-empowerment. She will never sell the chateau (*Udolpho*, 78); she withstands the temptation to run away with Valancourt (159); she exhibits strength and pride in the presence of Montoni (219, 379, 381, 394–95) and Morano (261, 263); and the narrator affirms, not only "the tenderness of her love," but also "the strength of her resolution" (628). She *earns* her happy ending.

But the ending? The characters' complicated, rather than straightforward, relation to the sublime and beautiful landscapes may help explain why, when Emily is happily returned to the nice home of her father with her nice new husband, Valancourt, the novel should end on a lugubrious series of negatives: "And, if the weak hand, that has recorded this tale, has, by its scenes, beguiled the mourner of one hour of sorrow, or, by its moral, taught him to sustain it—the effort, however humble, has not been vain, nor is the writer unrewarded" (*Udolpho*, 672). Emily ends up with her third choice. And it may help explain why, although the novel is seen as "rationalist" gothic, with the supernatural explained away at the end and most of the fainting fits caused by a momentary lack of courage or resolve, none of the *real* darkness of the preceding six hundred pages is dispelled with the explanations. The mountains, the castles, the Montonis, the banditti, the fact that fathers die, that human beings hear and see and interpret in mysterious ways, that life is fragmented, that even with an omniscient narrator we the readers are left in the dark—all this remains. Radcliffe no more tidies up the darkness than she produces transparent descriptions or unambiguous genderings. She makes description, not a background, not an ornament, but a self-referential system that begs for its own interpretation.

Historical Novels: Scott

In England, civilization has been so long complete, that our ideas of our ancestors are only to be gleaned from musty records and chronicles, the authors of which seem perversely to have conspired to suppress in their narratives all interesting details, in order to find room for flowers of monkish eloquence, or trite reflections upon morals.
—*Sir Walter Scott*, Ivanhoe *(1819)*

Scott, like Radcliffe, was praised for his detailed descriptions—for their novelty as well as their vividness. The *Monthly Magazine* finds that, in *Ivanhoe* (1819), "the exquisite description, and dramatic power of character is sufficient to redeem greater faults than are perceptible in the novels of this original author."[21] Says *Blackwood's Edinburgh Magazine*: "After the first hasty perusal of a work which unites so much novelty of representation with a depth of conception and a power of passion equal, at the least, to what had been exhibited in the best of its predecessors, it is no wonder that we should find ourselves left in a state of excitement not much akin to the spirit of remark or disquisition." The reviewer can hardly speak for pleasure. And he's not finished: "Never were the long-gathered stores of most extensive erudition applied to the purposes of imaginative genius with so much easy, lavish, and luxurious power—never was the illusion of fancy so complete—made up of so many minute elements,—and yet producing such entireness of effect."[22] *So many minute elements, such entireness of effect.* That is Description with a house in the country, if not as gentry with a landed estate.

I concentrate on *Ivanhoe* in this section partly because it is self-consciously contributing to the gothic tradition carved out by Walpole and Radcliffe, partly because its historical representation to some extent follows the anti-Whiggish line of Hume's *History of England*, partly because it so obviously derives from and shares in the culture of domestic tourism discussed in the previous chapter, and partly because, even for its contemporaries, the kind and quantity of its descriptions stand out. In reexamining what Scott brings to description, we will see again what description at any point in history is meant to supply the reader.

Ian Duncan suggests that "the heaviness of the preliminaries [in *Ivanhoe*] has much to do with the author's labour in putting together a new kind of fiction." He is referring, not only to Scott's introduction and his elaborate dedicatory epistle to the Reverend Dryasdust, but also implicitly to the sheer amount of time it takes in the first chapter to set up the stage, to create the space on which these "historical" events will be enacted: "Faster, lighter technologies of narration have made Scott's seem sluggish and encumbered, altogether too literary.... To be sure, once Scott's narrative takes off (by the Ashby tournament) all is fleet and glittering."[23] But six full pages (in Duncan's Oxford edition) are devoted to describing the time, the place, and the first characters, Wamba and Gurth, before anyone moves or speaks. In spite of Glenda Leeming's observation that, "when Richard wants news, there is a well-informed wandering minstrel to hand; when there is need of a quill pen in the forest, a grey goose is of course just passing overhead to be shot down by Robin Hood and rifled of its pinions,"[24] which suggests the kind of objects-to-hand embedded description of the earlier novels of Behn, Defoe, and Haywood, here the carpet really is descriptively rolled out *before* any narrative action. The Waverley novels—also noted for their descriptive powers—had made Scott the favorite author of his day; the first edition of *Ivanhoe* (eight thousand copies) sold out shortly after publication, and, by the end of 1820, a third edition was in production, "and at least five different theatrical versions had opened in London throughout the year" (Duncan, introduction to *Ivanhoe*, viii). The influence, popular and critical, seems inevitable. "Indeed all later novelists," said Sir H. J. C. Grierson, "have inherited from Scott, whether they write historical novels or not, this vital interest of the place and the time. For it is not only the historical novelist who has realized this sense of place and time as a vital part of his effect."[25] Virtually every other English novelist in the nineteenth century went in for the same descriptive "preliminaries": Dickens; Eliot; Gaskell; Trollope. There are exceptions, of course. *Jane Eyre* starts famously in medias res. But its description of the Red Room is every bit as elaborate as *Ivanhoe*'s description of Cedric's hall.

As with Radcliffe, Scott's "novelty" was, of course, culturally and literarily contextualized. Having admired and written on *The Castle of Otranto* and *The Mysteries of Udolpho*, Scott in the dedicatory epistle compared *Ivanhoe* to the "modern Gothic."[26] Duncan argues that "the example of the Gothic novel had been crucial for Scott, but where his Scottish novels had absorbed Gothic elements into a larger scheme of historical romance, *Ivanhoe* appeared to mark a ceremonial return to Gothic: a re-Gothicization of historical fiction" (introduction to *Ivanhoe*, x). That is, Scott *travels to* the gothic past rather than gothicizing (metaphorizing) modern life, attempting to make the past as visible as the present while retaining its idiosyncratic differences. And that is why critics so frequently compare Scott's novels to travel guides. James Kerr argues that, "in the early chapters of [*Waverley*], Scott serves as a sort of tour-guide, leading Waverley and the reader to the various attractions of his native country."[27] Duncan generalizes that most people now associate the Waverley novels with "the reinvention of Scotland for modern tourism."[28] Scott actually took a short trip to Scotland in 1817 while working on *Rob Roy* (a trip that led to "the guidebook legend that he composed it on the banks of Loch Lomond" [Duncan, introduction to *Rob Roy*, x]). But, like Radcliffe, he spun most of his descriptions from travel narratives, such as Defoe's *Tour thro' the whole Island of Great Britain* (1724–26), Edward Burt's *Letters from a Gentleman in the North of Scotland*, and the Reverend Patrick Grahame's *Sketches of Perthshire* (see Duncan, introduction to *Rob Roy*, x). Yet, also like Radcliffe, he did much more than lift them.

Graham Tulloch presents *Ivanhoe* as a sort of medieval tour guide rather than a history in the chronicle sense.[29] And, of course, Scott himself presents *Ivanhoe* that way, addressing in the dedicatory epistle Dryasdust's worries about the extent to which English readers will understand and like what he's doing:

> If you describe to [the English reader] a set of wild manners, and a state of primitive society existing in the Highlands of Scotland, he is much disposed to acquiesce in the truth of what is asserted. And reason good. If he

be of the ordinary class of readers, he has either never seen those remote districts at all, or he has wandered through those desolate regions in the course of a summer tour, eating bad dinners, sleeping on truckle beds, stalking from desolation to desolation, and fully prepared to believe the strangest things that could be told him of a people, wild and extravagant enough to be attached to scenery so extraordinary. But the same worthy person, when placed in his own snug parlour, and surrounded by all the comforts of an Englishman's fire-side, is not half so much disposed to believe that his own ancestors led a very different life from himself. (16)

Scott prepares his descriptions of historical and cultural *difference* in the face of presumed ignorance of and resistance to the past. Lukács, in comparing Scott's novels to those of earlier novelists, comments: "The great writers of the eighteenth century composed much more loosely. They were able to do so because they took the manners of their time for granted and could assume an immediate and obvious effect upon their readers."[30] Because he cannot assume a cultural storehouse and his description must supply it, Scott goes back to medieval England "full of minute details of medieval life... culled from the best authorities available to him: a mass of information about food, clothing, physical appearance, buildings, social classes, money, religious beliefs and superstitions" (Tulloch, xiv). "It is clear," says Lukács, "that the more remote an historical period and the conditions of life of its actors, the more the action must concern itself with bringing these conditions plastically before us" (*Historical Novel*, 43). Where in the later eighteenth century description served to visualize for the reader the expanding differences of *contemporary* society, in the early nineteenth Scott expanded the territory of strangeness to include the English past and attempted to make it home. As Ann Rigney argues, and as Thomas Babington Macaulay would understand, "Scott's thematic innovations must be seen in the context of a larger historiographical project to move beyond the sphere of politics and military operations into cultural and private spheres involving the population at large."[31]

As with Radcliffe, with Scott critics tend to agree that his descriptions are, in the words of Graham Tulloch, "not merely background decoration but often assume a central position in the story or the characterisation so that they achieve considerable prominence" (xiv). Alexander Welsh rather simply aligns Scott's topography with his characterization, as most critics do with Radcliffe: "The topographical stress of the Waverley Novels complements the contrast of two basic character types. The face of the land as well as the features of heroes and heroines physically represent the dualism of law and nature, reason and passion, sobriety and romance."[32] More complexly, James Kerr sees Waverley as "continually making a work of art out of the landscape," an Englishman assimilating and appropriating the Scottish landscape (24). But Scott also carves out larger and more detailed interiors, as in the descriptive preliminaries setting up Cedric's mansion in the third chapter of *Ivanhoe*:

> In a hall, the height of which was greatly disproportioned to its extreme length and width, a long oaken table formed of planks rough-hewn from the forest, and which had scarcely received any polish, stood ready prepared for the evening meal of Cedric the Saxon. The roof, composed of beams and rafters, had nothing to divide the apartment from the sky excepting the planking and thatch; there was a huge fire-place at either end of the hall, but as the chimneys were constructed in a very clumsy manner, at least as much of the smoke found its way into the apartment as escaped by the proper vent. The constant vapour which this occasioned, had polished the rafters and beams of the low-browed hall, by encrusting them with a black varnish of soot. On the sides of the apartment hung implements of war and of the chase, and there were at each corner folding doors, which gave access to other parts of the extensive building. (47)

Scott's description of the interior and exterior of Cedric's mansion, not to mention his clothes and his attendants, goes on for several pages, until all its corners, furniture, and inhabitants appear fully formed and minutely traced. Scott, like Radcliffe, creates a space ahead of time in which to place characters and their actions; he is fully aware of the power of accumulated detail to halt the reader in her narrativized tracks. Sir Leslie Stephen said that Scott's greatest achievement was "the *vivification* of history" (quoted in Grierson, 18); in supplying the cultural storehouse, Scott explains each object in the scene and its relation to the rest. He then, in his "plastic" way, gives social dimension to physical space:

> The other appointments of the mansion partook of the rude simplicity of the Saxon period, which Cedric piqued himself upon maintaining. The floor was composed of earth mixed with lime, trodden into such a hard substance, as is often employed in flooring our modern barns. For about one quarter of the length of the apartment, the floor was raised by a step, and this space, which was called the dais, was occupied only by the principal members of the family and visitors of distinction. For this purpose, a table richly covered with scarlet cloth was placed transversely

across the platform, from the middle of which run the longer and lower board, at which the domestics and inferior persons fed, down towards the bottom of the hall. The whole resembled the form of the letter T, or some of those ancient dinner-tables, which, arranged on the same principles, be still seen in the antique Colleges of Oxford or Cambridge. (*Ivanhoe*, 47)

Scott offers the dual perspective of the eighteenth-century historian, who positions the present in relation to the past. "Our modern barns" and the "antique colleges of Oxford" mark for the contemporary reader of *Ivanhoe* a sense of progress perhaps, a sense of temporal distance certainly. Mark Phillips compares Hume's technique to Scott's, arguing that, for both, "the manners of the past are only visible against the backdrop of present assumptions."[33] Preference at table was as rigorously prescribed in Scott's time as in Cedric's, but the trappings were different, and Scott was as interested in the trappings as in the somewhat longer-lasting social hierarchy. Scott has Cedric himself maintaining historical and cultural boundaries through spatial maintenance, with surfaces, with interior management. The description particularizes the space so that the particulars have meaning, on their own (as in Defoe's novels), but also in relation to each other. Visual space is filled in; the house is built, the carpet is laid, and the characters can now move in and begin their novelistic lives and actions.

For David Brown, "the effort of Scott's research in writing *Ivanhoe* notably fails to result in increased historical realism: in fact, the lack of realism is made more rather than less noticeable by the surfeit of bookish detail in the descriptive passages." Later authors who follow Scott's advice about research, Brown argues, such as Flaubert and Bulwer Lytton, end up in "a sterile externality which makes *Ivanhoe* look 'determinedly anti-antiquarian' by comparison."[34] But as Sir Leslie Stephen aptly put it: "We must begin by asking impartially what pleased men, and then inquire why it pleased them. We must not decide dogmatically that it ought to have pleased or displeased on the simple ground that it is or is not congenial to ourselves."[35]

Brown seems to miss the point, first, about Scott's (and *Ivanhoe*'s) massive nineteenth-century critical and popular success and, second, about the function of his descriptive detail. Scott most definitely "pleased men." And the vividness was much of it. The *Critical Review*, for example, "explicitly linked its appreciation for the vividness of Scott's portraits to the way in which characterization was embedded in action rather than ladled out in discrete passages of description" (Rigney, 155 nn. 60, 62). The reviewer for the *London Magazine*, after some hypothetical reservations about the

general reader's appreciation of *Ivanhoe* after the Waverley novels, embarks
on a description of Scott's descriptions that is every bit as charged with his
own readerly immediacy and full participation in the supplied storehouse as
Macaulay's description of Bunyan's spaces in *The Pilgrim's Progress*:

> The first paragraph of the present novel ... breathes upon us at once
> the mild fresh air of the English climate, and stamps the place of the
> fiction by presenting to our imaginations the rich and noble beauty of
> English scenery. The grassy glades of majestic forests—the broad short-
> stemmed oaks which the author, by a most skilful touch, associates with
> "the stately march of the Roman soldiery;"—gliding rivers, and pleasant
> towns, guarantee to us that we are indeed in "merry England." The very
> brook, so boisterous in his former compositions, is now hushed to the
> quiet tone of the new country; when interrupted in its course by some
> fallen druidical stones, the opposition to its course only gives "a feeble
> voice of murmur to the placid and elsewhere silent streamlet."

He concludes: "[O]ur author is penetrated with the characteristic aspect
and spirit of the objects amongst which he has come,—and this is enough to
satisfy us that he will acquit himself well. It will hold good in every sense, we
believe, if we affirm that, when *at home*, he is sure to be delightful."[36] One
of the primary functions of description, after making the familiar strange,
is to make the strange familiar. Scott is at home in his descriptions, and
so were the readers for whom description was itself settling down into a
comfortable domesticity.

Historiography: Hume and Gibbon

In musing on history writing, Thomas Babington Macaulay noted: "To call
up our ancestors before us with all their peculiarities of language, manners,
and garb, to show us over their houses, to seat us at their tables, to rum-
mage their old-fashioned wardrobes, to explain the uses of their ponderous
furniture, these parts of the duty which properly belongs to the historian
have been appropriated by the historical novelist."[37] But in fact, he has it
slightly wrong. The historian always rejected—much more loudly and for
much longer than the novelist—any "duty" toward ordinary detail or circumstantial description, *particularly* of domestic interiors. In history writing, terrain was described to contextualize battle strategies, and Star Chambers appear as sites of political decisions. Yet such was the domestication,
even gentrification, of description at the end of the eighteenth century and

into the nineteenth that fiction began to seem full and history empty. But it was not quite so descriptively empty as Macaulay complained: history writing, too, responded to the pressures of new ways of seeing, new kinds of surfaces, new worlds of goods, and its spaces acquired articulation, although its rhetoric disguised the difference. Thomas Carlyle credited Scott's novels, which, he said, "have taught all men this truth, which looks like a truism, and yet was as good as unknown to writers of history and others, till so taught: that the bygone ages of the world were actually filled by living men, not by protocols, state-papers, controversies, and abstractions of men. Not abstractions were they, not diagrams and theorems; but men, in buff or other coats and breeches, with colour in their cheeks, with passions in their stomach, and the idioms, features and vitalities of very men.... History will henceforth have to take thought of it."[38] And history did, in its own way.

Criticism from Horace and Aristotle to René Rapin (1621–87), Peter Whalley (1722–91), and, of course, Samuel Johnson (1706–84) catechized against ornament and superfluity even more fiercely in history writing. A 1680 translation of Rapin's Instructions pour l'histoire (1677) inquires rhetorically: "What Discernment and Recollection is there not requisite... to expose things at large or minutely, according as necessity or decorum require... and never to tire out the Reader by an excessive Uniformity?" The "grand Secret" of the historian, according to Rapin, is "to know how to make a prudent and judicious choice of the Circumstances, fit to give a great Idea of the thing... and by that minute dissection to render them capable of fastening on the Mind. A Collection of great and small Circumstances methodically intermix'd one with another, is of that nature when they are well chosen.... It is 'mean, frivolous, and minute Particularities, which debase a Subject; for he becomes childish, and indeed ridiculous, who insists too much on small things.'" No kings' vests or emperors' bucklers allowed: "Of what concern is it to me, to know whether Hannibal had a fair Sett of Teeth, provided his Historian discover to me the Grandeur of his Genius[?]"[39]

The historical critics repeat the charge of digression and interruption so familiar from the belletristic writers. Rapin cites the "frigidity" of "impertinent" descriptions (72), and Peter Whalley notes that, when descriptions are "too numerous, the Narration is embarrassed, and the Thread of the Story is unnaturally torn asunder."[40] Johnson criticizes Clarendon's history as a narration "not perhaps sufficiently rapid, but stopped too frequently by Particularities, which though they might strike the Author who was present at the Transactions, will not equally detain the Attention of Posterity" (Rambler, no. 122 [18 May 1751], 4:289–90). Description, that old obstacle, gets in the way, and the reader, losing plot or linearity or action in digression, just gets bored: "For what Art is there not requisite to prevent the distraction of the reader, and to keep him in a continual posture of Attention?" (Rapin, 44).

So descriptions in all the Best Models were kept "necessary, exact, succinct, elegant" (Rapin, 73). One of the favorites cited by both Rapin and Whalley is from Tacitus's *Annals*.[41] Tiberius retires to Capri,

> an Island disjoin'd from the point of the Cape of Surrentum by a channel of three miles. I should chiefly believe that he was taken with its solitude, as the sea above it is void of havens, as the stations for the smallest vessels are few and difficult, and as none could put in unperceiv'd by the guards. The genius of the climate is mild in winter, from the shelter of a mountain which intercepts the rigour of the winds: its summers are refresh'd by gales from the West; and the sea open all round it, makes a delightful view: from thence too was beheld a most lovely landskip, before the eruptions of Mount Vesuvius had chang'd the face of the prospect.[42]

Such a description draws the political lines: the open shoreline protected from secret invasions. It remarks favorably on the climate and the inhabitants' general seasonal experience; it offers a quick, undetailed bird's-eye view of mountains, open sea, lovely (now vanished) landscape. In short, it "specifies the Reasons which *Tiberius* had to retire thither, towards the end of his days, which makes it necessary: and being short, elegant, polite, as it is, having nothing superfluous, it may be said, that it is as it should be" (Rapin, 70). It is a *sketch*.

Such a call to "politeness" recalls the vocabulary of "barbarousness," "decorum," and "propriety" of sixteenth- and seventeenth-century criticism discussed in chapter 1. Sir Philip Sidney had suggested in 1595: "And euen *Historiographers*, although their lippes sound of things done, and veritie be written in their foreheads, haue bene glad to borrow both fashion and perchance weight of the Poets" (*Defence* [1575], B4v). Such a borrowing of "fashion" and "weight" obviously included the proprieties along the way. But, by the later eighteenth century, the historians were also absorbing some of the other critical fashions of the "poets." The rhetoric for eighteenth-century history writing apparently swallows all those dicta about circumstantial detail whole. In the lecture "Historical Writing," for example, Hugh Blair warns against "prolix detail" and repeats what he had said about poetry: "General facts make a slight impression on the mind. It is by means of circumstances and particulars *properly chosen*, that a narration becomes interesting and affecting to the Reader" (*Lectures*, 2:274). Yet, even as the phrase seems to repeat Rapinian strictures, the idea of what constitutes proper choice has undergone a sea change; as Mark Phillips notes: "[I]t is striking to see the great ancient histories applauded as 'picturesque' or 'interesting'" (42). More than a whiff of late eighteenth-century aesthetics mingles in the critical discourse and historical practice. The *Monthly Review* declared of Sir John Sinclair's *History of the Public Revenue* (1790):

> History, till of late, was chiefly employed in the recital of warlike transactions.... The *people* were not known; the circumstances that affected *their* domestic prosperity and happiness were entirely overlooked; and the records of many ages might have been perused without obtaining the least information concerning any fact that led to a knowledge of the internal economy of the state, or the private situation of individuals.
>
> Thanks, however, to the more enlightened spirit of modern times, things are much altered in this respect.[43]

Thanks to the study of manners pioneered by Voltaire in *Siècle de Louis XIV* (1751) and *Essai sur les moeurs* (1756), according to this reviewer, while history is not exactly rummaging in cupboards or exploring private dwellings, the geography of interest is clearly changing from the public to the private.

The invitation to greater spatial detail offered by the new interest in "manners"—including the touring of houses and the publishing of architectural observations—was answered even in historical writing. Detail, if still on the submerged side, was getting perceptibly more vivid. Compare, for example, Arthur Murphy's 1793 translation of Tacitus's description of Capri to the earlier version quoted above:

> [Capri was] a small island, separated from the promontory of Surentum by an arm of the sea, not more than three miles broad. Defended there from all intrusion, and delighted with the solitude of the place, [Tiberius] sequestered himself from the world, seeing, as may be imagined, many circumstances suited to his humour. Not a single port in the channel; the stations but few, and those accessible only to small vessels; no part of the island, where men could land unobserved by the sentinels; the climate inviting; in the winter, a soft and genial air, under the shelter of a mountain, that repels the inclemency of the winds; in the summer, the heat allayed by the western breeze; the sea presenting a smooth expanse, and opening a view of the bay of Naples, with a beautiful landscape on its borders: all these conspired to please the taste and genius of Tiberius. The

scene, indeed, has lost much of its beauty, the fiery eruptions of Mount
Vesuvius having, since that time, changed the face of the country.[44]

This description is literally longer than Gordon's translation seventy years
earlier. Although the difference in length may simply be the result of a difference in the talents of the translators, the fidelity to contemporary habits
is too striking to ignore. Murphy's sea is no longer just "open all round" but
presents "a smooth expanse"; the mild winter is elaborated into "a soft and
genial air"; the view is now particularly of Naples; the eruptions have gotten
"fiery"; and Tiberius here is a man of "taste" and "genius."

Whalley approved the seventeenth-century annalists' pruning of "Luxuriance and Superfluity," which he found to be increasingly cluttering up
the texts of eighteenth-century historians. But the annalist doesn't quite
make the grade as a historian because he also omits "Motives and Consequence[s]" (3–4). A gentleman in Sarah Fielding's Remarks on Clarissa (1749)
smugly produces a complete plot summary of Clarissa in a few paragraphs;
but, as Miss Gibson retorts: "[B]y his Rule of Writing, [an almanac] was the
best History of England, and Almanack-makers were the best Historians."[45]
Chronological narrations of great events needed a sort of thickening, and
that thickening, as many critics have noted, appropriated some of the novelistic strategies of the eighteenth century in absorbing details and rendering
scenes.

Harold Bond encapsulates the received wisdom about the difference between eighteenth- and nineteenth-century history writing: "One should not
come to Gibbon, as one does to Froude, Carlyle, or Michelet, for an imaginative re-creation of the past which the reader may experience vicariously."[46]
I do not propose to argue otherwise. What I want to propose is the extent to
which the increased cultural and narrative interest in the details of surfaces
and spaces was seeping into historical writing as well. David Womersley
notes that, in the first volume of The Decline and Fall of the Roman Empire
(1776), Gibbon's prose "appears to have passed through the mire of mere particularity to reach the commanding heights of true historical knowledge,"
but later, when Gibbon's "faith in the validity of those large, unified perspectives wanes, ... then the concrete is the grit around which he makes his
pearls."[47] Bond finds in the concrete grit, as it were, the most classical form
of description, one in which space is an undefined backdrop for action that
realizes its objects in narrative, and one that depends on the reader's cultural storehouse: "[In the battle scenes] there is movement, of course, but in
capturing the key features of the action, Gibbon has confined it and arrested
it in its moment of greatest vitality, stripped of superfluous detail. We do

not see the terrain nor do we know the time of day. . . . In the attack on Constantinople we see in the foreground a conflict of weapons—swords, spears, and battle-axes, and the reader fills in the human faces and cries which are left in the shadowy background" (73).

Yet Gibbon's descriptions are not purely classical; as Mark Phillips notes, the traditional rhetoric was covering a sea change of practice. G. W. Bowersock argues that Gibbon "treated the raw materials of ancient and mediaeval history much as a novelist treated the plot line," and, although he was not interested in art or architecture and had little visual imagination, he was excited by topography, and his description of Constantinople "is still one of the best ever written, even though he had never been there" (10, 13). Bowersock refers to Richard and Cosima Wagner in characterizing Gibbon's shaping of his material as dramatic rather than visual and points to his love of the classical French theater of Racine and Corneille. But, tellingly, Bowersock also describes the descriptions themselves as set pieces—"a scene for events that fired his imagination"; "a suitable stage for great events" (13, 14). And that, of course, is the nineteenth-century stock-in-trade. Topographical description entered into historical as well as novelistic writing in the eighteenth century to open up more visualized space for human action, for narrative itself.[48]

I will concentrate in this section on Hume, however, who, with William Robertson, provided English models for Gibbon: "Robertson has adorned the annals of his homeland with all the graces of the most vigorous eloquence. Hume, born to instruct and judge mankind, has carried into history the light of a profound and elegant philosophy."[49] David Wootton has argued that Hume, as a historian, positioned himself competitively against novelists; Everett Zimmerman counters that, in fact, Hume *incorporates* novelistic narrative techniques of "rendering . . . the private world of the historical agent."[50] Zimmerman focuses on Hume's sense of the constructedness of history writing, the "careful placement in time that is a feature of formal realism," the narrative connectedness through causality and contiguity, and the dual perspectives of "both trying to understand events as they appeared to contemporary spectators and trying, as well, to grasp the less public motives of participants in historical events" (236–39). But Zimmerman, Wootton, Phillips, and other analysts of Hume's historical techniques tend to focus on his crafting of contiguity in time; there is virtually no mention of Hume's use of space in his *History of England* (1754–62). In some ways, this is not surprising because, as Phillip Hicks points out, although some contemporaries claimed that Hume was writing history in a new manner, that "new manner" matched Voltaire's French classicism in "its avoidance of

trivial detail, its smooth, unbroken narrative, and its abundant reflections,"
with the result that most of his contemporaries "did not object to whatever
innovations Hume might have introduced into British historiography as in-
consistent with neoclassical standards for history."[51] But, as Phillips noted
about Blair, who managed to see classical models of history through a "picturesque" lens with no consciousness of anachronism, so the "new manner"
of writing history pioneered by Voltaire, and those interiors so carefully visualized by Richardson, Radcliffe, and Scott, opened up a conceptual space
for history writing to elaborate space as well as time.

Hume himself articulated most of the classical conventions about the
use of detail and description in narrative. He notes, for example, the use
of "minute circumstances" in poetry, "which, though to the historian they
seem superfluous, serve mightily to enliven the imagery and gratify the
fancy. If it be not necessary, as in the *Iliad*, to inform us each time the
hero buckles his shoes and ties his garters, it will be requisite, perhaps, to
enter into a greater detail than in the *Henriade*, where the events are run
over with such rapidity that we scarce have leisure to become acquainted
with the scene or action."[52] Hume disliked stylistic extravagance, arguing
for "simplicity and refinement in writing."[53] Yet, in history writing, he criticizes Clarendon's lack of detail in describing the execution of Charles I:
"Lord CLARENDON, when he approaches towards the apostrophe of the royal
party, supposes, that his narration then becomes infinitely disagreeable; and
he hurries over the king's death, without giving us one circumstance of it. He
considers it as too horrid a scene to be contemplated with any satisfaction, or
even without the utmost pain and aversion."[54] In general, as Mark Phillips
notes, eighteenth-century historical narratives move toward the mimetic:
"[T]hey concentrate on recording the concreteness of events . . . emphasizing
the satisfactions of detailed narrative" (23). Hume's devotion to neoclassical prescriptions was tempered by an eighteenth-century predilection for
looking more closely and rendering surfaces more exactly.

Hume's own historical descriptions thus offer notably more detail—
visual and spatial—than Clarendon's covering the same ground. In the account of Oliver Cromwell's last days, for example, Hume's version enters
more intimately into the scenes of horror, spacing out the linear narrative with precise details of objects, rooms, and states of mind. Clarendon
writes with the sort of "aloof generality" that, as Phillips argues, eighteenth-
century readers associated with "the dignity of history" (28):

> It had been observ'd in *England*, that, though from the dissolution of the
> last Parliament, all things seem'd to succeed, at home and abroad, to the

Protector's wish, and his power and greatness to be better establish'd than ever it had been, yet he never had the same serenity of mind he had been used to, after he had refused the Crown; but was out of countenance, and chagrin, as if he were conscious of not having been true to himself; and much more apprehensive of danger to his Person than he used to be. Insomuch as he was not easy of access, nor so much seen abroad; and seem'd to be in some disorder, when his Eyes found any Stranger in the room; upon whom they were still fixed. When he intended to go to *Hampton* Court, which was his principal delight and diversion, it was never known, till he was in the Coach, which way he would go; and he was still hem'd in by his Guards both before and behind; and the Coach in which he went, was always thronged as full as it could be, with his Servants; who were armed; and he seldom returned the same way he went; and rarely lodged two Nights together in one Chamber, but had many furnished and prepared, to which his own Key convey'd him and those he would have with him, when he had a mind to go to bed: which made his fears the more taken notice of, and publick, because he had never been accustom'd to those precautions.[55]

Hume revises, changing the sense of distance between reader and historical figure by refining and intensifying visual details and verbal patterns:

Death, too, which, with such signal intrepidity, he had braved in the field, being incessantly threatened by the poinards of fanatical or interested assassins, was ever present to his terrified apprehension, and haunted him in every scene of business or repose. Each action of his life betrayed the terrors under which he laboured. The aspect of strangers was uneasy to him: With a piercing and anxious eye he surveyed every face to which he was not daily accustomed. He never moved a step without strong guards attending him: He wore armour under his cloaths, and farther secured himself by offensive weapons, a sword, falchion, and pistols, which he always carried about him. He returned from no place by the direct road, or by the same way which he went. Every journey he performed with hurry and precipitation. Seldom he slept above three nights together in the same chamber: And he never let it be known beforehand what chamber he intended to choose, nor entrusted himself in any, which was not provided with back-doors, at which sentinels were carefully placed. Society terrified him, which he reflected on his numerous, unknown, and implacable enemies: Solitude astonished him, by withdrawing that protection which he found so necessary for his security.[56]

The various chambers are not themselves described in either account (although Hume's have back doors), but, where Clarendon ascribes motive and feeling from a distance ("as if," "seem'd to be"), Hume penetrates the psychological interior with Richardsonian confidence and emotional particularization: the adjectives and verbs "terrified," "haunted," "piercing and anxious," "hurry and precipitation," and "astonished" vivisect the Cromwellian soul. Phrases such as "every scene of business," "each action of his life," and "every journey" break into smaller bits the chronology implicit in Clarendon's "used to be," "still," and "always." Generalized objects such as "offensive weapons" are particularized into "a sword, falchion, and pistols." Where Clarendon's Cromwell is seen from without ("it had been observ'd," "the more taken notice of, and publick," and, in general, in the use of passive voice), Hume's is known from within, with the certainty of active verbs.

David Womersley argues, however, that Hume's predominant voice in the *History of England* is one of dispassion, composure, distance, with a general "refusal to attempt any duplication of the past's texture." This is not indifference (he notes that Hume's marked lack of judgment against the monks' torture of Elgiva "makes the writing gently, reticently elegiac" [23]) but intellectual control: "The essence of Hume's views on historical narrative is that composure, and the perspective conferred by distance, yields insight" (25). Hume himself had said: "There are different ways of examining the Mind, as well as the Body. One may consider it either as an Anatomist or as a Painter: either to discover its most secret Springs & Principles or to describe the Grace & Beauty of its Actions. I imagine it impossible to conjoin these two Views."[57] The historian is an anatomist, not a painter, because his object is not before him, reasons Womersley (although the anatomist surely needs a body as much as a painter). I suggest that, while Hume may not be a painterly historian in Macaulay's sense of rummaging for detail, he yet employs a strengthened rhetoric of visualness both in the scenes he opens up with greater detail than in earlier historians' versions and in the contrasting scenes of suppression.[58]

Hume employs the "objective," from-the-outside, passive-voiced historical narration, for particular purposes of perspective. The murder of Sir Edmund Berry Godfrey during the Popish Plot was never solved; Hume gathers up the forensic details of the corpse within the speculations of the authorities:

> This magistrate had been missing some days; and after much search, and many surmises, his body was found lying in a ditch at Primrose-Hill: The marks of strangling were thought to appear about his neck, and

some contusions on his breast: His own sword was sticking in the body; but as no considerable quantity of blood ensued on drawing it, it was concluded, that it had been thrust in after his death, and that he had not killed himself: He had rings on his fingers and money in his pocket: It was therefore inferred, that he had not fallen into the hands of robbers. (*History*, 6:341)

The reader is given the same information as the contemporary observer at the scene of the crime; the inferences of the officials are offered up for judgment along with the evidence. But, by the time we get to the political uses made of this murder, Hume reinstates readerly access into both the political agenda and the popular response: "In order to propagate the popular frenzy, several artifices were employed. The dead body of Godfrey was carried into the city, attended by vast multitudes. It was publicly exposed in the streets, and viewed by all ranks of men; and every one, who saw it, went away inflamed, as well by the mutual contagion of sentiments, as by the dismal spectacle itself" (6:342). Everett Zimmerman argues that Hume's ultimate structural preference for history writing was to impose a causal narrative onto the associative pattern of contiguity in time and space (239), and, here, the "contagion of sentiments" and the "dismal spectacle" combine to "inflame" "all ranks of men" gathered in the streets. Time is expanded in one direction by the "philosophical eye" that Hume believed "would depict the changing climate of opinion as it affected the interests, fears, and affections of humankind" (Phillips, 50) and in another by the space of detail, the spaces of *space*. As with the exhibition of Godfrey's body in the streets, Hume outlines the spaces that provide a spatial motive for public political action: for the execution of Lord Russell, "the scaffold was erected in Lincoln's Inn Fields, a place distant from the Tower; and it was probably intended, by conducting Russel through so many streets, to show the mutinous city their beloved leader, once the object of all their confidence, now exposed to the utmost rigours of the law" (*History*, 6:434).

Leo Braudy confesses that he is often bored by Hume's "undiscriminating" method of relying (particularly in the earlier-written Stuart volumes) too much on time itself to "provide the cohesion and continuity, as if the conjunctions of chronology told all" (*Narrative Form*, 87). He acknowledges Hume's causal, evidentiary, psychological, and rhetorical axes into the chronological line but insists that Hume eventually and unfortunately "withdraw[s] his narrative voice to allow the slow accretions of time to shape history" (49). On the one hand, Braudy does not adequately recognize the submerged but powerful *new* influences on and in Hume's

History—the increase in local detail, the spacing out of temporal scenes—and, on the other, he does not recognize the overt pull of the classical. As Phillips argues, the "prestige" of midcentury works of sentiment, social interest, and new geographic and ethnographic discoveries was "not accompanied by a movement to jettison classical models of historical narrative," and, in fact, convention "continued to entail that the best productions of modern letters would be held up to standards still deeply imbued with classical ideals, including...linearity and perspicuity" (8). Hume's *History* is an example of another genre quietly absorbing and employing the expanded territories of description precisely within the rhetoric of unadorned chronological narrative.

Macaulay had distinguished between two types of history in the mid-nineteenth century: one like a map, the other like a painted landscape. The painting gives us full visualization, but without accurate dimensions, distances, or angles. The map gives exact information, but no imaginative filling in (*Critical and Historical Essays*, 50–52). No historian, he claimed, had yet successfully combined the two approaches (as Ogilby had done for cartography in his road maps, we might think) because history writing is "under the jurisdiction of two hostile powers"—reason and imagination—"and, like other districts similarly situated, it is ill defined, ill cultivated, and ill regulated.... It may be laid down as a general rule, though subject to considerable qualifications and exceptions, that History begins in Novel and ends in Essay."[59] What Macaulay was historically marking, however, was, in part, the eighteenth-century remapping of the visual, the circumstantial, the surface, in narrative. The geographies of description and narrative, of visualization and factualization, of space and time, were in the process of redistricting. Although history writing would, for the most part, continue to ignore Macaulay's call for the spatially intimate, the circumstantially minute, the novelistically constructed, history nevertheless found itself spatially, circumstantially, and novelistically relocating from the classical world into eighteenth-century Britain.

✿

AFTERWORD: HUMPHRY REPTON

A knowledge of *arrangement or disposition* is, of all others, the most useful; and this must extend to external appendages as well as to internal accommodation.

—*Humphry Repton*, Observations on . . . Landscape Gardening *(1803)*

Humphry Repton (1752–1818), coiner of the term *landscape gardening* and master of domestic arrangements, seems a fitting figure with which to end this book. Like Hume, and Macaulay, and to some extent Ogilby, Repton was skeptical of the powers of a map in relation to a "painted landscape"—figuratively as well as literally. His early biographer J. C. Loudon claimed that he "found that a mere *map* was insufficient; as being no more capable of conveying an idea of the landscape, than the *ground-plan* of a house does of its *elevation*."[1] Repton did sketch rudimentary maps in his Red Books (those two-hundred-odd morocco-bound volumes of watercolor plans for various estates), but the maps were primarily just versions of estate surveys. The Red Books are really known for their combination of the before-and-after landscapes (with "slides" that could be lifted to dramatize the changes) and the carefully detailed and argued descriptions of what he envisioned. "Writing for Repton was a serious business," says Stephen Daniels.[2] Repton's written descriptions fill in even further the spaces imagined by his watercolors. In discussing Glemham Hall, for example, Repton was able to combine precise measurements, monetary estimates, and architectural character analysis: built of red brick, the hall has by the end of the eighteenth century, he finds, come to look too much like a workhouse; he recommends a whitewash.

Repton combines the historical and the visual, text and image, in the interests of both the aesthetic and the practical. Unlike the purists (and

231

his critics) Uvedale Price and Richard Payne Knight, who argued for the correspondence between landscape painting and landscape gardening, Repton agreed with his predecessor Capability Brown that nature was, in fact, something different from art; we move *inside* a landscape, changing perspective from all directions, encountering atmospheric differences, sheep, and mud. "Repton strove to present the perspectives of the land-agent, the kitchen-gardener, and the engineer" (Daniels, introduction, ix), not to mention the inhabitants of a house—mingling these perspectives into his own set of textual praxes. And, in so doing, said his contemporary William Mason, "he alters places on paper and makes them so picturesque that fine folks think that all the oaks etc. he draws on paper will grow exactly in the shape and fashion in which he delighted them."[3] Repton is, thus, an excellent visual figure of the descriptor, who alters places on paper, and his *Observations on the Theory and Practice of Landscape Gardening* summarizes much of what was experienced and articulated in later eighteenth-century Britain that contributed to the emerging prominence of that former nuisance, description.

In the *Observations*, Repton defends Lancelot ("Capability") Brown—who seemed much too tame and domesticated to rugged picturesquians such as Price and Knight—as a man and artist who combined "natural quickness of perception" with a "habitual correctness of observation" applied to "the higher requisites of the art, relating to *form*, to *proportion*, to *character*, and, above all, to *arrangement*" (167). Perception, observation, and arrangement have always been preconditions for any art, of course, but they were being culturally promoted in that famous eighteenth-century phenomenon of *taste*. And arrangement is "above all" because there was *so much to arrange*. Repton analyzes historical change in the great domestic house in England, from pre-Elizabethan houses, where "views from a window were of little consequence at a time when glass was hardly transparent," to the contemporary house, in which patrons and architects were so embarrassed by the existence of "offices" that they hid them with plantings (170–73) (fig. 16). He adds a footnote: "Such is the horror of seeing any building belong to the offices, that, in one instance, I was desired by the architect to plant a wood of trees on the earth which had been laid over the copper roofs of the kitchen offices, and which extended 300 feet in length from the house" (173n). In the current house, there is much to display, much to hide. But a mansion is not, he insists, like a prospect tower, whose only use is "to look out of the windows" (175). Organizing prospects is a matter that should come from within as well as without, determined, not simply by what is seen from the

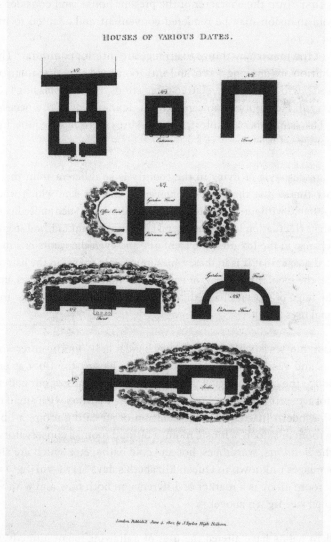

Figure 16. "Houses of Various Dates," in Humphry Repton, *Observations on the Theory and Practice of Landscape Gardening* (1803). Courtesy of the Newberry Library, Chicago.

windows, but also by what happens behind them or through them—"cold exposure to the north, the glaring blaze of a setting sun, or the frequent boisterous winds and rains" (180). But, in renovating old houses, the dignity of the old must be considered and respected when adapting it to the new. (Very Scottian.) In discussing changes to Michel Grove, for example, Repton inquires first "into the character of the present house, and consider[s] how far the old mansion may be rendered convenient and adapted to modern comforts" (176).

One of the many new things to arrange are interior contours: "The proposed addition of a drawing-room, and anti-room, and an eating-room of large dimensions, will alter those relative proportions, now so pleasing" (*Observations*, 176). He implies some regret but acknowledges the necessity of change. The demands of comfort, the pressures of *things*, require internal rearrangements:

> The present style of living in the country is so different from that of former times, that there are few houses of ancient date which would be habitable without great alterations and additions. Such indeed is the constant fluctuation in the habits and customs of mankind, and so great the change in the luxuries, the comforts, and even the wants of a more refined people that it is in these times impossible to live in the baronial castle, the secularized abbey, or even in the more modern palaces, built in the reign of Queen Elizabeth, preserving all the apartments to their original uses. (177)

In the past, houses (such as Cedric's) had a great hall "for the entertainment of friends and vassals; a large and lofty room, having the floor at one end raised above the common level, as at present in the halls of our colleges"; a gallery for reception, dancing; a chapel; and small parlors with small closets (177–78). Modern life requires the addition of an eating room, a library, a drawing room or saloon, a music room, a billiard room, a conservatory, "and lastly, the *Boudoirs*, wardrobes, hot and cold baths, &c. which are all modern appendages unknown in Queen Elizabeth's days" (178–79) (fig. 17). The drawing room alone is a marker of difference in both how and with what it is occupied (see fig. 10 above):

> Modern habits have altered the uses of a drawing-room: formerly the best room in the house was opened only a few days in each year, where the guests sat in a formal circle, but now the largest and best room in a gentleman's house is that most frequented and inhabited: it is filled with books, musical instruments, tables of every description, and whatever can contribute to the comfort or amusement of the guests, who form themselves into groups, at different parts of the room; and in winter, by the help of two fireplaces, the restraint and formality of the circle is done away. (*Observations*, 185)

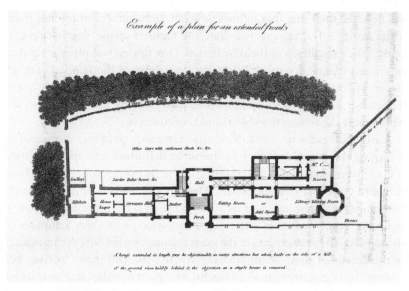

Figure 17. "Example of a plan for an extended front," in Humphry Repton, *Observations on the Theory and Practice of Landscape Gardening* (1803). Courtesy of the Newberry Library, Chicago.

More rooms, more perspectives; more furniture, more things to arrange; prospects within and without; the emphasis on variety and difference and surface rather than uniformity, symmetry, exactness. Caroline Bingley walks Elizabeth Bennett around the perimeters of the room to afford the gentlemen varying perspectives on their elegant figures. What moves and changes catches interest. The people, the furniture, the objects, the walls themselves move about. Any sort of cultural storehouse of objects or boundaries is deliberately complicated; the turn in the garden holds a deliberate surprise.

Two of Repton's contemporaries held two different views about his "slides." Loudon considered them false and misleading, raising improper expectations in their graphic depiction of otherness. Sir Walter Scott, on the other hand, saw them as miniature transformation scenes, theatrical, imaginative (see Carter, Goode, and Laurie, 21–22). Scott, like Radcliffe, used description as a sort of textual slide to lift up and see beyond the known into the past, into terra incognita rendered through the act of describing terra cognita. "Poetic creation, what is this too but *seeing* the thing sufficiently[?]" asked Thomas Carlyle (rhetorically). This book has tried to show that, in spite of late nineteenth- and twentieth-century skeptics, poets have, in fact, always seen sufficiently for themselves, although *sufficiently* has never meant "in the same way." For Carlyle, it is Shakespeare's "*word* that

will describe the thing that follows, of itself, from such clear intense sight
of the thing."[4] The tag can rehydrate the familiar image; description can
itemize the ingredients of the rehydration. Description was often measured
for *vraisemblance*, for its ability to *create* a sense of the familiar. Yet, in
the act of lifting up and looking at, as postmodernists have endlessly explained but Robert Hooke and Jonathan Swift already knew, the observer
appropriates the image, the object, and transforms it.

Carlyle's sense of seeing "sufficiently" can also include seeing *otherwise*,
of turning the everyday (which is almost by definition unseen) inside out,
as in Gulliver's account of his traveling box in Brobdingnag or Hooke's love
for his microscopic flea and louse.[5] Description can call up the ordinary,
the familiar, and remind us of its lines; it can also disintegrate familiarity
under the very pressure of sustained observation or the very lightness of
assumption. To what extent are the giant Despair and his wife domesticated
by the details of their bedtime chats (where Mrs. Diffidence advises her
husband to beat Christian and Hopeful to a pulp one day and to counsel
them to suicide the next) or by the fact that the giant sometimes has "fits"?
To what extent is the reassuring familiarity of La Vallée hollowed out by the
ghostly occupation of St. Aubert and the unrecognizability of Valancourt?[6]
Harriet Byron, like an upper-class Crusoe, makes her habitation more real
by counting its objects and coloring its rooms; Clarissa Harlowe cannot see
her walls and things because she is listening beyond them.

The spatial contours and object-presences of early novels seemed so certain they required no positioning before narrative, only positioning within
it, always immediately to hand. The vast spillage of things in the later eighteenth century demanded a different kind of accounting and assembling,
arrayed in rooms and texts as *settings for* human action. As Lukács said:
"These writers also knew quite well that it was not completeness of description that mattered—the enumeration of an object's constituents or of
a sequence of events forming a person's life—but the working-out of essential human and social determinants" (*Historical Novel*, 43). But, when the
"essential" human and social determinants no longer seemed *essential*, universal, the enumeration of an object's constituents swung more prominently
into interest. Or, to put it another way, "completeness of description" has always mattered, although the requirements for "complete" changed as much
as (and synchronically with) the taste for description itself. Woolf said of
Evelyn that "[t]he visible world was always close to him," that he used his
eyes ("Evelyn," 82). The visible world has always been present to those who
used their eyes; what was seen in different worlds is recorded by what was
described.

NOTES

All early modern texts are published in London, unless otherwise noted.

INTRODUCTION

1. Virginia Woolf, "Robinson Crusoe," in *The Common Reader, Second Series* (1932), ed. Andrew McNeillie (London: Hogarth, 1986), 54.

2. Dorothy Van Ghent, *The English Novel: Form and Function* (1953; reprint, New York: Harper & Row, 1961), 34–35.

3. George Puttenham, *The Art of English Poesie. Contriued into Three Bookes: The First of Poets and Poesie, the Second of Proportion, the Third of Ornament* (1589), 215.

4. Gérard Genette, *Figures of Literary Discourse*, trans. Alan Sheridan (New York: Columbia University Press, 1982), 134.

5. Samuel Johnson, "Preface to Shakespeare" (1765), in *Johnson on Shakespeare*, ed. Arthur Sherbo, with an introduction by Bertrand Bronson, vol. 7 of *The Yale Edition of the Works of Samuel Johnson*, ed. H. W. Liebert and A. T. Hazen, 16 vols. (New Haven, CT: Yale University Press, 1958–90), 111.

6. Samuel Johnson, *Rasselas* (1759), in *Rasselas and Other Tales*, ed. Gwin J. Kolb, vol. 16 of *The Yale Edition of the Works of Samuel Johnson*, 43.

7. Thomas Gray, "Some Remarks on the Poems of John Lydgate," in *The Works of Thomas Gray in Prose and Verse*, ed. Edmund Gosse (London: Macmillan, 1884), 1:392–93.

8. Hugh Blair, *Lectures on Rhetoric and Belles Lettres*, 2 vols. (London and Edinburgh, 1783), 2:372.

9. Philippe Hamon, "Rhetorical Status of the Descriptive," *Yale French Studies* 61 (1981): 4.

10. Virginia Woolf, "Rambling round Evelyn," in *The Common Reader, First Series* (1925), ed. Andrew McNeillie (London: Hogarth, 1984), 62.

11. Humphry Repton, *Observations on the Theory and Practice of Landscape Gardening. Including Some Remarks on Grecian and Gothic Architecture, collected from various manuscripts, in the possession of the different noblemen and*

gentlemen, for whose use they were originally written; the whole tending to establish fixed principles in the Respective arts (London, 1803), 169.

12. Michel Beaujour, "Some Paradoxes of Description," *Yale French Studies* 61 (1981): 28.

CHAPTER ONE

1. Hamon is quoted in José Manuel Lopes, *Foregrounded Description in Prose Fiction: Five Cross-Literary Studies* (Toronto: University of Toronto Press, 1995), 16.

2. John Bunyan, *The Pilgrim's Progress* (1678), ed. N. H. Keeble (1966; reprint; Oxford: Oxford University Press, 1984), 12. All quotations are from this edition.

3. See also Max Byrd, *London Transform'd: Images of the City in the Eighteenth Century* (New Haven, CT: Yale University Press, 1978): "[Defoe's London] remains somehow two-dimensional, an abstract environment so to speak, without colors or smells or windows or doors" (13); J. Donald Crowley, introduction to *The Life and Strange Surprizing Adventures of Robinson Crusoe,* by Daniel Defoe, ed. J. Donald Crowley (Oxford: Oxford University Press, 1972), emphasizing a lack of sensuousness in Defoe's writing (xv); G. A. Starr, introduction to *The Fortunes and Misfortunes of the Famous Moll Flanders,* by Daniel Defoe, ed. G. A. Starr (1971; reprint, Oxford: Oxford University Press, 1987), on Defoe's "paucity of visual detail" (xx); and Simon Varey, *Space and the Eighteenth-Century English Novel* (Cambridge: Cambridge University Press, 1990), on Defoe's vague, "generic" space (138).

4. Thomas Babington Macaulay, "*The Pilgrim's Progress, with a Life of John Bunyan,* by Robert Southey, Esq., LL.D., Poet-Laureate. Illustrated with Engravings. 8vo. London: 1830," *Edinburgh Review* 54 (December 1831): 452.

5. Charlotte Brontë, *Jane Eyre* (1847), ed. Richard J. Dunn, 3rd ed. (New York: Norton, 2001), 10–11.

6. Although we do learn in *Part II* that the arbor in the Enchanted Ground has a soft couch.

7. John Bender and Michael Marrinan, eds., *Regimes of Description: In the Archive of the Eighteenth Century* (Stanford, CA: Stanford University Press, 2005), 4.

8. *A Compendium of the Art of Logick and Rhetorick in the English Tongue. Containing all that Peter Ramus, Aristotle, and others have writ thereon: with Plaine Directions for the more easie understanding and practice of the same* (1651), 247.

9. Thomas Spencer, *The Art of Logick, Delivered in the Precepts of Aristotle and Ramus* (1628), 193.

10. *Dictionary of Philosophy,* ed. Dagobert D. Runes (Totowa, NJ: Littlefield, Adams, 1962), 77.

11. John B. Bender, *Spenser and Literary Pictorialism* (Princeton, NJ: Princeton University Press, 1972), 33, 35, 41–42.

12. Richard Rainolde, *A Booke Called the Foundacion of Rhetorike, because all other partes of Rhetorike are grounded thereupon, euery parte sette forthe in an Oracion vpon questions, verie profitable to bee knowen and redde* (Cambridge, 1563), lj–lij; Henry Peacham, *The Garden of Eloquence, Conteyning the Figures of Grammar and Rhetorick, from whence maye bee gathered all manner of Flowers,*

Coulors, Ornaments, Exornations, Formes and Fashions of speech, very profitable
for all those that be studious of Eloquence, and that made most Eloquent Poets and
Orators, and also helpeth much for the better understanding of the Holy Scriptures
(1577), Oiiii_v; Marmontel's definition in the *Encyclopédie* quoted in Hamon,
2–3.

13. Alexander Welsh, *Strong Representations: Narrative and Circumstantial Evidence in England* (Baltimore: Johns Hopkins University Press, 1991), ix.

14. Susan Stewart, *On Longing: Narratives of the Miniature, the Gigantic, the Souvenir, the Collection* (Baltimore: Johns Hopkins University Press, 1984; reprint, Durham, NC: Duke University Press, 1998), 26.

15. *Encyclopédie, ou Dictionnaire Raisonné des Sciences, des Arts et des Métiers, par une Societé de gens de Lettres*, ed. Denis Diderot, Jean Le Rond d'Alembert, et al., 17 vols. (Paris, 1751–65), 4:878.

16. Aristotle, *Poetics*, in *The Complete Works of Aristotle: The Revised Oxford Translation*, ed. Jonathan Barnes, 2 vols. (Princeton, NJ: Princeton University Press, 1984), 2:2322–23, sec. 1451a.

17. Edward S. Casey, "Literary Description and Phenomenological Method," *Yale French Studies* 61 (1981): 195.

18. Michael Riffaterre, "Descriptive Imagery," *Yale French Studies* 61 (1981): 125. This point, in its theoretical ahistoricism, strikes me as unintentionally more fixed within the historically determined theoretical discourse of the 1980s.

19. Mieke Bal, *Narratology: Introduction to the Theory of Narrative* (1978), 2nd ed. (Toronto: University of Toronto Press, 1997), 36.

20. Elizabeth Fowler, *Literary Character: The Human Figure in Early English Writing* (Ithaca, NY: Cornell University Press, 2003), 69.

21. T. J. Smiley, "The Theory of Descriptions," in *Proceedings of the British Academy*, vol. 67 (Oxford: Oxford University Press, 1981), 321.

22. Sir Philip Sidney, *The Defence of Poesie* (1595), I4–I4v.

23. Edmund Wilson, "Is Verse a Dying Technique?" in *The Triple Thinkers* (New York: Harcourt, Brace, 1938), 37. Wilson traces the ebb and flow of the aural vs. the visual over the centuries of English literature, finding the musical returning in the Renaissance and the "ocular sense … grown sharp again" with Pope (38).

24. Quoted in William H. Race, "Ekphrasis," in *The New Princeton Encyclopedia of Poetry and Poetics*, ed. Alex Preminger and T. V. F. Brogan (Princeton, NJ: Princeton University Press, 1993), 320.

25. Richard Sherry, *A Treatise of Schemes & Tropes very profytable for the better vnderstanding of good authors, gethered out of the best Grammarians & Oratours by Rychard Sherry Londoner. Whervnto is added a declamacion, That chyldren even strapt frō their infancie should be well and greatly broughte vp in learnynge. Written first in Latin by the most excellent and famous Clearke, Erasmus of Rotero* (1550), Ei.

26. The modern Anglicized forms of many of these Greek terms (e.g., *chronography, prosopography, topography*) have additional and, for us, more primary connotations than the rhetorical ones (*topographia*, e.g., would for sixteenth- and seventeenth-century readers mean an instance of topographical description within a poem or narrative, while *topography* also calls up a whole genre of place guides). For rhetorical and historical discussions, I retain the older forms of the words.

27. Aristotle, *Rhetoric*, in Barnes, ed., *Complete Works*, 2:2252, secs. 1411b–1412a: "By 'making them see things' I mean using expressions that represent things as in a state of activity... [as in] 'Thereat up sprang the Hellenes to their feet,' where 'up sprang' gives us activity as well as metaphor, for it at once suggests swiftness."

28. Ruth Helen Webb and Philip Weller, "Descriptive Poetry," in Preminger and Brogan, eds., *New Princeton Encyclopedia*, 284.

29. Phillip Damon, "History and Idea in Renaissance Criticism," in *Literary Criticism and Historical Understanding*, ed. Phillip Damon (New York: Columbia University Press, 1967), 33.

30. Douglas Kelly, *The Conspiracy of Allusion: Description, Rewriting, and Authorship from Macrobius to Medieval Romance* (Leiden: Brill, 1999), 43, 46, 47.

31. As Mary J. Carruthers puts it: "[M]edieval culture was fundamentally memorial, to the same profound degree that modern culture in the West is documentary" (*The Book of Memory: A Study of Memory in Medieval Culture* [Cambridge: Cambridge University Press, 1990], 8).

32. D. W. Robertson Jr., *A Preface to Chaucer* (Princeton, NJ: Princeton University Press, 1962), 247–48. B. E. C. Davis characterizes Chaucer's "larger pieces" as "catalogues of massed particulars in which he runs breathlessly from item to item, linked only by the formula 'I saw'; and even the figures of his foregrounds... are little more than summary sketches" because "formality in the design or structure of a word-portrait would be foreign to his purposes" (*Edmund Spenser* [Cambridge: Cambridge University Press, 1933], 161).

33. See, e.g., Edward W. Tayler, ed., *Literary Criticism of Seventeenth-Century England* (New York: Knopf, 1967), 5–6, 15.

34. Obadiah Walker, *Some Instructions Concerning the Art of Oratory* (1659), 1–2.

35. Page duBois, *History, Rhetorical Description, and the Epic from Homer to Spenser* (Cambridge: D. S. Brewer, 1982), 92.

36. Gordon Braden, "Riverrun: An Epic Catologue in *The Faerie Queene*," *English Literary Renaissance* 5, no. 1 (winter 1975): 25.

37. William G. Crane (introduction to *The Garden of Eloquence* [1593], by Henry Peacham [Gainesville, FL: Scholars' Facsimiles and Reprints, 1954], 9) explains that most of Peacham's explanations and examples come from sixteenth-century compilations of the works of Quintilian, Cornificius, and Cicero.

38. *The Artes of Logike and Rhetorike, plainely set foorth in the Englishe toonge, easie to be learned and practised: togeather with examples for the practice of the same for Methode in the gouernment of the familie, prescribed in the worde of God: And for the whole in the resolution or opening of certain parts of Scripture, according to the same* (1584), C4. This is roughly a translation of Aristotle and Ramus that is reproduced under different (or no) authors' names throughout the sixteenth and seventeenth centuries (see, e.g., the *Compendium*; and Thomas Hobbes, *The Art of Rhetoric, with a Discourse of the Laws of England* [1681]).

39. Alexander Pope, *The Iliad of Homer*, ed. Steven Shankman (Harmondsworth: Penguin, 1996), 129–30.

40. J. Daniel Kinney to Cynthia Wall, e-mail, 13 January 2000.

41. [John Newbery], *The Art of Poetry on a New Plan: Illustrated with a Great Variety of Examples from the Best English Poets; and of Translation from the Ancients: Together with such Reflections and Critical Remarks as may tend to form in our Youth an elegant Taste, and render the Study of this Part of the Belles Lettres more rational and pleasing*, 2 vols. (1762), 2:230.

42. P. G. Wodehouse, *Aunts Aren't Gentlemen* (London: Penguin, 1974), 123–24.

43. Thomas P. Roche Jr., *The Kindly Flame* (Princeton, NJ: Princeton University Press, 1964), 60.

44. Plato, *The Republic*, in *The Dialogues of Plato*, trans. Benjamin Jowett, 2 vols., 3rd ed. (1892; reprint, New York: Random House, 1937), 2:660 (bk. 3, sec. 397a).

45. Norman Friedman, "Imagery," in Preminger and Brogan, eds., *New Princeton Encyclopedia*, 560.

46. John Smith, *The Mysterie of Rhetorique Unvail'd, Wherein above 130 of The Tropes and Figures are severally derived from the Greek into English, together with lively Definitions and Variety of Latin/English/Scriptural Examples, Pertinent to each of them apart* (1657), 4.

47. 60. H. C., *Aristotle's Rhetoric: Or the True Grounds and principles of Oratory; Shewing, the Right Art of Pleading and Speaking in full Assemblies and Courts of Judicature. Made English by the Translators of the Art of Thinking. In Four Books* (1686), 176–77.

48. See Thomas Sebillet, *Art poêtique françoys* (1556), ed. F. Gaiffe (Paris, 1932).

49. Nicolas Boileau Despréaux, *The Art of Poetry* (1675), trans. Sir William Soames (1683), canto 3, lines 188–89.

50. Sir Thomas Pope Blount, *De re poetica; or, Remarks upon Poetry. With Characters and Censures of the Most Considerable Poets, Whether Ancient or Modern. Extracted out of the Best and Choicest Criticks* (1694), 103.

51. John Dryden, preface to *Du Fresnoy's De Arte Graphica. The Art of Painting, by C. A. Du Fresnoy. With Remarks. Translated into English, Together with an Original Preface containing a Parallel betwixt Painting and Poetry. By Mr. Dryden* (1695), xxxvi.

52. Thomas Rymer, *A Short View of Tragedy* (1693), 4.

53. Hobbes's *Art of Rhetoric* is basically the same translation of Aristotle and Ramus that is used by *The Artes of Logike and Rhetorike*, the *Compendium*, John Smith, and others.

54. Thomas Rymer, *Monsieur Rapin's Reflections on Aristotle's Treatise of Poesie. Containing the Necessary Rational and Universal Rules for Epick, Dramatick, and the other sorts of Poetry ... Made English by Mr. Rymer; by whom is added some Reflections on English Poets* (1694), 59.

55. Edward W. Tayler, *Literary Criticism of Seventeenth-Century England* (New York: Knopf, 1967), 23, quoting line 338 of John Donne's "Anatomie of the World: The First Anniversary" (1611).

56. Samuel Johnson, *The Rambler* (1750–52), ed. W. J. Bate and Albrecht B. Strauss, vols. 3–5 of *The Yale Edition of the Works of Samuel Johnson, Rambler*, no. 168 (26 October 1751), 5:128, 127.

57. Adam Smith, *Lectures on Rhetoric and Belles Lettres. Delivered in the University of Glasgow by Adam Smith, Reported by a Student in 1762–63*, ed. John M. Lothean (Carbondale: Southern Illinois University Press, 1971), 23, 30.

58. Quoted in Hamon, 8, citing the articles "Descriptif" and "Description" in the *Grand Dictionnaire Universel du XIXe siècle*, vol. 6.

59. Samuel Taylor Coleridge, *Biographia Literaria* (1817), ed. James Engell and W. Jackson Bate, 2 vols. (Princeton, NJ: Princeton University Press, 1983), 2:32.

60. The text at this point includes the note (without indication of whether the note is Boileau's or Soames's): "*Verse* of Scudery."

61. In a sense, this articulates a propriety that still lingers in upper-middle-class Britain: it verges on the ill-bred to compliment one's host on his house, to even appear to *notice* or *look at* one's surroundings.

62. In perfect fairness, it should be noted that Rymer is not an unambivalent champion of things French; he characterizes a description of Chapelain's as "perfect *French*. There is scarce any coming at a little sense, 'tis so encompass'd about with Words" (B7).

63. Joseph Addison and Richard Steele, *The Spectator*, ed. Donald F. Bond, 5 vols. (1965; reprint, Oxford: Clarendon, 1987), 3:567 (*Spectator*, no. 418, Monday, 30 June 1712).

64. Sir Joshua Reynolds, *The Works of Sir Joshua Reynolds, Knt.*, ed. Edmond Malone, 2 vols. (1797), 1:353–54 (*Idler*, no. 79, Saturday, 20 October 1759).

65. Edmund Burke, *A Philosophical Inquiry into the Origin of Our Ideas of the Sublime and Beautiful* (1757), ed. James T. Boulton (Notre Dame, IN: University of Notre Dame Press, 1958), 172.

66. Gray argues, in fact, that Homer was the father of circumstance, and that medieval writers "loved, I will not say tediousness, but length and a train of circumstances in narration," and that the "vulgar" still did—but so does "the mind" more generally because circumstance "gives an air of reality to facts, it fixes the attention, raises and keeps in suspense … expectation, and supplies the defects of … little and lifeless imagination[s]" ("Some Remarks," 393, 392). See also Thomas Gray, *Correspondence of Thomas Gray*, ed. Paget Toynbee and Leonard Whibley (1935), with corrections and additions by H. W. Starr, 3 vols. (Oxford: Clarendon, 1971): "Half a word fixed upon or near the spot, is worth a cart-load of recollection. When we trust to the picture that objects draw of themselves on our mind, we deceive ourselves; without accurate and particular observation, it is but ill-drawn at first, the outlines are soon blurred, the colours every day grow fainter; and at last, when we would produce it to any body, we are forced to supply its defects with a few strokes of our own imagination" (Gray to Palgrave, 6 September 1758, letter 278, p. 587).

67. Henry Home, Lord Kames, *Elements of Criticism* (1762), in *Literary Criticism in England, 1660–1800*, ed. Gerald Wester Chapman (New York: Knopf, 1966), 313.

68. W. J. T. Mitchell, *Iconology: Image, Text, Ideology* (Chicago: University of Chicago Press, 1986), 23. For a fuller analysis of the history of image epistemology, see 19–31.

69. Irvin Ehrenpreis, *Literary Meaning and Augustan Values* (Charlottesville: University Press of Virginia, 1974), 46–48.

70. John Graham, "Character and Description in the Romantic Novel," *Studies in Romanticism* 5 (1966): 210.

71. From William Blake's copy (British Library C.45.e.18) of *The Works of Sir Joshua Reynolds*, ed. Edmond Malone, 3 vols. (1798), Third Discourse, 1:52.

72. William Hazlitt, "On Certain Inconsistencies in Sir Joshua Reynolds' Discourses," in *Collected Works*, 12 vols. (1903), 6:132.

73. Henry James, "The Art of Fiction" (1884), in *Narrative/Theory*, ed. David H. Richter (New York: Longman, 1996), 48–49.

74. Defoe, *Moll Flanders*, ed. Starr, 195–96.

75. Charles Dickens, *Oliver Twist* (1837–38), ed. Kathleen Tillotson (1966; reprint, Oxford: Oxford University Press, 1990), 49.

76. Rachel Trickett, "'Curious Eye': Some Aspects of Visual Description in Eighteenth-Century Literature," in *Augustan Studies: Essays in Honor of Irvin Ehrenpreis*, ed. Douglas Lane Patey and Timothy Keegan (Newark: University of Delaware Press, 1985), 245.

77. Carol T. Christ, *The Finer Optic: The Aesthetic of Particularity in Victorian Poetry* (New Haven, CT: Yale University Press, 1975), 7–9, 12–14.

78. Georg Lukács, "Narrate or Describe?" (1936), in *Writer and Critic and Other Essays*, ed. Arthur Kahn (London: Merlin, 1970), 127.

79. Naomi Schor, *Reading in Detail: Aesthetics and the Feminine* (New York: Methuen, 1987), 22. Schor's work is important and influential but rather limited—overdetermined, in fact—in its viewpoint. While Reynolds and Burke certainly gendered the particular, they were not, in fact, all that influential in practice, particularly in literature; and Schor's book does not take into account the vast attention to detail in other "masculine" disciplines such as micrography, empiricism generally, topography, architecture, and the other cultural categories that I explore here; nor does her account match very well against the temporal shifts in attitude in favor of the particular in the nineteenth century.

80. Deidre Shauna Lynch, reader's report on this manuscript, November 2004.

CHAPTER TWO

1. John Stow, *A Survey of London. Contayning the Originall, Antiquity, Increase, Modern estate, and description of that Citie, written in the yeare 1598, by Iohn Stow Citizen of London. Since by the same Author increased, with diuers rare notes of Antiquity, and published in the yeare, 1603* (1603), A2v. All quotations are from this edition. I am using the 1603 rather than the 1598 edition as the last edition with Stow's own additions.

2. See, e.g., Ian W. Archer, *The Pursuit of Stability: Social Relations in Elizabethan London* (Cambridge: Cambridge University Press, 1991), 1–17, 257–60, and "The Nostalgia of John Stow," in *The Theatrical City: Culture, Theatre, and Politics in London, 1576–1649*, ed. D. L. Smith, R. Strier, and D. Bevington (Cambridge: Cambridge University Press, 1995); Barrett L. Beer, *Tudor England Observed: The World of John Stow* (Stroud: Alan Sutton, 1998), esp. chap. 6; Valerie Pearl, introduction to *The Survey of London*, by John Stow, ed. H. B. Wheatley (London: J. M. Dent, 1987); and M. J. Power, "John Stow and His London," *Journal of Historical Geography* 11 (1985): 1–20.

3. Patrick Collinson, "John Stow and Nostalgic Antiquarianism," in *Imagining Early Modern London: Perceptions and Portrayals of the City from Stow to Strype, 1598–1720*, ed. J. F. Merritt (Cambridge: Cambridge University Press, 2001), 35.

4. See Beer, 171–72; and J. F. Merritt, "The Reshaping of Stow's *Survey*: Munday, Strype, and the Protestant City," in Merritt, ed., *Imagining Early Modern London*, 87–88.

5. Richard Helgerson, *Forms of Nationhood: The Elizabethan Writing of England* (Chicago: University of Chicago Press, 1992), 132–33.

6. I have discussed Stow's street etymologies in relation to the cultural significance of pre-Fire London in *The Literary and Cultural Spaces of Restoration London* (Cambridge: Cambridge University Press, 1998), chap. 4, as well as in "Grammars of Space: The Language of London from Stow's *Survey* to Defoe's *Tour*," *Philological Quarterly* 76, no. 4 (fall 1997): 387–411. Here, I am pulling up some of the same details to point in a different direction.

7. The edition to which Merritt is referring is John Stow, *A Survey of London... Afterwards inlarged by... A. M. [Anthony Munday] in the yeere 1618. And now completely finished by A. M. [Anthony Munday] H. D. [Humphrey Dyson] and others, this present yeere 1633* (1633).

8. James Howell, *Londinopolis; An Historicall Discourse or Perlustration of the City of London* (1657), 7, 330.

9. Thomas De Laune, *The Present State of London, or Memorials Comprehending A Full and Succinct Account Of the Ancient and Modern State thereof* (1681), 97–98.

10. Edward Hatton, *A New View of London; Or, An Ample Account of that City, In Two Volumes, or Eight Sections. Being a more particular Description thereof than has hitherto been known to be published of any City in the World* (1708).

11. Presumably G. de Chuyes's *La Guide de Paris, contenant le nom & l'adresse de toutes les rues de ladite ville & faux-bourgs... Le tout rédigé par ordre alphabétique, etc. Liste générale des courriers* (Paris, 1654).

12. Even the title page of Strype's version expands the notice of things, giving a history (or description) of the life of Stow's work: "A SURVEY of the CITIES of London and Westminster, CONTAINING: The Original, Antiquity, Increase, Modern Estate and Government of those CITIES. By IOHN STOW, Citizen and Native of London. Written at first in the Year MDXCVIII. Since Reprinted and Augmented by the AUTHOR; And afterwards by A. M. [Anthony Munday] H. D. [Humphrey Dyson] and others. NOW LASTLY, Corrected, Improved, and very much Enlarged: And the SURVEY and HISTORY brought down from the Year 1633, (being near Fourscore Years since it was last printed) to the present Time; By JOHN STRYPE, M.A. a Native also of the said City. Illustrated with Exact Maps of the City and Suburbs, and of all the Wards; and likewise of the Out-Parishes of LONDON and WESTMINSTER: Together with many other fair Draughts of the more Eminent and Publick Edifices and Monuments. In SIX BOOKS, To which is prefixed, The LIFE of the AUTHOR, writ by the Editor. At the End is added, An APPENDIX of certain Tracts, Discourses and Remarks, concerning the State of the CITY of LONDON. TOGETHER WITH a Perambulation, or Circuit-Walk Four or Five Miles round about LONDON, to the Parish Churches: Describing the Monuments of the Dead there Interred: With other Antiquities observable in those Places. And concluding with a SECOND APPENDIX, as a Supply and Review: And a

Large INDEX of the Whole Work." See John Strype, *A Survey of the Cities of London and Westminster... Now Lastly, Corrected, Improved, and very much Enlarged: And the Survey and History brought down from the Year 1633, (being near Fourscore Years since it was last printed) to the present Time*, 2 vols. (1720).

13. Vanessa Harding, "City, Capital, and Metropolis: The Changing Shape of Seventeenth-Century London," in Merritt, ed., *Imagining Early Modern London*, 117, 143, 117.

14. John Aubrey, *Brief Lives*, ed. Oliver Lawson Dick (1949; reprint, Harmondsworth: Penguin, 1972), 289.

15. Carl Moreland and David Bannister, *Antique Maps* (London: Longman, 1983; 3rd ed., London: Phaidon, 1989; reprint, London: Phaidon, 1993), 25. Moreland and Bannister note that John Norden (1593–98) and Philip Symonson (1596), contemporaries of Saxton's, were the first to show roads on half a dozen county maps, but neither Speed nor the preparers of Camden's *Britannia* followed up on this, and, "in fact, the only works of any note in this field [of maps for travelers] were Norden's *An Intended Guyde for English Travailers* (1625), in which he demonstrated for the first time the use of triangular distance tables much as we use them today, and Matthew Simmons's *A Direction for the English Traviller*," the latter "a series of very small maps" (engraved by Jacob van Langeren) originally published in 1635 and republished in an enlarged edition by Thomas Jenner in 1643 (26).

16. Travel narratives are another obvious genre for this chapter—indeed, this book. Ogilby's *America* (*America: Being the Latest, and Most Accurate Description of the New World... Collected from most Authentick Authors, Augmented with later Observations, and Adorn'd with Maps and Sculptures* [1671]) supplies the kind of formulaic lists and details common to seventeenth- and eighteenth-century travel writing, largely compiled from other sources. His account of Virginia, e.g., comes largely from John Smith in its geography, zoology, and ethnography:

> The Countrey is generally even, the Soil fruitful, the Climate healthful, agreeable with *English* Constitutions.... Their peculiar Beasts are, the *Aroughena*, resembling a Badger; the *Assapanick* or *Flying-Squerril*; *Opassum*, a certain Beast having a Bag under her Belly, wherein she carrieth and suckleth her Young;... Their peculiar Fish are *Stingrais*.... [And there is] a great grim Fellow, all Painted over with Coal, mingled with Oyl; and many Snakes and Wesel skins stuff'd with Moss, and all their Tails ty'd together,... the Skins hanging round about his Head, Back, and Shoulders, and in a manner cover'd his Face; with a hellish voice, and a Rattle in his Hand. (195–96, 203)

But, for the purposes of this section, Ogilby's road map simply works better and more crisply, and maps are less studied in relation to their influence on literature.

17. Sir Herbert George Fordham notes that Ogilby's project was one of only two government admeasurement projects dealing with the national road system before the early twentieth century—in "striking contrast to the French system of centralized control and maintenance of the national roads, especially as developed in the eighteenth century" (*John Ogilby [1600–1676] His Britannia, and the British Itineraries of the Eighteenth Century* [London: Oxford University Press, 1925]), 157.

On the replacement of the old British mile by the statute mile, see Sir Herbert George Fordham, *Customary Acres and Their Historical Importance* (London, 1914), 157–58.

18. Quoted in Katherine S. Van Eerde, *John Ogilby and the Taste of His Times* (Folkestone: William Dawson & Sons, 1976), 134.

19. For an extensive print history of *Britannia* and its clones and offshoots, see Fordham, *John Ogilby.*

20. Howard Marchitello, *Narrative and Meaning in Early Modern England: Browne's Skull and Other Histories* (Cambridge: Cambridge University Press, 1997), 87.

21. J. B. Harley, "Silences and Secrecy: The Hidden Agenda of Cartography in Early Modern Europe," in *The New Nature of Maps: Essays in the History of Cartography*, ed. Paul Laxton (Baltimore: Johns Hopkins University Press, 2001) 107; Denis Wood, *The Power of Maps* (London: Routledge, 1993), 22–25; Marchitello, 87–91.

22. Jeremy Black, *Maps and History: Constructing Images of the Past* (New Haven, CT: Yale University Press, 1997), 7, 8. Edmond Halley's maps using isolines (lines connecting points of equal intensity of phenomena across geographic locations) also suggest a convergence of motion with place, maps with "narrative" lines, the representation of movement on a two-dimensional surface (see Lisa Jardine, *Ingenious Pursuits: Building the Scientific Revolution* [London: Little, Brown, 1999], 30–31).

23. Robert J. Mayhew, *Enlightenment Geography: The Political Languages of British Geography, 1650–1850* (London: Macmillan; New York: St. Martin's, 2000), 79; Helgerson, 332.

24. Roger Sharrock, *John Bunyan* (1954; rev. and corrected ed., London: Macmillan; New York: St. Martin's, 1968), 90; Henri Talon, "Space and the Hero in *The Pilgrim's Progress*: A Study of the Meaning of the Allegorical Universe" (1961), in *Bunyan: "The Pilgrim's Progress," a Casebook*, ed. Roger Sharrock (London: Macmillan, 1976), 158; Van Ghent, 22.

25. Henri Talon, *John Bunyan: The Man and His Works* (1948), trans. Barbara Wall (London: Rockliff, 1951), 186; Sharrock, *John Bunyan*, 90. Talon cites Charles G. Harper, *The Bunyan Country—Landmarks of "The Pilgrim's Progress"* (London: C. Palmer, 1928), 72.

26. See, e.g., Samuel Taylor Coleridge, *Coleridge on the Seventeenth Century*, ed. Roberta Florence Brinkley (Durham, NC: Duke University Press, 1955; reprint, New York: Greenwood, 1968), 480; U. Milo Kaufmann, *The Pilgrim's Progress and Traditions in Puritan Meditation* (New Haven, CT: Yale University Press, 1966), 16; and Talon, *John Bunyan*, 147.

27. James Turner, "Bunyan's Sense of Place," in *"The Pilgrim's Progress": Critical and Historical Views*, ed. Vincent Newey (Liverpool: Liverpool University Press, 1980), 97, 100, 103, 103.

28. The advertisement in *The Pilgrim's Progress... The sixth edition with additions* (1681) reads: "THE *Pilgrims Progress* having found good Acceptation among the People, to the carrying off the Fourth Impression, which had many Additions, more than any preceeding: And the Publisher observing, that many Persons desired to

have it illustrated with Pictures, hath endeavoured to gratifie them therein: And besides those that are ordinarily Printed to the Fifth Impression hath provided Thirteen Copper Cuts curiously Engraven for such as desire them."

29. N. H. Keeble, introduction to *The Pilgrim's Progress*, by Bunyan, ed. Keeble, xi.

30. Roger Sharrock, introduction to *The Pilgrim's Progress*, by John Bunyan, ed. Roger Sharrock (Harmondsworth: Penguin, 1965), 24.

31. Stanley Fish offers a very different argument, one that simply does not resonate with me as a reader or persuade me as a critic. He argues that "*The Pilgrim's Progress* is anti-progressive, both as a narrative and as a reading experience," that to accept "the presumptions that are inherent in the title" is to "spatializ[e] and trivializ[e] the way," and, therefore, that, to read properly, "we must actively resist the pressure of its temporal-spatial lines of cause and effect" ("Progress in *The Pilgrim's Progress*," in *Self-Consuming Artifacts: The Experience of Seventeenth-Century Literature* [Berkeley: University of California Press, 1972], 229). John R. Knott Jr. counters that "[t]o devalue this metaphor by considering it in purely formal terms is to explain away the reason for the extraordinary power of *The Pilgrim's Progress* over the imaginations of actual readers for several centuries" because Bunyan was employing "the sustaining metaphor of Puritan spiritual life in Bunyan's time" ("Bunyan's Gospel Day: A Reading of *The Pilgrim's Progress*" [1973], in Sharrock, ed., *Bunyan Casebook*, 221).

32. John Brown, *John Bunyan (1628–1688), His Life, Times, and Work* (1885), ed. Frank Mott Harrison (London: Hulbert, 1928), 18, 323.

33. [Thomas Sherman], *The Second Part of the Pilgrims Progress, From This present World of Wickeness* [sic] *and Misery, to An Eternity of Holiness and Felicity; Exactly Described under the Similitude of a Dream, Relation the Manner and Occasion of his setting out from, and difficult and dangerous Journey through the World; and safe Arrival at last to Eternal Happiness* (1682), n.p. For other examples of lavish contemporary landscape description, Turner (chap. 2) also points us to John Barclay, *Icon Animorum* (1614); Joseph Hall, "On a fair prospect," in *Occasional Meditations* (1633 ed.); and Barten Holyday, *A Survey of the World* (1661), A3.

CHAPTER THREE

1. With room enough and time, I would include other geographic writings. Miles Ogborn and Charles W. J. Withers examine, e.g., John Woodward's 1696 *Brief Instructions for Making Observations in All Parts of the World*, which, under the principal headings "At Sea," "Upon the Sea-Shores," and "At Land," "emphasized observation, recording, and detail" ("Travel, Trade, and Empire: Knowing Other Places, 1660–1800," in *A Concise Companion to the Restoration and Eighteenth Century*, ed. Cynthia Wall [Oxford: Blackwell, 2004], 23).

2. In a persuasive essay about the descriptive trajectory of natural history, Lorraine Daston argues: "[T]he prototypical scientific fact mutated between circa 1660 and 1730, from a singular and striking event that could be replicated only with great difficulty, if at all, to a large and uniform class of events that could be produced at will. The texture of description of nature changed accordingly, from long accounts

bristling with particulars to concise reports made deliberately bland by summary, repetition, and omission of details. Nature was not yet universal and eternal at the turn of the eighteenth century; my story of the transformation of the scientific fact is part of how it came to be so by mid-century" ("Description by Omission: Nature Enlightened and Obscured," in Bender and Marrinan, eds., *Regimes of Description,* 13). I do not argue with Daston about the history of natural history writing (although it is, I think, telling that, after a discussion of Robert Boyle's "militarily empirical" interest in the particular in the seventeenth century [21], her eighteenth-century examples are primarily from firm French Enlightenment members such as Charles Dufay); rather, my interest lies in how the early passionate interest in particularity and difference generated by the English natural philosophers migrated to and settled within eighteenth-century English literature.

3. Celia Fiennes and Daniel Defoe, other obvious choices for this chapter, reappear instead in chapter 7, in the section on domestic tourism.

4. See, e.g., Ian Hacking, *The Emergence of Probability: A Philosophical Study of Early Ideas about Probability, Induction, and Statistical Inference* (1975; reprint, Cambridge: Cambridge University Press, 1984); Jardine, *Ingenious Pursuits,* chap. 3; Barbara Shapiro, *A Culture of Fact: England, 1550–1720* (Ithaca, NY: Cornell University Press, 2000); and C. Wilson, *The Invisible World: Early Modern Philosophy and the Invention of the Microscope* (Princeton, NJ: Princeton University Press, 1995).

5. See, e.g., Svetlana Alpers, *The Art of Describing: Dutch Art in the Seventeenth Century* (London: John Murray, 1983); John Arthos, *The Language of Natural Description in Eighteenth-Century Poetry* (Ann Arbor: University of Michigan Press, 1949); Guy de la Bédoyère, *Particular Friends: The Correspondence of Samuel Pepys and John Evelyn* (Woodbridge: Boydell, 1997); M. Fournier, *The Fabric of Life: Microscopy and the Seventeenth Century* (Baltimore: Johns Hopkins University Press, 1996); Jardine, *Ingenious Pursuits;* Marjorie Hope Nicolson, *Newton Demands the Muse: Newton's "Opticks" and the Eighteenth Century Poets* (1946; reprint, Princeton, NJ: Princeton University Press, 1966), *Pepys' "Diary" and the New Science* (Charlottesville: University Press of Virginia, 1965), and *Science and Imagination* (1956), 2nd ed. (Ithaca, NY: Great Seal, 1962; reprint, Hamden, CT: Archon, 1976); Shapiro; and Ilse Vickers, *Defoe and the New Sciences* (Cambridge: Cambridge University Press, 1996).

6. J. Paul Hunter, among others, has reviewed the textual and historical influence of "occasional meditations" such as Boyle's, which "enjoyed enormous popularity in the second half of the seventeenth century among varied practitioners, not all of them Puritans" (*Before Novels: The Cultural Contexts of Eighteenth-Century English Fiction* [New York: Norton, 1990], 200).

7. As Lisa Jardine notes: "The charter thus acknowledged the key role of printers and engravers—those who produced the publications and visual images on which the Society's reputation largely depended for those outside the élite inner circle. The Society's official *Philosophical Transactions,* in which all its important scientific communications were circulated and preserved for posterity, have indeed largely shaped our view of its activities.... The engraved plates were just as influential" (*Ingenious Pursuits,* 83).

8. As Susan Stewart puts it: "[S]omehow it was the *writing* of the natural, the previously unreadable, which now stood revealed" (40).

9. Robert Hooke, *Micrographia Restaurata: Or, The Copper-Plates of Dr. Hooke's Wonderful Discoveries by the Microscope, Reprinted and Fully Explained: Whereby the most Valuable Particulars in that Celebrated Author's Micrographia Are brought together in a narrow Compass; and Intermixed, occasionally, with many Entertaining and Instructive Discoveries and Observations in Natural History* (1745), preface. The compiler actually thinks that Hooke's verbal descriptions are neither "instructive nor entertaining" because, "at the Time Dr. Hooke published this Work, a verbose and diffused Way of Writing was in fashion, which seems to us at present tedious and distasteful." But, although Hooke's method of verbal description may have lost fashion, his influence on the observation of surfaces and subspaces was explicitly continuing.

10. Robert Hooke, *Micrographia: Or Some Physiological Descriptions of Minute Bodies Made By Magnifying Glasses. With Observations and Inquiries thereupon* (1665), 210.

11. Unless you count Observation 32, "Of the Figure of several sorts of *Hair*, and of the texture of the *skin*," which begins: "Viewing some of the Hairs of my Head with a very good *Microscope*, I took notice of these particulars." Six indented points follow (*Micrographia* [1665], 156–57). If this observation is counted, Hooke's own hair is the only contender of importance to the flea.

12. "Physiological poetry" long preceded the invention of the microscope, and imagining miniature worlds has been a common favorite pastime of human imaginations. But as Nicolson points out: "[T]he microscope gave new direction to this kind of writing, introducing areas as novel as they were interesting. Matthew Prior's *Alma: or the Progress of the Mind* and Blackmore's *Creation* were to a later period what Fletcher's *Purple Island* had been to the earlier" (*Newton*, 178–79).

13. Robert Boyle, *Some Considerations touching the Usefulnesse of Experimental Naturall Philosophy. Propos'd in Familiar Discourses to a Friend, by way of Invitation to the Study* (1663), 3.

14. Kaufmann glosses further: "Even the one which might seem the most likely to have originated with Bunyan—the observation about the spring in high ground—can be found in William Spurstow's meditation 'On a Spring in an high ground,' in his *Spiritual Chymist* of 1666" (177).

15. Robert Boyle, *Occasional Reflections upon several Svbiects. Whereto is promis'd A Discourse About such kind of Thoughts* (1665), a6.

16. Robert Boyle, *The Works of the Honourable Robert Boyle, in Six Volumes* (1772), 6:525–26.

17. Jonathan Swift, *The Writings of Jonathan Swift*, ed. Robert A. Greenberg and William Bowman Piper (New York: Norton, 1973), 535–38.

18. Jonathan Swift, *Gulliver's Travels* (1726), ed. Paul Turner (1986; reprint, Oxford: Oxford University Press, 1998), 93.

19. "The Queen likewise ordered the thinnest Silks that could be gotten, to make me Cloaths; not much thicker than an *English* blanket, very cumbersome till I was accustomed to them" (*Gulliver*, 93). Hooke had pointed out that the finest piece of transparent lawn under the microscope turned into "a goodly piece of *coarse*

matting… being not unlike, both in shape and size, the bigger and coarser kind of *single Rope-yarn*, wherewith they usually make *Cables*" (*Micrographia* [1665], 7).

20. Quoted in Bill Brown, "Thing Theory," *Critical Inquiry* 28, no. 1 (autumn 2001): 6.

21. Hunter remarks on the ubiquity of diaries and the pressure to keep them: "Diaries proliferated in England and Scotland in the early seventeenth century and a little later in America. How many of them existed we have no way of knowing, but, judged by the great number that have survived, they must have been very common, perhaps almost universal among those who were both devout and literate, whatever their religious persuasion.… The perceived need to keep a record of one's daily life…was apparently very intense. Exhortations are ubiquitous.… Standard Guide books like *The Gentleman's Library* (1715) simply take the practice for granted and only explain its uses: 'as *Books* are Profitable, and *Reading* an Improvement, so much more will the *Reading* of our own Lives, a *Survey* of our Actions, and an Inspection into the Division of our *Time*, be an Advantage, as it certainly is a Duty'" (*Before Novels*, 305).

22. Guy de la Bédoyère, "Text Note," in *The Diary of John Evelyn*, ed. Guy de la Bédoyère (Bangor: Headstart History, 1994), 19.

23. E. S. De Beer, introduction to *The Diary of John Evelyn*, by John Evelyn, ed. E. S. De Beer, 6 vols. (Oxford: Clarendon, 1955), 1:70, 73.

24. John Miller, foreword to Bédoyère, ed., *The Diary of John Evelyn*, 3.

25. Evelyn, *Diary of John Evelyn*, ed. De Beer, 1:5 (*De Vita Propria*). All quotations are from this edition. The angle brackets are De Beer's.

26. John E. Crowley, *The Invention of Comfort: Sensibilities and Design in Early Modern Britain and Early America* (Baltimore: Johns Hopkins University Press, 2001), 71.

27. John Miller, e.g., suggests that Evelyn "was always on the periphery of events, not at the centre, a spectator rather than an actor. He rarely reveals his own opinion or feelings.… His diary is much less intimate, much more restrained, than that of his contemporary and friend, Samuel Pepys" (4).

28. Robert Latham, introduction to *The Illustrated Pepys*, ed. Robert Latham (1979; reprint, London: Penguin, 2000), 7.

29. Evelyn's diary was discovered in 1814 by the antiquarian William Bray and his associate, William Upcott, among the family papers at Wotton; its publication in 1816 led to the publication of some of Pepys's manuscripts in the Pepys Library at Magdalene College, Cambridge, in 1825 (much edited for presentability). Latham notes that it was the third edition of the diary, published in 1848–49, "about the same time as Macaulay's *History*," that "established the diary's popularity with the Victorian reading public" (introduction, 14).

30. See, e.g., Nicolson, *Pepys' "Diary" and the New Science* (Charlottesville: University Press of Virginia, 1965); John Bowle, *John Evelyn and His World* (London: Routledge & Kegan Paul, 1981); Bédoyère, *Particular Friends*; Stuart Sherman, *Telling Time: Clocks, Diaries, and English Diurnal Form, 1660–1785* (Chicago: University of Chicago Press, 1996); and Hunter, *Before Novels*. Note especially what is, perhaps, the Evelynian symmetry of "I went" or "To Lond:" with Pepys's "Up" and "so to bed" (see Sherman, *Telling Time*, 34, 44–45).

31. Samuel Pepys, *The Diary of Samuel Pepys*, ed. Robert Latham and William Matthews, 11 vols. (London: Bell & Hyman; New Haven, CT: Yale University Press, 1970–83), 4:354–55. All quotations are from this edition.

32. See Douglas Rigby and Elizabeth Rigby, *Lock, Stock and Barrel: The Story of Collecting* (Philadelphia: J. B. Lippincott, 1944): "Now it so happened that the system of arrangement devised by Pepys [for his books] was one peculiarly his own. Based entirely upon size rather than subject, it was both inconvenient and illogical for scholarly use. The temptation to break the will and ignore the gentleman's instructions, once he was safely out of the way, must, therefore, have been great. But Pepys himself had foreseen such a contingency; and to guard against it, he evolved an eternal spy system, in the hope that the jealously would live so long.... And so he decreed that once a year a delegation from Trinity College must visit the Pepys library at Magdalene, and there conduct a thorough investigation. As long as the vigilants from the rival school could uncover nothing unseemly, Magdalene was to keep the collection. But should the Trinity men ever find that so much as a single book had been moved from its proper place, or that any intruders had been foisted in among the original three thousand chosen volumes, then the entire library was immediately to be transferred to them!" (46).

33. Someone once suggested to me that he'd heard that the seventeenth- and early eighteenth-century English translations of Rabelais's *Gargantua and Pantagruel* (1588) actually *expanded* the original lists. I thought it an enchanting possibility, so I hunted up the English editions of 1694, 1737, and 1784 and counted nouns from the games in bk. 1, chap. 12, the blazon in bk. 3, chap. 38, and the meals in bk. 4, chap. 59. Sadly, I found no noun increases, except possibly in the blazon, in which 104 items appear in the 1588 and 1721 French editions and 124 in the 1737 and 1784 English editions.

34. Tony Bennett, *The Birth of the Museum: History, Theory, Politics* (London: Routledge, 1995), 96.

35. John Tradescant, *Musaeum Tradescantianum: Or, A Collection of Rarities Preserved at South-Lambeth neer London* (1656), a4, a4v.

36. "An Index for the Philosophical Transactions of An. 1667, beginning with Number 23, and ending with Numb. 32," in *Philosophical Transactions: Giving Some Accompt of the Present Undertakings, Studies, and Labours of the Ingenious in many Considerable Parts of the World* (1667), vol. 2, [n.p., but preceding p. 409].

37. Johann Amos Comenius, *Orbis Sensualium Pictus... Visible World, or, A Nomenclature, and Pictures of all The chiefe things that are in the World*, trans. Charles Hoole (1705), A3. Except for the preface of the 1777 edition, all quotations are from this edition.

38. W. Jones, preface to *Orbis Sensualium Pictus... Visible World, or, A Nomenclature, and Pictures of all The chiefe things that are in the World*, by Johann Amos Comenius, trans. Charles Hoole, 12th ed. (1777), a1.

39. J. Paul Hunter, "Form as Meaning: Pope and the Ideology of the Couplet," *The Eighteenth Century: Theory and Interpretation* 37, no. 3 (1996): 261.

40. See Krzysztof Pomian, *Collectors and Curiosities: Paris and Venice, 1500–1800*, trans. Elizabeth Wiles-Portier (Cambridge: Polity, 1990), chap. 1, "Collections," sec. 2, "The Invisible and the Visible," pp. 20–26.

41. Barbara M. Benedict, *Curiosity: A Cultural History of Early Modern Inquiry* (Chicago: University of Chicago Press, 2001), 162.

42. Alexander Pope, *The Rape of the Lock*, ed. Cynthia Wall (Boston: Bedford/ St. Martin's, 1998), canto 1, lines 129–30, 133–36.

43. William Hazlitt, *Lectures on the English Poets*, 4 vols. (London, 1818), 4:142.

44. Laura Brown, *Alexander Pope* (Oxford: Blackwell, 1985), 10–11. The whole passage is such valuable reading that it is worth repeating here: "The last line—'Puffs, Powders, Patches, Bibles, Billet-doux'—compactly summarizes the impression of arbitrary accumulation that dominates the whole passage. But despite this air of indiscriminacy, the list is carefully structured in sound and rhythm: it progresses from one- to two- to three-syllable units with a systematically cumulative effect, and the units are connected by the alliteration of the phonetically parallel plosives 'p' and 'b', which lead the reader's ear through the line. The final foreign word 'Billet-doux'—already typically made English by its second-position rhyme with 'Rows'—is even more insistently levelled through its smooth incorporation into the phonetic and metrical coherence of the line, as if real linguistic differences can readily be erased by the euphonious art of the heroic couplet. This powerful phonetic connection of words stands in diametrical opposition to the random relationship of things in the passage. The list does not distinguish 'Bibles' from 'Billet-doux,' a failure that in this poem indicates an implicit moral irresponsibility or disorder operating in contradiction to the poetic order of the line."

45. J. Jocelyn, *An Essay on Money and Bullion* (1718), in *Classic English Works on the History and Development of Economic Thought*, ed. W. E. Minchinton (Wakefield: S. R., 1970), 17, quoted in Brown, *Alexander Pope*, 12.

46. Barbara Benedict also addresses Belinda's dressing table, calling it a "female curiosity cabinet [that] exemplifies the collection of material relics in a world mesmerized by ownership. Whereas virtuosi's collections testify in absentia to ownership of land, expanding identity to vast territories, her armory frays her ownership of her own body" (77).

47. Leo Spitzer, "Milieu and Ambiance," in *Essays in Historical Semantics* (New York: S. F. Vanni, 1948), 300 n. 70.

CHAPTER FOUR

1. Ian Watt, *The Rise of the Novel* (Berkeley: University of California Press, 1957; reprint, Berkeley: University of California Press, 1965), 43.

2. Dorothy Van Ghent argues: "[E]ffective allegory has a triple achievement. The moral conceptions on which it rests must be culturally viable, or it will not find adequate metaphors for its meaning in our common experience; its primary appeal to the understanding of the reader must be through our common physical and psychological experience, for this provides it the image traits out of which its metaphors are constructed; and the images that it offers us must have the power of symbols, spontaneously to evoke feelings and emotions that naturally associate themselves with moral attitudes and specifically with those attitudes that make up the conceptual framework of the allegory" (25).

3. Sir Charles Firth, [s.t.] (1898), in Sharrock, ed., *Bunyan Casebook*, 102.

4. J. Paul Hunter has defined the Puritan sense of *emblem* as a way in which "to describe objects in the natural world which have spiritual significance. For Puritans, emblems become substitutes for icons. Unable to create objects to symbolize spiritual truths (because such action would usurp a divinely reserved prerogative), they permit themselves to isolate and interpret objects and events created by God" (*The Reluctant Pilgrim: Defoe's Emblematic Method and Quest for Form in "Robinson Crusoe"* [Baltimore: Johns Hopkins University Press, 1966], 29 n. 20).

5. C. S. Lewis, "The Vision of John Bunyan" (1969), in Sharrock, ed., *Bunyan Casebook*, 198.

6. Van Ghent says that, often, "the concepts Bunyan wishes to convey through his allegory do not relate themselves spontaneously with the realistic sense imagery" (22).

7. David J. Alpaugh, "Emblem and Interpretation in *The Pilgrim's Progress*," *ELH* 33, no. 3 (1966): 299.

8. Talon suggests that "Bunyan had noticed, like certain modern psychologists, that the conversion of women is usually less violent" and that, in general, as a minister he knew that "conversion could be calm and yet genuine" (*John Bunyan*, 159).

9. We don't see nearly so many things to eat in Behn, Haywood, or Aubin.

10. John Bunyan, *The Pilgrim's Progress . . . In Two Parts, Complete. The Two and Twentieth Edition, adorned with Twenty-Two Copper Plates, Engraven by J. Sturt* (1728), facing 2:43.

11. Roger Sharrock wonders just what Mr. Brisk is doing in the House Beautiful: "[C]learly, Bunyan is drifting once again from the world of allegory towards the sphere of realistic social observation. . . . These touches of nature are always breaking through to relieve the monotony of exemplary conduct" (*John Bunyan*, 145). See also Talon, *John Bunyan*, 161–62, 202; Firth, 100; and Van Ghent, 22–23.

12. Talon, like Macaulay, pulls out implicit details: "[In Gaius's inn,] the food is excellent and the sheets are scented with lavender, as Izaak Walton describes them. . . . It is even possible that Gaius' inn had its walls papered with ballads like the one where 'the compleat angler' slept, but Bunyan refrains from mentioning it" (*John Bunyan*, 164, 164 n. 77).

13. For more on historically accurate expectations of novelistic character, see, e.g., Deidre Shauna Lynch, *The Economy of Character: Novels, Market Culture, and the Business of Inner Meaning* (Chicago: University of Chicago Press, 1998); and Leo Braudy, "Penetration and Impenetrability in *Clarissa*," in *Modern Essays on Eighteenth-Century Literature*, ed. Leopold Damrosch Jr. (Oxford: Oxford University Press, 1988), 261–81.

14. Keeble's note to this scene in his edition (Bunyan, 281 n. 202) outlines the case for the Catholic Church but also cites Talon, who argues that, since anti-Catholicism does not feature much throughout *The Pilgrim's Progress*, the more likely candidate is rationalism (*John Bunyan*, 163).

15. Talon asserts: "This entire passage does not read like an allegory, nor like an old-time story in which the portraits, cracked with age, represent bloodless figures with stiff gestures, but like a romantic story very near to our own time. No other

moment of *The Pilgrim's Progress* confirms us more strongly in our conviction that, before Defoe, Bunyan was the father of the modern English novel" (*John Bunyan*, 164).

16. Jeffrey Kittay, "Descriptive Limits," *Yale French Studies* 61 (1981): 231–32.

17. Karl Marx, *Capital*, trans. Samuel Moore and Edward Aveling (Chicago: Charles H. Kerr, 1921), 1:88–91, reprinted in *The Life and Strange Surprizing Adventures of Robinson Crusoe of York, Mariner* (1719), by Daniel Defoe, ed. Michael Shinagel (1975), 2nd ed. (New York: Norton, 1994); Watt, 113; Van Ghent, 284; Maximilian E. Novak, *Economics and the Fiction of Daniel Defoe* (Berkeley: University of California Press, 1962); Sandra Sherman, *Finance and Fictionality in the Early Eighteenth Century: Accounting for Defoe* (Cambridge: Cambridge University Press, 1996); John O'Brien, "The Character of Credit: Daniel Defoe's Lady Credit, *The Fortunate Mistress* and the Resources of Inconsistency," *ELH* 63 (fall 1996): 603–31; Lydia H. Liu, "Robinson Crusoe's Earthenware Pot," *Critical Inquiry* 25, no. 4 (1999): 728–57, 729. See also Catherine Ingrassia, *Authorship, Commerce, and Gender in Early Eighteenth-Century England: A Culture of Paper Credit* (Cambridge: Cambridge University Press, 1998).

18. See my *Literary and Cultural Spaces*, chap. 6, and "Details of Space: Narrative Description in Early Eighteenth-Century Novels," *Eighteenth-Century Fiction* 10, no. 4 (July 1998): 387–405.

19. John Ballantyne, "Daniel de Foe," in *The Lives of the Novelists* (1810), ed. Sir Walter Scott (New York: E. P. Dutton/Everyman's Library, 1928), 381–82.

20. Arnold Kettle, "In Defence of *Moll Flanders*," in *Of Books and Humankind*, ed. John Butt (London: Routledge & Kegan Paul, 1964), 65, 59.

21. See Maximilian E. Novak, "Conscious Irony in *Moll Flanders*: Facts and Problems," *College English* 26 (December 1964): 198–204.

22. Marmontel's definition in the *Encyclopédie*, quoted in Hamon, 2–3.

23. Samuel Holt Monk, introduction to *The History and Remarkable Life of the Truly Honourable Col. Jacque commonly call'd Col Jack*, by Daniel Defoe, ed. Samuel Holt Monk (Oxford: Oxford University Press, 1965), xix.

24. Daniel Defoe, *A Journal of the Plague Year* (1722), ed. Cynthia Wall (Harmondsworth: Penguin, 2003), 79.

25. Horace Walpole, *The Castle of Otranto*, ed. W. S. Lewis, with a new introduction and notes by E. J. Clery (Oxford: Oxford University Press, 1996), 9. All quotations are from this edition.

26. "Je ne l'ai point écrit pour ce siècle-ci, qui ne veut que de la *raison froide*" (Walpole to Madame du Deffand, 13 March 1767, in Horace Walpole, *The Correspondence of Horace Walpole*, 48 vols., ed. W. S. Lewis et al. [Oxford: Oxford University Press; New Haven, CT: Yale University Press, 1937–83], 3:260).

27. *The Critical Review: Or, Annals of Literature* 19 (January 1765): 51.

28. Clara Reeve, *The Old English Baron* (1778), ed. James Trainer, with an introduction by James Watt (Oxford: Oxford University Press, 2003), app. 1, p. 138. All quotations are from this edition.

29. William Hazlitt, "On the English Novelists," in *Lectures on the English Comic Writers* (1819), in *The Complete Works of William Hazlitt*, ed. P. P. Howe, 21 vols. (London: J. M. Dent, 1930–34), 6:127.

30. Thomas Babington Macaulay, review of *Letters of Horace Walpole, Earl of Oxford, to Sir Horace Mann, British Envoy at the Court of Tuscany*, ed. Lord Dover, 3 vols. (London, 1833), *Edinburgh Review* 58 (October 1833): 300.

31. Caroline F. E. Spurgeon, preface to *The Castle of Otranto*, by Horace Walpole (London: Chatto & Windus, 1907), x.

32. Elizabeth Napier, *The Failure of Gothic: Problems of Disjunction in an Eighteenth-Century Literary Form* (Oxford: Clarendon, 1987), 81, 75, 76, 77, 97, 91.

33. It was, of course, Eve Kosofsky Sedgwick who pointed out that "an analysis of the thematic attention to surfaces changes the traditional view of the Gothic contribution to characterization and figuration in fiction" (*The Coherence of Gothic Conventions* [New York: Methuen, 1986], 142).

34. Horace Walpole, *Memoirs of King George II*, ed. John Brooke, 3 vols. (New Haven, CT: Yale University Press, 1985), 3:45.

35. W. S. Lewis, introduction to *The Castle of Otranto*, by Horace Walpole, ed. W. S. Lewis (1964; reprint, Oxford: Oxford University Press, 1982), xi.

36. W. S. Lewis, *Horace Walpole*, A. W. Mellon Lectures in the Fine Arts, Bollingen Series, vol. 35, no. 9 (New York: Pantheon, 1960), 161.

37. *The Monthly Review* 32 (January 1765): 97; *The Critical Review: Or, Annals of Literature* 19 (January 1765): 50–51.

38. Sir Walter Scott, ed., *The Novelist's Library*, vol. 5, *The Novels of Sterne, Goldsmith, Dr Johnson, Mackenzie, Horace Walpole, and Clara Reeve* (London: Hurst, Robinson; Edinburgh: Border, 1823), lxxviii.

39. Martin Kallich, *Horace Walpole* (New York: Twayne, 1971), 102.

40. E. J. Clery, introduction to *The Castle of Otranto*, by Walpole, ed. Lewis (1996), xviii.

41. *The Monthly Review* 32 (January 1765): 99.

42. In "*The Castle of Otranto*: A Shakespeareo-Political Satire" (in *Fictional Boundaries, Narrative Forms: Essays in Honor of Everett Zimmerman*, ed. Lorna Clymer and Robert Mayer [Newark: University of Delaware Press, in press]), I fold into this argument the idea that *The Castle of Otranto* is a subterranean satire on the cultural fetishization of Shakespeare as well as on patriarchal politics.

CHAPTER FIVE

1. This on-the-spot creation of space and objects of course comes out of older traditions. John Bender has noted that, in Spenser's *The Faerie Queene*, space "tends to be created *ad hoc* for special purposes in restricted settings which are arranged against a neutral, spaceless ground" (135). Elizabeth Fowler argues for many overlapping forms of space in medieval and Renaissance literature: Spenser, e.g., "draws upon an epic construct of space that frames action and character according to its places for exile, encounter, and territorial redemption. He draws on the scientific and natural philosophical views of space as generative, fateful, miraculous, cosmographic, and atomistic. He draws on an Ovidian mythography that assigns space the features of etiology, human passion, and politics.... There is a formal insistence that these multifarious modes of space are present together" (183). As throughout this book, I am arguing as much for a reseeing of eighteenth-century

strategies embedded in older rhetoric traditions as for novelistic innovations in narrative space.

2. Peacham's examples for the kinds of subject matter of prosopographia offer their own interesting miniature of the reasons critics mistrusted description. The categories "Parentage," "Nation," "Kinde," "Age," and "Education" remain succinct; "Habite of body," however, runs on a bit: "A tall and slender yong man, very fayre of complexion, grave eyed, yellowe beared [*sic*], in a Doublet of greene Satten, Hose of Scarlet, a black Velvet Cappe, with a fayre whyte Feather, a bewtifull and rich chayne about his necke, fayre ringes of [*sic*] his hande, &" (Oii$_v$). As with the instances of prosopographia discussed in this chapter, we do seem to see the tendency of description to swell out of bounds. As if recognizing this himself, Peacham in his later edition of 1593 brings "Habite of body" firmly back in line with its briefer neighbors.

3. For a compelling essay on the visual dynamics and gender reversals of the sensualized scene of the duchess and Germanicus in Delarivière Manley's *The New Atalantis* (1709), see Toni Bowers, "Sex, Lies, and Invisibility: Amatory Fiction from the Restoration to Mid-Century," in *The Columbia History of the Novel*, ed. John Richetti, John Bender, Deirdre David, and Michael Seidel (New York: Columbia University Press, 1994), 50–72.

4. Aphra Behn, *The Fair Jilt: or, the History of Prince Tarquin and Miranda* (1688), in *The Histories and Novels of the Late Ingenious Mrs Behn: In One Volume* (1696), 26. This text is mispaginated: 1–34, 145–178. The printer, S. Briscoe, obviously patched two printings together.

5. Aphra Behn, *The Lucky Mistake. A New Novel* (1689), in ibid., 358.

6. For example, *Fantomina* has been included in Robert DeMaria Jr., ed., *British Literature, 1640–1789: An Anthology* (1996; rev. ed., Oxford: Blackwell, 2001); and a new edition of the novel, Alexander Pettit, Margaret Case Croskery, and Anna C. Patchias, eds., *Fantomina* (Peterborough, ON: Broadview, 2004), has just appeared.

7. Eliza Haywood, *Idalia: or, the Unfortunate Mistress*, 3rd ed. (1725), 16.

8. J. Paul Hunter, *Occasional Form: Henry Fielding and the Chains of Circumstance* (Baltimore: Johns Hopkins University Press, 1975), 151, 146.

9. Kathryn R. King reminds us that, in the early eighteenth century, "the terms 'novel' and 'romance' were often paired or used interchangeably, and far from pointing toward contrasting sets of imaginative possibilities they stood together for an entire tradition of continental and English love-centered fiction, a tradition which would have included the ten volumes of *Clélie* (1654–61) and Behn's 'little histories' in the seventeenth century and the lengthy scandal fictions of Manley in the next—as well as [a] host of new and translated shorter amatory fictions calling themselves novels" ("The Novel before Novels [with a Glance at Mary Hearne's *Fables of Desertion*]," in *Eighteenth-Century Genre and Culture: Serious Reflections on Occasional Forms; Essays in Honor of J. Paul Hunter*, ed. Dennis Todd and Cynthia Wall [Newark: University of Delaware Press; London: Associated University Presses, 2001], 38–39).

10. Penelope Aubin, *The Life of Madam de Beaumont, a French Lady; Who lived in a Cave in Wales above fourteen Years undiscovered....* (1721), 83–84.

11. See, e.g., *Rambler*, no. 200 (discussed in chapter 7).

12. Mary Davys, *Familiar Letters betwixt a Gentleman and a Lady*, in *The Works of Mrs. Davys: Consisting of Plays, Novels, Poems, and Familiar Letters*, vol. 2 (1725), 275–76.

13. Robert A. Day, introduction to *Familiar Letters Betwixt a Gentleman and a Lady (1725)*, by Mary Davys, Augustan Reprint Society, no. 54 (Los Angeles: William Andrews Clark Memorial Library, University of California, 1955), 2.

14. Quoted in T. C. Duncan Eaves and Ben D. Kimpel, *Samuel Richardson: A Biography* (Oxford: Clarendon, 1971), 496–97.

15. Thomas Keymer notes: "Richardson's well-known admission to Hill that he 'seldom read but as a Printer' is far from suggesting the narrow literary horizons sometimes attributed to him by critics. By virtue of his activity and scope as master printer, and of the wide range of literary connections arising from it, he must be credited instead with a finger kept right on the pulse of fashion and innovation in the rapidly expanding book market of his day" (introduction to *Pamela*, by Samuel Richardson, ed. Thomas Keymer and Alice Wakeley [Oxford: Oxford University Press, 2001], xii). For recent excellent work on the deliberate effects of the dash and other punctuation in eighteenth-century printing, see Janine Barchas, "Sarah Fielding's Dashing Style and Eighteenth-Century Print Culture," *ELH* 64 (1996): 633–56.

16. Samuel Richardson, *Pamela: Or, Virtue Rewarded. In a Series of Familiar Letters from a Beautiful Young Damsel, To her Parents*, 2 vols. (1740), 1:12 (*Pamela; or, Virtue Rewarded*, ed. Thomas Keymer and Alice Wakeley [Oxford: Oxford University Press, 2001], 19). All quotations are taken from the first edition, but, for convenience, citations give page numbers from both editions.

17. Philippa Tristram, *Living Space in Fact and Fiction* (London: Routledge, 1989), 245.

18. See Cynthia Wall, "Gendering Rooms: Domestic Architecture and Literary Acts," *Eighteenth-Century Fiction* 5, no. 4 (July 1993): 360–67, and "The Spaces of *Clarissa* in Text and Film," in *Eighteenth-Century Fiction on Screen*, ed. Robert Mayer (Cambridge: Cambridge University Press, 2002).

19. Samuel Richardson, *Clarissa. Or, The History of a Young Lady: Comprehending the Most Important Concerns of Private Life*, ed. William Warburton, 7 vols. (1747–48), 6:157–58 (*Clarissa* [1747–48], ed. Angus Ross [Harmondsworth: Penguin, 1985], 1064–65). All quotations are taken from the first edition, but, for convenience, citations give page numbers from both editions.

20. John Samuel Bullen, *Time and Space in the Novels of Samuel Richardson*, Monograph Series, vol. 12, no. 2 (Logan: Utah State University Press, July 1965), 32–33.

CHAPTER SIX

1. Carole Fabricant has argued that, from the landowner's point of view, Fanny Price, in Austen's *Mansfield Park* (1814), was the ideal visitor: she could visit Sotherton and eagerly view its rooms and prospects and treasures "without making any material claim upon it, the acquisitiveness suggested by the description taking place on an aesthetic and metaphorical level only" ("The Literature of Domestic Tourism and the Public Consumption of Private Property," in *The New Eighteenth*

Century, ed. Felicity Nussbaum and Laura Brown [New York: Methuen, 1987], 254].

2. At one point, one of the Harrels' creditors, Mr. Hobson, argues against Cecilia's pleading for the widowed Mrs. Harrel: "What have we creditors to do with a man's family? Suppose I am a cabinet-maker? When I send in my chairs, do I ask who is to sit upon them? No; it's all one to me whether it's the gentleman's progeny or his friends, I must be paid for the chairs the same, use them who may" [Frances Burney, *Cecilia, or Memoirs of an Heiress* [1782], ed. Peter Sabor and Margaret Anne Doody [Oxford: Oxford University Press, 1988], 448].

3. See Julia Epstein, *The Iron Pen: Frances Burney and the Politics of Women's Writing* [Madison: University of Wisconsin Press, 1989], 159.

4. For a good condensed account of the changing economic and social systems in Britain, see Hoh-cheung Mui and Lorna H. Mui, *Shops and Shopkeeping in Eighteenth-Century England* [Montreal: McGill-Queen's University Press; London: Routledge, 1989], 12ff. For the more related studies that constitute the epigraph to this section, see John Brewer and Roy Porter, eds., *Consumption and the World of Goods* [London: Routledge, 1993]; J. G. A. Pocock, *Virtue, Commerce, and History: Essays on Political Thought and History, Chiefly in the Eighteenth Century* [Cambridge: Cambridge University Press, 1985]; Laura Brown, *The Ends of Empire: Women and Ideology in Early Eighteenth-Century English Literature* [Ithaca, NY: Cornell University Press, 1993]; David H. Solkin, *Painting for Money: The Visual Arts and the Public Sphere in Eighteenth-Century England* [New Haven, CT: Yale University Press, for the Paul Mellon Centre for Studies in British Art, 1993]; Crowley, *The Invention of Comfort*; Lynch, *The Economy of Character*; Alistair M. Duckworth, *The Improvement of the Estate: A Study of Jane Austen's Novels* [Baltimore: Johns Hopkins University Press, 1971]; Bennett, *The Birth of the Museum*; John Brewer and Susan Staves, eds., *Early Modern Conceptions of Property* [London: Routledge, 1996]; Susan Staves, *Married Women's Separate Property in England, 1660–1833* [Cambridge, MA: Harvard University Press, 1990]; Colin Campbell, *The Romantic Ethic and the Spirit of Modern Consumerism* [Oxford: Blackwell, 1987]; John Elsner and Roger Cardinal, eds., *The Cultures of Collection* [Cambridge, MA: Harvard University Press, 1994]; Robin Myers and Michael Harris, eds., *Property of a Gentleman: The Formation, Organisation and Dispersal of the Private Library, 1620–1920* [Winchester: St. Paul's Bibliographies, 1991]; Daniel Roche, *A History of Everyday Things: The Birth of Consumption in France, 1600–1800* [1997], trans. Brian Pearce [Cambridge: Cambridge University Press, 2000]; Roland Barthes, "Le monde-objet," in *Essais critiques* [Paris: du Seuil, 1964], 19–28; and Stewart, *On Longing*.

5. A misused as well as overused term, as J. A. Downie points out in "Public and Private: The Myth of the Bourgeois Public Sphere," in Wall, ed., *Concise Companion*, 58–79.

6. Simon Schama, "Perishable Commodities: Dutch Still-Life Painting and the 'Empire of Things,'" in Brewer and Porter, eds., *Consumption*, 479.

7. See, e.g., James Raven, "Defending Conduct and Property: The London Press and the Luxury Debate," in Brewer and Staves, eds., *Conceptions*, 301–19.

8. Peter Stallybrass and Ann Rosalind Jones, "Fetishizing the Glove in Renaissance Europe," *Critical Inquiry* 28, no. 1 [autumn 2001]: 116.

9. Elizabeth Burton, *The Georgians at Home* (1967; reprint, London: Arrow, 1973), 122.

10. Chandra Mukerji, *From Graven Images: Patterns of Modern Materialism* (New York: Columbia University Press, 1983), 21.

11. See John Brewer, *The Pleasures of the Imagination: English Culture in the Eighteenth Century* (New York: Farrar Straus Giroux, 1997): "As many foreign commentators and visitors to England recognized, the rise of the arts in England was the triumph of a commercial and urban society, not the achievement of a royal court" (xxiv).

12. Carole Shammas, "Changes in English and Anglo-American Consumption from 1550 to 1800," in Brewer and Porter, eds., *Consumption*, 177.

13. Lorna Weatherill, "The Meaning of Consumer Behaviour in Late Seventeenth- and Early Eighteenth-Century England," in ibid., 208.

14. Charles Dickens, *Great Expectations* (1860–61), ed. Angus Calder (Harmondsworth: Penguin, 1985), 229 (chap. 25).

15. T. H. Breen, "The Meanings of Things: Interpreting the Consumer Economy in the Eighteenth Century," in Brewer and Porter, eds., *Consumption*, 258.

16. See Warren Hunting Smith, *Architecture in English Fiction* (New Haven, CT: Yale University Press, 1934; reprint, Hamden, CT: Archon, 1970); and James H. Bunn, "The Aesthetics of British Mercantilism," *New Literary History* 11 (1980): 303–21.

17. Henri Lefebvre, *The Production of Space* (1974), trans. Donald Nicholson-Smith (Oxford: Blackwell, 1991), 213, 212, 101, 209.

18. These innovations were, according to Breen, also well established in America: "By mid-century these 'trifles' had thus become part of a new visual landscape. Colonists could view the imported manufactures on display in urban stores and rural shops" (253).

19. So attributes the *Oxford Dictionary of Quotations*.

20. Much of what follows on the space of the shop and the shopwindow is derived from Cynthia Wall, "Window Shopping" (paper presented at the conference "Monuments and Dust," London, 2001; available online at http://www.iath.virginia.edu/london/Archive/On-line-pubs/2001/paper4.html), which focuses primarily on nineteenth-century shops.

21. James B. Jefferys, *Retail Trading in Britain, 1850–1950* (Cambridge: Cambridge University Press, 1954), 37.

22. Daniel Defoe, *The Complete English Tradesman, in Familiar Letters* (1725), 315.

23. Plate glass was introduced in 1827, and, between 1830 and 1860, the size of shopwindow glass panes zoomed from seven feet high by three feet wide to fourteen feet high by eight feet wide (see Bill Evans and Andrew Lawson, *A Nation of Shopkeepers* [London: Plexus, 1981], 120–21).

24. Sophie von la Roche, *Sophie in London, 1786: Being the Diary of Sophie von la Roche*, trans. and ed. Clare Williams (London: J. Cape, 1933), 87, quoted in Dorothy Davis, *A History of London Shopping* (London: Routledge & Kegan Paul, 1966), 191.

25. Quoted in Neil McKendrick, "Josiah Wedgwood: An Eighteenth-Century Entrepreneur in Salesmanship and Marketing Techniques," *Economic History Review*, 2nd ser., 12, no. 3 (April 1960): 419.

26. T. R. Nevett, *Advertising in Britain: A History* (London: Heinemann, 1982), 8, 11.

27. Peter Briggs, "'News from the Little World': A Critical Glance at Eighteenth-Century British Advertising," *Studies in Eighteenth-Century Culture* 23 (1993): 30; C. Y. Ferdinand, "Selling It to the Provinces: News and Commerce round Eighteenth-Century Salisbury," in Brewer and Porter, eds., *Consumption*, 398.

28. Breen is quoting from *Account of the Robberies Committed by John Morrison. And his Accomplices, in and Near Philadelphia, 1750: Together with the Manner of their being discover'd, their Behaviour on their Tryalls, in the Prison after Sentence, and then at the Place of Execution* (Philadelphia, 1751).

29. Jonathan Lamb, "Modern Metamorphoses and Disgraceful Tales," *Critical Inquiry* 28 (2001): 133–66. See also Cynthia Wall, "The English Auction: Narratives of Dismantlings," *Eighteenth-Century Studies* 31, no. 1 (1997): 1–25, esp. 14–18.

30. The Hon. John Byng, *The Torrington Diaries: Containing the Tours through England and Wales of the Hon. John Byng (Later Fifth Viscount Torrington) Between the Years 1781 and 1794*, ed. C. Bruyn Andrews, 4 vols. (London: Eyre & Spottiswoode, 1934), 1:208.

31. James Ralph, *The Touch-Stone: Or, Historical, Critical, Political, Philosophical and Theological Essays on the reigning Diversions of the Town. Design'd for the Improvement of all Authors, Spectators, and Actors of Operas, Plays, and Masquerades. In which every thing antique, or modern, relating to Musick, Poetry, Dancing, Pantomimes, Choruses, Cat-Calls, Audiences, Judges, Criticks, Balls, Ridottos, Assemblies, New Oratory, Circus, Bear-Garden, Gladiators, Prize-Fighters, Italian Strollers, Mountebank Stages, Cock-pits, Puppet-Shews, Fairs, and Publick Auctions, is occasionally handled. By a Person of Taste and some Quality* (1728), 231–32.

32. For a more fully detailed history of the English auction, see my "The English Auction," 3–7.

33. Henry Fielding, *The Historical Register for the Year 1736*, ed. William W. Appleton (Lincoln: University of Nebraska Press, 1967), act 2, "The Auction," pp. 28–35.

34. Samuel Baker gave his business to his nephew, John Sotheby, who renamed it in 1780.

35. Albert Braunmuller to Cynthia Wall, e-mail, 25 November 1999.

36. John Lawler, *Book Auctions in England in the Seventeenth Century (1676–1700)* (London: Elliot Stock, 1898), xx. Lawler adds: "The first [such catalogs] have no reference to condition or binding, but it was soon found to be of great advantage to have a book well bound, and Millington and the later auctioneers introduced references to the binding, and in some instances distinguished a book as 'edito optima' or 'charta magna.' All the early auctioneers had a considerable degree of learning, and made their titles and classifications chiefly in Latin."

37. Joseph Farington, *The Diary of Joseph Farington*, ed. Kenneth Garlick and Angus Macintyre, 17 vols. (New Haven, CT: Yale University Press, 1978–98), 3:979 (4 February 1798).

38. John Nichols, *Literary Anecdotes of the Eighteenth Century; comprizing Biographical Memoirs of William Bowyer, Printer, F.S.A.*, 9 vols. (London: Nichols,

Son, & Bentley, 1812–15), 3:624n. The description comes from a 1788 note to Richard Gough.

39. James Boswell, *Boswell: The Applause of the Jury, 1782–1785*, ed. Irma S. Lustig and Frederick A. Pottle (New York: McGraw-Hill, 1981), 337 (15 August 1785).

40. My thanks to Catherine Rodriguez for this bibliographic information.

41. Paraphrased in Antoinette Marie Sol, *Textual Promiscuities: Eighteenth-Century Critical Rewriting* (Lewisburg, PA: Bucknell University Press, 2002), 162.

42. Mrs. A. Woodfin, *The Auction: A Modern Novel. In Two Volumes* (1770).

CHAPTER SEVEN

1. Jane Austen, *Mansfield Park: A Novel*, 2nd ed., 3 vols. (London: J. Murray, 1816), 1:176–77, 176.

2. Lisa Jardine, *Worldly Goods: A New History of the Renaissance* (New York: Nan A. Talese/Doubleday, 1996), 16.

3. James Ayres, *Domestic Interiors: The British Tradition, 1500–1850* (New Haven, CT: Yale University Press, 2003), 165.

4. See, e.g., Roche on furniture in Alsace (*History of Everyday Things*, 180); and Ayres on window blinds (81ff.) and chairs (171ff.).

5. Caroline Lybbe Powys, *Passages from the Diaries of Mrs. Philip Lybbe Powys of Hardwick House, Oxon. A.D. 1756 to 1808*, ed. Emily J. Climenson (London: Longmans, Green, 1899), 6.

6. Batty Langley, *The Builder's Chest-Book; Or A Complete Key to the Five Orders of Columns in Architecture* (1727), 129–36.

7. Robert Adam and James Adam, *The Works in Architecture of Robert and James Adam, Esquires* (1773), preface, 3.

8. Mary Granville Delany, *The Autobiography and Correspondence of Mary Granville, Mrs. Delany*, 1st and 2nd ser., ed. the Right Honourable Lady Llanover, 6 vols. (London: Richard Bentley, 1861–62), 5:35 (16 September 1774).

9. Adam Smith, *The Theory of Moral Sentiments* (1759), ed. Knud Haakonssen (Cambridge: Cambridge University Press, 2002), 210.

10. Charles Dickens, *Our Mutual Friend* (1864–65), ed. Michael Cotsell (Oxford: Oxford University Press, 1989), 55–56.

11. Jane Schneider, "Fantastical Colors in Foggy London: The New Fashion Potential of the Late Sixteenth Century," in *Material London, ca. 1600*, ed. Lena Cowen Orlin (Philadelphia: University of Pennsylvania Press, 2000), 121–22, 117.

12. Paul D. McGlynn, "Samuel Johnson and the Illusions of Popular Culture," *Modern Language Studies* 10 (1980): 32.

13. John Bender, like John Keats, subordinates the importance of travelers' description to readers' visualization. Bender argues that, generally, "description lacks pictorial force":

Descriptive detail accumulates without compelling the reader to a fresh visualization and reevaluation of successive images in a developing context.

Keats recognizes this tendency of description to reduce and simplify experience when he refuses to catalog his experiences as a traveler, "unless perhaps I do it in the manner of the Laputan printing press—that is I put down Mountains, Rivers Lakes, dells, glens, Rocks, and Clouds, With beautiful enchanting, gothic picturesque fine, delightful, enchanting, Grand, sublime—a few Blisters &ᶜ—and now you have our journey thus far." As Keats implies, description has no inherent narrative content, but a narrative or proto-narrative structure can be easily imposed upon it. It does not exclude narrative, as we might at first suppose. It can also be ordered discursively or logically. Description is formally neutral, but of course in most literature it is not formless. (33)

But Keats would not have had the travel vocabulary to disparage without the sharp rise in popularity of domestic and foreign travel narratives; and both travel writers and novelists used their accumulated detail precisely in order to create pictorial force and fresh visualizations.

14. John Harris, "English Country House Guides, 1740–1840," in *Concerning Architecture: Essays on Architectural Writers and Writing Presented to Nikolaus Pevsner*, ed. John Summerson (Baltimore: Penguin, 1968), 69.

15. Celia Fiennes, *The Illustrated Journeys of Celia Fiennes, 1685–c. 1712*, ed. Christopher Morris (London: Macdonald, 1982; new ed., Stroud: Alan Sutton, 1995), 32.

16. Christopher Morris, introduction to ibid., 10–31, 30.

17. Daniel Defoe, *A Tour through the Whole Island of Great Britain* (1724–26), ed. P. N. Furbank, W. R. Owens, and A. J. Coulson (New Haven, CT: Yale University Press, 1991), 250.

18. George B. Clarke, introduction to *The Beauties of Stow* (1750), by George Bickham, William Andrews Clark Memorial Library Publication, nos. 185–86 (Los Angeles: University of California Press, 1977), x, xi.

19. Bickham, *The Beauties of Stow*, 23–24.

20. George Bickham and P. Norbury, *A Short Account of the Principal Seats and Gardens in and about Richmond and Kew* (Brentford, n.d.), 11, 8, 7.

21. William Mavor, *New Description of Blenheim, The Seat of His Grace the Duke of Marlborough* (1793), 25.

22. It is worth remembering from the previous chapter that artwork and household goods generally had separate auction catalogs; art had a separate audience in terms of wealth and class, although the house guides bridge the gap to some extent.

23. Esther Moir, *The Discovery of Britain: The English Tourists, 1540–1840* (London: Routledge & Kegan Paul, 1964), 63, 71.

24. Samuel Richardson, *Sir Charles Grandison* (1753–54), ed. Jocelyn Harris (Oxford: Oxford University Press, 1972), 272 (pt. 3, p. 272 [vol. 7, letter 5]).

25. Malcolm Kelsall, *The Great Good Place: The Country House and English Literature* (New York: Columbia University Press, 1993), 94.

26. This scene has been discussed by Neil Hultgren, whose observations are reprinted in my "Teaching Space in *Sir Charles Grandison*," in *Approaches to*

Teaching Richardson, ed. Jocelyn Harris and Lisa Zunshine (New York: Modern Language Association, in press).

CHAPTER EIGHT

1. Henry Fielding, *The History of Tom Jones, a Foundling* (1749), ed. Fredson Bowers, with an introduction by Martin Battestin (Middletown, CT: Wesleyan University Press, 1975), 42.

2. For a good synopsis of the twentieth-century status of literary description, see Lopes, 3, 9–10.

3. Myra Reynolds, *The Treatment of Nature in English Poetry between Pope and Wordsworth* (Chicago: University of Chicago Press, 1909), 215. Reynolds does an admirably systematic job of surveying about forty-five eighteenth-century novels, but the survey often comes down to a "she has it, he doesn't" checklist, with relatively little explanation of why or in what relation.

4. Review of *The Poetical Works of Anne* [sic] *Radcliffe. St Alban's Abbey; a metrical Romance. With other Poems*, 2 vols. (London, 1834), *Edinburgh Review* 59 (July 1834): 327–41.

5. See, e.g., Gary Kelly, *Women, Writing, and Revolution, 1790–1827* (Oxford: Clarendon, 1993); Robert Mighall, *A Geography of Victorian Gothic Fiction: Mapping History's Nightmares* (Oxford: Oxford University Press, 1999); and Michael Gamer, *Romanticism and the Gothic: Genre, Reception, and Canon Formation* (Cambridge: Cambridge University Press, 2000).

6. James Trainer, introduction to *The Old English Baron*, by Clara Reeve, ed. James Trainer (1967; reprint, Oxford: Oxford University Press, 1977), xiii, xii n. 2.

7. James Watt, introduction to *The Old English Baron*, ed. Trainer (2003), xv.

8. J. M. S. Tompkins, *The Popular Novel in England, 1770–1800* (London: Constable, 1932), 229–30.

9. John Dunlop, *The History of Fiction: being a Critical Account of the most celebrated Prose Works of Fiction, from the earliest Greek Romances to the Novels of the Present Age*, 3 vols. (London: Longman, Hurst, Reise, Orme, & Brown, 1814), 3:384.

10. Matthew G. Lewis, *The Life and Correspondence of M. G. Lewis*, 2 vols. (London: Henry Colburn, 1839), 1:122–24 (18 May 1794).

11. Christopher MacLachlan, introduction to *The Monk*, by Matthew Lewis, ed. Christopher MacLachlan (London: Penguin, 1998), vii.

12. See *British Critic* 4 (August 1794): 110–21; *The Gentleman's Magazine* 64, pt. 2 (September 1794): 834; *The Critical Review*, 2nd ser., 11 (August 1794): 361–72; *Analytical Review* 19 (June 1794): 140–45; *The Monthly Review*, n.s., 15 (November 1794): 278–83; and *European Magazine and London Review* 25 (June 1794): 433–40.

13. Sir Walter Scott, *Miscellaneous Prose Works of Sir Walter Scott, Bart.*, 3 vols. (Edinburgh: Robert Cadell, 1841–47), 1:314.

14. Clara Frances McIntyre, *Ann Radcliffe in Relation to Her Time*, Yale Studies in English, ed. Albert S. Cook, vol. 62 (New Haven, CT: Yale University Press, 1920), 59–60.

264 NOTES TO PAGES 208–218

15. Rhoda L. Flaxman, *Victorian Word-Painting and Narrative: Toward the Blending of Genres* (Ann Arbor: UMI Research, 1987), 11.

16. Ann Radcliffe, *The Mysteries of Udolpho* (1794), ed. Bonamy Dobrée, with an introduction by Terry Castle (1966; reprint, Oxford: Oxford University Press, 1970), 1. All quotations are from this edition.

17. Deborah D. Rogers, introduction to *The Critical Response to Ann Radcliffe*, ed. Deborah D. Rogers (Westport, CT: Greenwood, 1994), xxxiv.

18. Daniel Cottom, *The Civilized Imagination: A Study of Ann Radcliffe, Jane Austen, and Sir Walter Scott* (Cambridge: Cambridge University Press, 1985), 35.

19. Edmund Burke defines the source of the sublime as "whatever is fitted in any sort to excite the ideas of pain, and danger, that is to say, whatever is in any sort terrible, or is conversant about terrible objects, or operates in a manner analogous to terror," and he specifically connects the sublime with power and the masculine, comparing our feelings toward our fathers (reverence, awe, respect) with those toward our mothers or grandfathers (love and contempt). Beauty is "the soft green of the soul," and Burke waxes most eloquent about its attractions when he contemplates the female breast. But it depends for its attractions, in part, on its weakness, modesty, vulnerability (pt. 1, sec. 7, p. 39; pt. 3, sec. 10, p. 111).

20. In "The Gothic Mirror" (in *The [M]other Tongue: Essays in Feminist Psychoanalytic Interpretation*, ed. Shirley Nelson Garner, Claire Kahane, and Madelon Sprengnether [Ithaca, NY: Cornell University Press, 1985], 335–36), Claire Kahane argues along the related lines of "a helpless daughter confronting the erotic power of a father or a brother, with the mother noticeably absent." Gothic spaces for Kahane are more womblike, the castle as a site of confrontation between the daughter and the absent mother. But, to me, such a reading takes Emily's "helplessness" too much at face value.

21. *The Monthly Magazine; or, British Register* 49, pt. 1 (1 February 1820): 71.

22. *Blackwood's Edinburgh Magazine* 6, no. 33 (December 1819): 262–63, 263.

23. Ian Duncan, introduction to *Ivanhoe*, by Sir Walter Scott, ed. Ian Duncan (Oxford: Oxford University Press, 1996), x, ix–x.

24. Glenda Leeming, introduction to *Ivanhoe* (London: Panther, 1969), 10–11.

25. Sir H. J. C. Grierson, introduction to *Ivanhoe* (London: Collins, 1952), 18.

26. Scott, *Ivanhoe* (1819), ed. Duncan, 21. All quotations are from this edition.

27. James Kerr, *Fiction against History: Scott as Storyteller* (Cambridge: Cambridge University Press, 1989), 24.

28. Ian Duncan, introduction to *Rob Roy*, by Sir Walter Scott, ed. Ian Duncan (Oxford: Oxford University Press, 1998), vii.

29. Graham Tulloch, introduction to *Ivanhoe*, by Sir Walter Scott, ed. Graham Tulloch (London: Penguin, 1998), xiv.

30. Georg Lukács, *The Historical Novel* (1955), trans. Hannah Mitchell and Stanley Mitchell (London: Merlin, 1962; reprint, Harmondsworth: Penguin, 1981), 42.

31. Ann Rigney, *Imperfect Histories: The Elusive Past and the Legacy of Romantic Historicism* (Ithaca, NY: Cornell University Press, 2001), 36.

32. Alexander Welsh, *The Hero of the Waverley Novels, with New Essays on Scott* (1963; expanded ed., Princeton, NJ: Princeton University Press, 1992), 56.

33. Mark Salber Phillips, *Society and Sentiment: Genres of Historical Writing in Britain, 1740–1820* (Princeton, NJ: Princeton University Press, 2000), 53.

34. David Brown, *Walter Scott and the Historical Imagination* (London: Routledge & Kegan Paul, 1979), 177.

35. Sir Leslie Stephen, *English Literature and Society in the Eighteenth Century* (London: Duckworth, 1904), 5.

36. *The London Magazine* 1, no. 1 (January 1820): 79.

37. Thomas Babington Macaulay, *Critical and Historical Essays Contributed to the Edinburgh Review* (London: Longman, Brown, Green, & Longmans, 1850), 51.

38. Thomas Carlyle, *Thomas Carlyle's Essay on Sir Walter Scott*, ed. Arnold Smith (London: J. M. Dent, 1925), 101.

39. René Rapin, *Instructions for History: with a Character of the most Considerable Historians, Antient and Modern. Out of the French, by J. Davies of Kidwelly* (1680), 45, 53–54, 78.

40. [Peter Whalley], *An Essay on the Manner of Writing History* (1746), 17.

41. Although G. W. Bowersock has noted that the (twentieth-century) historian Sir Ronald Syme's style, which he describes as "unusual," is "an English reworking of the inconcinnity of Tacitus," so a rhetorical reputation has moved from propriety to awkwardness and disproportion ("Gibbon's Historical Imagination" [Stanford, CA: Stanford Humanities Center, 1988], 4).

42. Cornelius Tacitus, *The Works of Tacitus*, trans. T. Gordon, 2 vols. (1723), 1, pt. 4:199–200.

43. *The Monthly Review*, 2nd ser., 3 (1790): 93–94.

44. Cornelius Tacitus, *The Works of Cornelius Tacitus: by Arthur Murphy, Esq.*, 4 vols. (1793), 1:305–6.

45. Sarah Fielding, *Remarks on Clarissa Addressed to the Author. Occasioned by some critical Conversations on the Characters and Conduct of that Work* (1749), 5.

46. Harold L. Bond, *The Literary Art of Edward Gibbon* (Oxford: Clarendon, 1960), 68.

47. David Womersley, *The Transformation of "The Decline and Fall of the Roman Empire"* (Cambridge: Cambridge University Press, 1988), 278.

48. A descriptive example is Gibbon's translation of Poggius looking on the ruins of Rome: "The path of victory is obliterated by vines, and the benches of the senators are concealed by a dunghill. Cast your eyes on the Palatine hill, and seek, among the shapeless and enormous fragments, the marble theatre, the obelisks, the colossal statues, the porticoes of Nero's palace: survey the other hills of the city, the vacant space is interrupted only by ruins and gardens. The forum of the Roman people where they assembled to enact their laws and elect their magistrates, is now inclosed for the cultivation of pot-herbs, or thrown open for the reception of swine and buffaloes. The public and private edifices, that were founded for eternity, lie prostrate, naked, and broken, like the limbs of a mighty giant; and the ruin is the more visible, from the stupendous relics that have survived the injuries of time and fortune" (Edward Gibbon, *The History of the Decline and Fall of the Roman Empire* [1776–88], 6:620).

49. Edward Gibbon, *Mémoires littéraires de la Grande Bretagne* (1768–69), quoted in Bowersock, 7.

50. David Wootton, "David Hume, 'the Historian,'" in *The Cambridge Companion to Hume*, ed. David Fate Norton (Cambridge: Cambridge University Press, 1993), 281–82; Everett Zimmerman, *The Boundaries of Fiction: History and the Eighteenth-Century British Novel* (Ithaca, NY: Cornell University Press, 1996), 245–46.

51. Phillip Hicks, *Neoclassical History and English Culture from Clarendon to Hume* (London: Macmillan, 1996), 199.

52. David Hume, *An Inquiry concerning Human Understanding* (1748), ed. Tom L. Beauchamp (Oxford: Clarendon, 2000), 35.

53. David Hume, "Simplicity and Refinement in Writing," in *Essays Moral, Political, and Literary*, ed. Eugene F. Miller (1985; reprint, Indianapolis: Liberty Classics, 1987). See also John J. Richetti, *Philosophical Writing: Locke, Berkeley, Hume* (Cambridge, MA: Harvard University Press, 1983), 189; and, less persuasively, Leo Braudy, *Narrative Form in History and Fiction* (Princeton, NJ: Princeton University Press, 1970), 48–49, 87–88.

54. David Hume, "Of Tragedy," in Miller, ed., *Essays*, 223.

55. Edward Hyde, Earl of Clarendon, *The History of the Rebellions and Civil Wars in England, begun in the Year 1641*, 3 vols. (Oxford, 1702), 1:504 (bk. 15, mistakenly bound in vol. 1 instead of vol. 3 in this edition).

56. David Hume, *The History of England, from the Invasion of Julius Caesar to the Revolution in 1688* (1778), ed. William B. Todd, 6 vols. (Indianapolis: Liberty, 1983), 6:105.

57. David Hume, *The Letters of David Hume*, ed. J. Y. T. Greig, 2 vols. (Oxford: Clarendon, 1932), 1:32, quoted in Womersley, 23.

58. Braudy emphasizes the stylistic differences between the Stuart volumes, written first, and the medieval volumes, in which Hume "emphasizes the continuity of historical narrative at the expense of the outstanding historical character," and in which he gradually "withdraw[s] his narrative voice to allow the slow accretions of time to shape history" (*Narrative Form*, 49).

59. Thomas Babington Macaulay, "HISTORY. *The Romance of History*. By Henry Neele. London, 1828," in *Reviews, Essays, and Poems* (London: Ward, Lock, & Tyler, n.d.), 323.

AFTERWORD

1. J. C. Loudon, *The Landscape Gardening and Landscape Architecture of the Late Humphry Repton, Esq.* (1840; reprint, Farnborough: Gregg International, 1969).

2. Stephen Daniels, introduction to *Humphry Repton: The Red Books for Brandsbury and Glemham Hall* (Washington, DC: Dumbarton Oaks, 1994), ix.

3. Quoted in George Carter, Patrick Goode, and Kedrun Laurie, *Humphry Repton, Landscape Gardener, 1752–1818* (Norwich: Sainsbury Centre for the Visual Arts, 1982), 21.

4. Thomas Carlyle, "The Hero as Poet," in *On Heroes, Hero-Worship, and the Heroic in History*, ed. Michael K. Goldberg (Berkeley and Los Angeles: University of California Press, 1993), 89.

5. Susan Fraiman's current project on "shelter writing" and domestic description revisits the "everyday" of Henri Lefebvre and Michel de Certeau along the feminist critical lines of Rita Felski and Mary McLeod, arguing that "this body of theory deals in the everyday only insofar as (shades of Bachelard here?) it is somehow aesthetically or politically ennobled" ("From *Crusoe* to *Queer Eye*: Towards a Feminist Poetics of Interior Design" [Carolyn G. Heilbrun Memorial Lecture, City University of New York, 5 March 2004]).

6. See Terry Castle, "The Spectralization of the Other in *The Mysteries of Udolpho*," in Nussbaum and Brown, eds., *New Eighteenth Century*.

BIBLIOGRAPHY

Note: *All early modern texts are published in London, unless otherwise noted.*

PRIMARY SOURCES

Account of the Robberies Committed by John Morrison. And his Accomplices, in and Near Philadelphia, 1750: Together with the Manner of their being discover'd, their Behaviour on their Tryalls, in the Prison after Sentence, and then at the Place of Execution. Philadelphia, 1751.

Adam, Robert, and James Adam, *The Works in Architecture of Robert and James Adam, Esquires.* 1773.

Addison, Joseph, and Richard Steele. *The Spectator.* 1711–12. Edited by Donald F. Bond. 5 vols. 1965. Reprint, Oxford: Clarendon, 1987.

Analytical Review 19 (June 1794): 140–45.

Aristotle. *Poetics.* In *The Complete Works of Aristotle: The Revised Oxford Translation,* ed. Jonathan Barnes, vol. 2. Princeton, NJ: Princeton University Press, 1984.

———. *Rhetoric.* In *The Complete Works of Aristotle: The Revised Oxford Translation,* ed. Jonathan Barnes, vol. 2. Princeton, NJ: Princeton University Press, 1984.

The Artes of Logike and Rhetorike, plainely set foorth in the Englishe toongue, easie to be learned and practised: togeather with examples for the practise of the same for Methode in the gouernment of the familie, prescribed in the worde of God: And for the whole in the resolution or opening of certain parts of Scripture, according to the same. 1584.

Aubin, Penelope. *The Life and Adventures of the Lady Lucy.* 1726.

———. *The Life of Charlotta Du Pont, An English Lady; Taken from her own Memoirs.* 1723.

———. *The Life of Madam de Beaumont, a French Lady; Who lived in a Cave in Wales above fourteen Years undiscovered....* 1721.

————. *The Noble Slaves: or, the Lives and Adventures of Two Lords and Two Ladies, Who were Shipwrecked, and cast upon a desolate Island, near the East Indies, in the Year 1710*. Dublin, [1730].

————. *The Strange Adventures of the Count de Vinevil And his Family*. 1721.

Aubrey, John. *Brief Lives*. Edited by Oliver Lawson Dick. 1949. Reprint, Harmondsworth: Penguin, 1972.

Austen, Jane. *Mansfield Park: A Novel*. 2nd ed. 3 vols. London: J. Murray, 1816.

————. *Mansfield Park*. Edited by Marilyn Butler. Oxford: Oxford University Press, 1970.

Ballantyne, John. "Daniel de Foe." In *The Lives of the Novelists* (1810), ed. Sir Walter Scott. New York: E. P. Dutton/Everyman's Library, 1928.

Barbauld, Anna Laetitia. *The British Novelists*. 50 vols. London, 1810.

Beattie, James. *Elements of Moral Science*. Philadelphia, 1792.

Behn, Aphra. *Agnes de Castro: or, the Force of Generous Love. Written in French by a Lady of Quality. Made English by Mrs. Behn*. 1688. In *The Histories and Novels of the Late Ingenious Mrs Behn: In One Volume*. 1696.

————. *The Fair Jilt; or, the History of Prince Tarquin and Miranda*. 1688. In *The Histories and Novels of the Late Ingenious Mrs Behn: In One Volume*. 1696.

————. *The Histories and Novels of the Late Ingenious Mrs Behn: In One Volume*. 1696.

————. *Love Letters from a Noble Man to his Sister: Mixt With the History of their Adventures*. 1685.

————. *The Lucky Mistake. A New Novel*. 1689. In *The Histories and Novels of the Late Ingenious Mrs Behn: In One Volume*. 1696.

Bickham, George. *The Beauties of Stow*. 1750. With an introduction by George B. Clarke. William Andrews Clark Memorial Library Publication, nos. 185–86. Los Angeles: University of California Press, 1977.

Bickham, George, and P. Norbury. *A Description of the Gardens and Buildings at Kew*. Brentford, n.d.

————. *A Short Account of the Principal Seats and Gardens in and about Richmond and Kew*. Brentford, n.d.

Blackwood's Edinburgh Magazine. Vol. 6, no. 33 (December 1819).

Blair, Hugh. *Lectures on Rhetoric and Belles Lettres*. 2 vols. London and Edinburgh, 1783.

Blount, Sir Thomas Pope. *De re poetica: or, Remarks upon Poetry. With Characters and Censures of the Most Considerable Poets, Whether Ancient or Modern. Extracted out of the Best and Choicest Criticks*. 1694.

Bohun, Edmund. *A Geographical Dictionary*. 1688, 1689–90, 1710.

Boileau Despréaux, Nicolas. *The Art of Poetry*. 1675. Translated by Sir William Soames. 1683.

Boswell, James. *Boswell: The Applause of the Jury, 1782–1785*. Edited by Irma S. Lustig and Frederick A. Pottle. New York: McGraw-Hill, 1981.

————. *Boswell: The English Experiment, 1785–1798*. Edited by Irma S. Lustig and
Frederick A. Pottle. New York: McGraw-Hill, 1986.

————. *The Life of Johnson*. 1791. Edited by R. W. Chapman. With an introduction
by Pat Rogers. Oxford: Oxford University Press, 1980.

Bowen, Emanuel. *Britannia Depicta or Ogilby Improv'd*. 1720–64.

Boyle, Robert. *Occasional Reflections upon several Svbiects. Whereto is promis'd A
Discourse About such kind of Thoughts*. 1665.

————. *Some Considerations touching the Usefulnesse of Experimental Naturall
Philosophy. Propos'd in Familiar Discourses to a Friend, by way of Invitation to
the Study of it*. Oxford, 1663.

————. *The Works of the Honourable Robert Boyle, in Six Volumes*. 1772.

*A Brief of the Art of Rhetorick. Containing in substance all that Aristotle hath
written in this Three Books of that Subject, Except onely what is not applicable
to the English Tongue*. 1651.

British Critic 4 (August 1794): 110–21.

Brontë, Charlotte. *Jane Eyre*. 1847. Edited by Richard J. Dunn. 3rd ed. New York:
Norton, 2001.

Bunyan, John. *The Pilgrim's Progress from This world, to That which is to come:
Delivered under the Similitude of a Dream Wherein is Discovered, The manner
of his setting out, His Dangerous Journey; And safe Arrival at the Desired
Countrey*. 1678.

————. *The Pilgrim's Progress . . . The sixth edition with additions*. 1681.

————. *The Pilgrim's Progress . . . In Two Parts, Complete. The Two and Twentieth
Edition, adorned with Twenty-Two Copper Plates, Engraven by J. Sturt*. 1728.

————. *The Pilgrim's Progress*. 1678. Edited by James Blanton Wharey. Revised by
Roger Sharrock. Oxford: Clarendon, 1960.

————. *The Pilgrim's Progress*. 1678. Edited by N. H. Keeble. 1966. Reprint, Oxford:
Oxford University Press, 1984.

Burke, Edmund. *A Philosophical Inquiry into the Origin of Our Ideas of the
Sublime and Beautiful*. 1757. Edited by James T. Boulton. Notre Dame, IN:
Notre Dame University Press, 1958.

Burney, Frances. *Cecilia, or Memoirs of an Heiress*. 1782. Edited by Peter Sabor and
Margaret Anne Doody. Oxford: Oxford University Press, 1988.

————. *Evelina; or, The History of a Young Lady's Entrance into the World*. 1778.
Edited by Edward A. Bloom. Oxford: Oxford University Press, 1968.

Byng, John, the Hon. *The Torrington Diaries: Containing the Tours through England
and Wales of the Hon. John Byng (Later Fifth Viscount Torrington) Between the
Years 1781 and 1794*. Edited by C. Bruyn Andrews. 4 vols. London: Eyre &
Spottiswoode, 1934.

Bysshe, Edward. *The Art of English Poetry*. 1702.

Carlyle, Thomas. "The Hero as Poet." In *On Heroes, Hero-Worship, and the Heroic
in History*. Edited by Michael K. Goldberg. Berkeley and Los Angeles: University
of California Press, 1993.

————. *Lectures on the History of Literature, Delivered by Thomas Carlyle, April to July 1838*. New York: Scribner's, 1892.

————. *Thomas Carlyle's Essay on Sir Walter Scott*. Edited by Arnold Smith. London: J. M. Dent, 1925.

Cary, John. *Cary's New Itinerary; or, An Accurate Delineation of the Great Roads, both Direct and Cross, through England and Wales*. 1798.

Chippendale, Thomas. *The Gentleman and Cabinet-Maker's Director, being a large collection of the Most Elegant and Useful Designs of Household Furniture in the Most Fashionable taste*. 1754. 3rd ed. 1762.

Clavell, Robert. *The General Catalogue of Books, Printed in England Since the Dreadful Fire of London MDCLXVI*. 1677.

Coleridge, Samuel Taylor. *Biographia Literaria*. 1817. Edited by James Engell and W. Jackson Bate. 2 vols. Princeton, NJ: Princeton University Press, 1983.

————. *Coleridge on the Seventeenth Century*. Edited by Roberta Florence Brinkley. Durham, NC: Duke University Press, 1955. Reprint, New York: Greenwood, 1968.

Comenius, Johann Amos. *Orbis Sensualium Pictus . . . Visible World, or, A Nomenclature, and Pictures of all The chiefe things that are in the World*. Translated by Charles Hoole. 1659, 1664, 1672, 1689, 1705, 1729, 1777.

A Compendium of the Art of Logick and Rhetorick in the English Tongue. Containing all that Peter Ramus, Aristotle, and others have writ thereon: with Plaine Directions for the more easie understanding and practice of the same. 1651.

The Critical Review: Or, Annals of Literature. By a Society of Gentlemen. January–June 1765.

Davys, Mary. *The Accomplished Rake, or, The Modern Fine Gentleman. Being An Exact Description of the Conduct and Behavior of a Person of Distinction*. 1727.

————. *Familiar Letters Betwixt a Gentleman and a Lady*. In *The Works of Mrs. Davys: Consisting of Plays, Novels, Poems, and Familiar Letters*, vol. 2. 1725.

————. *Familiar Letters Betwixt a Gentleman and a Lady (1725)*. With an introduction by Robert A. Day. Augustan Reprint Society, no. 54. Los Angeles: William Andrews Clark Memorial Library, University of California, Los Angeles, 1955.

————. *The Reform'd Coquet; a Novel*. In *The Works of Mrs. Davys: Consisting of Plays, Novels, Poems, and Familiar Letters*, vol. 2. 1725.

Defoe, Daniel. *The Complete English Tradesman, in Familiar Letters*. 1725.

————. *The Fortunes and Misfortunes of the Famous Moll Flanders*. 1722. Edited by G. A. Starr. 1971. Reprint, Oxford: Oxford University Press, 1987.

————. *The History and Remarkable Life of the Truly Honourable Col. Jacque commonly call'd Col Jack*. Edited by Samuel Holt Monk. Oxford: Oxford University Press, 1965.

————. *A Journal of the Plague Year*. 1722. Edited by Cynthia Wall. Harmondsworth: Penguin, 2003.

———. *The Life and Strange Surprizing Adventures of Robinson Crusoe.* 1719. Edited by J. Donald Crowley. Oxford: Oxford University Press, 1972.

———. *The Life and Strange Surprizing Adventures of Robinson Crusoe of York, Mariner.* 1719. Edited by Michael Shinagel. 1975. 2nd ed. New York: Norton, 1994.

———. *Robinson Crusoe.* 1719. Edited by John Richetti. Harmondsworth: Penguin, 2002.

———. *A Tour through the Whole Island of Great Britain.* 1724–26. Edited by P. N. Furbank, W. R. Owens, and A. J. Coulson. New Haven, CT: Yale University Press, 1991.

Delany, Mary Granville. *The Autobiography and Correspondence of Mary Granville, Mrs. Delany.* 1st and 2nd ser. Edited by the Right Honourable Lady Llanover. 6 vols. London: Richard Bentley, 1861–62.

De Laune, Thomas. *Angliae Metropolis: Or, The Present State of London... First Written by the late Ingenious Tho: Delaune Gent. and Continu'd to this present Year, by a careful hand.* 1690.

———. *The Present State of London, or Memorials Comprehending A Full and Succinct Account Of the Ancient and Modern State thereof.* 1681.

Dickens, Charles. *Great Expectations.* 1860–61. Edited by Angus Calder. Harmondsworth: Penguin, 1985.

———. *Oliver Twist.* 1837–38. Edited by Kathleen Tillotson. 1966. Reprint, Oxford: Oxford University Press, 1990.

———. *Our Mutual Friend.* 1864–65. Edited by Michael Cotsell. Oxford: Oxford University Press, 1989.

Dryden, John. Preface to *Du Fresnoy's De Art Graphica. The Art of Painting, by C. A. Du Fresnoy. With Remarks. Translated into English, Together with an Original Preface containing a Parallel betwixt Painting and Poetry. By Mr. Dryden.* 1695.

Dufresnoy, Charles-Alphonse. *The Art of Painting.* 1716.

Dunlop, John. *The History of Fiction: being a Critical Account of the most celebrated Prose Works of Fiction, from the earliest Greek Romances to the Novels of the Present Age.* 3 vols. London: Longman, Hurst, Reise, Orme, & Brown, 1814.

Encyclopédie, ou Dictionnaire Raisonné des Sciences, des Arts et des Métiers, par une Societé de gens de Lettres. Edited by Denis Diderot, Jean Le Rond d'Alembert, et al. 17 vols. Paris, 1751–65.

European Magazine and London Review 25 (June 1794): 433–40.

Evelyn, John. *The Diary of John Evelyn.* Edited by E. S. De Beer. 6 vols. Oxford: Clarendon, 1955.

———. *The Diary of John Evelyn.* Edited by Guy de la Bédoyère. Bangor: Headstart History, 1994.

Farington, Joseph. *The Diary of Joseph Farington.* Edited by Kenneth Garlick and Angus Macintyre. 17 vols. New Haven, CT: Yale University Press, 1978–98.

Fielding, Henry. *The Historical Register for the Year 1736*. Edited by William W.
    Appleton. Lincoln: University of Nebraska Press, 1967.
———. *The History of Tom Jones, a Foundling*. 1749. Edited by Fredson Bowers.
    With an introduction by Martin Battestin. Middletown, CT: Wesleyan
    University Press, 1975.
Fielding, Sarah. *Remarks on Clarissa Addressed to the Author. Occasioned by some
    critical Conversations on the Characters and Conduct of that Work*. 1749.
Fiennes, Celia. *The Illustrated Journeys of Celia Fiennes, 1685–c. 1712*. Edited by
    Christopher Morris. London: Macdonald, 1982. New ed., Stroud: Alan Sutton,
    1995.
The Gentleman's Magazine 64, pt. 2 (September 1794): 834.
Gibbon, Edward. *The History of the Decline and Fall of the Roman Empire*. 6 vols.
    1776–88.
———. *The Decline and Fall of the Roman Empire*. With an introduction by Hugh
    Trevor-Roper. 6 vols. London: Everyman's Library, 1994.
———. *Mémoires Littéraires de la Grande Bretagne*. 1768–69.
Goldsmith, Oliver. *The Art of Poetry on a New Plan*. 1762.
Gough, Richard. *British Topography*. 1780.
———. *The Progress of Selling Books*. 1788.
Gray, Thomas. *Correspondence of Thomas Gray*. Edited by Paget Toynbee and
    Leonard Whibley. 1935. With corrections and additions by H. W. Starr. 3 vols.
    Oxford: Clarendon, 1971.
———. "Some Remarks on the Poems of John Lydgate." In *The Works of Thomas
    Gray in Prose and Verse*, ed. Edmund Gosse, 1:387–409. London: Macmillan,
    1884.
The Great Historical, Geographical and Poetical Dictionary. 1640 [1740?].
H. C. *Aristotle's Rhetoric: Or the True Grounds and Principles of Oratory; Shewing,
    the Right Art of Pleading and Speaking in full Assemblies and Courts of
    Judicature. Made English by the Translators of the Art of Thinking. In Four
    Books*. 1686.
Harris, James. *Three Treatises*. 1744.
Hatton, Edward. *A New View of London; Or, An Ample Account of that City, In
    Two Volumes, or Eight Sections. Being a more particular Description thereof
    than has hitherto been known to be published of any City in the World*. 1708.
Haywood, Eliza. *The British Recluse: Or, Secret History of Cleomira, supposed
    dead. A Novel*. 1725.
———. *Fantomina: or, Love in a Maze. Being a Secret History of an Amour Between
    Two Persons of Condition*. 1725.
———. *Idalia: or, the Unfortunate Mistress. A Novel. In Three Parts*. 3rd ed. 1725.
———. *The Injur'd Husband; or, Mistaken Resentment*. 2nd ed. 1725.
———. *Love in Excess; or the Fatal Inquiry, a Novel*. 1729.
———. *The Secret Histories, Novels, and Poems, Written by Mrs. Eliza Haywood*.
    2 vols. 2nd ed. 1725.

————. *The Surprise: or, Constancy rewarded*. 2nd ed. 1725.

Hazlitt, William. *Lectures on the English Poets*. 4 vols. London, 1818.

————. "On Certain Inconsistencies in Sir Joshua Reynolds' Discourses." In *Collected Works*. 12 vols. 1903.

————. "On the English Novelists." In *Lectures on the English Comic Writers*. 1819. In *The Complete Works of William Hazlitt*, ed. P. P. Howe. 21 vols. London: J. M. Dent, 1930–34.

Heylyn, Peter. *Microcosmus, or a Little Description of the Great World. A Treatise Historicall, Geographicall, Politicall, Theologicall*. Oxford, 1621.

Hobbes, Thomas. *The Art of Rhetoric, with a Discourse of the Laws of England*. 1681.

Hogarth, William. *An Analysis of Beauty*. 1753.

Home, Henry, Lord Kames. *Elements of Criticism*. 1762. In *Literary Criticism in England, 1660–1800*, ed. Gerald Wester Chapman. New York: Knopf, 1966.

Hooke, Robert. *Micrographia: Or Some Physiological Descriptions of Minute Bodies Made By Magnifying Glasses. With Observations and Inquiries thereupon*. 1665.

————. *Micrographia Restaurata: Or, The Copper-Plates of Dr. Hooke's Wonderful Discoveries by the Microscope, Reprinted and Fully Explained: Whereby the most Valuable Particulars in that Celebrated Author's Micrographia Are brought together in a narrow Compass; and Intermixed, occasionally, with many Entertaining and Instructive Discoveries and Observations in Natural History*. 1745.

Howell, James. *Londinopolis; An Historicall Discourse or Perlustration of the City of London*. 1657.

Hume, David. *An Enquiry concerning Human Understanding*. 1748. Edited by Tom L. Beauchamp. Oxford: Clarendon, 2000.

————. *The History of England, from the Invasion of Julius Caesar to the Revolution in 1688*. 1778. Edited by William B. Todd. 6 vols. Indianapolis: Liberty, 1983.

————. *The Letters of David Hume*. Edited by J. Y. T. Grieg. 2 vols. Oxford: Clarendon, 1932.

————. "Of Tragedy." In *Essays Moral, Political, and Literary*. Edited by Eugene F. Miller. 1985. Reprint, Indianapolis: Liberty Classics, 1987.

————. "Simplicity and Refinement in Writing." In *Essays Moral, Political, and Literary*. Edited by Eugene F. Miller. 1985. Reprint, Indianapolis: Liberty Classics, 1987.

Hyde, Edward, Earl of Clarendon. *The History of the Rebellions and Civil Wars in England, begun in the Year 1641*. 3 vols. Oxford, 1702.

"An Index for the Philosophical Transactions of An. 1667, beginning with Number 23, and ending with Numb. 32." In *Philosophical Transactions: Giving Some Accompt of the Present Undertakings, Studies, and Labours of the Ingenious in many Considerable Parts of the World*, vol. 2. 1667.

Ireland, John. *Hogarth Illustrated*. 1791.

Johnson, Samuel. "Preface to Shakespeare." 1765. In *Johnson on Shakespeare*, ed. Arthur Sherbo, with an introduction by Bertrand Bronson. Vol. 7 of *The Yale Edition of the Works of Samuel Johnson*, ed. H. W. Liebert and A. T. Hazen. 16 vols. New Haven, CT: Yale University Press, 1958–90.

———. *The Rambler*. 1750–52. Edited by W. J. Bate and Albrecht B. Strauss. Vols. 3–5 of *The Yale Edition of the Works of Samuel Johnson*, ed. H. W. Liebert and A. T. Hazen. 16 vols. New Haven, CT: Yale University Press, 1958–90.

———. *Rasselas*. 1759. In *Rasselas and Other Tales*, ed. Gwin J. Kolb. Vol. 16 of *The Yale Edition of the Works of Samuel Johnson*, ed. H. W. Liebert and A. T. Hazen. 16 vols. New Haven, CT: Yale University Press, 1958–90.

Jones, W. Preface to *Orbis Sensualium Pictus... Visible World, or, A Nomenclature, and Pictures of all The chiefe things that are in the World*, by Johann Amos Comenius, trans. Charles Hoole, 12th ed. 1777.

Langley, Batty. *The Builder's Chest-Book; Or A Complete Key to the Five Orders of Columns in Architecture*. 1727.

———. *The Builder's Director, or Bench-Mate*. 1751.

Langley, Batty, and Thomas Langley. *The Builder's Jewel: or the Youth's Instructor*. 1757.

Lenglet-Dufresnoy, Nicholas. *The Geography of Children: Or, a Short and Easy Method of Teaching or Learning Geography*. 1737.

———. *A New Method of Studying History, Geography, and Chronology*. Translated by Richard Rawlinson. 1730.

Lessing, Gotthold Ephraim. *Laokoön*. 1766.

Lewis, Matthew G. *The Life and Correspondence of M. G. Lewis*. 2 vols. London: Henry Colburn, 1839.

———. *The Monk*. 1796. Edited by Howard Anderson. Oxford: Oxford University Press, 1995.

———. *The Monk*. 1796. Edited by Christopher MacLachlan. London: Penguin, 1998.

Locke, John. *Two Treatises of Government*. Edited by Peter Laslett. Cambridge: Cambridge University Press, 1988.

The London Gazette.

The London Magazine. Vol. 1 (January–June 1820).

Loudon, J. C. *The Landscape Gardening and Landscape Architecture of the Late Humphry Repton, Esq.* 1840. Reprint, Farnborough: Gregg International, 1969.

Macaulay, Thomas Babington. *Critical and Historical Essays Contributed to the Edinburgh Review*. London: Longman, Brown, Green, & Longmans, 1850.

———. "HISTORY. *The Romance of History*. By Henry Neele. London, 1828." In *Reviews, Essays, and Poems*. London: Ward, Lock, & Tyler, n.d.

———. "*The Pilgrim's Progress, with a Life of John Bunyan*, by Robert Southey, Esq., LL.D., Poet-Laureate. Illustrated with Engravings. 8vo. London: 1830." *Edinburgh Review* 54 (December 1831): 450–61.

————. Review of *Letters of Horace Walpole, Earl of Oxford, to Sir Horace Mann, British Envoy at the Court of Tuscany*, ed. Lord Dover, 3 vols. (London, 1833). *Edinburgh Review* 58 (October 1833): 227–58.

Manley, Delarivière. *The New Atalantis*. 1709.

Mavor, William. *New Description of Blenheim, The Seat of His Grace the Duke of Marlborough*. 1793.

Miller, James. *Harlequin-Horace, or, The Art of Modern Poetry*. 1731.

The Monthly Magazine; or, British Register. Vol. 49 (February 1820).

The Monthly Review. Vol. 32 (January–June 1765).

Moreri, Louis. *Le grand dictionnaire historique*. Lyons, 1674. 19th ed., Paris, 1743–49.

The Morning Chronicle. June 1769.

The Morning Post. November 1772.

A New and Accurate Description of the Present Great Roads and the Principal Cross Roads of England and Wales. R. & J. Dodsley, printers, 1756.

[Newbery, John]. *The Art of Poetry on a New Plan: Illustrated with a Great Variety of Examples from the Best English Poets; and of Translation from the Ancients: Together with such Reflections and Critical Remarks as may tend to form in our Youth an elegant Taste, and render the Study of this Part of the Belles Lettres more rational and pleasing*. 2 vols. 1762.

Newton, John. *An Introduction to the Art of Rhetorick*. 1671.

Nichols, John. *Literary Anecdotes of the Eighteenth Century; comprizing Biographical Memoirs of William Bowyer, Printer, F. S. A.* 9 vols. London: Nichols, Son, & Bentley, 1812–15.

Norden, John. *An Intended Guyde for English Travailers*. 1625.

Ogilby, John. *Africa: Being an Accurate Description of the Regions of Aegypt, Barbary, Lybia, and Billedulgerid, The Land of Negroes, Guinee, Aetheopia, and the Abyssines . . . Collected and Translated from Most Authentick Authors, and Augmented with Later Observations; Illustrated with Notes, and Adorn'd with peculiar Maps, and proper Sculptures*. 1670.

————. *America: Being the Latest, and Most Accurate Description of the New World . . . Collected from most Authentick Authors, Augmented with later Observations, and Adorn'd with Maps and Sculptures*. 1671.

————. *Asia, The First Part. Being An Accurate Description of Persia . . . the Great Mogul . . . [and] India . . . Collected and translated from most Authentick Authors, and Augmented with later Observations; Illustrated with Notes, and Adorn'd with peculiar Maps and proper Sculptures*. 1673.

————. *Britannia, Volume the First: Or, An Illustration of the Kingdom of England and Dominion of Wales: By a Geographical and Historical Description of the Principal Roads Thereof*. 1675.

Peacham, Henry. *The Garden of Eloquence, Conteyning the Figures of Grammer and Rhetorick, from whence maye bee gathered all manner of Flowers, Coulors,*

Ornaments, Exornations, Formes and Fashions of speech, very profitable for all those that be studious of Eloquence, and that made most Eloquent Poets and Orators, and also helpeth much for the better understanding of the Holy Scriptures. 1577.

————. The Garden of Eloqvence, Conteining the Most Excellent Ornaments, Exornations, Lightes, flowers, and formes of speech, commonly called the figures of "Rhetorike" . . . Corrected and amended by the first Author. 1593.

Pepys, Samuel. The Diary of Samuel Pepys. Edited by Robert Latham and William Matthews. 11 vols. London: Bell & Hyman; New Haven, CT: Yale University Press, 1970–83.

————. The Illustrated Pepys. Edited by Robert Latham. 1979. Reprint, London: Penguin Books, 2000.

Plato. The Republic. In The Dialogues of Plato, trans. Benjamin Jowett, vol. 2. 3rd ed. 1892. Reprint, New York: Random House, 1937.

Pope, Alexander. The Iliad of Homer. 1715–20. Edited by Steven Shankman. Harmondsworth: Penguin, 1996.

————. The Rape of the Lock. 1714. Edited by Cynthia Wall. Boston: Bedford/St. Martin's, 1998.

————. The Works of Alexander Pope. 1727.

Potter, John. The Traveller's Pocket-Book; or, Ogilby and Morgan's Book of the Roads Improved and Amended. 20th ed. 1780.

Powys, Caroline Lybbe. Passages from the Diaries of Mrs. Philip Lybbe Powys of Hardwick House, Oxon. A.D. 1756 to 1808. Edited by Emily J. Climenson. London: Longmans, Green, 1899.

Public Advertiser.

Puttenham, George. The Art of English Poesy. Contriued into Three Bookes: The First of Poets and Poesie, the Second of Proportion, the Third of Ornament. 1589.

Radcliffe, Ann. The Mysteries of Udolpho, A Romance; Interspersed with Some Pieces of Poetry. 4 vols. 5th ed. London, 1803.

————. The Mysteries of Udolpho. 1794. Edited by Bonamy Dobrée. With an introduction by Terry Castle. 1966. Reprint, Oxford: Oxford University Press, 1970.

Rainolde, Richard. A Booke Called the Foundacion of Rhetorike, because all other partes of Rhetorike are grounded thereupon, euery parte sette forthe in an Oracion vpon questions, verie profitable to bee knowen and redde. Cambridge, 1563.

Ralph, James. The Touch-Stone: Or, Historical, Critical, Political, Philosophical and Theological Essays on the reigning Diversions of the Town. Design'd for the Improvement of all Authors, Spectators, and Actors of Operas, Plays, and Masquerades. In which every thing antique, or modern, relating to Musick, Poetry, Dancing, Pantomimes, Choruses, Cat-Calls, Audiences, Judges, Criticks, Balls, Ridottos, Assemblies, New Oratory, Circus, Bear-Garden,

Gladiators, Prize-Fighters, Italian Strollers, Mountebank Stages, Cock-pits, Puppet-Shews, Fairs, and Publick Auctions, is occasionally handled. By a Person of Taste and some Quality. 1728.

Rapin, René. Instructions for History: with a Character of the most Considerable Historians, Antient and Modern. Out of the French, by J. Davies of Kidwelly. 1680. A translation of Instructions pour l'histoire (1677).

[_____]. The Modest Critick; or, Remarks Upon the Most Eminent Historians, Antient and Modern. 1689.

Reeve, Clara. The Old English Baron. 1778. Edited by James Trainer. 1967. Reprint, Oxford: Oxford University Press, 1977.

_____. The Old English Baron. 1778. Edited by James Trainer. With an introduction by James Watt. Oxford: Oxford University Press, 2003.

Reminiscences of an Old Draper. London, 1876.

Repton, Humphry. Fragments on the Theory of Landscape Gardening. London, 1816.

_____. Humphry Repton: The Red Books for Brandsbury and Glemham Hall. With an introduction by Stephen Daniels. Washington, DC: Dumbarton Oaks, 1994.

_____. Observations on the Theory and Practice of Landscape Gardening. Including Some Remarks on Grecian and Gothic Architecture, collected from various manuscripts, in the possession of the different noblemen and gentlemen, for whose use they were originally written; the whole tending to establish fixed principles in the Respective arts. London, 1803.

Review of The Poetical Works of Anne [sic] Radcliffe. St Alban's Abbey; a metrical Romance. With other Poems, 2 vols. (London, 1834), Edinburgh Review 59 (July 1834): 327–41.

Reynolds, Sir Joshua. The Works of Sir Joshua Reynolds, Knt. Edited by Edmond Malone. 2 vols. 1797.

Rhetoric; or, the Principles of Oratory Delineated. 1736.

Richardson, Samuel. Clarissa. Or, The History of a Young Lady: Comprehending the Most Important Concerns of Private Life. Edited by William Warburton. 7 vols. 1747–48.

_____. Clarissa. 1747–48. Edited by Angus Ross. Harmondsworth: Penguin, 1985.

_____. Pamela: Or, Virtue Rewarded. In a Series of Familiar Letters from a Beautiful Young Damsel, To her Parents. 2 vols. 1740.

_____. Pamela; or, Virtue Rewarded. Edited by Thomas Keymer and Alice Wakeley. Oxford: Oxford University Press, 2001.

_____. Prefaces, Hints of Prefaces and Postscripts. With an introduction by R. S. Brissenden. Augustan Reprint Society, no. 103. Los Angeles: William Andrews Clark Memorial Library, University of California, Los Angeles, 1964.

_____. The Richardson-Stinstra Correspondence and Stinstra's Prefaces to Clarissa. Edited by William C. Slattery. Carbondale: Southern Illinois University Press, 1969.

_____. Sir Charles Grandison. 1753–54. Edited by Jocelyn Harris. Oxford: Oxford University Press, 1972.

Roche, Sophie von la. *Sophie in London, 1786: Being the Diary of Sophie von la Roche.* Translated and edited by Clare Williams. London: J. Cape, 1933.

Rymer, Thomas. *Monsieur Rapin's Reflections on Aristotle's Treatise of Poesie. Containing the Necessary Rational and Universal Rules for Epick, Dramatick, and the other sorts of Poetry ... Made English by Mr. Rymer; by whom is added some Reflections on English Poets.* 1694.

———. *A Short View of Tragedy.* 1693.

Scott, Sir Walter. Introduction to *The Castle of Otranto, A Gothic Story*, by Horace Walpole. London: John Ballantyne; Edinburgh: Longman, 1811.

———. *Ivanhoe; A Romance.* 1819. In *Historical Romances of the Author of Waverly.* Edinburgh: Archibald Constable; London: Hurst Robinson, 1822.

———. *Ivanhoe.* 1819. With an introduction by Sir H. J. C. Grierson. London: Collins, 1952.

———. *Ivanhoe.* 1819. Edited by Ian Duncan. Oxford: Oxford University Press, 1996.

———. *Ivanhoe.* 1819. Edited by Graham Tulloch. London: Penguin, 1998.

———. *Miscellaneous Prose Works of Sir Walter Scott, Bart.* Edinburgh, n.d.

———, ed. *The Novelist's Library.* Vol. 5, *The Novels of Sterne, Goldsmith, Dr Johnson, Mackenzie, Horace Walpole, and Clara Reeve.* London: Hurst, Robinson; Edinburgh: Border, 1823.

———. *Rob Roy.* 1817. Edited by Ian Duncan. Oxford: Oxford University Press, 1998.

Sebillet, Thomas. *Art poêtique françoys.* 1556. Edited by F. Gaiffe. Paris, 1932.

Serle, John. *A Plan of Mr. Pope's Garden, As it was left at his Death: With a Plan and Perspective View of the Grotto.* 1745.

Sheridan, Richard Brinsley. *The School for Scandal.* 1777. Edited by C. J. L. Price. Oxford: Oxford University Press, 1971.

[Sherman, Thomas.] *The Second Part of the Pilgrims Progress, From This present World of Wickeness* [sic] *and Misery, to An Eternity of Holiness and Felicity; Exactly Described under the Similitude of a Dream, Relation the Manner and Occasion of his setting out from, and difficult and dangerous Journey through the World; and safe Arrival at last to Eternal Happiness.* 1682.

[———]. *The Pilgrim's Progress, From This Present World of Wickedness and Misery, to an Eternity of Holiness and Felicity. The Second Part.* Glasgow, 1736.

Sherry, Richard. *A Treatise of Schemes & Tropes very profytable for the better vnderstanding of good authors, gethered out of the best Grammarians & Oratours by Rychard Sherry Londoner. Whervnto is added a declamacion, That chyldren even strapt frō their infancie should be well and greatly broughte vp in learning. Written first in Latin by the most excellent and famous Clearke, Erasmus of Rotero.* 1550.

Sidney, Sir Philip. *The Defence of Poesie.* 1595.

———. *The Defense of Poesy.* 1595. Glasgow, 1752.

———. *An Apology for Poetry.* 1595. Edited by Geoffrey Shepherd. Revised by R. W. Maslen. 3rd ed. 1973. Reprint, Manchester: Manchester University Press, 2002.

Simmons, Matthew. *A Direction for the English Traviller.* 1635.

Smith, Adam. *Lectures on Rhetoric and Belles Lettres. Delivered in the University of Glasgow by Adam Smith, Reported by a Student in 1762–63*. Edited by John M. Lothean. Carbondale: Southern Illinois University Press, 1971.

———. *The Theory of Moral Sentiments.* 1759. Edited by Knud Haakonssen. Cambridge: Cambridge University Press, 2002.

Smith, Charlotte. *The Old Manor House. A Novel.* 2nd ed. 4 vols. 1793.

———. *The Old Manor House.* 1793. Edited by Anne Henry Ehrenpreis. With an introduction by Judith Phillips Stanton. Oxford: Oxford University Press, 1989.

———. *The Old Manor House.* 1793. Edited by Jacqueline M. Labbe. Peterborough, Ont.: Broadview, 2002.

Smith, John. *The Mysterie of Rhetorique Unvail'd, Wherein above 130 of The Tropes and Figures are severally derived from the Greek into English, together with lively Definitions and Variety of Latin/English/Scriptural Examples, Pertinent to each of them apart.* 1657.

Spence, Joseph. *Anecdotes, Observations and Characters of Books and Men.* Edited by Bonamy Dobrée. Carbondale: Southern Illinois University Press, 1964.

Spencer, Thomas. *The Art of Logick, Delivered in the Precepts of Aristotle and Ramus.* 1628.

Stirling, John. *A System of Rhetorick.* 1788.

Stow, John. *A Svrvay of London. Contayning the Originall, Antiquity, Increase, Modern estate, and description of that Citie, written in the yeare 1598, by Iohn Stow Citizen of London.* 1598.

———. *A Survay of London. Contayning the Originall, Antiquity, Increase, Modern estate, and description of that Citie, written in the yeare 1598, by Iohn Stow Citizen of London. Since by the same Author increased, with diuers rare notes of Antiquity, and published in the yeare, 1603.* 1603.

———. *A Survey of London... Afterwards inlarged by... A. M. [Anthony Munday] in the yeere 1618. And now completely finished by A. M. [Anthony Munday] H. D. [Humphrey Dyson] and others, this present yeere 1633.* 1633.

———. *A Survey of London by John Stow.* Edited by Charles Lethbridge Kingsford. 2 vols. 1908. Reprint, Oxford: Clarendon, 1971.

———. *The Survey of London.* Edited by H. B. Wheatley. With an introduction by Valerie Pearl. London: Dent, 1987.

———. *A Survey of London, Written in the Year 1598.* Edited by Henry Morley. With an introduction by Antonia Fraser. Stroud: Alan Sutton, 1994.

Strange, Sir Robert. *An Inquiry into the Rise and Establishment of the Royal Academy of Arts.* 1773.

Strype, John. *A Survey of the Cities of London and Westminster... Now Lastly, Corrected, Improved, and very much Enlarged: And the Survey and History brought down from the Year 1633, (being near Fourscore Years since it was last printed) to the present Time.* 2 vols. 1720.

Swift, Jonathan. *Gulliver's Travels.* 1726. Edited by Paul Turner. 1986. Reprint, Oxford: Oxford University Press, 1998.

————. *The Writings of Jonathan Swift*. Edited by Robert A. Greenberg and William
    Bowman Piper. New York: Norton, 1973.

Tacitus, Cornelius. *The Works of Tacitus*. Translated by T. Gordon. 2 vols.
    1723.

————. *The Works of Cornelius Tacitus: by Arthur Murphy, Esq.* 4 vols. 1793.

Taylor, John. *Records of My Life*. 2 vols. London, 1832.

Tradescant, John. *Musaeum Tradescantianum: Or, A Collection of Rarities.
    Preserved at South-Lambeth neer London*. 1656.

Tradesman. July 1809.

Turner, Thomas. *The Diary of a Georgian Shopkeeper*. Edited by G. H. Jennings.
    Oxford: Oxford University Press, 1979.

Voltaire [François Marie Arouet]. *Essai sur les moeurs*. Paris, 1756.

————. *Siècle de Louis XIV*. Paris, 1751.

Walker, Obadiah. *Some Instructions Concerning the Art of Oratory*. 1659.

Walpole, Horace. *The Castle of Otranto*. 1764. Edited by Sir Walter Scott. London:
    John Ballantyne; Edinburgh: Longman, 1811.

————. *The Castle of Otranto*. 1764. Edited by W. S. Lewis. 1964. Reprint, Oxford:
    Oxford University Press, 1982.

————. *The Castle of Otranto*. 1764. Edited by W. S. Lewis. With a new introduction
    and notes by E. J. Clery. Oxford: Oxford University Press, 1996.

————. *The Correspondence of Horace Walpole*. Edited by W. S. Lewis et al. 48 vols.
    Oxford: Oxford University Press; New Haven, CT: Yale University Press,
    1937–83.

————. *Memoirs of King George II*. Edited by John Brooke. 3 vols. New Haven, CT:
    Yale University Press, 1985.

Wedgwood, Josiah. *Letters of Josiah Wedgwood*. 2 vols. London, 1903.

[Whalley, Peter]. *An Essay on the Manner of Writing History*. 1746.

Wilkins, John. *An Essay Towards a Real Character, and a Philosophical Language*.
    1668.

Woodfin, Mrs. A. *The Auction: A Modern Novel. In Two Volumes*. 1770.

SECONDARY SOURCES

Alexander, David. *Retailing in England during the Industrial Revolution*. London:
    Athlone, 1970.

Alpaugh, David J. "Emblem and Interpretation in *The Pilgrim's Progress*." *ELH* 33,
    no. 3 (1966): 299–314.

Alpers, Svetlana. *The Art of Describing: Dutch Art in the Seventeenth Century*.
    London: John Murray, 1983.

Anderson, James. *Sir Walter Scott and History*. Edinburgh: Edina, 1981.

Archer, Ian W. "The Nostalgia of John Stow." In *The Theatrical City: Culture,
    Theatre, and Politics in London, 1576–1649*, ed. D. L. Smith, R. Strier, and
    D. Bevington. Cambridge: Cambridge University Press, 1995.

———. *The Pursuit of Stability: Social Relations in Elizabethan England.*
Cambridge: Cambridge University Press, 1991.

Ariés, Philippe, and Roger Chartier, eds. *A History of Private Life.* Vol. 3.
Cambridge, MA: Belknap/Harvard University Press, 1989.

Arthos, John. *The Language of Natural Description in Eighteenth-Century Poetry.*
Ann Arbor: University of Michigan Press, 1949.

Ayres, James. *Domestic Interiors: The British Tradition, 1500–1850.* New Haven,
CT: Yale University Press, 2003.

Bachelard, Gaston. *The Poetics of Space.* 1958. Translated by Maria Jolas. Boston:
Beacon, 1969.

Bal, Mieke. *Narratology: Introduction to the Theory of Narrative.* 1978. 2nd ed.
Toronto: University of Toronto Press, 1997.

Ballaster, Rosalind. *Seductive Forms: Women's Amatory Fiction from 1684 to 1740.*
Oxford: Clarendon, 1992.

Barchas, Janine. "Sarah Fielding's Dashing Style and Eighteenth-Century Print
Culture." *ELH* 64 (1996): 633–56.

Barthes, Roland. "Le monde-objet." In *Essais critiques,* 19–28. Paris: du Seuil, 1964.

Bartsch, Shadi. *Decoding the Ancient Novel: The Reader and the Role of
Description in Heliodorus and Achilles Tatius.* Princeton, NJ: Princeton
University Press, 1989.

Baudrillard, Jean. *The System of Objects.* Translated by James Benedict. London:
Verso, 1996.

Beaujour, Michel. "Some Paradoxes of Description." *Yale French Studies* 61 (1981):
25–59.

Bédoyère, Guy de la. *Particular Friends: The Correspondence of Samuel Pepys and
John Evelyn.* Woodbridge: Boydell, 1997.

———. "Text Note." In *The Diary of John Evelyn,* ed. Guy de la Bédoyère. Bangor:
Headstart History, 1994.

Beer, Barrett L. *Tudor England Observed: The World of John Stow.* Stroud: Alan
Sutton, 1998.

Bender, John B. *Spenser and Literary Pictorialism.* Princeton, NJ: Princeton
University Press, 1972.

Bender, John, and Michael Marrinan, eds. *Regimes of Description: In the Archive of
the Eighteenth Century.* Stanford, CA: Stanford University Press, 2005.

Benedict, Barbara M. *Curiosity: A Cultural History of Early Modern Inquiry.*
Chicago: University of Chicago Press, 2001.

Benjamin, Walter. *Walter Benjamin: Selected Writings.* Translated by Edmund
Jephcott, Howard Eiland, et al. Edited by Howard Eiland and Michael W.
Jennings. Cambridge, MA: Harvard University Press, 2002.

———. "The Work of Art in the Age of Mechanical Reproduction." In
Illuminations: Essays and Reflections (1955), trans. Harry Zohn, ed. Hannah
Arendt. New York: Schocken, 1969.

Bennett, J. A. W. *Essays on Gibbon.* Cambridge: privately printed, 1980.

Bennett, Tony. *The Birth of the Museum: History, Theory, Politics.* New York: Routledge, 1995.

Beresiner, Yasha. "John Ogilby." In *British County Maps: Reference and Price Guide.* N.p.: Antique Collectors' Club, n.d.

Bermingham, Ann. "The Aesthetics of Ignorance: The Accomplished Woman in the Culture of Connoisseurship." *Oxford Art Journal* 16, no. 2 (1993): 3–20.

Black, J. B. *The Art of History: A Study of Four Great Historians of the Eighteenth Century.* 1926. Reprint, New York: Russell & Russell, 1965.

Black, Jeremy. *Maps and History: Constructing Images of the Past.* New Haven, CT: Yale University Press, 1997.

Bland, D. S. "Endangering the Reader's Neck: Background Description in the Novel." In *The Theory of the Novel*, ed. Philip Stevick, 313–31. New York: Free Press, 1947.

Blunden, Edmund. "Edward Gibbon and His Age." Arthur Skemp Memorial Lecture. Bristol: University of Bristol, 1935.

Bond, Harold L. *The Literary Art of Edward Gibbon.* Oxford: Clarendon, 1960.

Bowers, Toni. "Sex, Lies, and Invisibility: Amatory Fiction from the Restoration to Mid-Century." In *The Columbia History of the Novel*, ed. John Richetti, John Bender, Deirdre David, and Michael Seidel, 50–72. New York: Columbia University Press, 1994.

Bowersock, G. W. "Gibbon's Historical Imagination." Stanford, CA: Stanford Humanities Center, 1988. A reprint, with the text slightly augmented, of "Gibbon's Historical Imagination," *American Scholar* 57 (winter 1988): 33–47.

Bowle, John. *John Evelyn and His World.* London: Routledge & Kegan Paul, 1981.

Braden, Gordon. "Riverrun: An Epic Catalogue in *The Faerie Queene.*" *English Literary Renaissance* 5, no. 1 (winter 1975): 25–48.

Braudy, Leo. *Narrative Form in History and Fiction.* Princeton, NJ: Princeton University Press, 1970.

———. "Penetration and Impenetrability in *Clarissa.*" In *Modern Essays on Eighteenth-Century Literature*, ed. Leopold Damrosch Jr., 261–81. Oxford: Oxford University Press, 1988.

Breen, T. H. "The Meanings of Things: Interpreting the Consumer Economy in the Eighteenth Century." In *Consumption and the World of Goods*, ed. John Brewer and Roy Porter, 249–60. London: Routledge, 1993.

Brewer, John. *The Pleasures of the Imagination: English Culture in the Eighteenth Century.* New York: Farrar Straus Giroux, 1997.

Brewer, John, and Roy Porter, eds. *Consumption and the World of Goods.* London: Routledge, 1993.

Brewer, John, and Susan Staves, eds. *Early Modern Conceptions of Property.* London: Routledge, 1996.

Briggs, Peter. "'News from the Little World': A Critical Glance at Eighteenth-Century British Advertising." *Studies in Eighteenth-Century Culture* 23 (1993): 29–45.

Brown, Bill. "Thing Theory." *Critical Inquiry* 28, no. 1 (autumn 2001): 1–22.

Brown, David. *Walter Scott and the Historical Imagination.* London: Routledge & Kegan Paul, 1979.

Brown, John. *Bunyan's Home.* London: Ernest Nister; New York: E. P. Dutton, n.d.

———. *John Bunyan (1628–1688), His Life, Times, and Work.* 1885. Edited by Frank Mott Harrison. London: Hulbert, 1928.

Brown, Laura. *Alexander Pope.* Oxford: Blackwell, 1985.

———. *The Ends of Empire: Women and Ideology in Early Eighteenth-Century English Literature.* Ithaca, NY: Cornell University Press, 1993.

Bryant, Frank Egbert. *On the Limits of Descriptive Writing Apropos of Lessing's Laocoön.* Ann Arbor, MI: Ann Arbor, 1906.

Bullen, John Samuel. *Time and Space in the Novels of Samuel Richardson.* Monograph Series, vol. 12, no. 2. Logan: Utah State University Press, July 1965.

Bunn, James H. "The Aesthetics of British Mercantilism." *New Literary History* 11 (1980): 303–21.

Burton, Elizabeth. *The Georgians at Home.* 1967. Reprint, London: Arrow, 1973.

Butor, Michel. *Inventory.* Translated by Richard Howard. New York: Simon & Schuster, 1961.

Byrd, Max. *London Transform'd: Images of the City in the Eighteenth Century.* New Haven, CT: Yale University Press, 1978.

Campbell, Colin. *The Romantic Ethic and the Spirit of Modern Consumerism.* Oxford: Blackwell, 1987.

Carruthers, Mary J. *The Book of Memory: A Study of Memory in Medieval Culture.* Cambridge: Cambridge University Press, 1990.

Carruthers, Mary J., and Jan M. Ziolkowski, eds. *The Medieval Craft of Memory: An Anthology of Texts and Pictures.* Philadelphia: University of Pennsylvania Press, 2002.

Carter, George, Patrick Goode, and Kedrun Laurie. *Humphry Repton, Landscape Gardener, 1752–1818.* Norwich: Sainsbury Centre for the Visual Arts, 1982.

Casey, Edward S. "Literary Description and Phenomenological Method." *Yale French Studies* 61 (1981): 176–201.

Cassady, Ralph, Jr. *Auctions and Auctioneers.* Berkeley: University of California Press, 1967.

Castle, Terry. "The Spectralization of the Other in *The Mysteries of Udolpho.*" In *The New Eighteenth Century: Theory, Politics, English Literature,* ed. Felicity Nussbaum and Laura Brown. New York: Methuen, 1987.

Castronovo, David. *The English Gentleman: Images and Ideals in Literature and Society.* New York: Ungar, 1987.

Chapman, Gerald Wester, ed. *Literary Criticism in England, 1660–1800.* New York: Knopf, 1966.

Chatman, Seymour. *Coming to Terms: The Rhetoric of Narrative in Fiction and Film.* Ithaca, NY: Cornell University Press, 1990.

Christ, Carol T. *The Finer Optic: The Aesthetic of Particularity in Victorian Poetry*. New Haven, CT: Yale University Press, 1975.

Christ, Carol T., and John O. Jordan, eds. *Victorian Literature and the Victorian Visual Imagination*. Berkeley and Los Angeles: University of California Press, 1995.

Clarke, George B. Introduction to *The Beauties of Stow* (1750), by George Bickham. William Andrews Clark Memorial Library Publication, nos. 185–86. Los Angeles: University of California Press, 1977.

Clery, E. J. Introduction to *The Castle of Otranto* (1764), by Horace Walpole, ed. W. S. Lewis. Oxford: Oxford University Press, 1996.

———. *The Rise of Supernatural Fiction, 1762–1800*. Cambridge: Cambridge University Press, 1995.

Clifford, James. *The Predicament of Culture: Twentieth-Century Ethnography, Literature, and Art*. Cambridge, MA: Harvard University Press, 1988.

Clutton-Brock, Arthur. "Description in Poetry." In *Essays and Studies by Members of the English Association*, ed. H. C. Beeching, 2:91–103. Oxford: Clarendon, 1911.

Cohen, Ralph. *The Art of Discrimination: Thomson's "The Seasons" and the Language of Criticism*. London: Routledge & Kegan Paul, 1964.

Collinson, Patrick. "John Stow and Nostalgic Antiquarianism." In *Imagining Early Modern London: Perceptions and Portrayals of the City from Stow to Strype, 1598–1720*, ed. J. F. Merritt. Cambridge: Cambridge University Press, 2001.

Colson, Percy. *A Story of Christie's*. London: Sampson Low, 1950.

Colvin, H. M. "Aubrey's *Chronologia Architectonica*." In *Concerning Architecture: Essays on Architectural Writers and Writing Presented to Nikolaus Pevsner*, ed. John Summerson. Baltimore: Penguin, 1968.

Cottom, Daniel. *The Civilized Imagination: A Study of Ann Radcliffe, Jane Austen, and Sir Walter Scott*. Cambridge: Cambridge University Press, 1985.

Crane, William G. Introduction to *The Garden of Eloquence* (1593), by Henry Peacham, 5–23. Gainesville, FL: Scholars' Facsimiles and Reprints, 1954.

Crowley, J. Donald. Introduction to *The Life and Strange Surprizing Adventures of Robinson Crusoe*, by Daniel Defoe, ed. J. Donald Crowley. Oxford: Oxford University Press, 1972.

Crowley, John E. *The Invention of Comfort: Sensibilities and Design in Early Modern Britain and Early America*. Baltimore: Johns Hopkins University Press, 2001.

Damon, Phillip. "History and Idea in Renaissance Criticism." In *Literary Criticism and Historical Understanding*, ed. Phillip Damon. New York: Columbia University Press, 1967.

Damrosch, Leo. *Fictions of Reality in the Age of Hume and Johnson*. Madison: University of Wisconsin Press, 1989.

Daniels, Stephen. "Goodly Prospects: English Estate Portraiture, 1670–1730." In *Mapping the Landscape: Essays on Art and Cartography*, ed. Nicholas Alfrey and Stephen Daniels. Nottingham: University Art Gallery, Castle Museum, 1990.

———. *Humphry Repton: Landscape Gardening and the Geography of Georgian England*. New Haven, CT: Yale University Press, 1999.

———. Introduction to *Humphry Repton: The Red Books for Brandsbury and Glemham Hall*. Washington, DC: Dumbarton Oaks, 1994.

Daston, Lorraine. "Description by Omission: Nature Enlightened and Obscured." In *Regimes of Description: In the Archive of the Eighteenth Century*, ed. John Bender and Michael Marrinan. Stanford, CA: Stanford University Press, 2005.

Davis, B. E. C. *Edmund Spenser*. Cambridge: Cambridge University Press, 1933.

Davis, Dorothy. *A History of London Shopping*. London: Routledge & Kegan Paul, 1966.

Day, Robert A. Introduction to *Familiar Letters Betwixt a Gentleman and a Lady (1725)*, by Mary Davys. Augustan Reprint Society, no. 54. Los Angeles: William Andrews Clark Memorial Library, University of California, 1955.

De Beer, E. S. Introduction to *The Diary of John Evelyn*, ed. E. S. De Beer, vol. 1. Oxford: Clarendon, 1955.

Debray-Genette, Raymonde. "Traversées de l'espace descriptif." *Poétique* 51 (1982): 329–44.

Delassaux, Victor, and John Elliott. *Street Architecture: A Series of Shop Fronts and Façades, Characteristic of and Adapted to Different Branches of Commerce*. London: John Weale, Holborn, 1855.

Derrida, Jacques. *The Truth in Painting*. Translated by Geoff Bennington and Ian McLeod. Chicago: University of Chicago Press, 1987.

Dictionary of Philosophy. Edited by Dagobert D. Runes. Totowa, NJ: Littlefield, Adams, 1962.

Donker, Marjorie, and George M. Muldrow. *Dictionary of Literary-Rhetorical Conventions in the English Renaissance*. Westport, CT: Greenwood, 1982.

Downes, Kerry. "John Evelyn and Architecture: A First Inquiry." In *Concerning Architecture: Essays on Architectural Writers and Writing Presented to Nikolaus Pevsner*, ed. John Summerson. Baltimore: Penguin, 1968.

Downie, J. A. "Public and Private: The Myth of the Bourgeois Public Sphere." In *A Concise Companion to the Restoration and Eighteenth Century*, ed. Cynthia Wall, 58–79. Oxford: Blackwell, 2004.

duBois, Page. *History, Rhetorical Description, and the Epic from Homer to Spenser*. Cambridge: D. S. Brewer, 1982.

Duckworth, Alistair M. *The Improvement of the Estate: A Study of Jane Austen's Novels*. Baltimore: Johns Hopkins University Press, 1971.

Duncan, Ian. Introduction to *Ivanhoe*, by Sir Walter Scott, ed. Ian Duncan. Oxford: Oxford University Press, 1996.

————. Introduction to *Rob Roy*, by Sir Walter Scott, ed. Ian Duncan. Oxford: Oxford University Press, 1998.

Eaves, T. C. Duncan, and Ben D. Kimpel. *Samuel Richardson: A Biography*. Oxford: Clarendon, 1971.

Edwards, A. Trystan. *The Architecture of Shops*. London: Chapman & Hall, 1933.

Edwards, Philip. "The Journey in *The Pilgrim's Progress*." In *The Pilgrim's Progress: Critical and Historical Views*, ed. Vincent Newey, 111–17. Liverpool: Liverpool University Press, 1980.

Ehrenpreis, Irvin. *Literary Meaning and Augustan Values*. Charlottesville: University Press of Virginia, 1974.

Elledge, Scott. "The Background and Development in English Criticism of the Theories of Generality and Particularity." *PMLA* 62 (1947): 147–82.

Elsner, John, and Roger Cardinal, eds. *The Cultures of Collection*. Cambridge, MA: Harvard University Press, 1994.

Epstein, Julia. *The Iron Pen: Frances Burney and the Politics of Women's Writing*. Madison: University of Wisconsin Press, 1989.

Evans, Bill, and Andrew Lawson. *A Nation of Shopkeepers*. London: Plexus, 1981.

Fabricant, Carole. "The Literature of Domestic Tourism and the Public Consumption of Private Property." In *The New Eighteenth Century*, ed. Felicity Nussbaum and Laura Brown. New York: Methuen, 1987.

Ferdinand, C. Y. "Selling It to the Provinces: News and Commerce round Eighteenth-Century Salisbury." In *Consumption and the World of Goods*, ed. John Brewer and Roy Porter, 393–411. London: Routledge, 1993.

Firth, Sir Charles. [s.t.]. 1898. In *Bunyan: "The Pilgrim's Progress," a Casebook*, ed. Roger Sharrock, 81–103. London: Macmillan, 1976. The essay originally formed the introduction to *Pilgrim's Progress* (London: Methuen, 1898); it was published separately as *John Bunyan*, English Association Pamphlet no. 19 (London, 1911), and reprinted in *Authors and Poets: Bibliographies, Criticism and Comment: The English Association Pamphlets and a Presidential Address* (London, 1968), 39–64.

Fish, Stanley. "Progress in *The Pilgrim's Progress*." In *Self-Consuming Artifacts: The Experience of Seventeenth-Century Literature*, 224–64. Berkeley: University of California Press, 1972.

Fiske, John. "Cultural Studies and the Culture of Everyday Life." In *Cultural Studies*, ed. Lawrence Grossberg, Cory Nelson, and Paula Treichler. London: Routledge, 1992.

Flaxman, Rhoda L. *Victorian Word-Painting and Narrative: Toward the Blending of Genres*. Ann Arbor: UMI Research, 1987.

Flint, Christopher. "Speaking Objects: The Circulation of Stories in Eighteenth-Century Prose Fiction." *PMLA* 113 (1998): 212–26.

Fordham, Sir Herbert George. *Customary Acres and Their Historical Importance*. London, 1914.

———. *John Ogilby (1600–1676) His Britannia, and the British Itineraries of the Eighteenth Century*. London: Oxford University Press, 1925. Reprinted from the *Transactions of the Bibliographical Society*.

———. *Notes on British and Irish Itineraries and Road Books*. Hertford: Stephen Austin, 1912.

Fournier, M. *The Fabric of Life: Microscopy and the Seventeenth Century*. Baltimore: Johns Hopkins University Press, 1996.

Fowler, Alastair. *The Country House Poem: A Cabinet of Seventeenth-Century Estate Poems and Related Items*. Edinburgh: Edinburgh University Press, 1994.

Fowler, Elizabeth. *Literary Character: The Human Figure in Early English Writing*. Ithaca, NY: Cornell University Press, 2003.

Fraiman, Susan. "From *Crusoe* to *Queer Eye*: Towards a Feminist Poetics of Interior Design." Carolyn G. Heilbrun Memorial Lecture, City University of New York, 5 March 2004.

Frank, Joseph. "Spatial Form in Modern Literature." *Sewanee Review* 53 (1945): 221–46, 433–56.

Freud, Sigmund. "Das Unheimliche." In *Gesammelte Werke*, ed. Anna Freud et al. London: Imago, 1947.

Friedman, Norman. "Imagery." In *The New Princeton Encyclopedia of Poetry and Poetics*, ed. Alex Preminger and T. V. F. Brogan. Princeton, NJ: Princeton University Press, 1993.

Galperin, William. *The Return of the Visible in British Romanticism*. Baltimore: Johns Hopkins University Press, 1993.

Gamer, Michael. *Romanticism and the Gothic: Genre, Reception, and Canon Formation*. Cambridge: Cambridge University Press, 2000.

Gamwell, Lynn, and Richard Wells, eds. *Sigmund Freud and Art*. New York: Harry N. Abrams, 1989.

Gay, Peter. *Style in History*. New York: Basic, 1974.

Gelley, Alexander. "The Represented World: Toward a Phenomenological Theory of Description in the Novel." *Journal for Aesthetic and Art Criticism* 37, no. 4 (1979): 415–22.

Genette, Gérard. *Figures of Literary Discourse*. Translated by Alan Sheridan. New York: Columbia University Press, 1982.

Gilmour, Robin. *The Idea of the Gentleman in the Victorian Novel*. London: Allen & Unwin, 1981.

Girouard, Mark. *Life in the English Country House*. New Haven, CT: Yale University Press, 1978.

Graham, John. "Character and Description in the Romantic Novel." *Studies in Romanticism* 5 (1966): 208–18.

Grant, Aline. *Ann Radcliffe: A Biography*. Denver: Alan Swallow, 1951.

Grierson, Sir H. J. C. Introduction to *Ivanhoe*, by Sir Walter Scott. London: Collins, 1952.

Habermas, Jürgen. *The Structural Transformation of the Public Sphere.* 1962.
    Translated by Thomas Burger. Cambridge, MA: MIT Press, 1989.
Hacking, Ian. *The Emergence of Probability: A Philosophical Study of Early Ideas
    about Probability, Induction, and Statistical Inference.* 1975. Reprint,
    Cambridge: Cambridge University Press, 1984.
Hagstrum, Jean. "Pictures to the Heart: The Psychological Picturesque in Ann
    Radcliffe's *The Mysteries of Udolpho.*" In *Greene Centennial Studies,* ed. Paul J.
    Korshin and Robert R. Allen. Charlottesville: University Press of Virginia, 1984.
Hamon, Philippe. "Rhetorical Status of the Descriptive." Translated by Patricia
    Baudoin. *Yale French Studies* 61 (1981): 1–26.
Harding, Vanessa. "City, Capital, and Metropolis: The Changing Shape of
    Seventeenth-Century London." In *Imagining Early Modern London: Perceptions
    and Portrayals of the City from Stow to Strype, 1598–1720,* ed. J. F. Merritt.
    Cambridge: Cambridge University Press, 2001.
Hardy, Barbara. "The Objects in *Mansfield Park.*" In *Jane Austen: Bicentenary
    Essays,* ed. John Halperin, 180–96. Cambridge: Cambridge University Press,
    1975.
——. "Objects in Novels." In *Forms of Prose Fiction,* ed. J. Paul Hunter. Special
    issue, *Genre* 10 (winter 1977): 485–500.
Harley, J. B. "Deconstructing the Map." In *The New Nature of Maps: Essays in the
    History of Cartography,* ed. Paul Laxton. Baltimore: Johns Hopkins University
    Press, 2001.
——. "*Imago Mundi*: The First Fifty Years and the Next Ten." *Cartographica* 23,
    no. 3 (1986): 1–15.
——. "Silences and Secrecy: The Hidden Agenda of Cartography in Early Modern
    Europe." In *The New Nature of Maps: Essays in the History of Cartography,* ed.
    Paul Laxton. Baltimore: Johns Hopkins University Press, 2001.
Harper, Charles G. *The Bunyan Country—Landmarks of "The Pilgrim's Progress."*
    London: C. Palmer, 1928.
Harris, John. *The Artist and the Country House: A History of County House and
    Garden View Painting in Britain, 1540–1870.* London: Sotheby Parke Bernet,
    1979.
——. "English Country House Guides, 1740–1840." In *Concerning Architecture:
    Essays on Architectural Writers and Writing Presented to Nikolaus Pevsner,* ed.
    John Summerson. Baltimore: Penguin, 1968.
Heidegger, Martin. "Building Dwelling Thinking." 1951. In *Basic Writings,* ed.
    David Farrell Krell. New York: Harper & Row, 1977.
Helgerson, Richard. *Forms of Nationhood: The Elizabethan Writing of England.*
    Chicago: University of Chicago Press, 1992.
Herbert, John. *Inside Christie's.* New York: St. Martin's, 1990.
Hermann, Frank. "The Emergence of the Book Auctioneer as a Professional." In
    Property of a Gentleman, ed. Robin Myers and Michael Harris. Winchester:
    St. Paul's Bibliographies, 1991.

Hicks, Phillip. *Neoclassical History and English Culture from Clarendon to Hume.*
    London: Macmillan, 1996.
Howell, Robert. "Fictional Objects: How They Are and How They Aren't." *Poetics* 8
    (1979): 129–77.
Hunter, J. Paul. *Before Novels: The Cultural Contexts of Eighteenth-Century
    English Fiction.* New York: Norton, 1990.
———. "Form as Meaning: Pope and the Ideology of the Couplet." *The Eighteenth
    Century: Theory and Interpretation* 37, no. 3 (1996): 257–70. Reprinted in
    Ideology and Form, ed. David Richter (Lubbock: Texas Tech Press, 1999).
———. *Occasional Form: Henry Fielding and the Chains of Circumstance.*
    Baltimore: Johns Hopkins University Press, 1975.
———. *The Reluctant Pilgrim: Defoe's Emblematic Method and Quest for Form in
    "Robinson Crusoe."* Baltimore: Johns Hopkins University Press, 1966.
Impey, Oliver, and Arthur McGregor, eds. *The Origins of Museums.* 1985. Reprint,
    Poughkeepsie, NY: House of Stratus, 2001.
Ingrassia, Catherine. *Authorship, Commerce, and Gender in Early
    Eighteenth-Century England: A Culture of Paper Credit.* Cambridge: Cambridge
    University Press, 1998.
Irwin, Michael. *Picturing: Description and Illusion in the Nineteenth-Century
    Novel.* London: George Allen & Unwin, 1979.
James, Henry. "The Art of Fiction." 1884. In *Narrative/Theory*, ed. David H.
    Richter, 42–56. New York: Longman, 1996.
Jardine, Lisa. *Ingenious Pursuits: Building the Scientific Revolution.* London: Little,
    Brown, 1999.
———. *Worldly Goods: A New History of the Renaissance.* New York: Nan A.
    Talese/Doubleday, 1996.
Jefferys, James B. *Retail Trading in Britain, 1850–1950.* Cambridge: Cambridge
    University Press, 1954.
Jones, Catherine. *Literary Memory: Scott's Waverley Novels and the Psychology of
    Narrative.* Lewisburg, PA: Bucknell University Press, 2003.
Kahane, Claire. "The Gothic Mirror." In *The (M)other Tongue: Essays in Feminist
    Psychoanalytic Interpretation*, ed. Shirley Nelson Garner, Claire Kahane, and
    Madelon Sprengnether. Ithaca, NY: Cornell University Press, 1985.
Kallich, Martin. *Horace Walpole.* New York: Twayne, 1971.
Kaufmann, U. Milo. *The Pilgrim's Progress and Traditions in Puritan Meditation.*
    New Haven, CT: Yale University Press, 1966.
Kaul, Suvir. *Thomas Gray and Literary Authority: Ideology and Poetics in
    Eighteenth-Century England.* Oxford: Oxford University Press, 1992.
Keeble, N. H. Introduction to *The Pilgrim's Progress*, by John Bunyan, ed. N. H.
    Keeble. Oxford: Oxford University Press, 1984.
Kelly, Douglas. *The Conspiracy of Allusion: Description, Rewriting, and Authorship
    from Macrobius to Medieval Romance.* Leiden: Brill, 1999.
Kelly, Gary. *Women, Writing, and Revolution, 1790–1827.* Oxford: Clarendon, 1993.

Kelsall, Malcolm. *The Great Good Place: The Country House and English Literature*. New York: Columbia University Press, 1993.

Kerr, James. *Fiction against History: Scott as Storyteller*. Cambridge: Cambridge University Press, 1989.

Kestner, Joseph A. *The Spatiality of the Novel*. Detroit: Wayne State University Press, 1978.

Kettle, Arnold. "In Defence of *Moll Flanders*." In *Of Books and Humankind*, ed. John Butt, 55–67. London: Routledge & Kegan Paul, 1964.

Keymer, Thomas. Introduction to *Pamela*, by Samuel Richardson, ed. Thomas Keymer and Alice Wakeley. Oxford: Oxford University Press, 2001.

King, Kathryn R. "The Novel before Novels (with a Glance at Mary Hearne's Fables of Desertion)." In *Eighteenth-Century Genre and Culture: Serious Reflections on Occasional Forms; Essays in Honor of J. Paul Hunter*, ed. Dennis Todd and Cynthia Wall. Newark: University of Delaware Press; London: Associated University Presses, 2001.

Kittay, Jeffrey. "Descriptive Limits." *Yale French Studies* 61 (1981): 225–43.

Knott, John R., Jr. "Bunyan's Gospel Day: A Reading of *The Pilgrim's Progress*." 1973. In *Bunyan: "The Pilgrim's Progress," a Casebook*, ed. Roger Sharrock, 221–43. London: Macmillan, 1976.

Kuiper, Koenraad. "The Oral Tradition in Auction Speech." *American Speech* 67, no. 3 (fall 1992): 279–89.

Lamb, Jonathan. "Modern Metamorphoses and Disgraceful Tales." *Critical Inquiry* 28 (2001): 133–66.

Latham, Robert. Introduction to *The Illustrated Pepys*, ed. Robert Latham. 1979. Reprint, London: Penguin, 2000.

Lawler, John. *Book Auctions in England in the Seventeenth Century (1676–1700)*. London: Elliot Stock, 1898.

Leavis, F. R. "Bunyan's Resoluteness." 1969. In *Bunyan: "The Pilgrim's Progress," a Casebook*, ed. Roger Sharrock, 204–20. London: Macmillan, 1976.

Leeming, Glenda. Introduction to *Ivanhoe*, by Sir Walter Scott. London: Panther, 1969.

Lefebvre, Henri. *The Production of Space*. 1974. Translated by Donald Nicholson-Smith. Oxford: Blackwell, 1991.

Lewis, C. S. "The Vision of John Bunyan." 1969. In *Bunyan: "The Pilgrim's Progress," a Casebook*, ed. Roger Sharrock. 195–203. London: Macmillan, 1976.

Lewis, W. S. *Horace Walpole*. A. W. Mellon Lectures in the Fine Arts, Bollingen Series, vol. 35, no. 9. New York: Pantheon, 1960.

———. *Horace Walpole's Library*. Cambridge: Cambridge University Press, 1958.

———. Introduction to *The Castle of Otranto*, by Horace Walpole, ed. W. S. Lewis. 1964. Reprint, Oxford: Oxford University Press, 1982.

Liu, Lydia H. "Robinson Crusoe's Earthenware Pot." *Critical Inquiry* 25, no. 4 (1999): 728–57.

Lopes, José Manuel. *Foregrounded Description in Prose Fiction: Five Cross-Literary Studies*. Toronto: University of Toronto Press, 1995.

Lukács, Georg. *The Historical Novel*. 1955. Translated by Hannah Mitchell and Stanley Mitchell. London: Merlin, 1962. Reprint, Harmondsworth: Penguin, 1981.

———. "Narrate or Describe?" 1936. In *Writer and Critic and Other Essays*. Edited and translated by Arthur Kahn. London: Merlin, 1970.

Lynch, Deidre Shauna. *The Economy of Character: Novels, Market Culture, and the Business of Inner Meaning*. Chicago: University of Chicago Press, 1998.

MacLachlan, Christopher. Introduction to *The Monk*, by Matthew Lewis, ed. Christopher Maclauchlan. London: Penguin, 1998.

Marchitello, Howard. *Narrative and Meaning in Early Modern England: Browne's Skull and Other Histories*. Cambridge: Cambridge University Press, 1997.

Marillier, H. C. *Christies, 1766 to 1925*. London: Constable, 1926.

Markley, Robert. "Language, Power, and Sexuality in Cleland's *Fanny Hill*." *Philological Quarterly* 63, no. 3 (summer 1984): 343–56.

Martin, Paul. *Popular Collecting and the Everyday Self*. London: Leicester University Press, 1999.

Mason, Philip. *The English Gentleman: The Rise and Fall of an Ideal*. New York: William Morrow, 1982.

Matheson, C. S. "'A Shilling Well Laid Out': The Royal Academy's Early Public." In *Art on the Line: The Royal Academy Exhibition at Somerset House, 1780–1836*, ed. David H. Solkin. New Haven, CT: Yale University Press, 2001.

Mayhew, Robert J. *Enlightenment Geography: The Political Languages of British Geography, 1650–1850*. London: Macmillan; New York: St. Martin's, 2000.

McClellan, Andrew. *Inventing the Louvre: Art, Politics, and the Origins of the Modern Museum in Eighteenth-Century Paris*. Cambridge: Cambridge University Press, 1994.

McGlynn, Paul D. "Samuel Johnson and the Illusions of Popular Culture." *Modern Language Studies* 10 (1980): 28–35.

McIntyre, Clara Frances. *Ann Radcliffe in Relation to Her Time*. Yale Studies in English, ed. Albert S. Cook, vol. 62. New Haven, CT: Yale University Press, 1920.

McKendrick, Neil. "Josiah Wedgwood: An Eighteenth-Century Entrepreneur in Salesmanship and Marketing Techniques." *Economic History Review*, 2nd ser., 12, no. 3 (1960): 408–33.

McKillop, Alan Dugald. *The Early Masters of English Fiction*. Lawrence: University Press of Kansas, 1956.

Merleau-Ponty, Maurice. *The Phenomenology of Perception*. Translated by C. Smith. New York: Humanities, 1962.

Merritt, J. F. "The Reshaping of Stow's *Survey*: Munday, Strype, and the Protestant City." In *Imagining Early Modern London: Perceptions and Portrayals of the*

City from Stow to Strype, 1598–1720, ed. J. F. Merritt. Cambridge: Cambridge University Press, 2001.

Mighall, Robert. *A Geography of Victorian Gothic Fiction: Mapping History's Nightmares.* Oxford: Oxford University Press, 1999.

Miller, John. Foreword to *The Diary of John Evelyn,* ed. Guy de la Bédoyère. Bangor: Headstart History, 1994.

Mintz, Sidney. "The Changing Roles of Food in the Study of Consumption." In *Consumption and the World of Goods,* ed. John Brewer and Roy Porter, 261–73. London: Routledge, 1993.

Mitchell, W. J. T. *Iconology: Image, Text, Ideology.* Chicago: University of Chicago Press, 1986.

——. "Romanticism and the Life of Things: Fossils, Totems, and Images." *Critical Inquiry* 28 (2001): 167–84.

——. "Spatial Form in Literature: Toward a General Theory." *Critical Inquiry* (spring 1980): 539–67.

Moir, Esther. *The Discovery of Britain: The English Tourists, 1540–1840.* London: Routledge & Kegan Paul, 1964.

Monk, Samuel Holt. Introduction to *The History and Remarkable Life of the Truly Honourable Col. Jacque commonly call'd Col. Jack,* by Daniel Defoe, ed. Samuel Holt Monk. London: Oxford University Press, 1965.

Montgomery, Robert Langford. *The Reader's Eye: Studies in Didactic Literary Theory from Dante to Tasso.* Berkeley and Los Angeles: University of California Press, 1979.

Moran, Michael G., ed. *Eighteenth-Century British and American Rhetorics and Rhetoricians: Critical Studies and Sources.* Westport, CT: Greenwood, 1994.

Moreland, Carl, and David Bannister. *Antique Maps.* London: Longman, 1983. 3rd ed., London: Phaidon, 1989. Reprint, London: Phaidon, 1993.

Morris, Christopher. Introduction to *The Illustrated Journeys of Celia Fiennes, 1685–c. 1712,* ed. Christopher Morris. London: Macdonald, 1982. New ed., Stroud: Alan Sutton, 1995.

Morrissey, Lee. *From the Temple to the Castle: An Architectural History of British Literature, 1660–1760.* Charlottesville: University Press of Virginia, 1999.

Mosher, Harold F., Jr. "Towards a Poetics of 'Descriptivized' Narration." *Poetics Today* 12, no. 3 (fall 1991): 425–45.

Mui, Hoh-cheung, and Lorna H. Mui. *Shops and Shopkeeping in Eighteenth-Century England.* Montreal: McGill-Queen's University Press; London: Routledge, 1989.

Muir, Edwin. *Scott and Scotland: The Predicament of the Scottish Writer.* London: George Routledge & Sons, 1936.

Mukerji, Chandra. *From Graven Images: Patterns of Modern Materialism.* New York: Columbia University Press, 1983.

Mullaney, Steven. "Strange Things, Gross Terms, Curious Customs: The Rehearsal of Cultures in the Late Renaissance." *Representations* 3 (1983): 40–67.

Myers, Robin, and Michael Harris, eds. *Property of a Gentleman: The Formation,
    Organisation and Dispersal of the Private Library, 1620–1920*. Winchester:
    St. Paul's Bibliographies, 1991.
Nagel, Sidney R. "Shadows and Ephemera." *Critical Inquiry* 28 (2001):
    23–39.
Napier, Elizabeth. *The Failure of Gothic: Problems of Disjunction in an
    Eighteenth-Century Literary Form*. Oxford: Clarendon, 1987.
Nevett, T. R. *Advertising in Britain: A History*. London: Heinemann, 1982.
Nicolson, Marjorie Hope. *Newton Demands the Muse: Newton's "Opticks" and the
    Eighteenth Century Poets*. 1946. Reprint, Princeton, NJ: Princeton University
    Press, 1966.
———. *Pepys' "Diary" and the New Science*. Charlottesville: University Press of
    Virginia, 1965.
———. *Science and Imagination*. 1956. 2nd ed., Ithaca, NY: Great Seal, 1962.
    Reprint, Hamden, CT: Archon, 1976.
North, Michael, and David Ormrod, eds. *Art Markets in Europe, 1400–1800*.
    Brookfield: Ashgate, 1999.
Novak, Maximilian E. "Conscious Irony in *Moll Flanders*: Facts and Problems."
    College English 26 (December 1964): 198–204.
———. *Economics and the Fiction of Daniel Defoe*. Berkeley: University of
    California Press, 1962.
O'Brien, John. "The Character of Credit: Daniel Defoe's Lady Credit, *The
    Fortunate Mistress* and the Resources of Inconsistency." *ELH* 63 (fall 1996):
    603–31.
Ogborn, Miles, and Charles W. J. Withers. "Travel, Trade, and Empire: Knowing
    Other Places, 1660–1800." In *A Concise Companion to the Restoration and
    Eighteenth Century*, ed. Cynthia Wall. Oxford: Blackwell, 2004.
Olivecrona, Karl. "Appropriation in the State of Nature: Locke on the Origin of
    Property." In *John Locke: Critical Assessments*, ed. Richard Ashcraft. 4 vols.
    London: Routledge, 1991.
Orlin, Lena Cowen. *Elizabethan Households: An Anthology*. Washington, DC:
    Folger Shakespeare Library, 1995.
———. *Private Matters and Public Culture in Post-Reformation England*. Ithaca,
    NY: Cornell University Press, 1994.
Parker, Blandford. *The Triumph of Augustan Poetics: English Literary Culture from
    Butler to Johnson*. Cambridge: Cambridge University Press, 1998.
Parks, Stephen, ed. *Poets and Men of Letters*. Vol. 9 of *Sale Catalogues of Libraries
    of Eminent Persons*, ed. A. N. L. Munby. London: Sotheby Parke-Bernet
    Publications, 1972.
Paulson, Ronald. *Emblem and Expression: Meaning in English Art in the Eighteenth
    Century*. Cambridge, MA: Harvard University Press, 1975.
———. *Hogarth: His Life, Art, and Times*. 2 vols. New Haven, CT: Yale University
    Press, 1971.

————. *Popular and Polite Art in the Age of Hogarth and Fielding*. Notre Dame, IN: Notre Dame University Press, 1979.

Pearce, Susan, and Ken Arnold, eds. *The Collector's Voice: Critical Readings in the Practice of Collecting*. 4 vols. Burlington, VT: Ashgate, 2000.

————. *Museums, Objects, and Collecting: A Cultural Study*. Washington, DC: Smithsonian Institution Press, 1992.

Pearl, Valerie. Introduction to *The Survey of London*, by John Stow, ed. H. B. Wheatley. London: Dent, 1987.

Phillips, Mark Salber. *Society and Sentiment: Genres of Historical Writing in Britain, 1740–1820*. Princeton, NJ: Princeton University Press, 2000.

Pocock, J. G. A. *Virtue, Commerce, and History: Essays on Political Thought and History, Chiefly in the Eighteenth Century*. Cambridge: Cambridge University Press, 1985.

Pomian, Krzysztof. *Collectors and Curiosities: Paris and Venice, 1500–1800*. Translated by Elizabeth Wiles-Portier. Cambridge: Polity, 1990.

Poovey, Mary. *A History of the Modern Fact: Problems of Knowledge in the Sciences of Wealth and Society*. Chicago: University of Chicago Press, 1998.

Power, M. J. "John Stow and His London." *Journal of Historical Geography* 11 (1985): 1–20.

Quayle, Thomas. *Poetic Diction: A Study of Eighteenth-Century Verse*. London: Methuen, 1924.

Race, William H. "Ekphrasis." In *The New Princeton Encyclopedia of Poetry and Poetics*, ed. Alex Preminger and T. V. F. Brogan. Princeton, NJ: Princeton University Press, 1993.

Raven, James. "Defending Conduct and Property: The London Press and the Luxury Debate." In *Early Modern Conceptions of Property*, ed. John Brewer and Susan Staves, 301–19. London: Routledge, 1996.

Redford, George. *Art Sales: A History of Sales of Pictures and Other Works of Art*. London: Whitefriars, 1888.

Reynolds, Myra. *The Treatment of Nature in English Poetry between Pope and Wordsworth*. Chicago: University of Chicago Press, 1909.

Ricardou, Jean. "La description créatrice: Une course contre le sens." In *Problèmes du nouveau roman*, 91–111. Paris: de Seuil, 1967.

Rice, Matthew. *Traditional Houses of Rural Britain*. New York: Cross River, 1991.

Richetti, John J. *Philosophical Writing: Locke, Berkeley, Hume*. Cambridge, MA: Harvard University Press, 1983.

————. *Popular Fiction before Richardson*. 1969. Reprint, Oxford: Clarendon, 1992.

Riffaterre, Michael. "Descriptive Imagery." *Yale French Studies* 61 (1981): 107–25.

Rigby, Douglas, and Elizabeth Rigby. *Lock, Stock and Barrel: The Story of Collecting*. Philadelphia: J. B. Lippincott, 1944.

Rigney, Ann. *Imperfect Histories: The Elusive Past and the Legacy of Romantic Historicism*. Ithaca, NY: Cornell University Press, 2001.

Roberts, S. C. *An Eighteenth-Century Gentleman and Other Essays*. Cambridge: Cambridge University Press, 1930.

Roberts, William. *Memorials of Christies: A Record of Art Sales from 1766 to 1896*. 2 vols. London: G. Bell, 1897.

Robertson, D. W., Jr. *A Preface to Chaucer*. Princeton, NJ: Princeton University Press, 1962.

Robinson, Forrest. *The Shape of Things Known: Sidney's "Apology" in its Philosophical Tradition*. Cambridge, MA: Harvard University Press, 1972.

Roche, Daniel. *A History of Everyday Things: The Birth of Consumption in France, 1600–1800*. 1997. Translated by Brian Pearce. Cambridge: Cambridge University Press, 2000.

Roche, Thomas P., Jr. *The Kindly Flame*. Princeton, NJ: Princeton University Press, 1964.

Rogers, Deborah D., ed. Introduction to *The Critical Response to Ann Radcliffe*, ed. Deborah D. Rogers. Westport, CT: Greenwood, 1994.

Röstvig, Maren-Sofie. *The Background of English Neo-Classicism*. Oslo: Universitetsforlaget, 1961.

Schama, Simon. "Perishable Commodities: Dutch Still-Life Painting and the 'Empire of Things.'" In *Consumption and the World of Goods*, ed. John Brewer and Roy Porter, 478–88. London: Routledge, 1993.

Schneider, Jane. "Fantastical Colors in Foggy London: The New Fashion Potential of the Late Sixteenth Century." In *Material London, ca. 1600*, ed. Lena Cowen Orlin, 109–27. Philadelphia: University of Pennsylvania Press, 2000.

Scholes, Robert, and Robert Kellogg. *The Nature of Narrative*. Oxford: Oxford University Press, 1966.

Schor, Naomi. *Reading in Detail: Aesthetics and the Feminine*. New York: Methuen, 1987.

Sedgwick, Eve Kosofsky. *The Coherence of Gothic Conventions*. New York: Methuen, 1986.

Shammas, Carole. "Changes in English and Anglo-American Consumption from 1550 to 1800." In *Consumption and the World of Goods*, ed. John Brewer and Roy Porter, 177–205. London: Routledge, 1993.

Shapiro, Barbara J. *A Culture of Fact: England, 1550–1720*. Ithaca, NY: Cornell University Press, 2000.

Sharrock, Roger, ed. *Bunyan: "The Pilgrim's Progress," a Casebook*. London: Macmillan, 1976.

———. Introduction to *Pilgrim's Progress*, by John Bunyan, ed. James Blanton Wharey, rev. Roger Sharrock. Oxford: Clarendon, 1960.

———. Introduction to *The Pilgrim's Progress*, by John Bunyan, ed. Roger Sharrock. Rev. and corrected ed. Harmondsworth: Penguin, 1965.

———. *John Bunyan*. 1954. Rev. and corrected ed., London: Macmillan; New York: St. Martin's Press, 1968.

Shaw, Harry E. *The Forms of Historical Fiction: Sir Walter Scott and His Successors.* Ithaca, NY: Cornell University Press, 1983.

———. *Narrating Reality: Austen, Scott, Eliot.* Ithaca, NY: Cornell University Press, 1999.

Sherman, Sandra. *Finance and Fictionality in the Early Eighteenth Century: Accounting for Defoe.* Cambridge: Cambridge University Press, 1996.

Sherman, Stuart. *Telling Time: Clocks, Diaries, and English Diurnal Form, 1660–1785.* Chicago: University of Chicago Press, 1996.

Smiley, T. J. "The Theory of Descriptions." In *Proceedings of the British Academy,* vol. 67, pp. 321–37. Oxford: Oxford University Press, 1981.

Smiten, Jeffrey R., et al. *Spatial Form in Narrative.* Ithaca, NY: Cornell University Press, 1981.

Smith, Barbara Herrnstein. *Contingencies of Value: Alternative Perspectives for Critical Theory.* Cambridge, MA: Harvard University Press, 1988.

Smith, Warren Hunting. *Architecture in English Fiction.* New Haven, CT: Yale University Press, 1934. Reprint, Hamden, CT: Archon, 1970.

Snyder, Joel. "Benjamin on Reproducibility and Aura: A Reading of 'The Work of Art in the Age of Its Technical Reproducibility.'" In *Benjamin: Philosophy, Aesthetics, History,* ed. Gary Smith. Chicago: University of Chicago Press, 1983.

Sol, Antoinette Marie. *Textual Promiscuities: Eighteenth-Century Critical Rewriting.* Lewisburg, PA: Bucknell University Press, 2002.

Solkin, David H. *Painting for Money: The Visual Arts and the Public Sphere in Eighteenth-Century England.* New Haven, CT: Yale University Press, for the Paul Mellon Centre for Studies in British Art, 1993.

Spitzer, Leo. "Milieu and Ambiance." In *Essays in Historical Semantics,* 179–255. New York: S. F. Vanni, 1948.

Spurgeon, Caroline F. E. Preface to *The Castle of Otranto,* by Horace Walpole. London: Chatto & Windus, 1907.

Stafford, Barbara. *Voyage into Substance.* Cambridge, MA: MIT Press, 1984.

Stallybrass, Peter, and Ann Rosalind Jones. "Fetishizing the Glove in Renaissance Europe." *Critical Inquiry* 28, no. 1 (autumn 2001): 114–32.

Starr, G. A. Introduction to *The Fortunes and Misfortunes of the Famous Moll Flanders,* by Daniel Defoe, ed. G. A. Starr. 1971. Reprint, Oxford: Oxford University Press, 1987.

Starr, G. Gabrielle. "Objects, Imaginings, and Facts: Going beyond Genre in Behn and Defoe." *Eighteenth-Century Fiction* 16, no. 4 (July 2004): 499–518.

Staves, Susan. *Married Women's Separate Property in England, 1660–1833.* Cambridge, MA: Harvard University Press, 1990.

Steegman, John. *The Artist and the Country House: Descriptive Notes by Dorothy Stroud on the Houses Illustrated in the Paintings.* New York: Scribner's, 1949.

Stephen, Sir Leslie. *English Literature and Society in the Eighteenth Century.* London: Duckworth, 1904.

Stewart, Susan. *On Longing: Narratives of the Miniature, the Gigantic, the Souvenir, the Collection*. Baltimore: Johns Hopkins University Press, 1984. Reprint, Durham, NC: Duke University Press, 1998.

Stocking, Marion Kingston. *Evidence of the Imagination: Studies of Interactions between Life and Art in English Romantic Literature*. New York: New York University Press, 1978.

Straub, Kristina. "Reconstructing the Gaze: Voyeurism in Richardson's *Pamela*." *Studies in Eighteenth-Century Culture* 18 (1988): 419–31.

Sutton, Denys. "'The King of Epithets': A Study of James Christie." *Apollo* 84 (November 1966): 364–75.

Talon, Henri. *John Bunyan: The Man and His Works*. 1948. Translated by Barbara Wall. London: Rocklift, 1951.

———. "Space and the Hero in *The Pilgrim's Progress*: A Study of the Meaning of the Allegorical Universe." 1961. In *Bunyan: "The Pilgrim's Progress," a Casebook*, ed. Roger Sharrock, 158–67. London: Macmillan, 1976.

Tatar, Maria M. "The Houses of Fiction: Toward a Definition of the Uncanny." *Comparative Literature* 33 (1981): 167–82.

Tayler, Edward W., ed. *Literary Criticism of Seventeenth-Century England*. New York: Knopf, 1967.

Thomas, Nicholas. *Entangled Objects: Exchange, Material Culture, and Colonialism in the Pacific*. Cambridge, MA: Harvard University Press, 1991.

Thompson, A. Hamilton. "Thomson and Natural Description in Poetry." In *The Cambridge History of English Literature*, vol. 10, ed. Sir A. W. Ward and A. R. Waller. Cambridge: Cambridge University Press, 1913.

Tillotson, Geoffrey. *Augustan Poetic Diction*. London: Athlone, 1964.

Todorov, Tzvetan. *The Fantastic: A Structural Approach to a Literary Genre*. 1970. Translated by Richard Howard. Ithaca, NY: Cornell University Press, 1975.

Tompkins, J. M. S. *The Popular Novel in England, 1770–1800*. London: Constable, 1932.

Trainer, James. Introduction to *The Old English Baron*, by Clara Reeve, ed. James Trainer. 1967. Reprint, Oxford: Oxford University Press, 1977.

Trickett, Rachel. "'Curious Eye': Some Aspects of Visual Description in Eighteenth-Century Literature." In *Augustan Studies: Essays in Honor of Irvin Ehrenpreis*, ed. Douglas Lane Patey and Timothy Keegan, 239–52. Newark: University of Delaware Press, 1985.

Tristram, Philippa. *Living Space in Fact and Fiction*. London: Routledge, 1989.

Trumpener, Katie. *Bardic Nationalism: The Romantic Novel and the British Empire*. Princeton, NJ: Princeton University Press, 1997.

Tulloch, Graham. Introduction to *Ivanhoe*, by Sir Walter Scott, ed. Graham Tulloch. London: Penguin, 1998.

Turner, James. "Bunyan's Sense of Place." In *"The Pilgrim's Progress": Critical and Historical Views*, ed. Vincent Newey, 91–110. Liverpool: Liverpool University Press, 1980.

————. *The Politics of Landscape: Rural Scenery and Society in English Poetry, 1630–1660*. Oxford: Blackwell, 1979.

Twitchell, James B. *Lead Us into Temptation: The Triumph of American Materialism*. New York: Columbia University Press, 1999.

Van Eerde, Katherine S. *John Ogilby and the Taste of His Times*. Folkestone: William Dawson & Sons, 1976.

Van Ghent, Dorothy. *The English Novel: Form and Function*. 1953. Reprint, New York: Harper & Row, 1961.

Varey, Simon. *Space and the Eighteenth-Century English Novel*. Cambridge: Cambridge University Press, 1990.

Vickers, Ilse. *Defoe and the New Sciences*. Cambridge: Cambridge University Press, 1996.

Wall, Cynthia. "*The Castle of Otranto*: A Shakespeareo-Political Satire." In *Fictional Boundaries, Narrative Forms: Essays in Honor of Everett Zimmerman*, ed. Lorna Clymer and Robert Mayer. Newark: University of Delaware Press, in press.

————, ed. *A Concise Companion to the Restoration and Eighteenth Century*. Oxford: Blackwell, 2004.

————. "Details of Space: Narrative Description in Early Eighteenth-Century Novels." *Eighteenth-Century Fiction* 10, no. 4 (July 1998): 387–405.

————. "The English Auction: Narratives of Dismantlings." *Eighteenth-Century Studies* 31, no. 1 (1997): 1–25.

————. "Gendering Rooms: Domestic Architecture and Literary Acts." *Eighteenth-Century Fiction* 5, no. 4 (July 1993): 349–72.

————. "Grammars of Space: The Language of London from Stow's *Survey* to Defoe's *Tour*." *Philological Quarterly* 76, no. 4 (fall 1997): 387–411.

————. *The Literary and Cultural Spaces of Restoration London*. Cambridge: Cambridge University Press, 1998.

————. "The Spaces of *Clarissa* in Text and Film." In *Eighteenth-Century Fiction on Screen*, ed. Robert Mayer. Cambridge: Cambridge University Press, 2002.

————. "Teaching Space in *Sir Charles Grandison*." In *Approaches to Teaching Richardson*, ed. Jocelyn Harris and Lisa Zunshine. New York: Modern Language Association, in press.

————. "Window Shopping." Paper presented at the conference "Monuments and Dust," London, 2001. Available online at http://www.iath.virginia.edu/london/Archive/On-line-pubs/2001/paper4.html.

Watt, Ian. *The Rise of the Novel*. Berkeley: University of California Press, 1957. Reprint, Berkeley: University of California Press, 1965.

Watt, James. Introduction to *The Old English Baron*, by Clara Reeve, ed. James Trainer. Oxford: Oxford University Press, 2003.

Weatherill, Lorna. "The Meaning of Consumer Behaviour in Late Seventeenth-and Early Eighteenth-Century England." In *Consumption and the World of Goods*, ed. John Brewer and Roy Porter, 206–77. London: Routledge, 1993.

Webb, Ruth Helen, and Philip Weller. "Descriptive Poetry." In *The New Princeton Encyclopedia of Poetry and Poetics*, ed. Alex Preminger and T. V. F. Brogan. Princeton, NJ: Princeton University Press, 1993.

Welsh, Alexander. *The Hero of the Waverley Novels, with New Essays on Scott*. 1963. Expanded ed., Princeton, NJ: Princeton University Press, 1992.

———. *Strong Representations: Narrative and Circumstantial Evidence in England*. Baltimore: Johns Hopkins University Press, 1991.

White, Hayden. *The Content of the Form: Narrative Discourse and Historical Representation*. Baltimore: Johns Hopkins University Press, 1987.

Whitley, William T. *Artists and Their Friends in England, 1700–1799*. 2 vols. London: Medici Society, 1928.

Williams, Anne Patricia. "Description and Tableau in the Eighteenth-Century British Sentimental Novel." *Eighteenth-Century Fiction* 8, no. 4 (July 1996): 465–84.

Wilson, C. *The Invisible World: Early Modern Philosophy and the Invention of the Microscope*. Princeton, NJ: Princeton University Press, 1995.

Wilson, Edmund. "Is Verse a Dying Technique?" In *The Triple Thinkers*. New York: Harcourt, Brace, 1938.

Wimsatt, William K., Jr. "The Structure of the 'Concrete Universal' in Literature." *PMLA* 62 (1947): 262–80.

Wodehouse, P. G. *Aunts Aren't Gentlemen*. London: Penguin, 1974.

Womersley, David. *The Transformation of "The Decline and Fall of the Roman Empire."* Cambridge: Cambridge University Press, 1988.

Wood, Denis. *The Power of Maps*. London: Routledge, 1993.

Woolf, Virginia. "Defoe." In *The Common Reader, First Series*. 1925. Edited by Andrew McNeillie. London: Hogarth, 1984.

———. "Rambling round Evelyn." In *The Common Reader, First Series*. 1925. Edited by Andrew McNeillie. London: Hogarth, 1984.

———. "*Robinson Crusoe*." In *The Common Reader, Second Series*. 1932. Edited by Andrew McNeillie. London: Hogarth, 1986.

Wootton, David. "David Hume, 'the Historian.'" In *The Cambridge Companion to Hume*, ed. David Fate Norton. Cambridge: Cambridge University Press, 1993.

Zimmerman, Everett. *The Boundaries of Fiction: History and the Eighteenth-Century British Novel*. Ithaca, NY: Cornell University Press, 1996.

INDEX

Note: Numbers in italic refer to illustrations.

criticism, literary: Augustan, 81; classical, 15–18, 22, 25, 28, 31, 32, 208; discourse linguists, 38, 202; neoclassical, 226; New, 38, 202; nineteenth-century, 109; psychoanalytic, 213; Russian formalism, 38, 202; twentieth-century, 8, 109, 154–58, 198, 202, 208, 209
Cromwell, Oliver, 226–28
Crowley, J. Donald, 84, 238n3
Crowley, John, 150, 186, 190, 258n4
cultural storehouse, 6, 8, 9, 11, 33, 35, 77, 165, 177, 200, 217, 220, 235. *See also* Beaujour, Michel

Daily Advertiser, 163, 165. *See also* newspapers
Daily Post, 163. *See also* newspapers
Damon, Phillip, 18
Daniels, Stephen, 231, 232
Dante Alighieri, 97
Darwin, Charles, 154, 155
Daston, Lorraine, 247n2
Davis, B. E. C., 240n32
Davis, Dorothy, 259n24
Davys, Mary, 4, 124, 135–37; *Familiar Letters betwixt a Gentleman and a Lady*, 135–37
Day, Robert A., 137
De Beer, E. S., 83
decor/decoration. *See* houses; interior design
decorum, 28–31, 34, 222, 242n61. *See also* description; gentility/gentrification
Defoe, Daniel, 1, 3, 4, 38, 42, 108–14, 124, 138, 142, 155, 161, 178, 190, 195, 202, 204, 215, 219, 248n3; *Colonel Jack*, 207; *Complete English Tradesman*, 160, 161, 164; *Journal of the Plague Year*, 97, 109, 113, 155, 159; *Moll Flanders*, 1, 36–37, 96, 97, 109, 110, 111–12, 138, 155, 161, 163, 178, 207; *Robinson Crusoe*, 1, 13, 40, 42, 97, 108–9, 110, 112–13, 155, 178, 189, 207, 236; *Roxana*, 109; *Tour thro' the whole Island of Great Britain*, 191, 216
Delany, Mary, 5, 153, 178, 184, 186–87, 193, 194, 195–96
De Laune, Thomas, 43; *Angliae Metropolis*, 48; *Present State of London*, 43, 47–48
description: chronographia, 2, 16, 239n26; classical, 15–19, 31; and decorum, 14, 28–31; definitions of, 7, 10, 11–15, 113; and details, 2, 96–122; and diaries, 82–88; and differentiation, 206, 217; distrust of,

1, 25–27, 124, 126, 198; domestication, 199, 220; eighteenth-century, 22, 95, 123; as emblematic, 2, 96–113; and empiricism, 70–82, 88–90; ethopoeia, 2; and generals, 2, 208; gentrification of, 5, 28, 34, 40, 150, 174–75, 178, 206, 220; history of, 1, 2, 7–40; of houses, 5, 46, 47, 49, 81, 83–84, 86, 87–88, 177–200, 203–20, 231–36; as interruption/refrigeration, 1, 27, 124, 126, 221; landscape, 124, 130–31, 203, 207–11; medieval, 18–19, 31; as neutral, 262n13; nineteenth-century, 36–40, 84, 214–20; as object, 1, 10, 11, 25–27; as obstacle, 25–27, 124, 221; as ornament, 2; as particulars, 2; pathopeia, 16; pictorial, 10; portrait, 2; as power, 144; pragmatographia, 12, 16, 21–22, 94, 99, 139, 239n26; prosopographia, 2, 16, 105, 107, 123, 127, 131, 132, 143, 239n26, 255n2; prosopopeia, 2, 16, 239n26; realism, 82; Renaissance, 31, 41, 45; as representation, 2; as respite, 24–25, 88; rhetoric about, 4; self-, 4; as set-pieces, 225; seventeenth-century, 22, 41, 95, 123; status of, 10, 11, 18, 31–40; theories of, 154–58; things stand in for, 2; topographia, 2, 16, 41, 43–53, 198, 239n26; twentieth-century, 38–39
descriptor, 74, 232
detail: accidentals, 2; architectural, 44, 48, 117, 140, 156, 202; circumstantial (*see* circumstance); and Defoe, 110–12; and empiricism, 70–82, 88–90; as gendered, 39; lack of, 226; and novels, 9, 87; of place, 88; rise of, 31–40, 41, 42; as "setting for," 4; superfluous, 221–22, 224. *See also* description; surfaces
dialect, 139
dialogue, 16
diaries, 3, 41, 71, 77, 82–88, 155, 189, 194, 203; diarists, 77, 82–88. *See also* Byng, John; Delany, Mary; Evelyn, John; journals; Pepys, Samuel; travel narratives
Dickens, Charles, 1, 154, 216; *Great Expectations*, 153; *Hard Times*, 34; *Oliver Twist*, 37; *Our Mutual Friend*, 185–86
diction, 28, 208
Dictionary of Philosophy, 12, 13, 14
Diderot, Denis. See *Encyclopédie*